CANDORVILLE

Thank God For

DARRIN BELL

Andrews McMeel
Publishing

Kansas City

Other Books by Darrin Bell

Rudy Park: The People Must Be Wired (with Theron Heir)
Peace, Love, and Lattes: A Rudy Park Collection (with Theron Heir)

**For Grandpa Roscoe, for Laura, and for a shy little kid
who wanted to talk to the whole world**

05 06 07 08 09 BBG 10 9 8 7 6 5 4 3 2

ISBN-13: 978-0-7407-5442-5
ISBN-10: 0-7407-5442-4

Library of Congress Control Number: 2005925267

www.andrewsmcmeel.com

Candorville can be viewed on the Internet at
www.candorville.com.

ATTENTION: SCHOOLS AND BUSINESSES

Andrews McMeel books are available at quantity discounts with bulk purchase for educational, business, or sales promotional use. For information, please write to: Special Sales Department, Andrews McMeel Publishing, 4520 Main Street, Kansas City, Missouri 64111.

WHY?

a Foreword by
Lemont Brown

Why do some people grow up without a father? Why do some of them end up in the boardroom while others end up in the Big House? Is it because the system is stacked against them, or is it because some people make wise decisions and others don't (or is it a little of both)?

Why do women earn less than men who do the same job? Why are courts biased against men in custody battles? Why are some people more likely to help a stray dog than a homeless mother? Why do some homeless people think the world owes them a free ride?

Why do I get pulled over all the time when I don't speed? Why do so many minorities either believe they have no business commenting on politics or feel the only politics they should concern themselves with are matters of race? Why do so many Americans not care about politics at all when politics determine the amount of freedom they can enjoy and the quality of their lives?

Why does television news suck?

Why do so many Black musicians make music that belittles Black women and glorifies ignorance, greed, and other behavior that's destructive to the Black community? Why do those musicians get more attention than the constructive ones? Why do so many young minorities accuse those who choose to study, who are polite, and who speak proper English of "acting White"?

Why do corporations get unfettered access to our leaders, while actual *people* are corralled into "Free Speech Zones" where no one can hear them? Why do CEOs who steal the life savings of millions of people go free while someone who steals $20 from a liquor store goes to jail? Why do some people think it's okay to steal?

Why do so many liberals disagree with what America stands for? Why do so many conservatives disagree with what America stands for? What does America stand for?

Why do stunning golden sunsets turn even the most run-down tenement into a living, glowing work of art? Why do friends sometimes feel more like family than family? Why do people stick by their friends when their friends are wrong? Is loyalty more important than doing what's right?

Why ask any of these questions? Why ask them on the comics pages every morning? Don't kids read the comics pages? What will happen if kids are encouraged to ask "why"? Does asking "why" mean kids are learning to hate America, or does asking "why" mean kids are learning to be Americans?

Is it worth loving your country if that love is blind? Is it better to love with your eyes open?

What makes *Candorville*, the chronicle of my life, qualified to answer all of those questions?

The answer is nothing. *Candorville* is no more qualified than any of you. *Candorville* does not have all the answers—but it does have a lot of questions. And maybe—just maybe—that's more important.

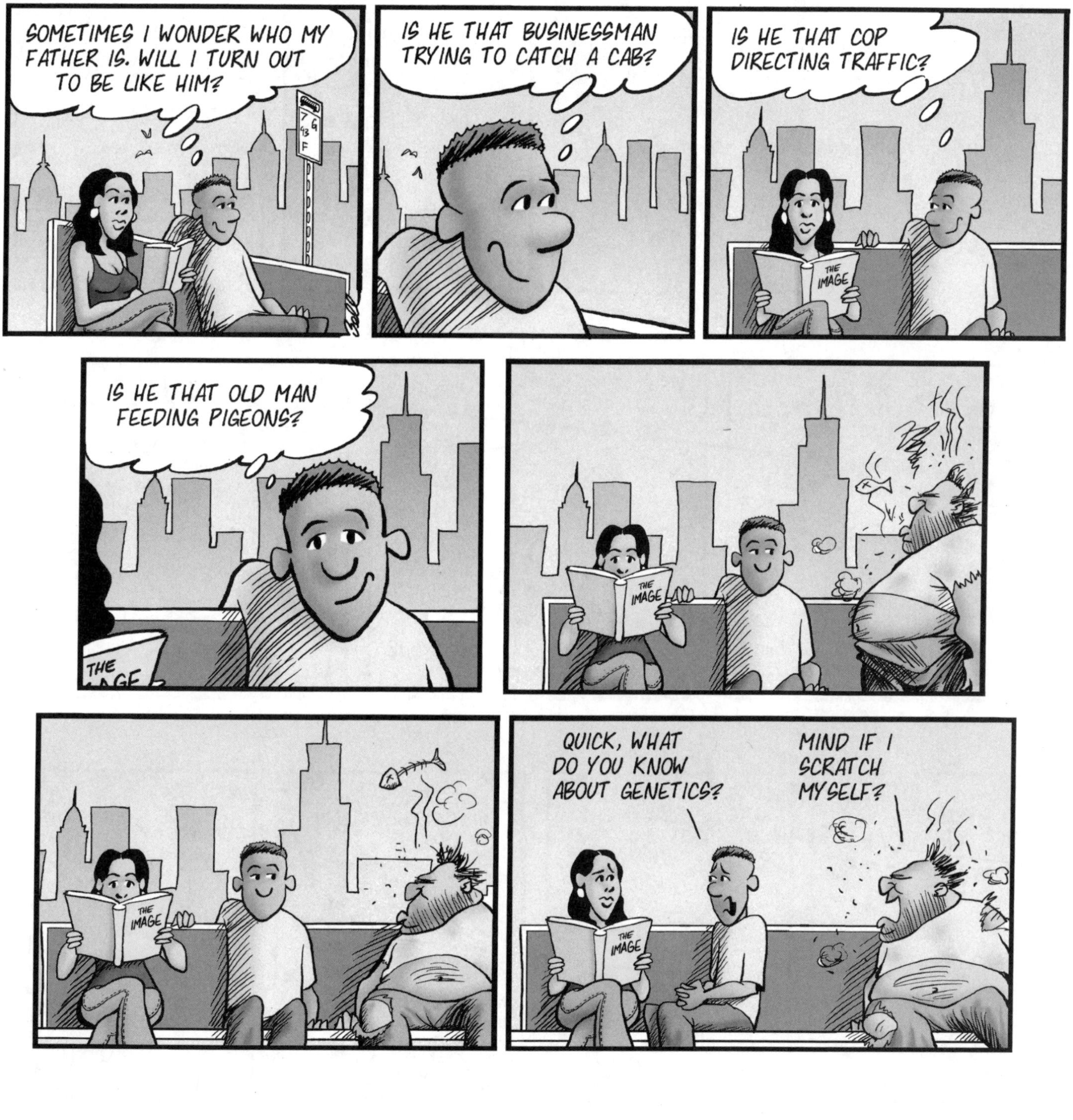
SOMETIMES I WONDER WHO MY FATHER IS. WILL I TURN OUT TO BE LIKE HIM?
IS HE THAT BUSINESSMAN TRYING TO CATCH A CAB?
IS HE THAT COP DIRECTING TRAFFIC?
THE IMAGE
IS HE THAT OLD MAN FEEDING PIGEONS?
THE
THE IMAGE
THE IMAGE
QUICK, WHAT DO YOU KNOW ABOUT GENETICS?
MIND IF I SCRATCH MYSELF?
THE IMAGE

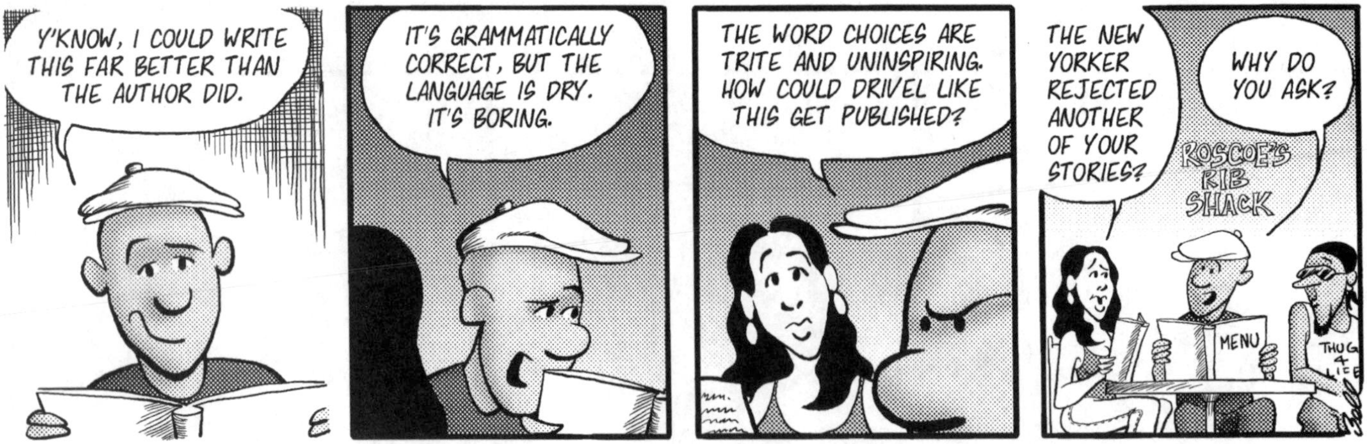
Y'KNOW, I COULD WRITE THIS FAR BETTER THAN THE AUTHOR DID.
IT'S GRAMMATICALLY CORRECT, BUT THE LANGUAGE IS DRY. IT'S BORING.
THE WORD CHOICES ARE TRITE AND UNINSPIRING. HOW COULD DRIVEL LIKE THIS GET PUBLISHED?
THE NEW YORKER REJECTED ANOTHER OF YOUR STORIES?
WHY DO YOU ASK?
ROSCOE'S RIB SHACK
MENU
THUG 4 LIFE

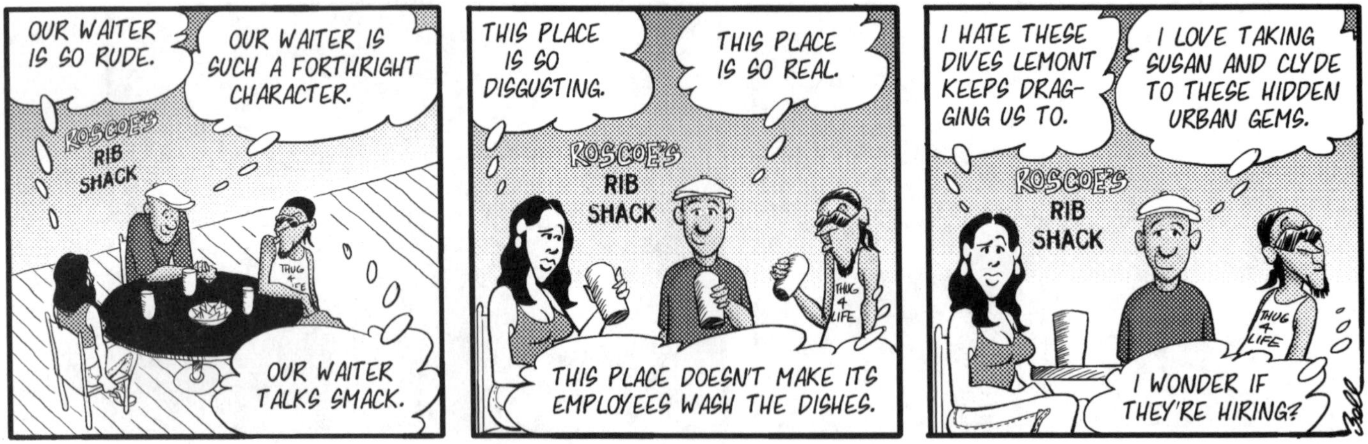
OUR WAITER IS SO RUDE.
OUR WAITER IS SUCH A FORTHRIGHT CHARACTER.
ROSCOE'S RIB SHACK
OUR WAITER TALKS SMACK.
THIS PLACE IS SO DISGUSTING.
THIS PLACE IS SO REAL.
ROSCOE'S RIB SHACK
THIS PLACE DOESN'T MAKE ITS EMPLOYEES WASH THE DISHES.
I HATE THESE DIVES LEMONT KEEPS DRAGGING US TO.
I LOVE TAKING SUSAN AND CLYDE TO THESE HIDDEN URBAN GEMS.
ROSCOE'S RIB SHACK
I WONDER IF THEY'RE HIRING?

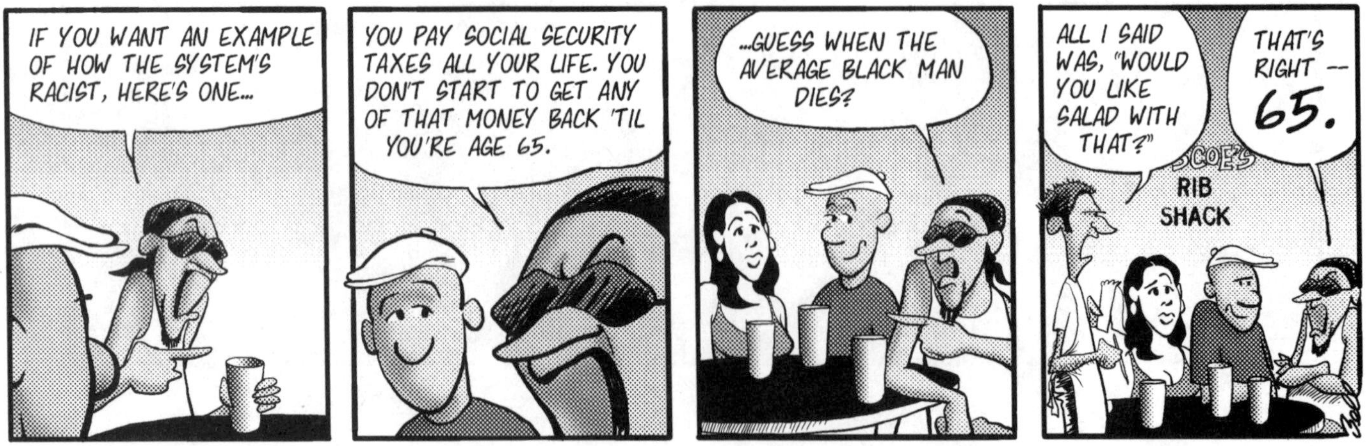
IF YOU WANT AN EXAMPLE OF HOW THE SYSTEM'S RACIST, HERE'S ONE...
YOU PAY SOCIAL SECURITY TAXES ALL YOUR LIFE. YOU DON'T START TO GET ANY OF THAT MONEY BACK 'TIL YOU'RE AGE 65.
...GUESS WHEN THE AVERAGE BLACK MAN DIES?
ALL I SAID WAS, "WOULD YOU LIKE SALAD WITH THAT?"
THAT'S RIGHT -- 65.
RIB SHACK

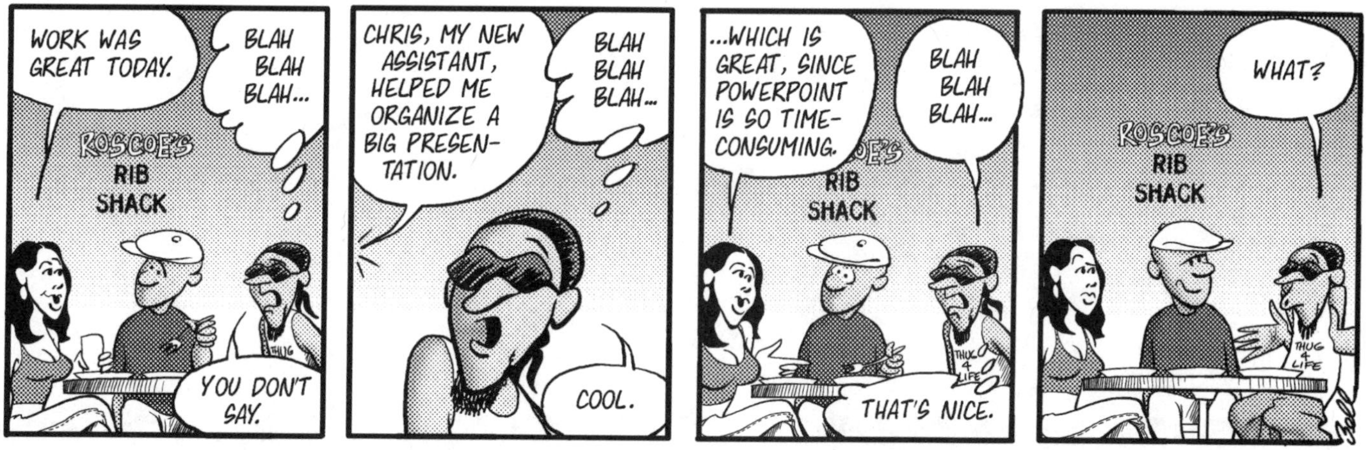
WORK WAS GREAT TODAY.
BLAH BLAH BLAH...
ROSCOE'S RIB SHACK
YOU DON'T SAY.
CHRIS, MY NEW ASSISTANT, HELPED ME ORGANIZE A BIG PRESENTATION.
BLAH BLAH BLAH...
COOL.
...WHICH IS GREAT, SINCE POWERPOINT IS SO TIME-CONSUMING.
BLAH BLAH BLAH...
THAT'S NICE.
WHAT?
ROSCOE'S RIB SHACK
THUG 4 LIFE

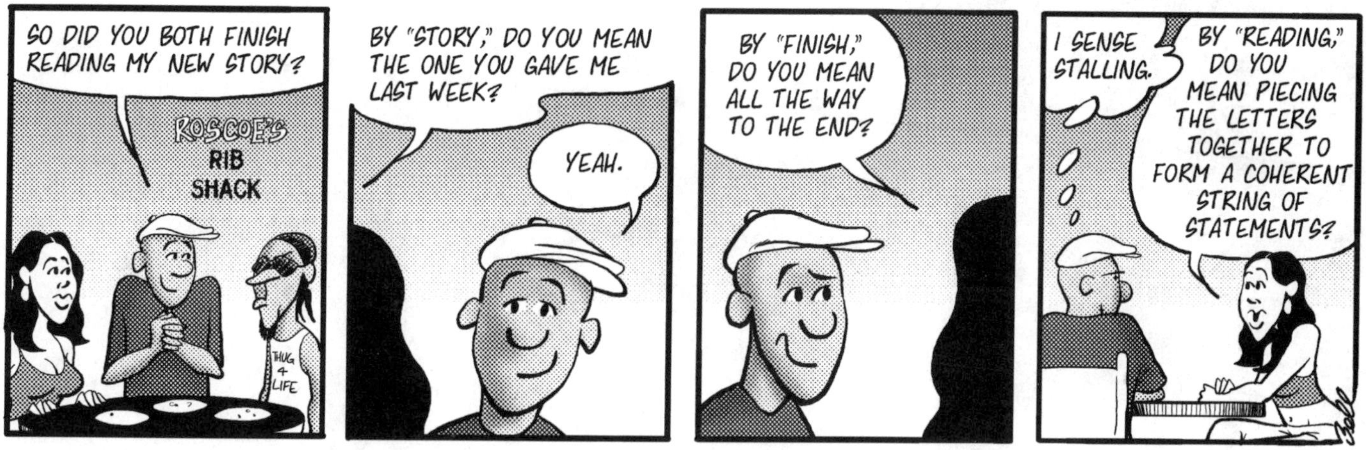
SO DID YOU BOTH FINISH READING MY NEW STORY?
ROSCOE'S RIB SHACK
THUG 4 LIFE
BY "STORY," DO YOU MEAN THE ONE YOU GAVE ME LAST WEEK?
YEAH.
BY "FINISH," DO YOU MEAN ALL THE WAY TO THE END?
I SENSE STALLING.
BY "READING," DO YOU MEAN PIECING THE LETTERS TOGETHER TO FORM A COHERENT STRING OF STATEMENTS?

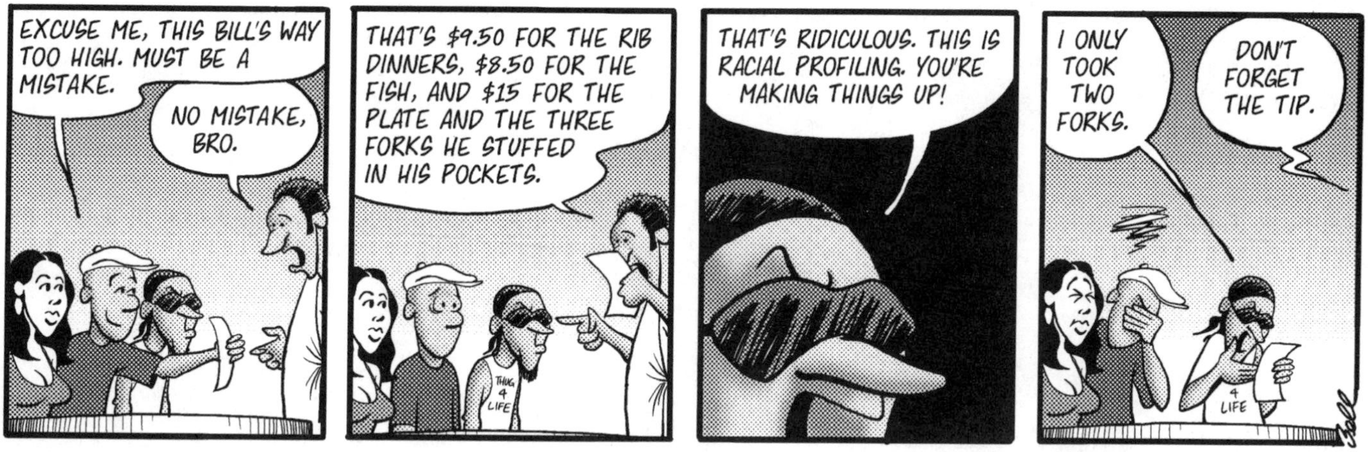
EXCUSE ME, THIS BILL'S WAY TOO HIGH. MUST BE A MISTAKE.
NO MISTAKE, BRO.
THAT'S $9.50 FOR THE RIB DINNERS, $8.50 FOR THE FISH, AND $15 FOR THE PLATE AND THE THREE FORKS HE STUFFED IN HIS POCKETS.
THUG 4 LIFE
THAT'S RIDICULOUS. THIS IS RACIAL PROFILING. YOU'RE MAKING THINGS UP!
I ONLY TOOK TWO FORKS.
DON'T FORGET THE TIP.

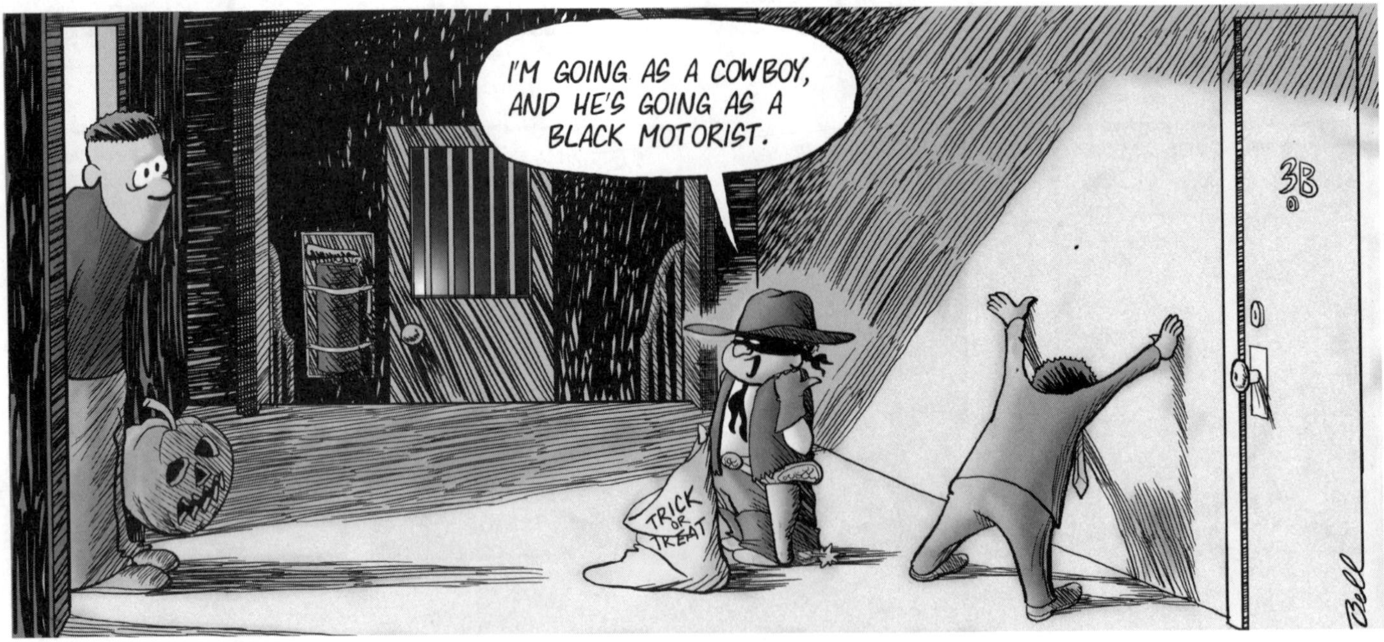
I'M GOING AS A COWBOY, AND HE'S GOING AS A BLACK MOTORIST.
3B
TRICK OR TREAT
Bell

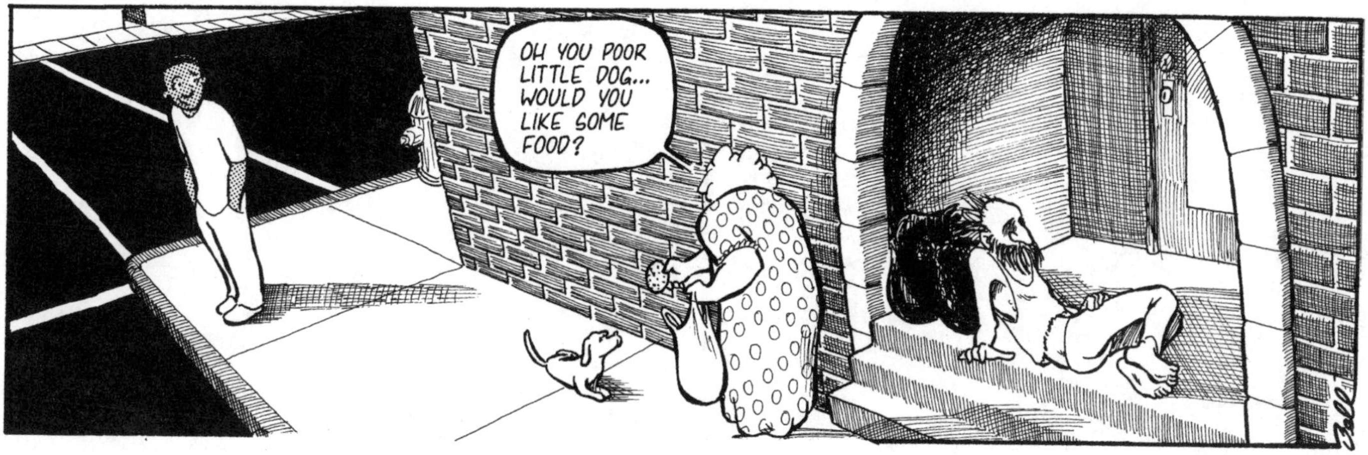
OH YOU POOR LITTLE DOG... WOULD YOU LIKE SOME FOOD?
BELL

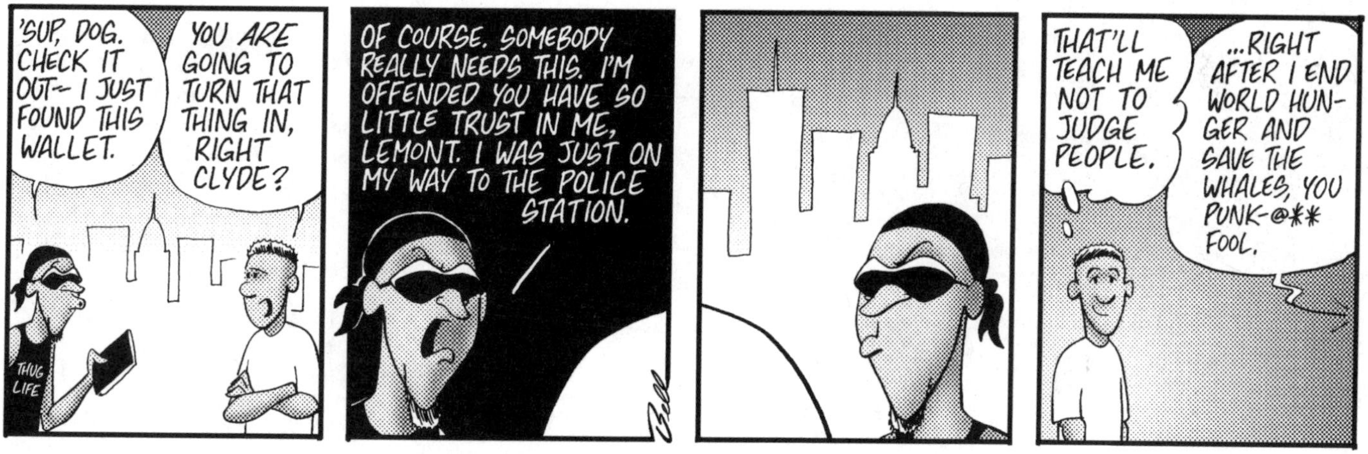
'SUP, DOG. CHECK IT OUT-- I JUST FOUND THIS WALLET.
YOU ARE GOING TO TURN THAT THING IN, RIGHT CLYDE?
THUG LIFE
OF COURSE. SOMEBODY REALLY NEEDS THIS. I'M OFFENDED YOU HAVE SO LITTLE TRUST IN ME, LEMONT. I WAS JUST ON MY WAY TO THE POLICE STATION.
BELL
THAT'LL TEACH ME NOT TO JUDGE PEOPLE.
...RIGHT AFTER I END WORLD HUNGER AND SAVE THE WHALES, YOU PUNK-@** FOOL.

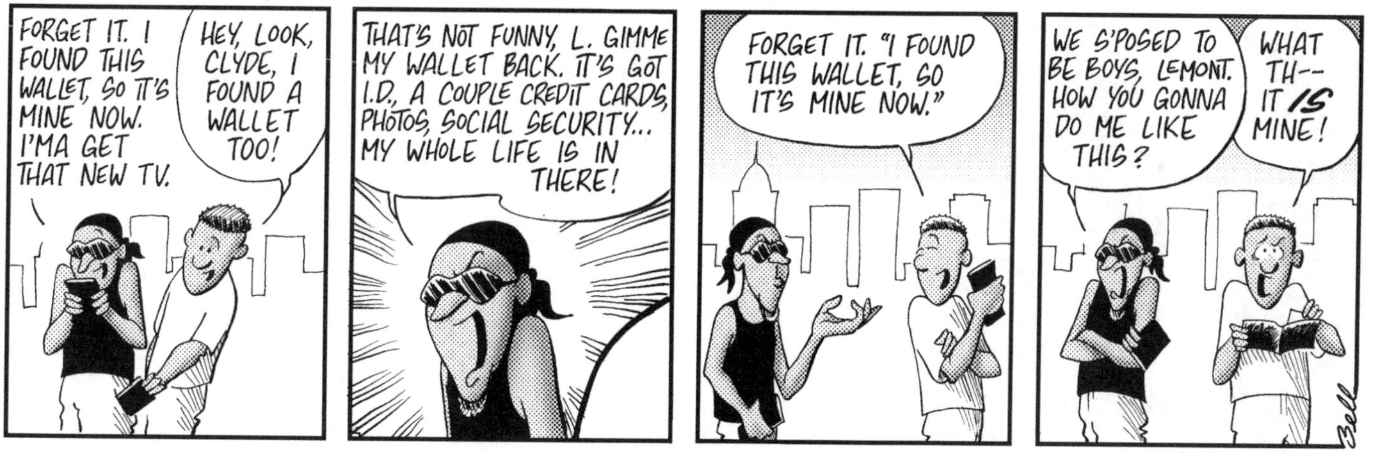
FORGET IT. I FOUND THIS WALLET, SO IT'S MINE NOW. I'MA GET THAT NEW TV.
HEY, LOOK, CLYDE, I FOUND A WALLET TOO!
THAT'S NOT FUNNY, L. GIMME MY WALLET BACK. IT'S GOT I.D., A COUPLE CREDIT CARDS, PHOTOS, SOCIAL SECURITY... MY WHOLE LIFE IS IN THERE!
FORGET IT. "I FOUND THIS WALLET, SO IT'S MINE NOW."
WE S'POSED TO BE BOYS, LEMONT. HOW YOU GONNA DO ME LIKE THIS?
WHAT TH-- IT IS MINE!
BELL

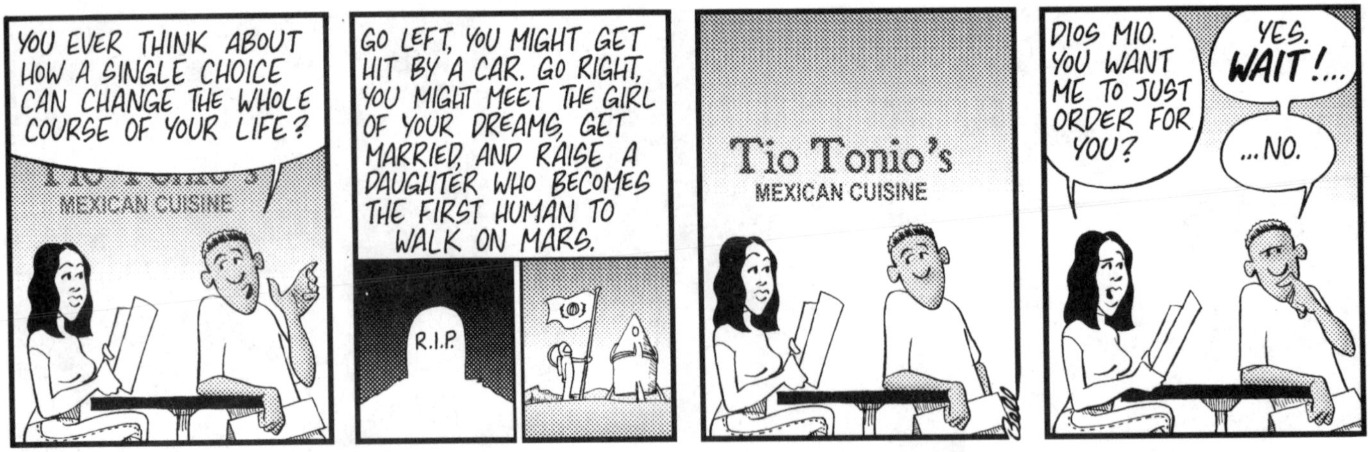
YOU EVER THINK ABOUT HOW A SINGLE CHOICE CAN CHANGE THE WHOLE COURSE OF YOUR LIFE?
MEXICAN CUISINE
GO LEFT, YOU MIGHT GET HIT BY A CAR. GO RIGHT, YOU MIGHT MEET THE GIRL OF YOUR DREAMS, GET MARRIED, AND RAISE A DAUGHTER WHO BECOMES THE FIRST HUMAN TO WALK ON MARS.
R.I.P.
Tio Tonio's
MEXICAN CUISINE
DIOS MIO. YOU WANT ME TO JUST ORDER FOR YOU?
YES. WAIT!...
...NO.

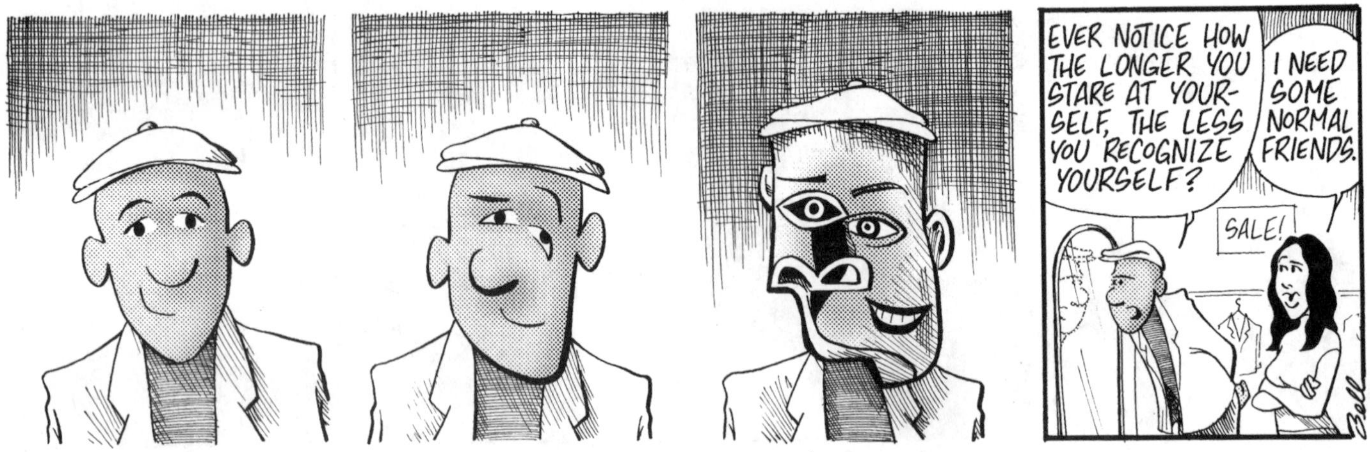
EVER NOTICE HOW THE LONGER YOU STARE AT YOURSELF, THE LESS YOU RECOGNIZE YOURSELF?
I NEED SOME NORMAL FRIENDS.
SALE!

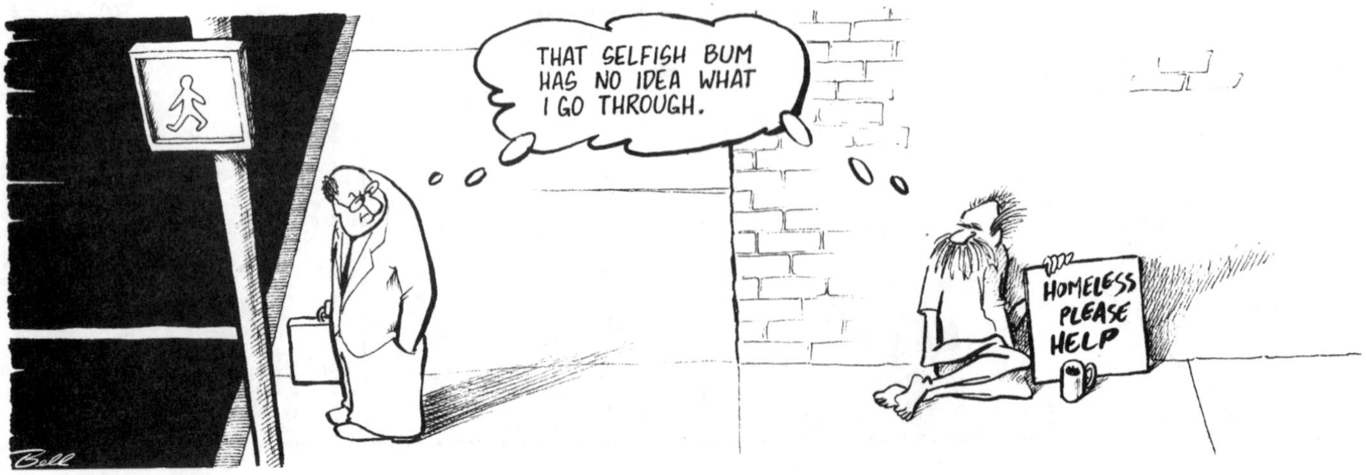
THAT SELFISH BUM HAS NO IDEA WHAT I GO THROUGH.
HOMELESS PLEASE HELP

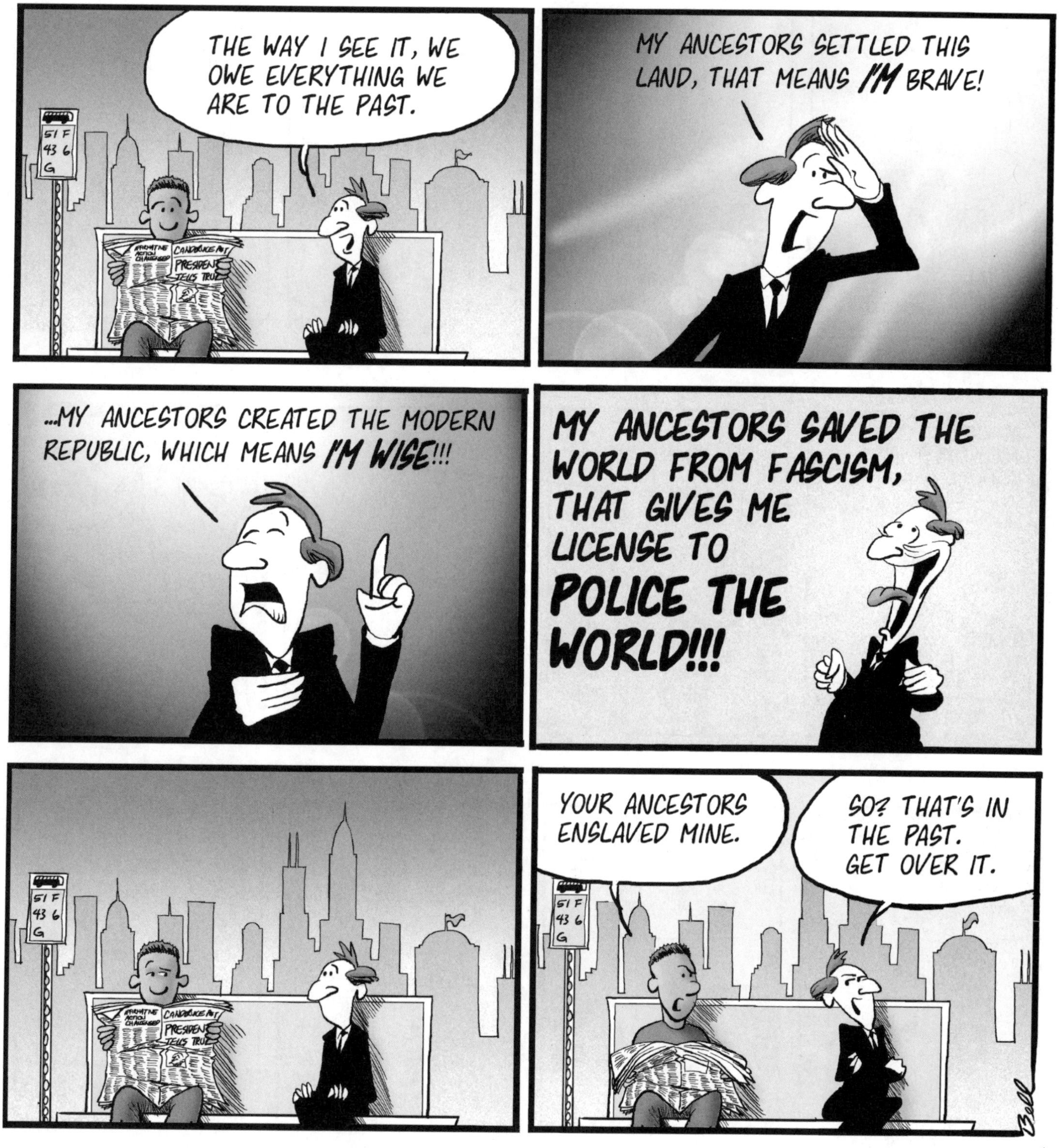
THE WAY I SEE IT, WE OWE EVERYTHING WE ARE TO THE PAST.
MY ANCESTORS SETTLED THIS LAND, THAT MEANS I'M BRAVE!
...MY ANCESTORS CREATED THE MODERN REPUBLIC, WHICH MEANS I'M WISE!!!
MY ANCESTORS SAVED THE WORLD FROM FASCISM, THAT GIVES ME LICENSE TO POLICE THE WORLD!!!
YOUR ANCESTORS ENSLAVED MINE.
SO? THAT'S IN THE PAST. GET OVER IT.
Bell

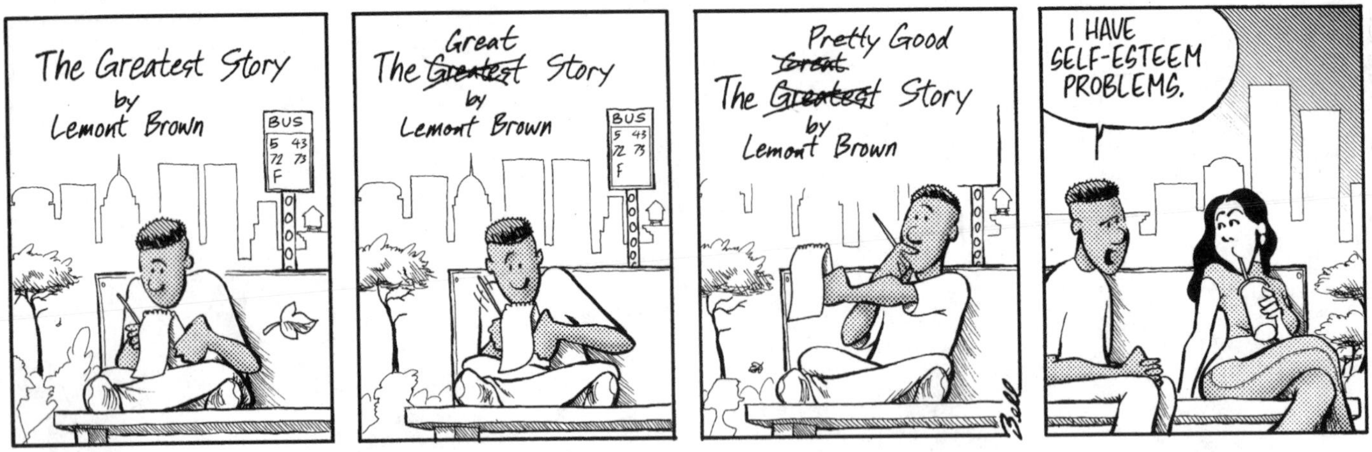
The Greatest Story
by
Lemont Brown
BUS
5 43
72 73
F
The Great ~~Greatest~~ Story
by
Lemont Brown
BUS
5 43
72 73
F
The Pretty Good ~~Great~~ ~~Greatest~~ Story
by
Lemont Brown
I HAVE SELF-ESTEEM PROBLEMS.

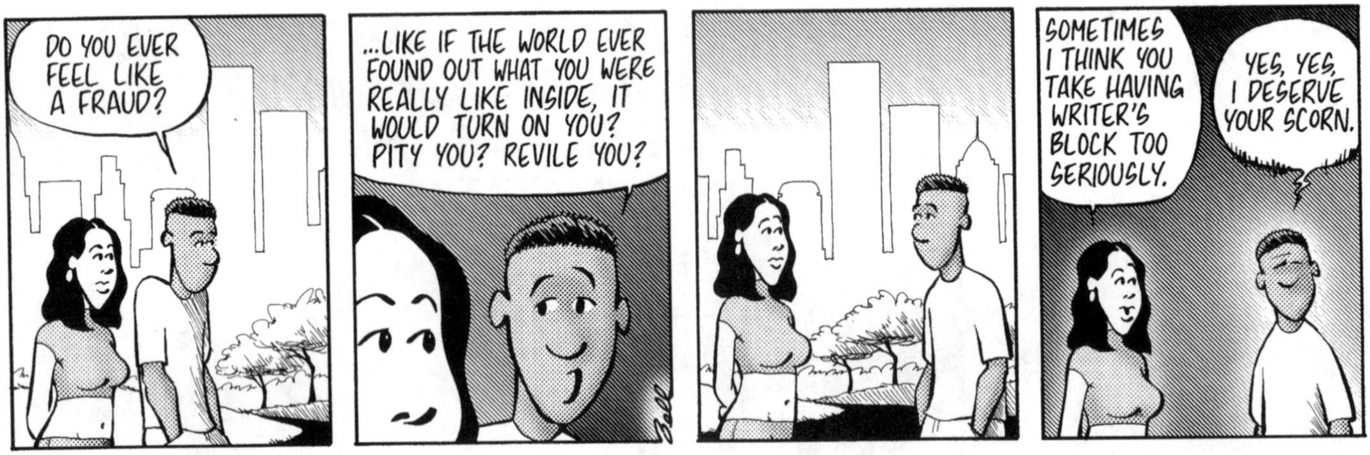
DO YOU EVER FEEL LIKE A FRAUD?
...LIKE IF THE WORLD EVER FOUND OUT WHAT YOU WERE REALLY LIKE INSIDE, IT WOULD TURN ON YOU? PITY YOU? REVILE YOU?
SOMETIMES I THINK YOU TAKE HAVING WRITER'S BLOCK TOO SERIOUSLY.
YES, YES, I DESERVE YOUR SCORN.

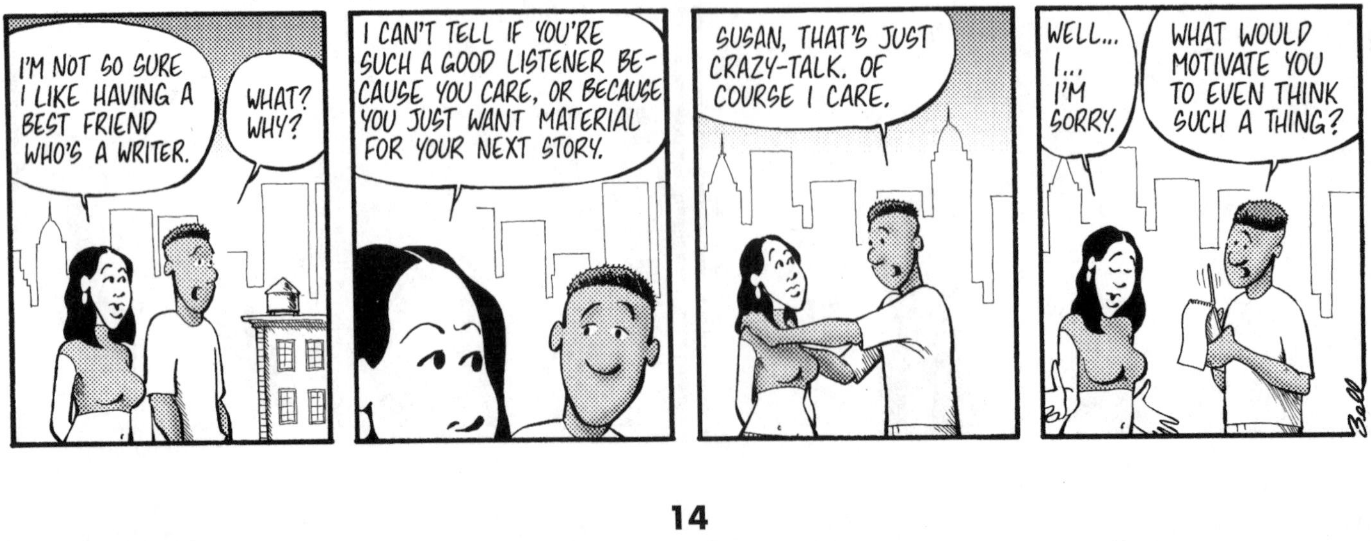
I'M NOT SO SURE I LIKE HAVING A BEST FRIEND WHO'S A WRITER.
WHAT? WHY?
I CAN'T TELL IF YOU'RE SUCH A GOOD LISTENER BECAUSE YOU CARE, OR BECAUSE YOU JUST WANT MATERIAL FOR YOUR NEXT STORY.
SUSAN, THAT'S JUST CRAZY-TALK. OF COURSE I CARE.
WELL... I... I'M SORRY.
WHAT WOULD MOTIVATE YOU TO EVEN THINK SUCH A THING?

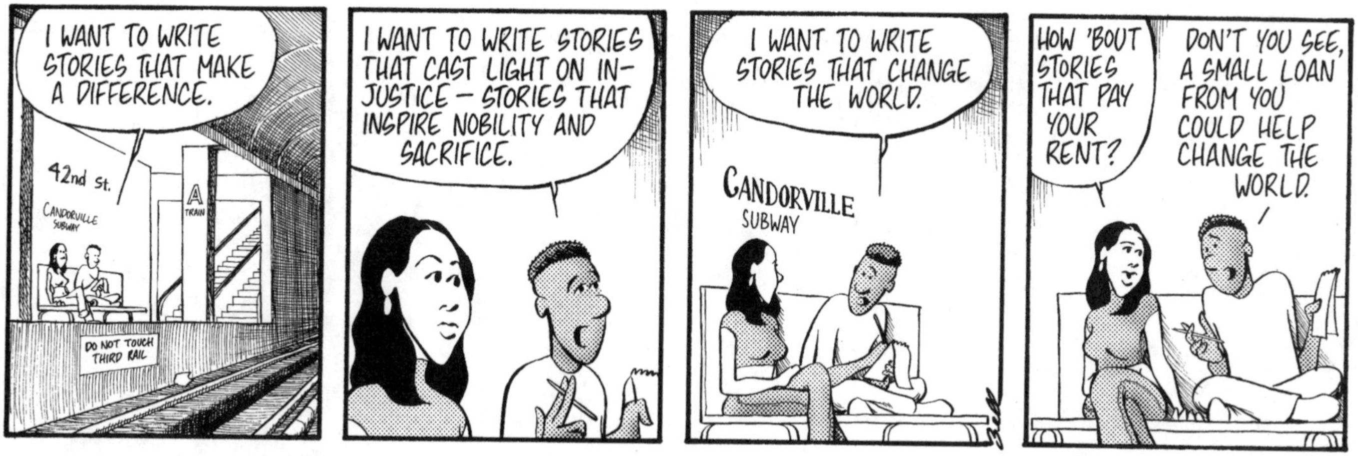
I WANT TO WRITE STORIES THAT MAKE A DIFFERENCE.
42nd St.
CANDORVILLE SUBWAY
A TRAIN
DO NOT TOUCH THIRD RAIL
I WANT TO WRITE STORIES THAT CAST LIGHT ON INJUSTICE — STORIES THAT INSPIRE NOBILITY AND SACRIFICE.
I WANT TO WRITE STORIES THAT CHANGE THE WORLD.
CANDORVILLE SUBWAY
HOW 'BOUT STORIES THAT PAY YOUR RENT?
DON'T YOU SEE, A SMALL LOAN FROM YOU COULD HELP CHANGE THE WORLD.

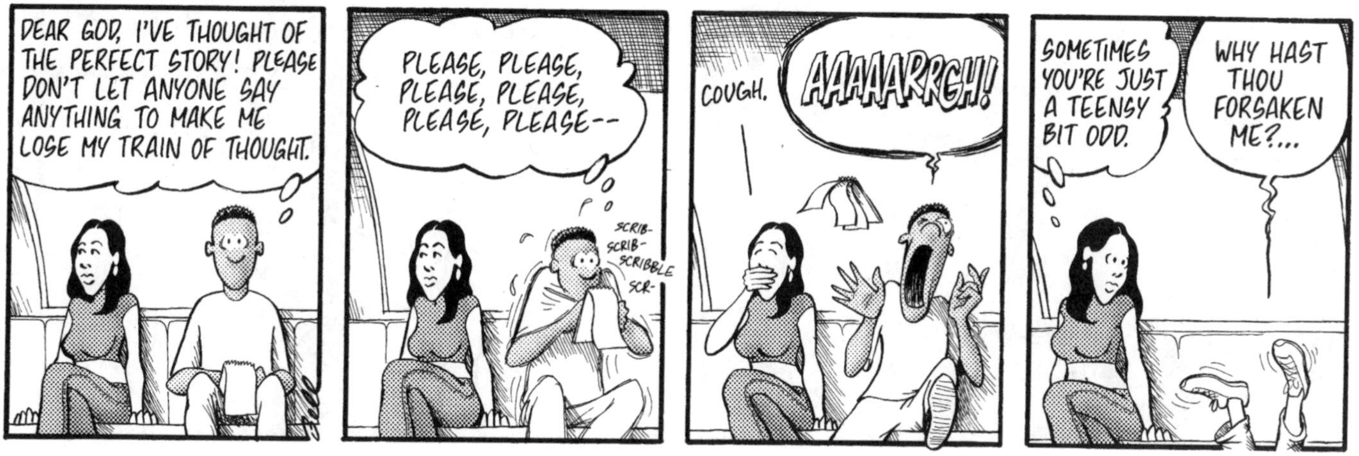
DEAR GOD, I'VE THOUGHT OF THE PERFECT STORY! PLEASE DON'T LET ANYONE SAY ANYTHING TO MAKE ME LOSE MY TRAIN OF THOUGHT.
PLEASE, PLEASE, PLEASE, PLEASE, PLEASE, PLEASE--
SCRIB- SCRIB- SCRIBBLE SCR-
COUGH.
AAAAARRGH!
SOMETIMES YOU'RE JUST A TEENSY BIT ODD.
WHY HAST THOU FORSAKEN ME?...

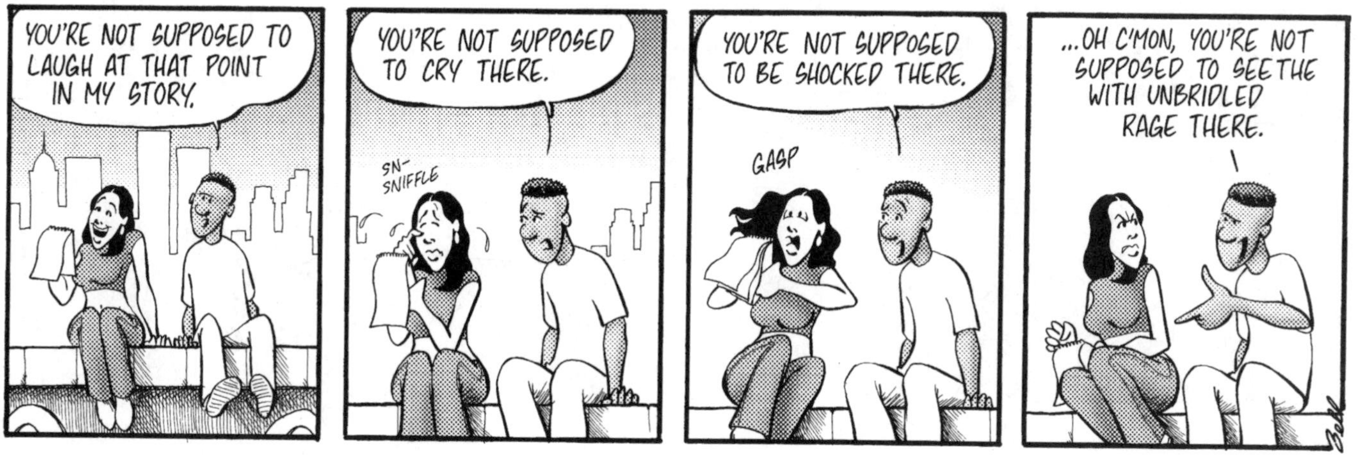
YOU'RE NOT SUPPOSED TO LAUGH AT THAT POINT IN MY STORY.
YOU'RE NOT SUPPOSED TO CRY THERE.
SN- SNIFFLE
YOU'RE NOT SUPPOSED TO BE SHOCKED THERE.
GASP
...OH C'MON, YOU'RE NOT SUPPOSED TO SEETHE WITH UNBRIDLED RAGE THERE.

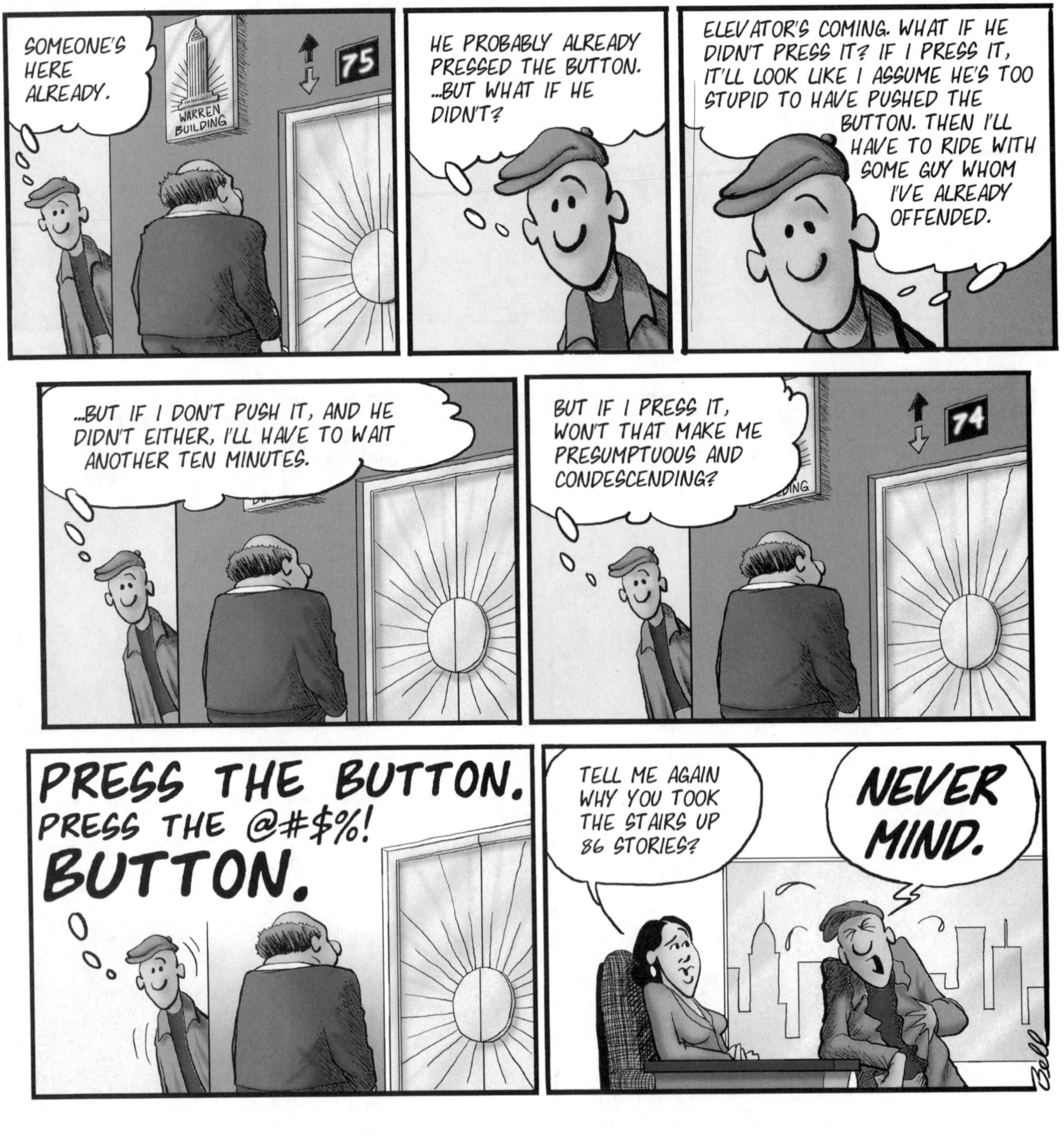
SOMEONE'S HERE ALREADY.
WARREN BUILDING
75
HE PROBABLY ALREADY PRESSED THE BUTTON. ...BUT WHAT IF HE DIDN'T?
ELEVATOR'S COMING. WHAT IF HE DIDN'T PRESS IT? IF I PRESS IT, IT'LL LOOK LIKE I ASSUME HE'S TOO STUPID TO HAVE PUSHED THE BUTTON. THEN I'LL HAVE TO RIDE WITH SOME GUY WHOM I'VE ALREADY OFFENDED.
...BUT IF I DON'T PUSH IT, AND HE DIDN'T EITHER, I'LL HAVE TO WAIT ANOTHER TEN MINUTES.
BUT IF I PRESS IT, WON'T THAT MAKE ME PRESUMPTUOUS AND CONDESCENDING?
74
PRESS THE BUTTON. PRESS THE @#$%! BUTTON.
TELL ME AGAIN WHY YOU TOOK THE STAIRS UP 86 STORIES?
NEVER MIND.
Bell

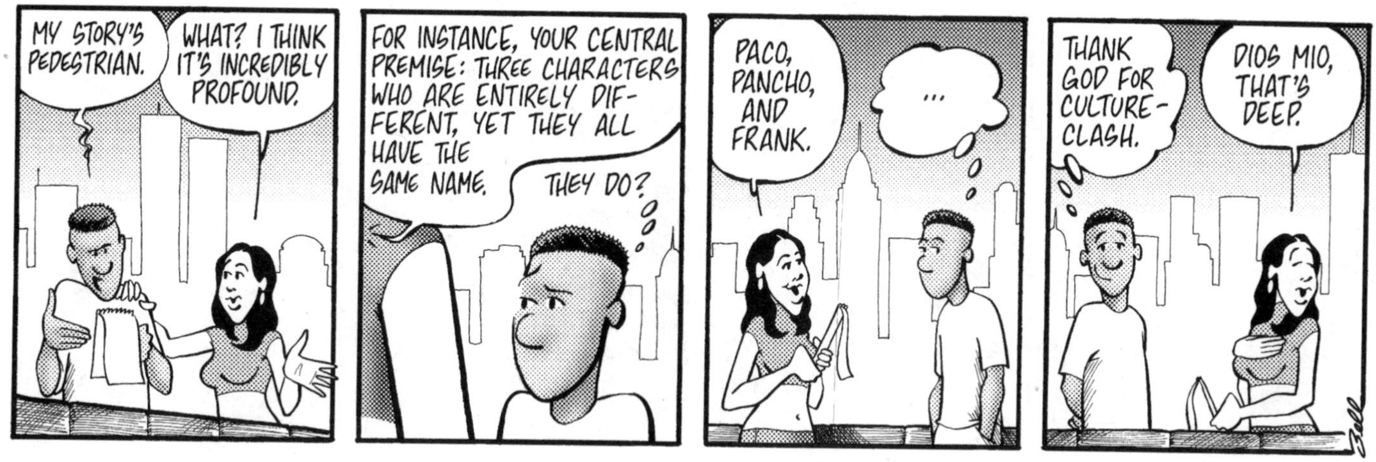
MY STORY'S PEDESTRIAN.
WHAT? I THINK IT'S INCREDIBLY PROFOUND.
FOR INSTANCE, YOUR CENTRAL PREMISE: THREE CHARACTERS WHO ARE ENTIRELY DIF-FERENT, YET THEY ALL HAVE THE SAME NAME.
THEY DO?
PACO, PANCHO, AND FRANK.
...
THANK GOD FOR CULTURE-CLASH.
DIOS MIO, THAT'S DEEP.

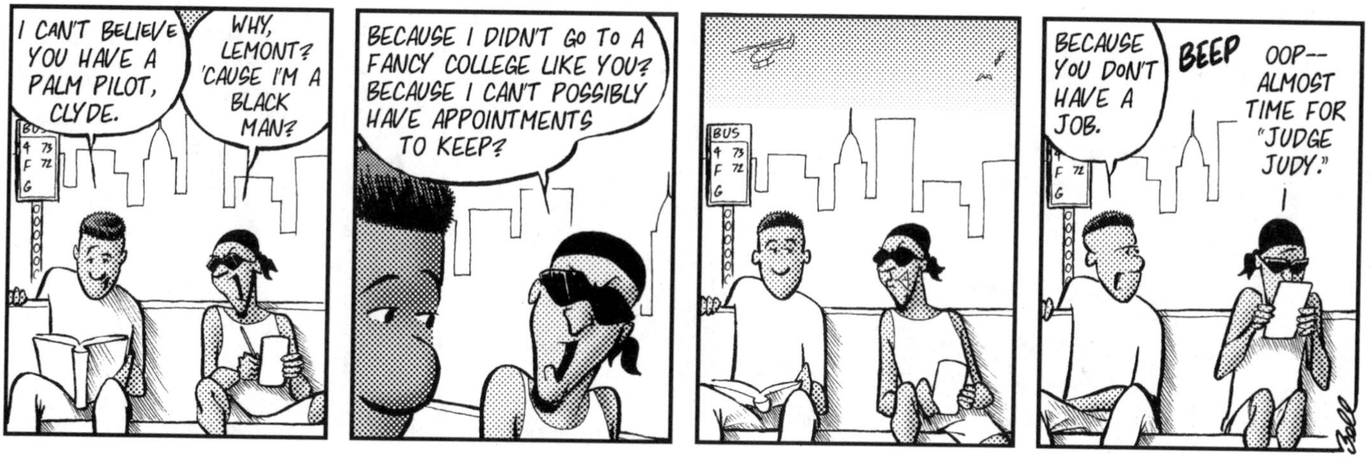
I CAN'T BELIEVE YOU HAVE A PALM PILOT, CLYDE.
WHY, LEMONT? 'CAUSE I'M A BLACK MAN?
BUS 4 73 F 72 G
BECAUSE I DIDN'T GO TO A FANCY COLLEGE LIKE YOU? BECAUSE I CAN'T POSSIBLY HAVE APPOINTMENTS TO KEEP?
BUS 4 73 F 72 G
BECAUSE YOU DON'T HAVE A JOB.
BEEP
OOP-- ALMOST TIME FOR "JUDGE JUDY."

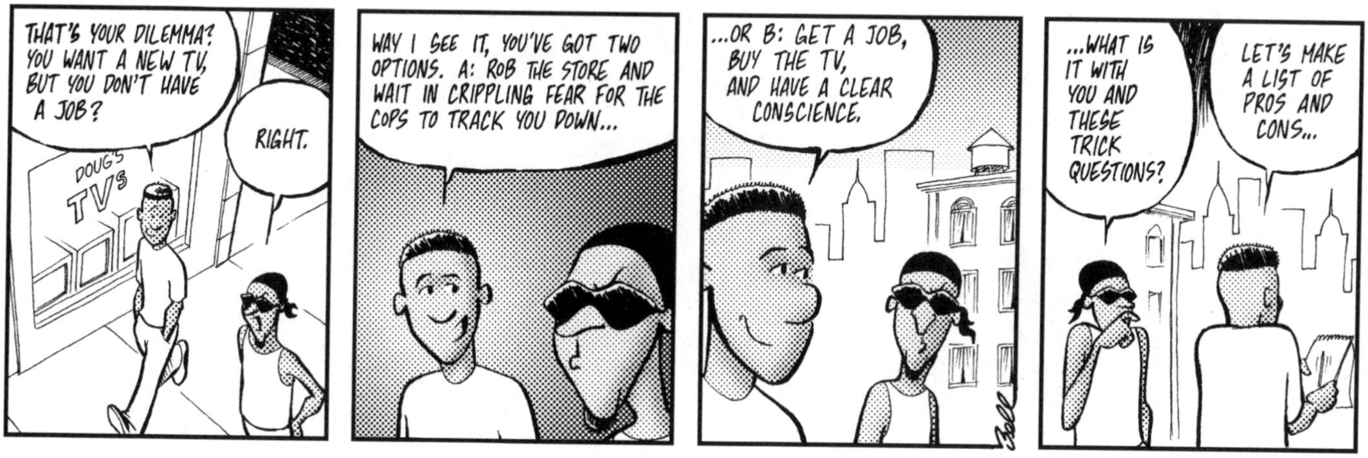
THAT'S YOUR DILEMMA? YOU WANT A NEW TV, BUT YOU DON'T HAVE A JOB?
RIGHT.
DOUG'S TVs
WAY I SEE IT, YOU'VE GOT TWO OPTIONS. A: ROB THE STORE AND WAIT IN CRIPPLING FEAR FOR THE COPS TO TRACK YOU DOWN...
...OR B: GET A JOB, BUY THE TV, AND HAVE A CLEAR CONSCIENCE.
...WHAT IS IT WITH YOU AND THESE TRICK QUESTIONS?
LET'S MAKE A LIST OF PROS AND CONS...

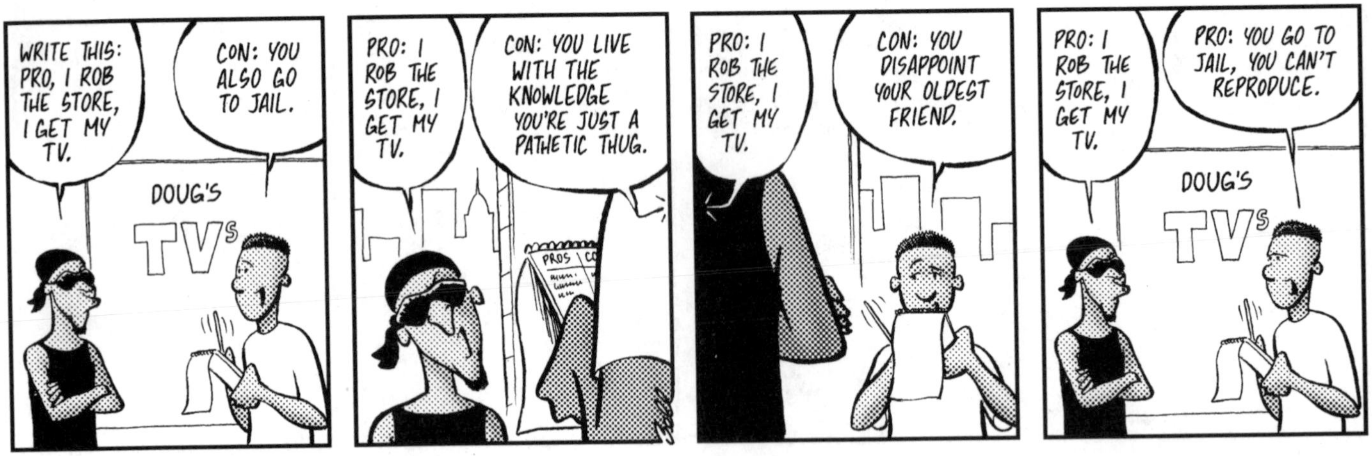
WRITE THIS: PRO, I ROB THE STORE, I GET MY TV.
CON: YOU ALSO GO TO JAIL.
DOUG'S TVs
PRO: I ROB THE STORE, I GET MY TV.
CON: YOU LIVE WITH THE KNOWLEDGE YOU'RE JUST A PATHETIC THUG.
PROS
PRO: I ROB THE STORE, I GET MY TV.
CON: YOU DISAPPOINT YOUR OLDEST FRIEND.
PRO: I ROB THE STORE, I GET MY TV.
PRO: YOU GO TO JAIL, YOU CAN'T REPRODUCE.
DOUG'S TVs

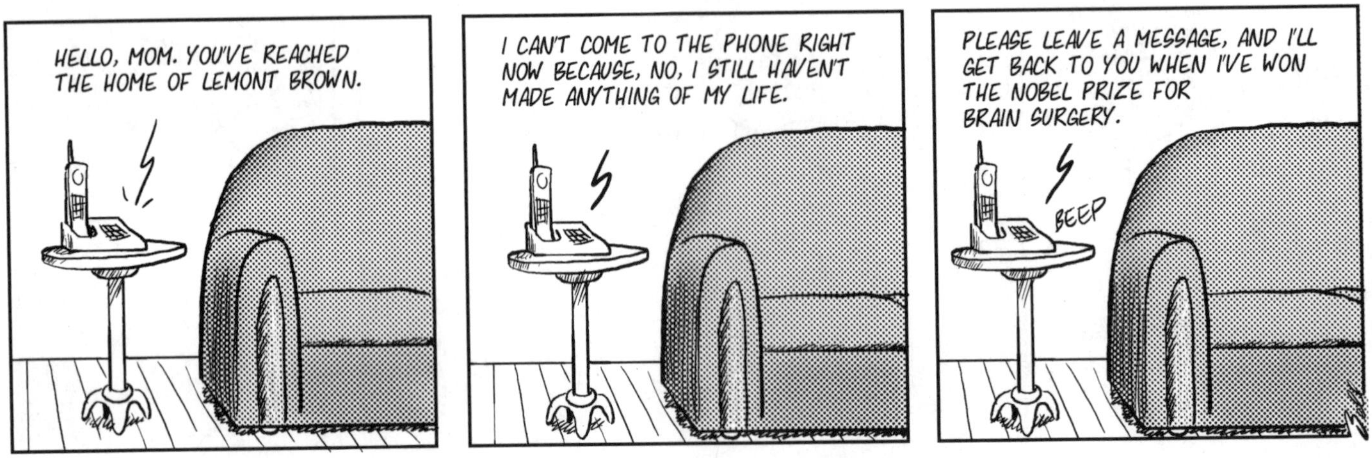
HELLO, MOM. YOU'VE REACHED THE HOME OF LEMONT BROWN.
I CAN'T COME TO THE PHONE RIGHT NOW BECAUSE, NO, I STILL HAVEN'T MADE ANYTHING OF MY LIFE.
PLEASE LEAVE A MESSAGE, AND I'LL GET BACK TO YOU WHEN I'VE WON THE NOBEL PRIZE FOR BRAIN SURGERY.
BEEP

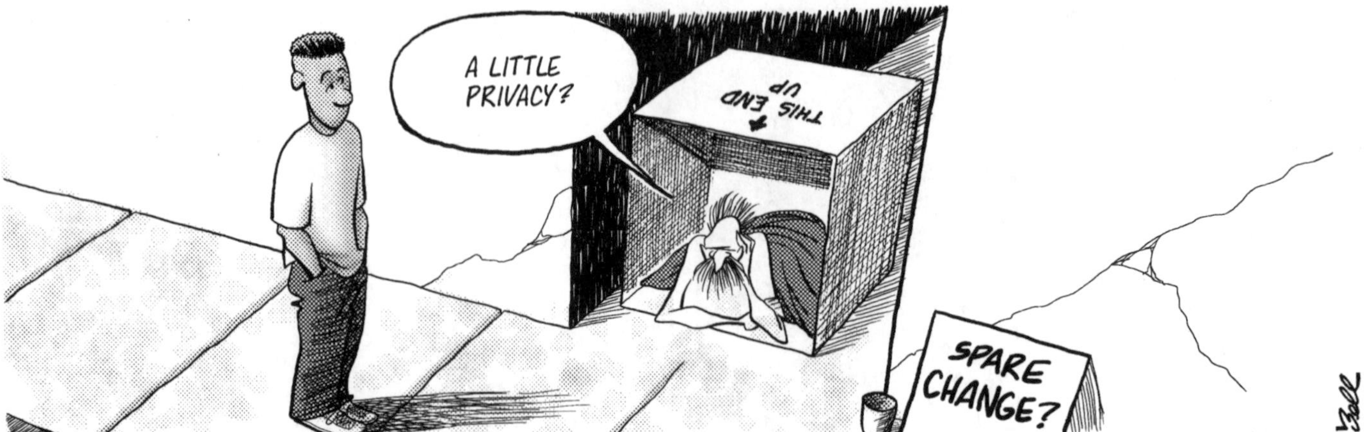
A LITTLE PRIVACY?
THIS END UP
SPARE CHANGE?

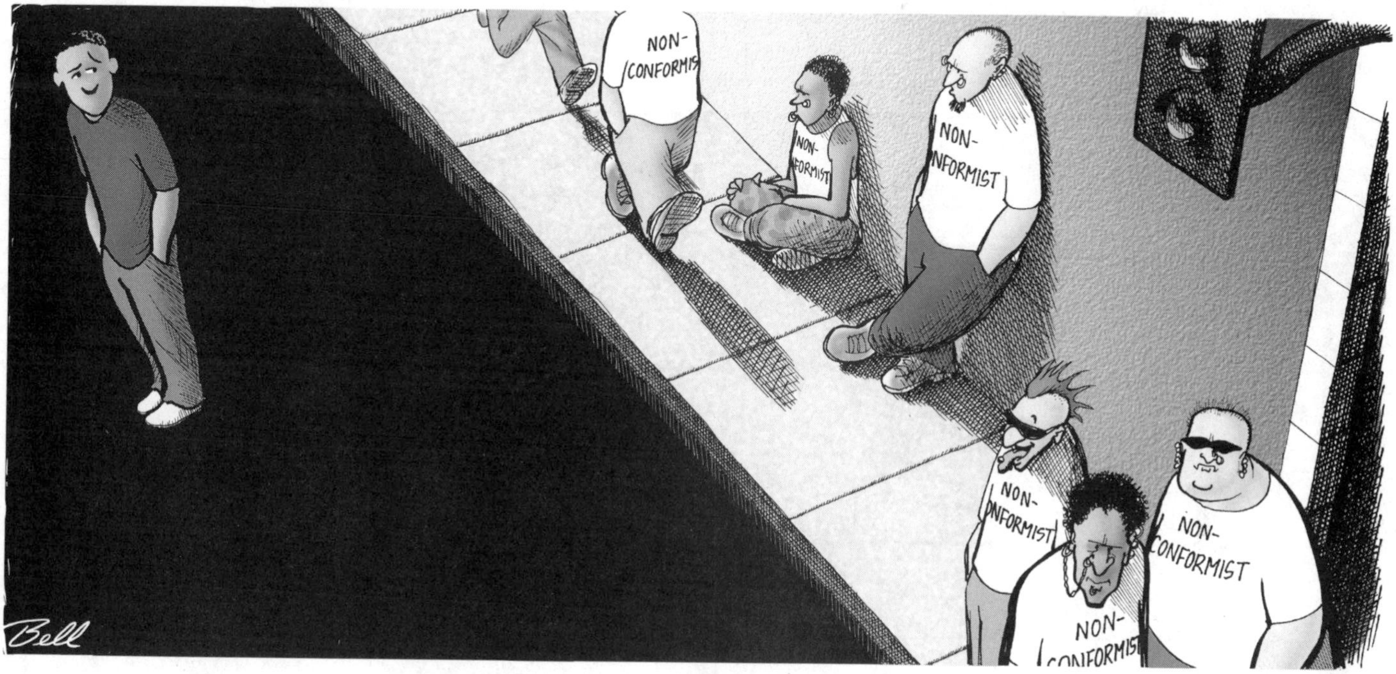
NON-
CONFORMIS
NON-
FORMIST
NON-
NFORMIST
NON-
NFORMIST
NON-
CONFORMIST
NON-
CONFORMIST
Bell

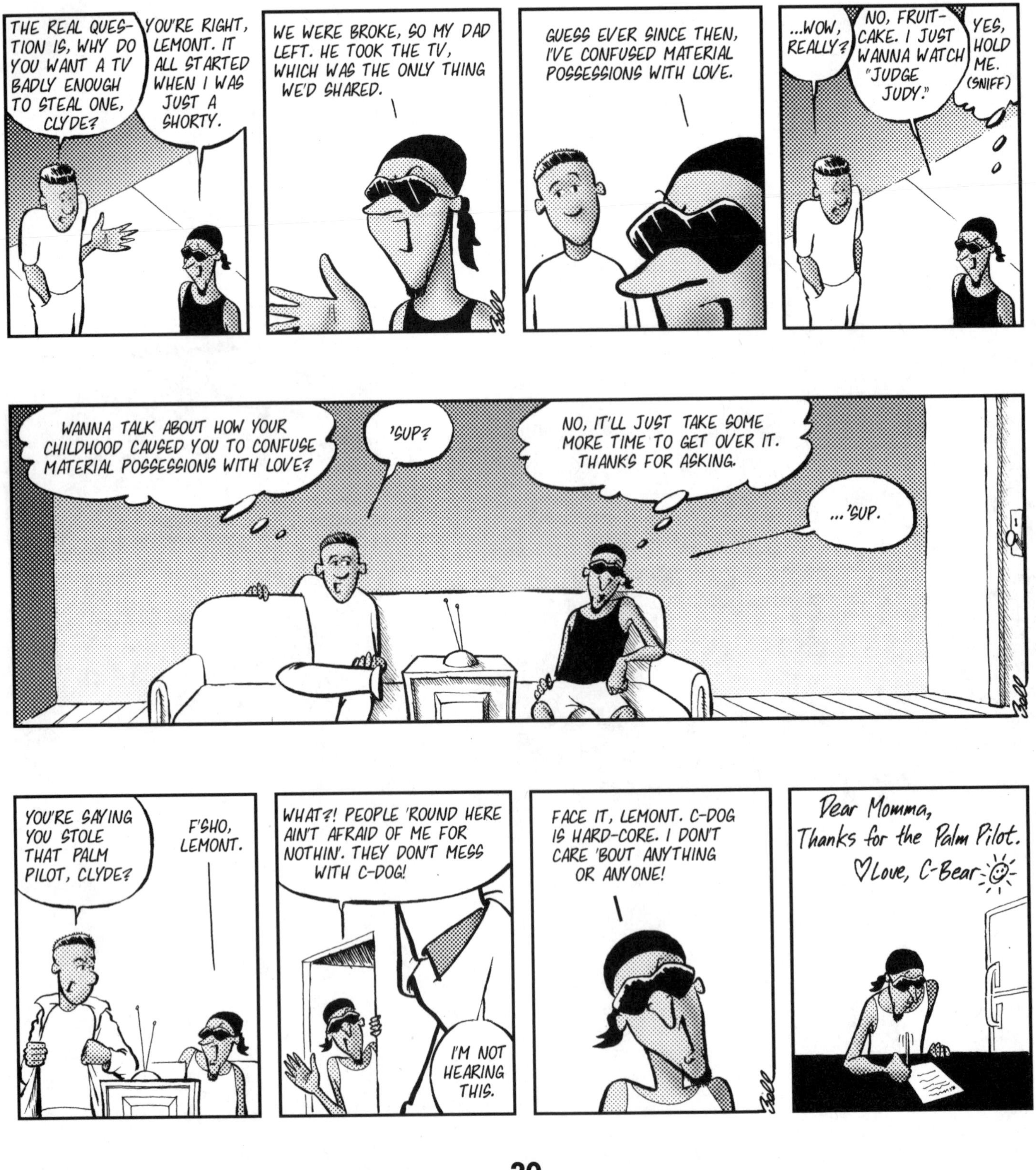
THE REAL QUESTION IS, WHY DO YOU WANT A TV BADLY ENOUGH TO STEAL ONE, CLYDE?
YOU'RE RIGHT, LEMONT. IT ALL STARTED WHEN I WAS JUST A SHORTY.
WE WERE BROKE, SO MY DAD LEFT. HE TOOK THE TV, WHICH WAS THE ONLY THING WE'D SHARED.
GUESS EVER SINCE THEN, I'VE CONFUSED MATERIAL POSSESSIONS WITH LOVE.
...WOW, REALLY?
NO, FRUITCAKE. I JUST WANNA WATCH "JUDGE JUDY."
YES, HOLD ME. (SNIFF)
WANNA TALK ABOUT HOW YOUR CHILDHOOD CAUSED YOU TO CONFUSE MATERIAL POSSESSIONS WITH LOVE?
'SUP?
NO, IT'LL JUST TAKE SOME MORE TIME TO GET OVER IT. THANKS FOR ASKING.
...'SUP.
YOU'RE SAYING YOU STOLE THAT PALM PILOT, CLYDE?
F'SHO, LEMONT.
WHAT?! PEOPLE 'ROUND HERE AIN'T AFRAID OF ME FOR NOTHIN'. THEY DON'T MESS WITH C-DOG!
I'M NOT HEARING THIS.
FACE IT, LEMONT. C-DOG IS HARD-CORE. I DON'T CARE 'BOUT ANYTHING OR ANYONE!
Dear Momma,
Thanks for the Palm Pilot.
♡Love, C-Bear

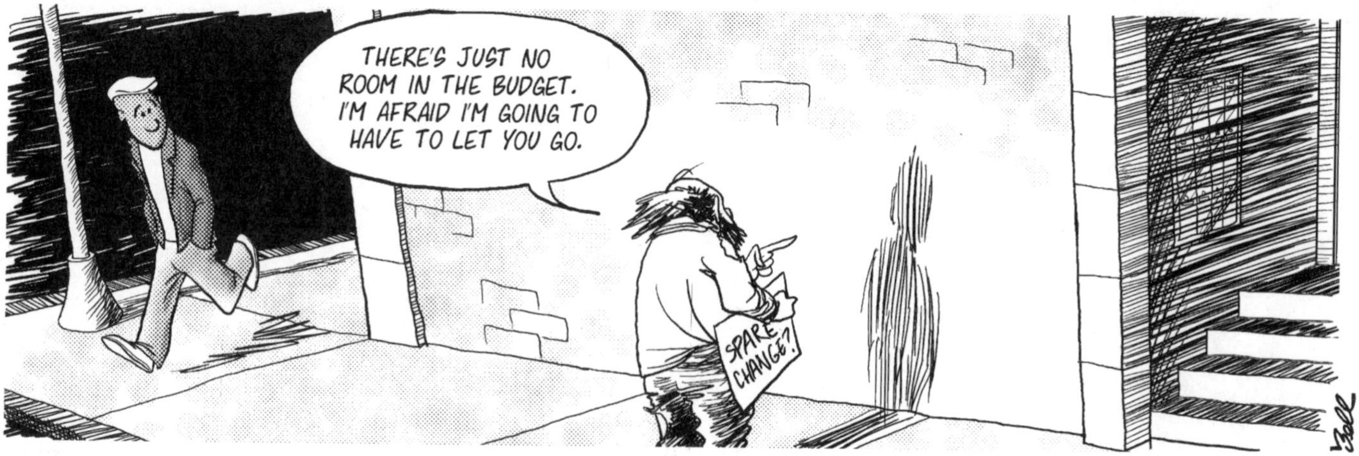
THERE'S JUST NO ROOM IN THE BUDGET. I'M AFRAID I'M GOING TO HAVE TO LET YOU GO.
SPARE CHANGE?

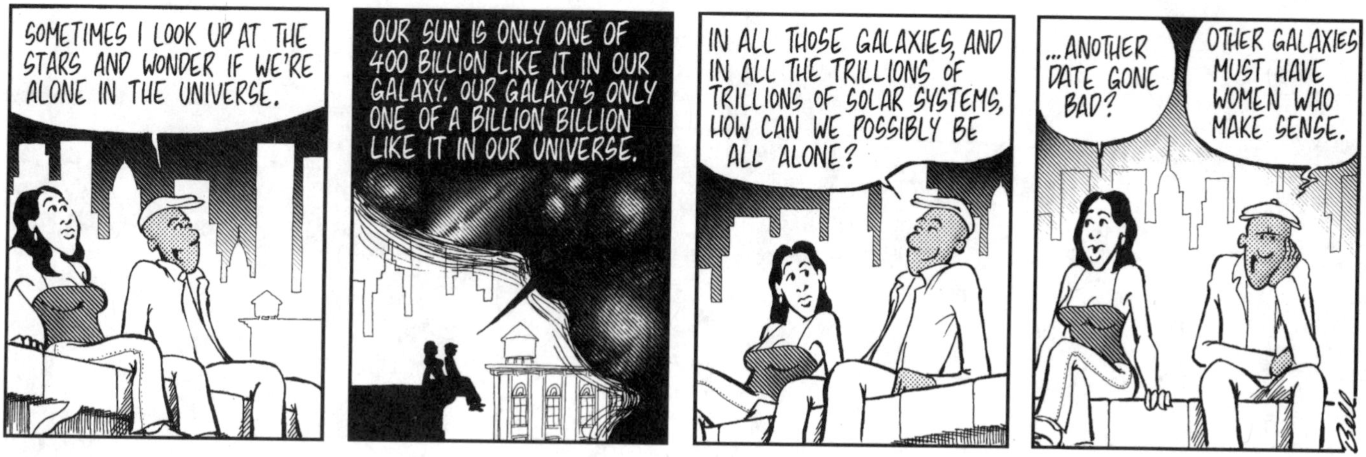
SOMETIMES I LOOK UP AT THE STARS AND WONDER IF WE'RE ALONE IN THE UNIVERSE.
OUR SUN IS ONLY ONE OF 400 BILLION LIKE IT IN OUR GALAXY. OUR GALAXY'S ONLY ONE OF A BILLION BILLION LIKE IT IN OUR UNIVERSE.
IN ALL THOSE GALAXIES, AND IN ALL THE TRILLIONS OF TRILLIONS OF SOLAR SYSTEMS, HOW CAN WE POSSIBLY BE ALL ALONE?
...ANOTHER DATE GONE BAD?
OTHER GALAXIES MUST HAVE WOMEN WHO MAKE SENSE.

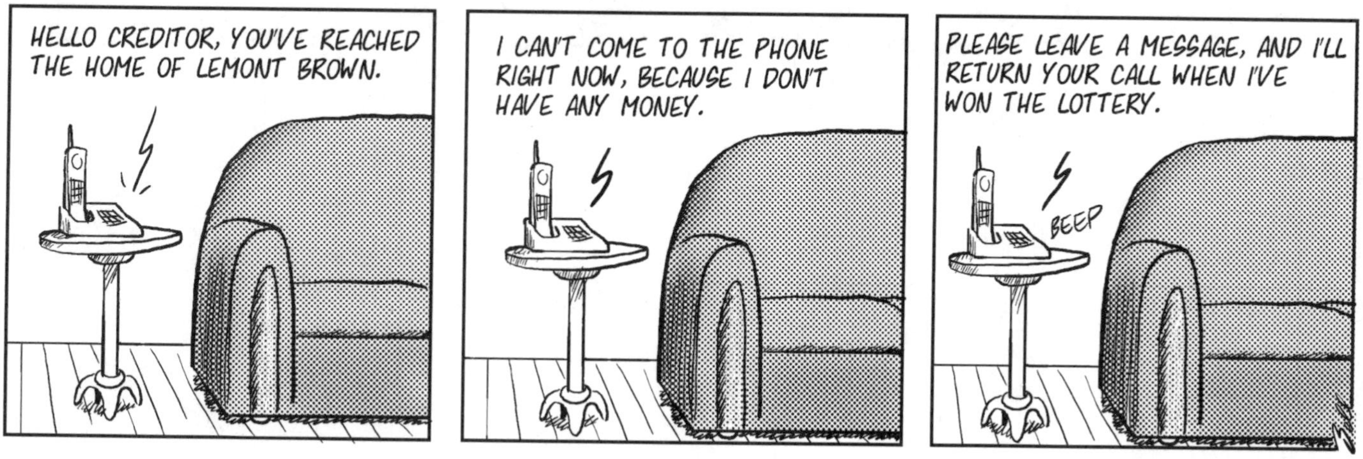
HELLO CREDITOR, YOU'VE REACHED THE HOME OF LEMONT BROWN.
I CAN'T COME TO THE PHONE RIGHT NOW, BECAUSE I DON'T HAVE ANY MONEY.
PLEASE LEAVE A MESSAGE, AND I'LL RETURN YOUR CALL WHEN I'VE WON THE LOTTERY.
BEEP

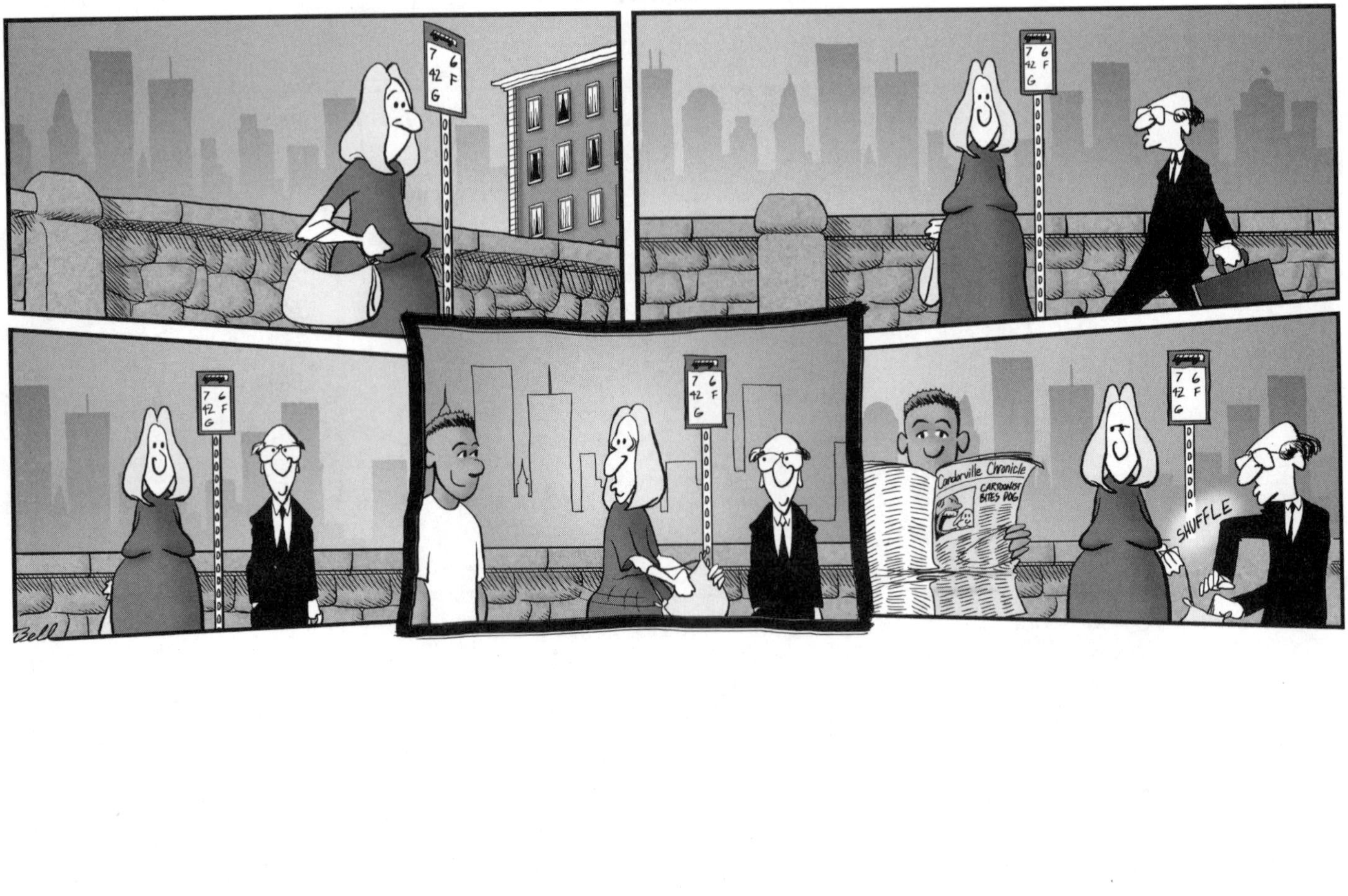

Canderville Chronicle
CARTOONIST BITES DOG
SHUFFLE

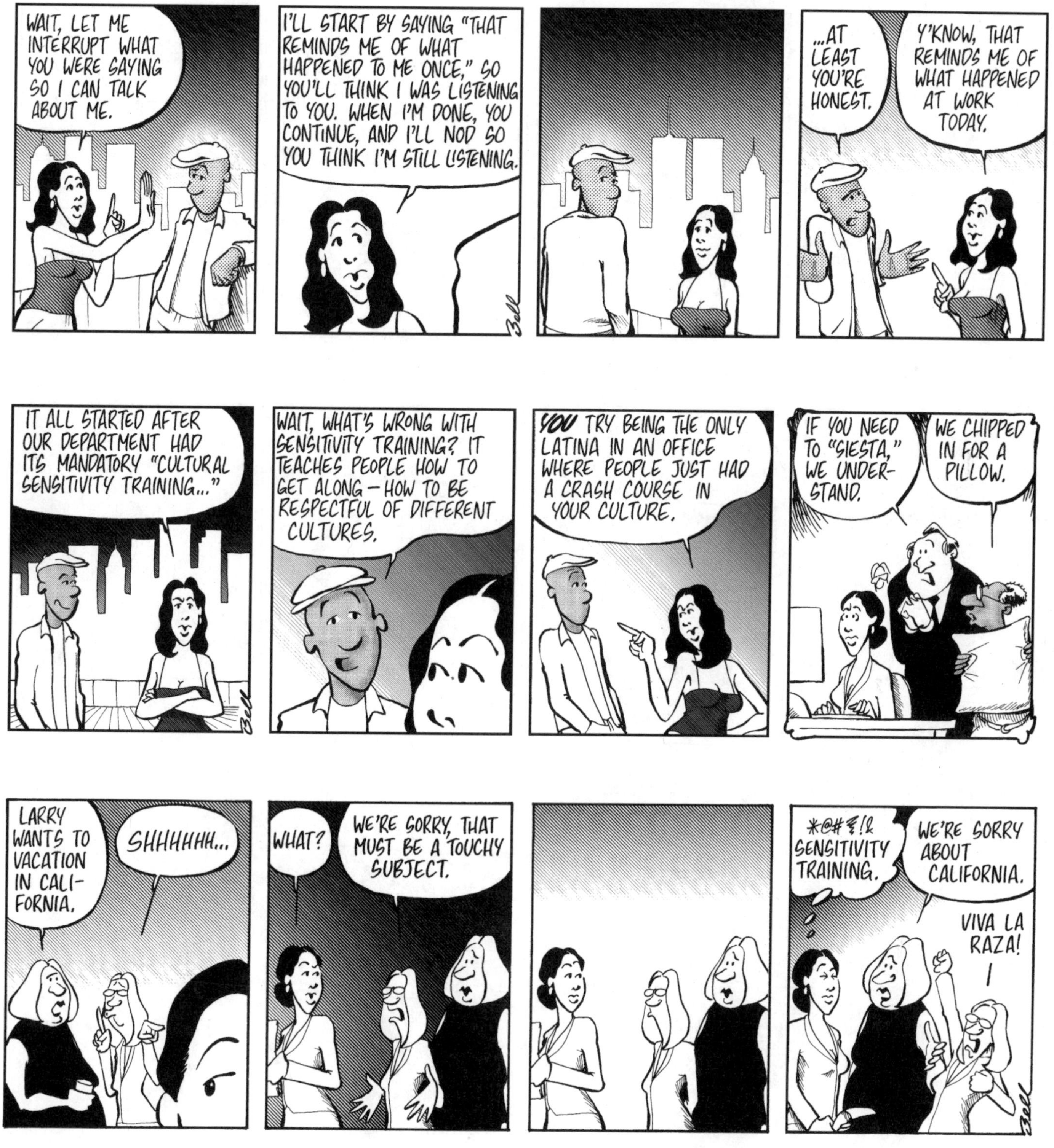
WAIT, LET ME INTERRUPT WHAT YOU WERE SAYING SO I CAN TALK ABOUT ME.
I'LL START BY SAYING "THAT REMINDS ME OF WHAT HAPPENED TO ME ONCE," SO YOU'LL THINK I WAS LISTENING TO YOU. WHEN I'M DONE, YOU CONTINUE, AND I'LL NOD SO YOU THINK I'M STILL LISTENING.
...AT LEAST YOU'RE HONEST.
Y'KNOW, THAT REMINDS ME OF WHAT HAPPENED AT WORK TODAY.
IT ALL STARTED AFTER OUR DEPARTMENT HAD ITS MANDATORY "CULTURAL SENSITIVITY TRAINING..."
WAIT, WHAT'S WRONG WITH SENSITIVITY TRAINING? IT TEACHES PEOPLE HOW TO GET ALONG — HOW TO BE RESPECTFUL OF DIFFERENT CULTURES.
YOU TRY BEING THE ONLY LATINA IN AN OFFICE WHERE PEOPLE JUST HAD A CRASH COURSE IN YOUR CULTURE.
IF YOU NEED TO "SIESTA," WE UNDERSTAND.
WE CHIPPED IN FOR A PILLOW.
LARRY WANTS TO VACATION IN CALIFORNIA.
SHHHHHH...
WHAT?
WE'RE SORRY, THAT MUST BE A TOUCHY SUBJECT.
*@#§!& SENSITIVITY TRAINING.
WE'RE SORRY ABOUT CALIFORNIA.
VIVA LA RAZA!

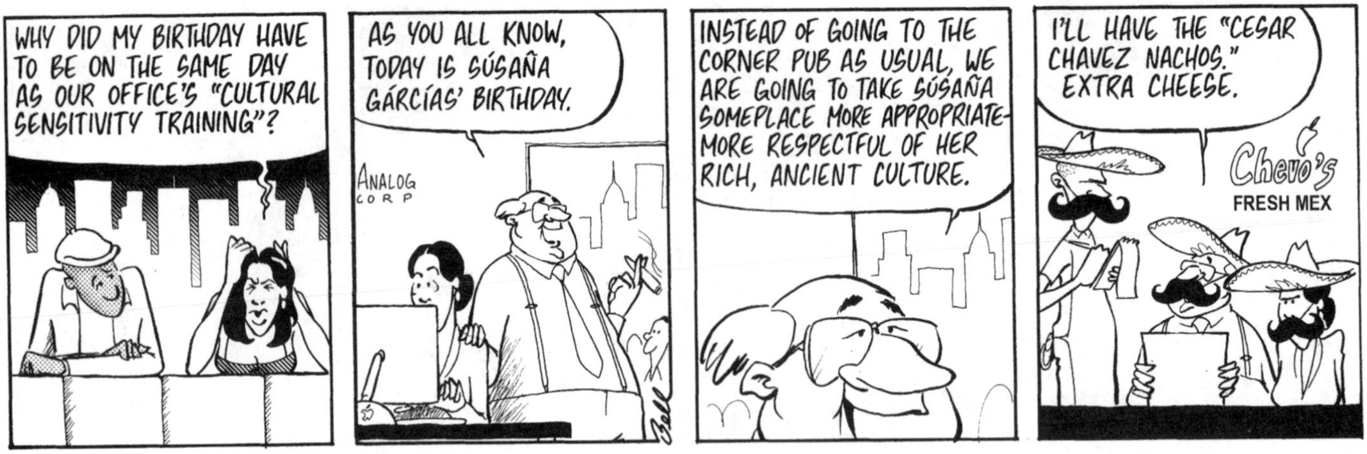
WHY DID MY BIRTHDAY HAVE TO BE ON THE SAME DAY AS OUR OFFICE'S "CULTURAL SENSITIVITY TRAINING"?
AS YOU ALL KNOW, TODAY IS SÚSAÑA GÁRCÍAS' BIRTHDAY.
ANALOG CORP
INSTEAD OF GOING TO THE CORNER PUB AS USUAL, WE ARE GOING TO TAKE SÚSAÑA SOMEPLACE MORE APPROPRIATE-MORE RESPECTFUL OF HER RICH, ANCIENT CULTURE.
I'LL HAVE THE "CESAR CHAVEZ NACHOS." EXTRA CHEESE.
Chevo's
FRESH MEX
Bell

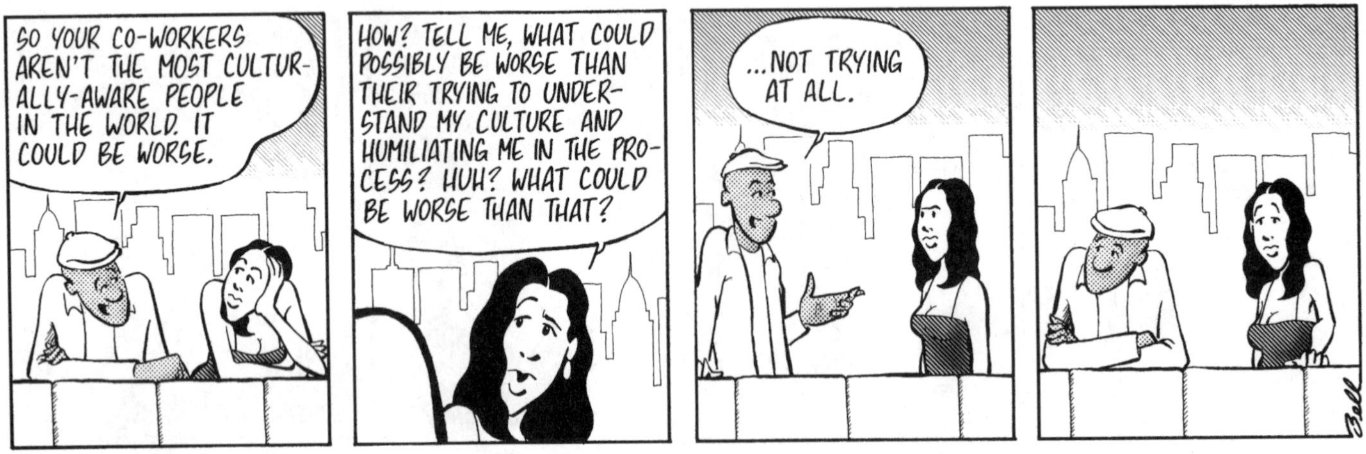
SO YOUR CO-WORKERS AREN'T THE MOST CULTURALLY-AWARE PEOPLE IN THE WORLD. IT COULD BE WORSE.
HOW? TELL ME, WHAT COULD POSSIBLY BE WORSE THAN THEIR TRYING TO UNDERSTAND MY CULTURE AND HUMILIATING ME IN THE PROCESS? HUH? WHAT COULD BE WORSE THAN THAT?
...NOT TRYING AT ALL.
Bell

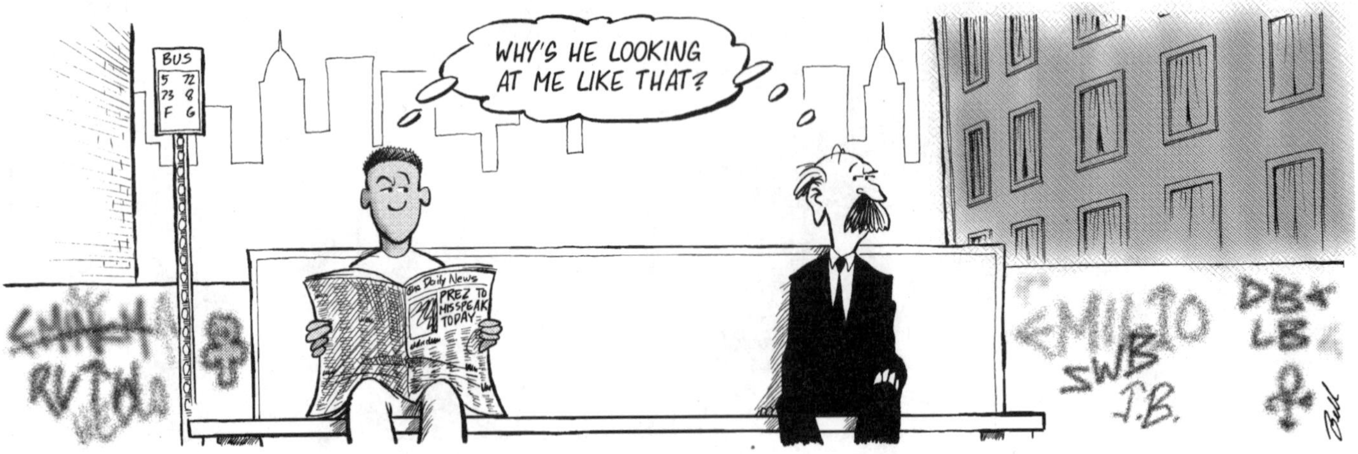
BUS
5 72
73 8
F G
WHY'S HE LOOKING AT ME LIKE THAT?
Daily News
PREZ TO MISSPEAK TODAY
EMILIO
SWB
J.B.
DB
LB
Bell

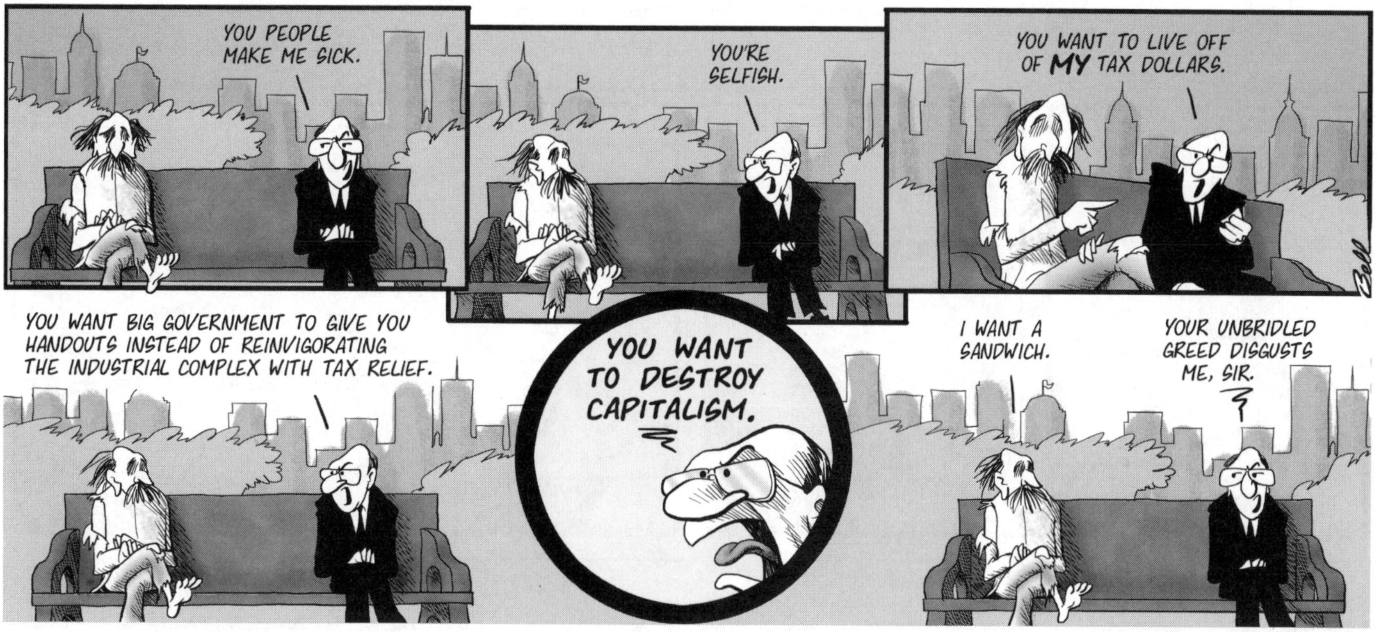
YOU PEOPLE MAKE ME SICK.
YOU'RE SELFISH.
YOU WANT TO LIVE OFF OF MY TAX DOLLARS.
YOU WANT BIG GOVERNMENT TO GIVE YOU HANDOUTS INSTEAD OF REINVIGORATING THE INDUSTRIAL COMPLEX WITH TAX RELIEF.
YOU WANT TO DESTROY CAPITALISM.
I WANT A SANDWICH.
YOUR UNBRIDLED GREED DISGUSTS ME, SIR.

DOWN WITH POLITICAL CORRECTNESS

I ASSUME YOU REALIZE THAT IT'S NOW POLITICALLY CORRECT TO CONDEMN POLITICAL CORRECTNESS.

DOWN WITH POLITICAL CORRECT...

DEAR FATHER, SOME SAY INTERRACIAL DATING IS A TRADE-OFF.

THE BLACK MAN SEEKS HIGHER SOCIAL STATUS, AND THE WHITE WOMAN WANTS MATERIAL ADVANCEMENT.

MOM, NEXT TIME YOU SAY GRACE.

PASS THE TURNIPS.

MAYBE IF HE KNEW I WAS BROKE...

SLURRRP

SORRY I DIDN'T WANT TO STAY AT YOUR FOLKS' FOR DINNER. WE CAN GET SOMETHING ON THE WAY TO THE MOVIE.

WHY DID YOU WANT TO GO, LEMONT?

YOUR DAD'S A RACIST BUFFOON.

I THOUGHT WE'D GET TO KNOW EACH OTHER BETTER ON OUR OWN.

THAT'S SWEET.

...AND I DIDN'T LIKE THE LOOKS OF THAT PUTRID SLOP YOUR MOM CONCOCTED.

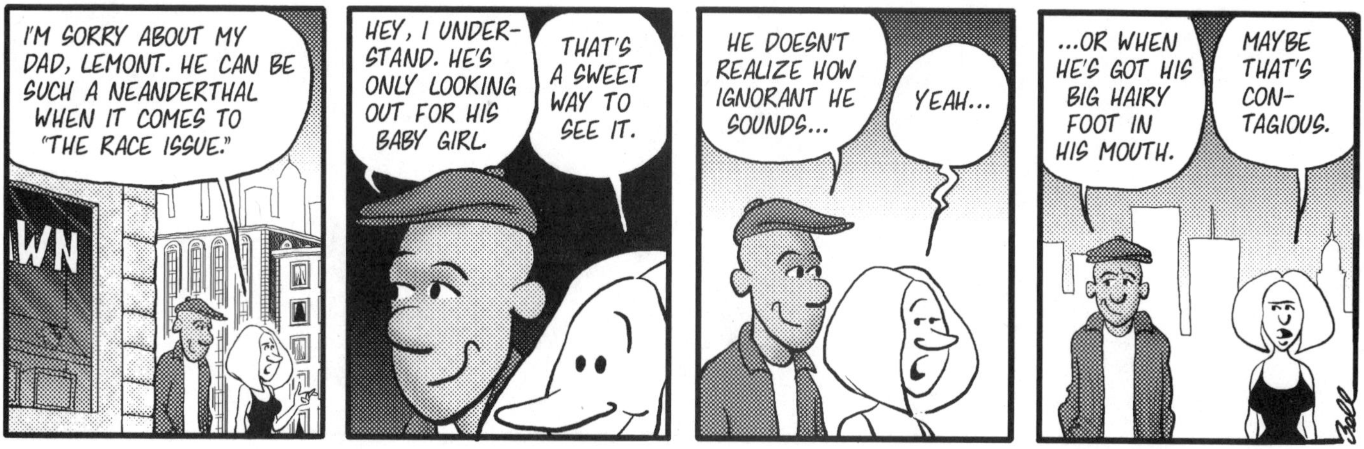
I'M SORRY ABOUT MY DAD, LEMONT. HE CAN BE SUCH A NEANDERTHAL WHEN IT COMES TO "THE RACE ISSUE."
HEY, I UNDERSTAND. HE'S ONLY LOOKING OUT FOR HIS BABY GIRL.
THAT'S A SWEET WAY TO SEE IT.
HE DOESN'T REALIZE HOW IGNORANT HE SOUNDS...
YEAH...
...OR WHEN HE'S GOT HIS BIG HAIRY FOOT IN HIS MOUTH.
MAYBE THAT'S CONTAGIOUS.

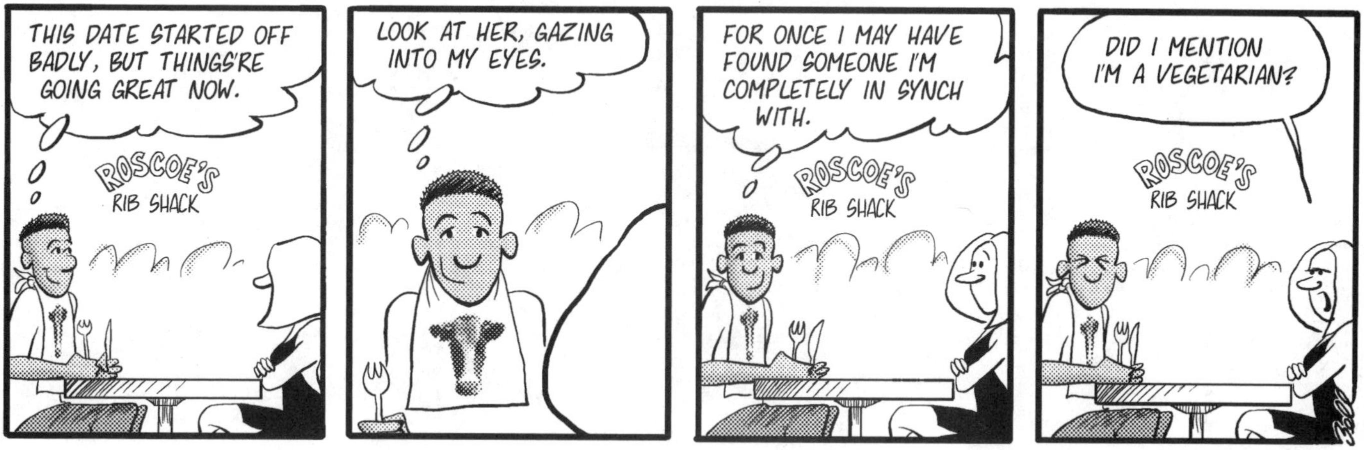
THIS DATE STARTED OFF BADLY, BUT THINGS'RE GOING GREAT NOW.
ROSCOE'S
RIB SHACK
LOOK AT HER, GAZING INTO MY EYES.
FOR ONCE I MAY HAVE FOUND SOMEONE I'M COMPLETELY IN SYNCH WITH.
ROSCOE'S
RIB SHACK
DID I MENTION I'M A VEGETARIAN?
ROSCOE'S
RIB SHACK

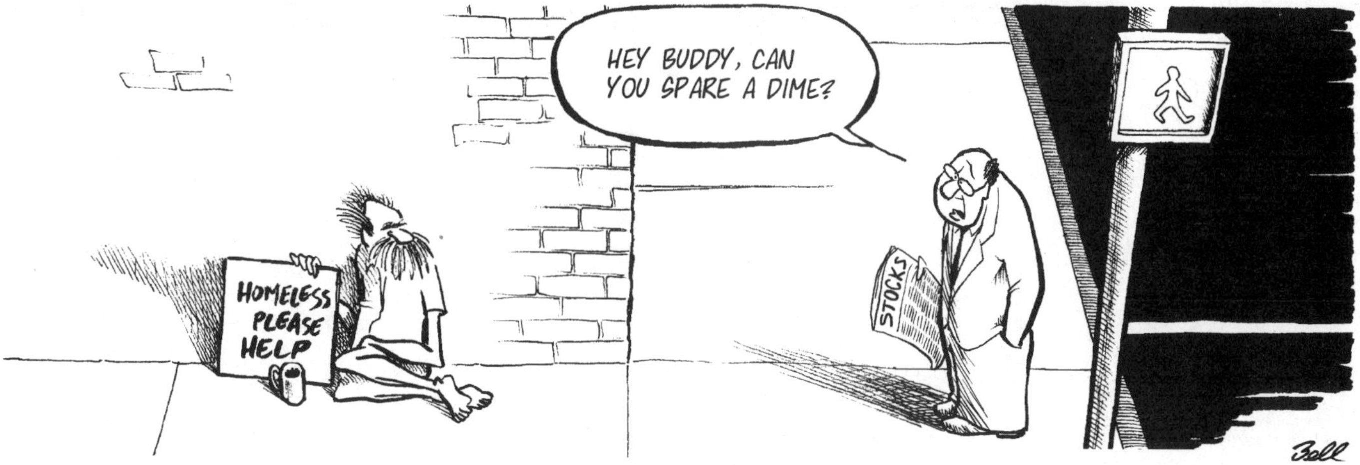
HOMELESS PLEASE HELP
HEY BUDDY, CAN YOU SPARE A DIME?
STOCKS

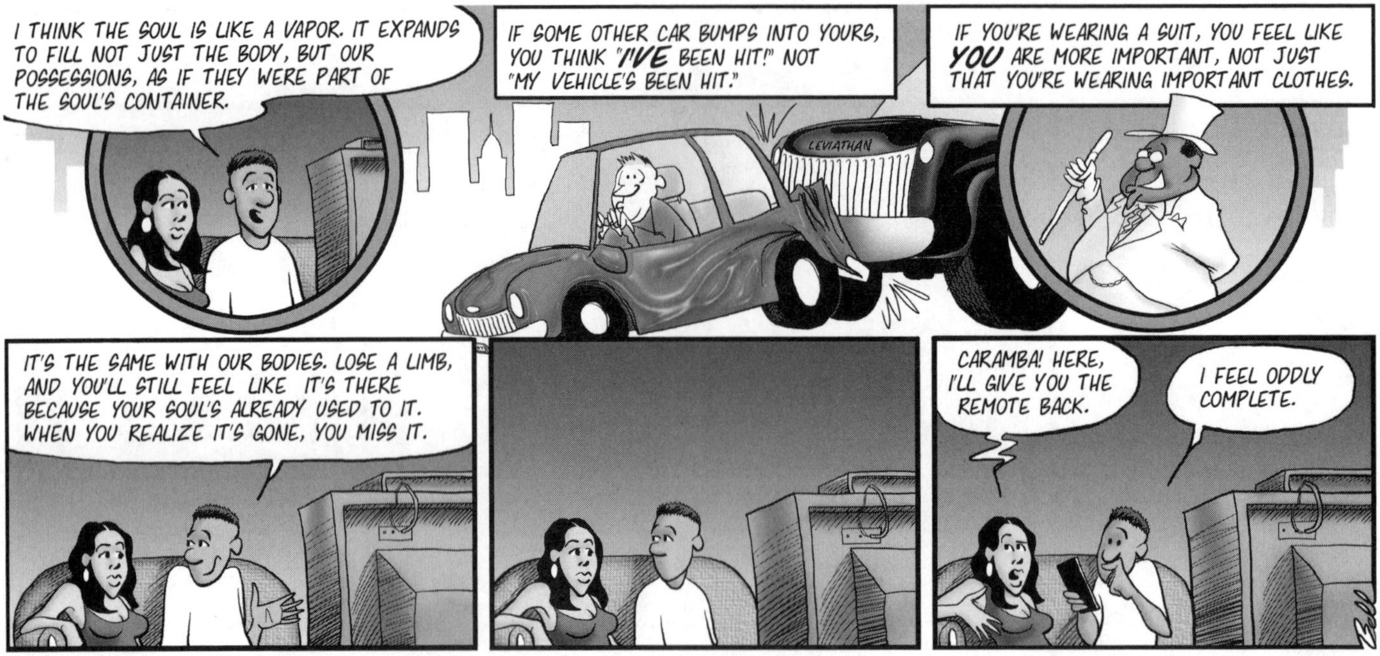
I THINK THE SOUL IS LIKE A VAPOR. IT EXPANDS TO FILL NOT JUST THE BODY, BUT OUR POSSESSIONS, AS IF THEY WERE PART OF THE SOUL'S CONTAINER.
IF SOME OTHER CAR BUMPS INTO YOURS, YOU THINK "I'VE BEEN HIT!" NOT "MY VEHICLE'S BEEN HIT."
LEVIATHAN
IF YOU'RE WEARING A SUIT, YOU FEEL LIKE YOU ARE MORE IMPORTANT, NOT JUST THAT YOU'RE WEARING IMPORTANT CLOTHES.
IT'S THE SAME WITH OUR BODIES. LOSE A LIMB, AND YOU'LL STILL FEEL LIKE IT'S THERE BECAUSE YOUR SOUL'S ALREADY USED TO IT. WHEN YOU REALIZE IT'S GONE, YOU MISS IT.
CARAMBA! HERE, I'LL GIVE YOU THE REMOTE BACK.
I FEEL ODDLY COMPLETE.

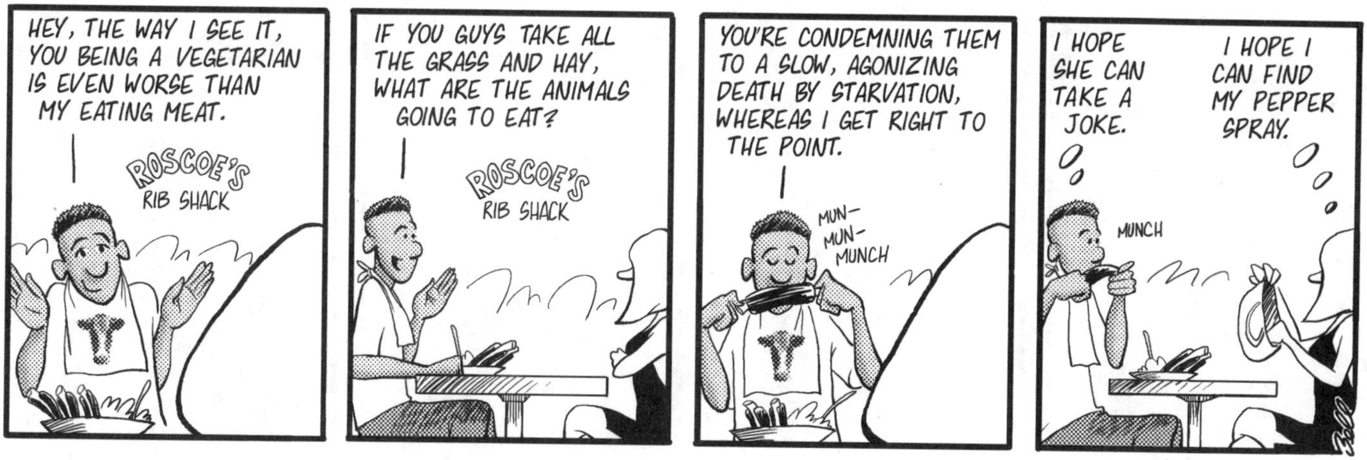
HEY, THE WAY I SEE IT, YOU BEING A VEGETARIAN IS EVEN WORSE THAN MY EATING MEAT.
ROSCOE'S RIB SHACK
IF YOU GUYS TAKE ALL THE GRASS AND HAY, WHAT ARE THE ANIMALS GOING TO EAT?
ROSCOE'S RIB SHACK
YOU'RE CONDEMNING THEM TO A SLOW, AGONIZING DEATH BY STARVATION, WHEREAS I GET RIGHT TO THE POINT.
MUN- MUN- MUNCH
I HOPE SHE CAN TAKE A JOKE.
MUNCH
I HOPE I CAN FIND MY PEPPER SPRAY.

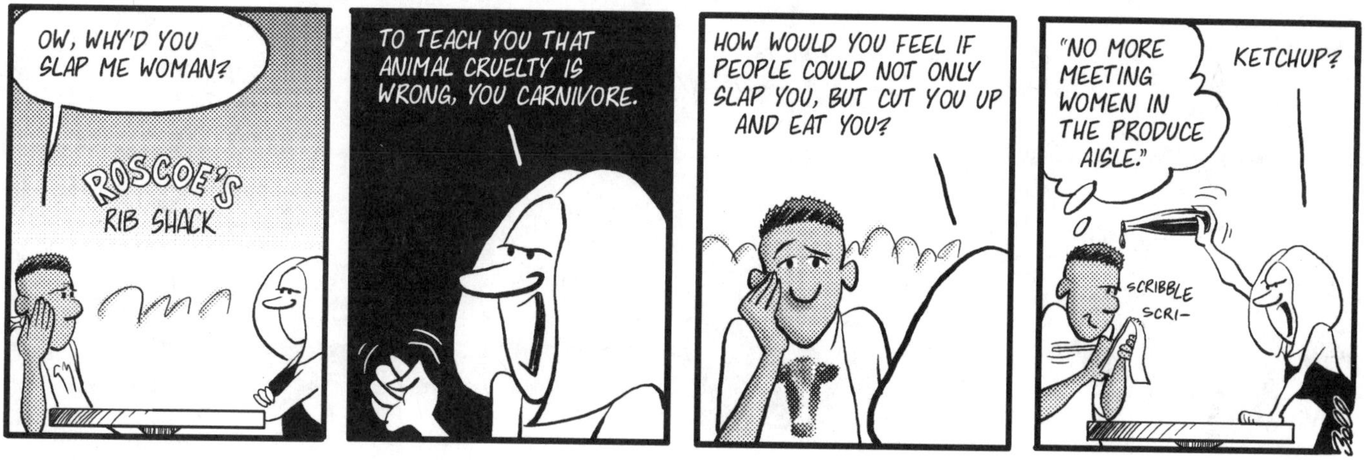
OW, WHY'D YOU SLAP ME WOMAN?
ROSCOE'S RIB SHACK
TO TEACH YOU THAT ANIMAL CRUELTY IS WRONG, YOU CARNIVORE.
HOW WOULD YOU FEEL IF PEOPLE COULD NOT ONLY SLAP YOU, BUT CUT YOU UP AND EAT YOU?
"NO MORE MEETING WOMEN IN THE PRODUCE AISLE."
KETCHUP?
SCRIBBLE SCRI-

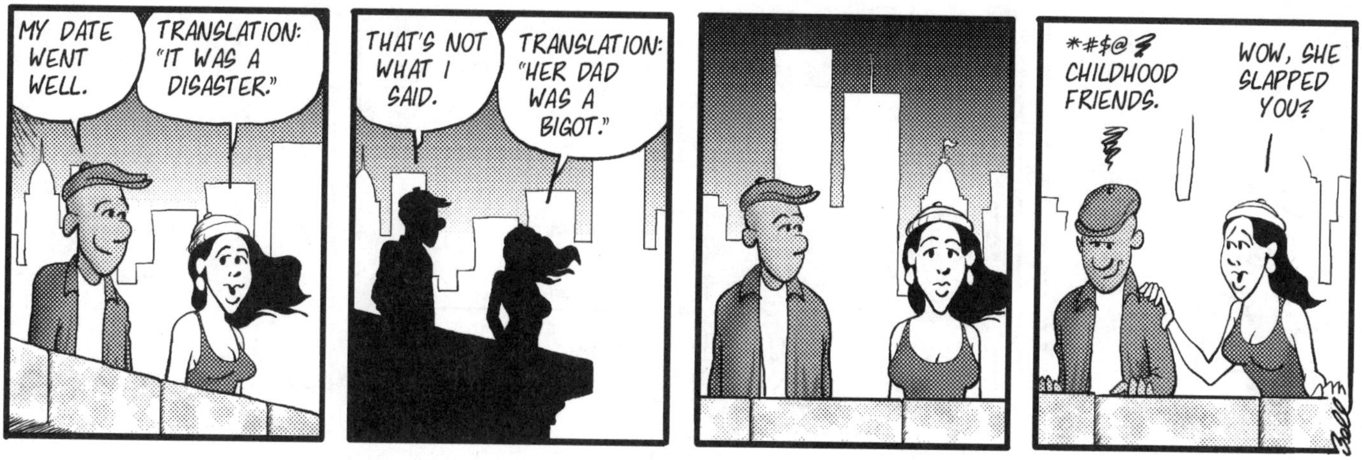
MY DATE WENT WELL.
TRANSLATION: "IT WAS A DISASTER."
THAT'S NOT WHAT I SAID.
TRANSLATION: "HER DAD WAS A BIGOT."
*#$@?
CHILDHOOD FRIENDS.
WOW, SHE SLAPPED YOU?

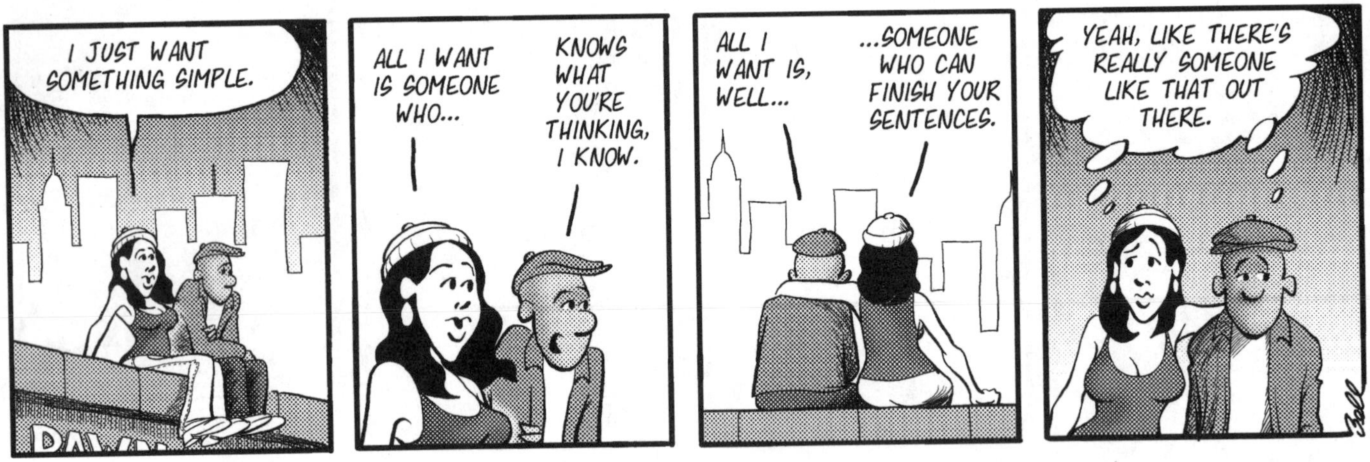
I JUST WANT SOMETHING SIMPLE.
ALL I WANT IS SOMEONE WHO...
KNOWS WHAT YOU'RE THINKING, I KNOW.
ALL I WANT IS, WELL...
...SOMEONE WHO CAN FINISH YOUR SENTENCES.
YEAH, LIKE THERE'S REALLY SOMEONE LIKE THAT OUT THERE.

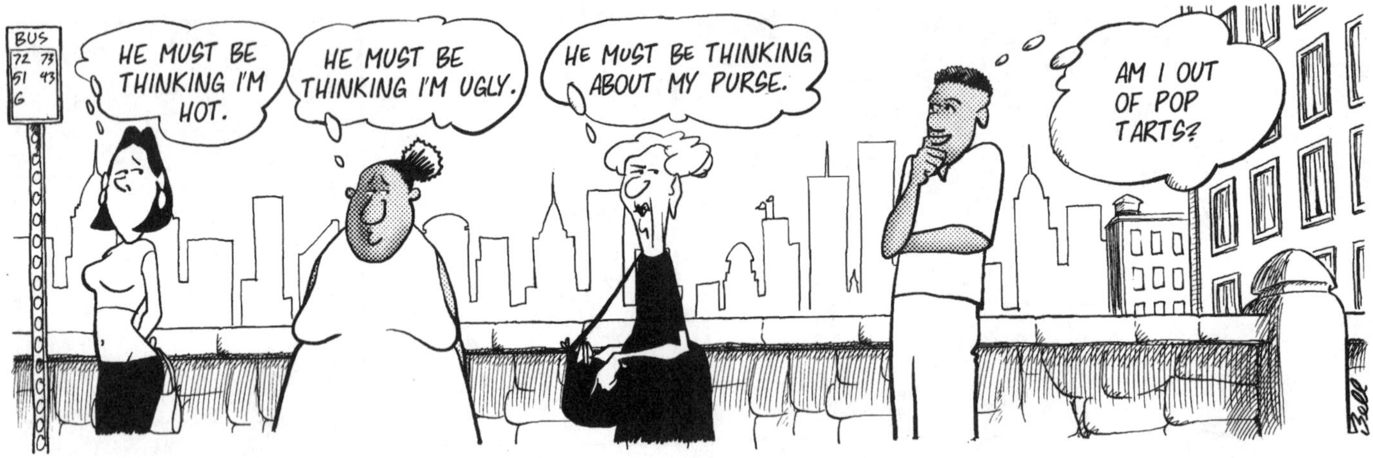
BUS
72 73
51 43
G
HE MUST BE THINKING I'M HOT.
HE MUST BE THINKING I'M UGLY.
HE MUST BE THINKING ABOUT MY PURSE.
AM I OUT OF POP TARTS?

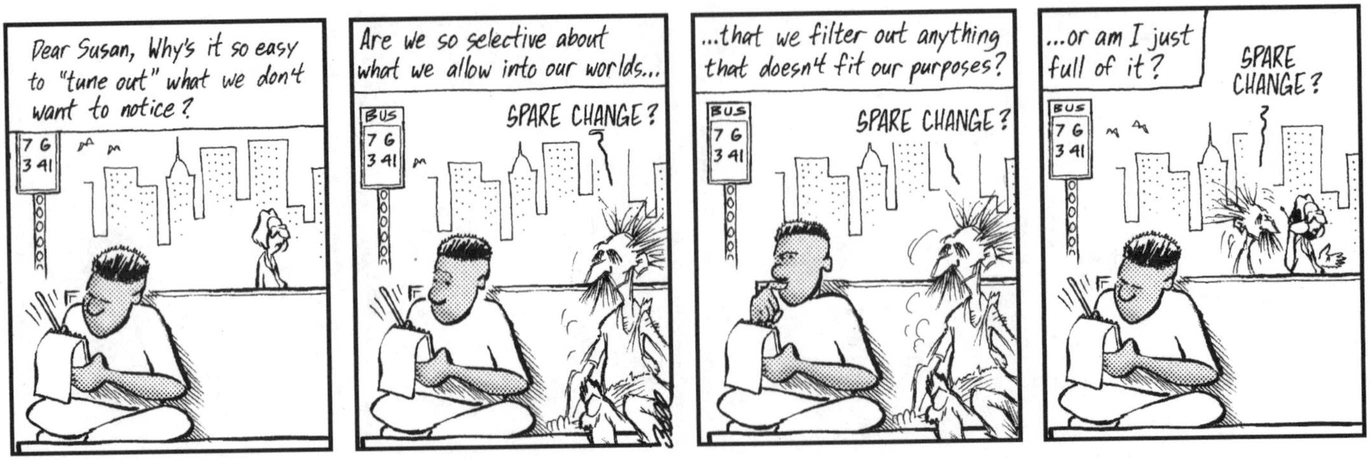
Dear Susan, Why's it so easy to "tune out" what we don't want to notice?
Are we so selective about what we allow into our worlds...
SPARE CHANGE?
...that we filter out anything that doesn't fit our purposes?
SPARE CHANGE?
...or am I just full of it?
SPARE CHANGE?

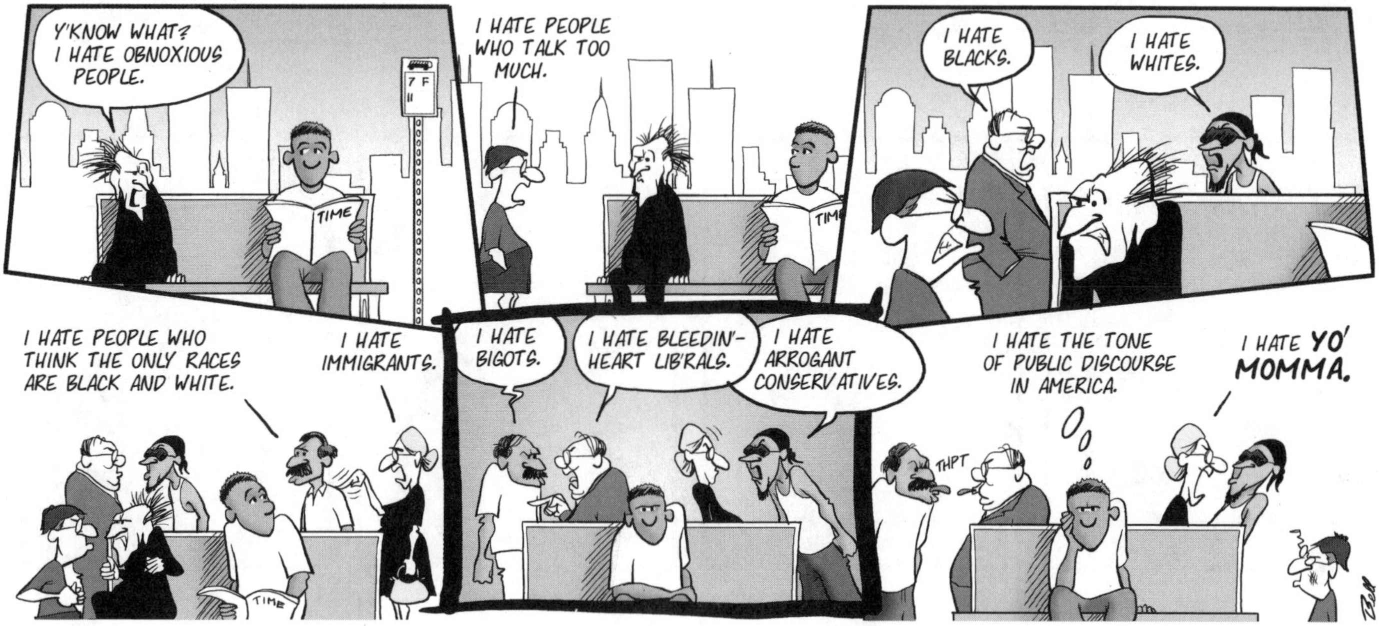

Y'KNOW WHAT? I HATE OBNOXIOUS PEOPLE.
TIME
I HATE PEOPLE WHO TALK TOO MUCH.
I HATE BLACKS.
I HATE WHITES.
I HATE PEOPLE WHO THINK THE ONLY RACES ARE BLACK AND WHITE.
I HATE IMMIGRANTS.
TIME
I HATE BIGOTS.
I HATE BLEEDIN'-HEART LIB'RALS.
I HATE ARROGANT CONSERVATIVES.
THPT
I HATE THE TONE OF PUBLIC DISCOURSE IN AMERICA.
I HATE **YO' MOMMA.**

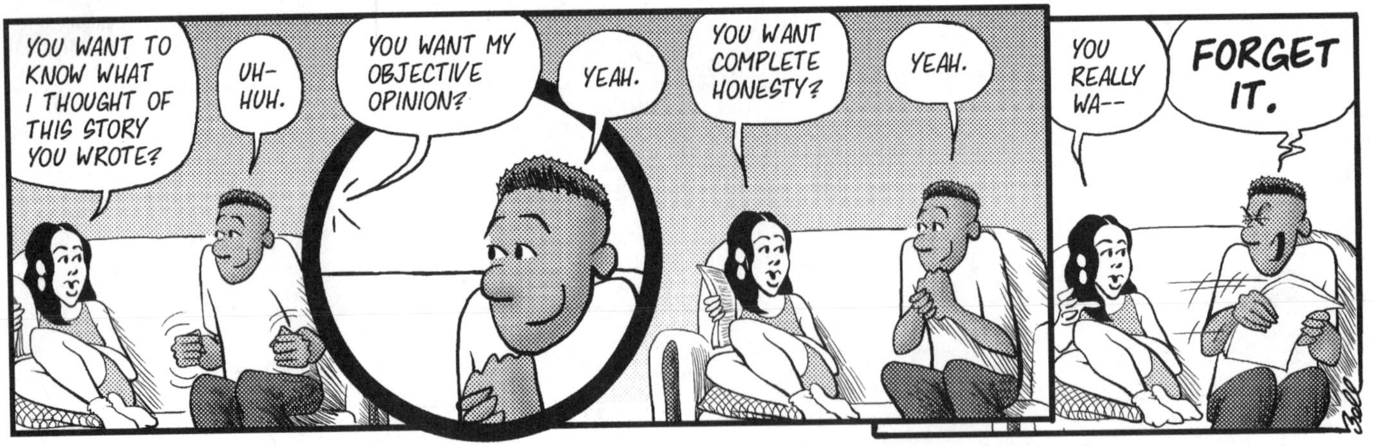
YOU WANT TO KNOW WHAT I THOUGHT OF THIS STORY YOU WROTE?
UH-HUH.
YOU WANT MY OBJECTIVE OPINION?
YEAH.
YOU WANT COMPLETE HONESTY?
YEAH.
YOU REALLY WA--
FORGET IT.

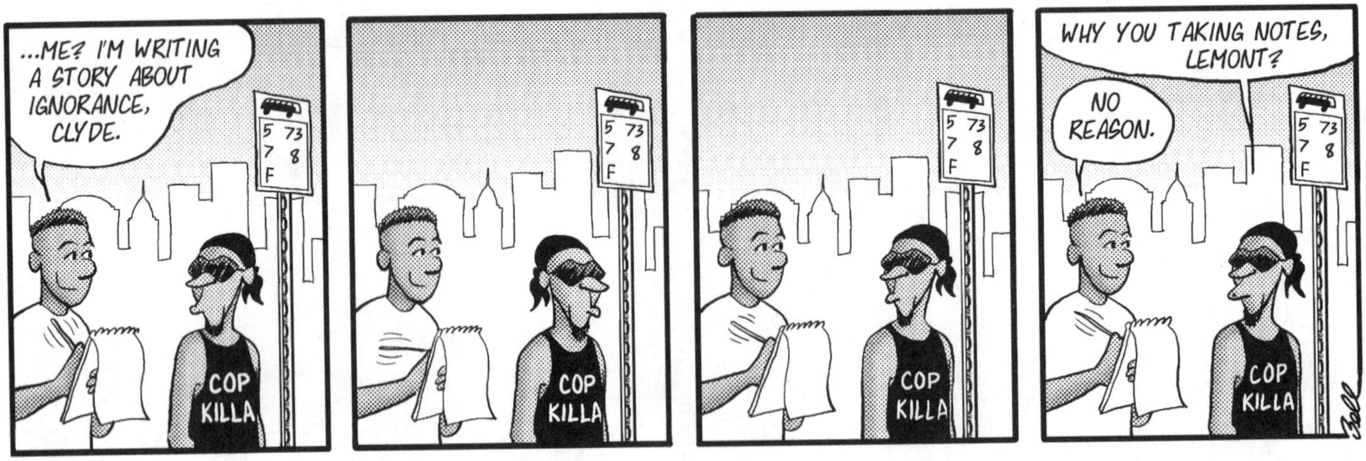
...ME? I'M WRITING A STORY ABOUT IGNORANCE, CLYDE.
COP KILLA
WHY YOU TAKING NOTES, LEMONT?
NO REASON.

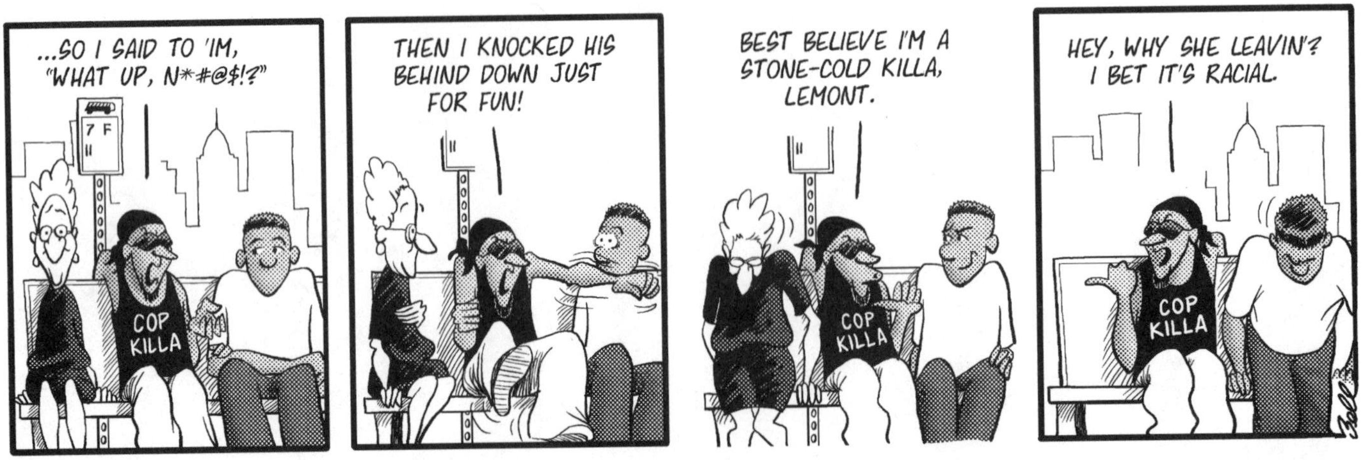
...SO I SAID TO 'IM, "WHAT UP, N*#@$!?"
COP KILLA
THEN I KNOCKED HIS BEHIND DOWN JUST FOR FUN!
BEST BELIEVE I'M A STONE-COLD KILLA, LEMONT.
HEY, WHY SHE LEAVIN'? I BET IT'S RACIAL.

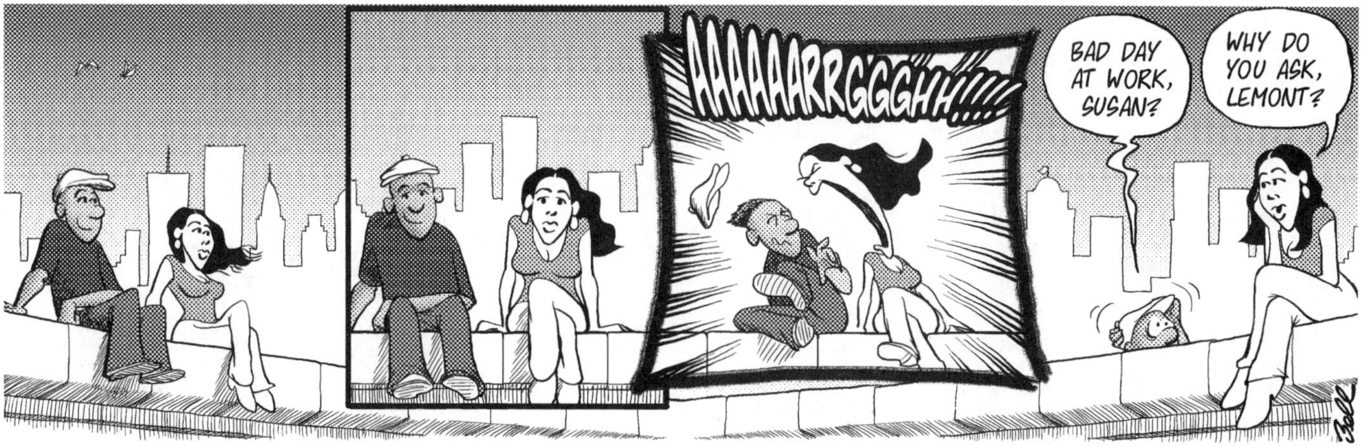
AAAAAARRGGGHH!!!!!
BAD DAY AT WORK, SUSAN?
WHY DO YOU ASK, LEMONT?

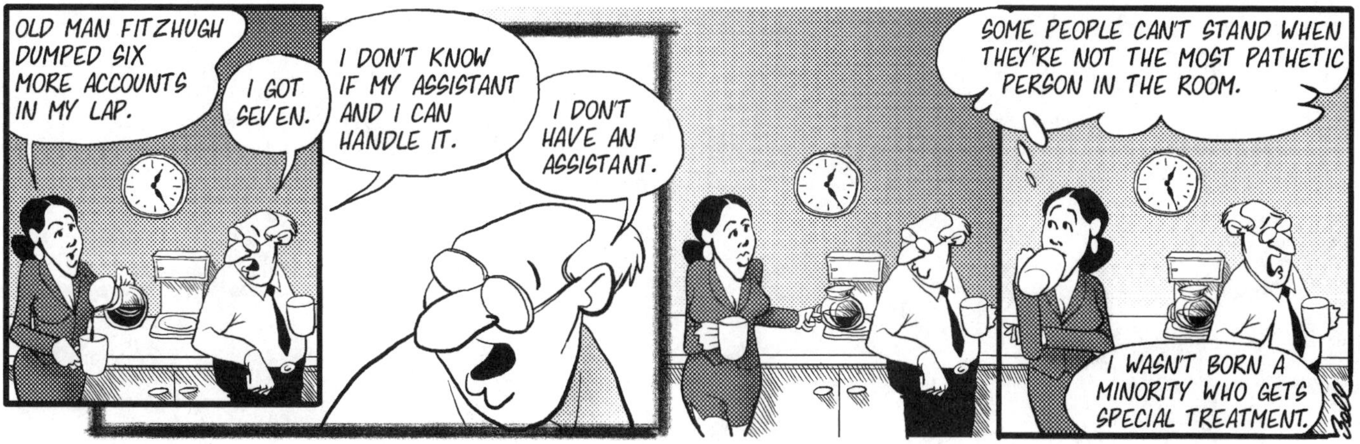
OLD MAN FITZHUGH DUMPED SIX MORE ACCOUNTS IN MY LAP.
I GOT SEVEN.
I DON'T KNOW IF MY ASSISTANT AND I CAN HANDLE IT.
I DON'T HAVE AN ASSISTANT.
SOME PEOPLE CAN'T STAND WHEN THEY'RE NOT THE MOST PATHETIC PERSON IN THE ROOM.
I WASN'T BORN A MINORITY WHO GETS SPECIAL TREATMENT.

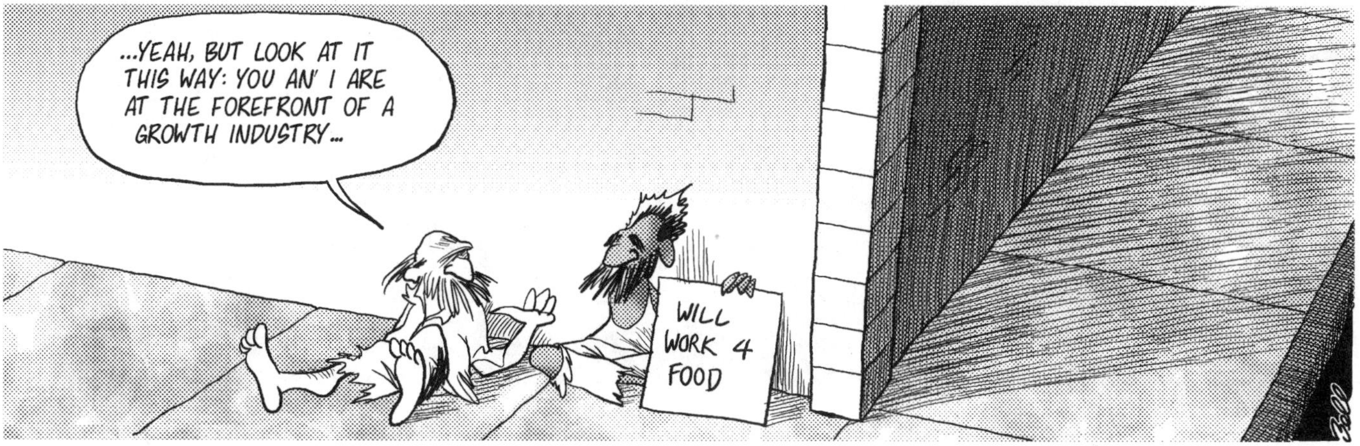
...YEAH, BUT LOOK AT IT THIS WAY: YOU AN' I ARE AT THE FOREFRONT OF A GROWTH INDUSTRY...
WILL WORK 4 FOOD

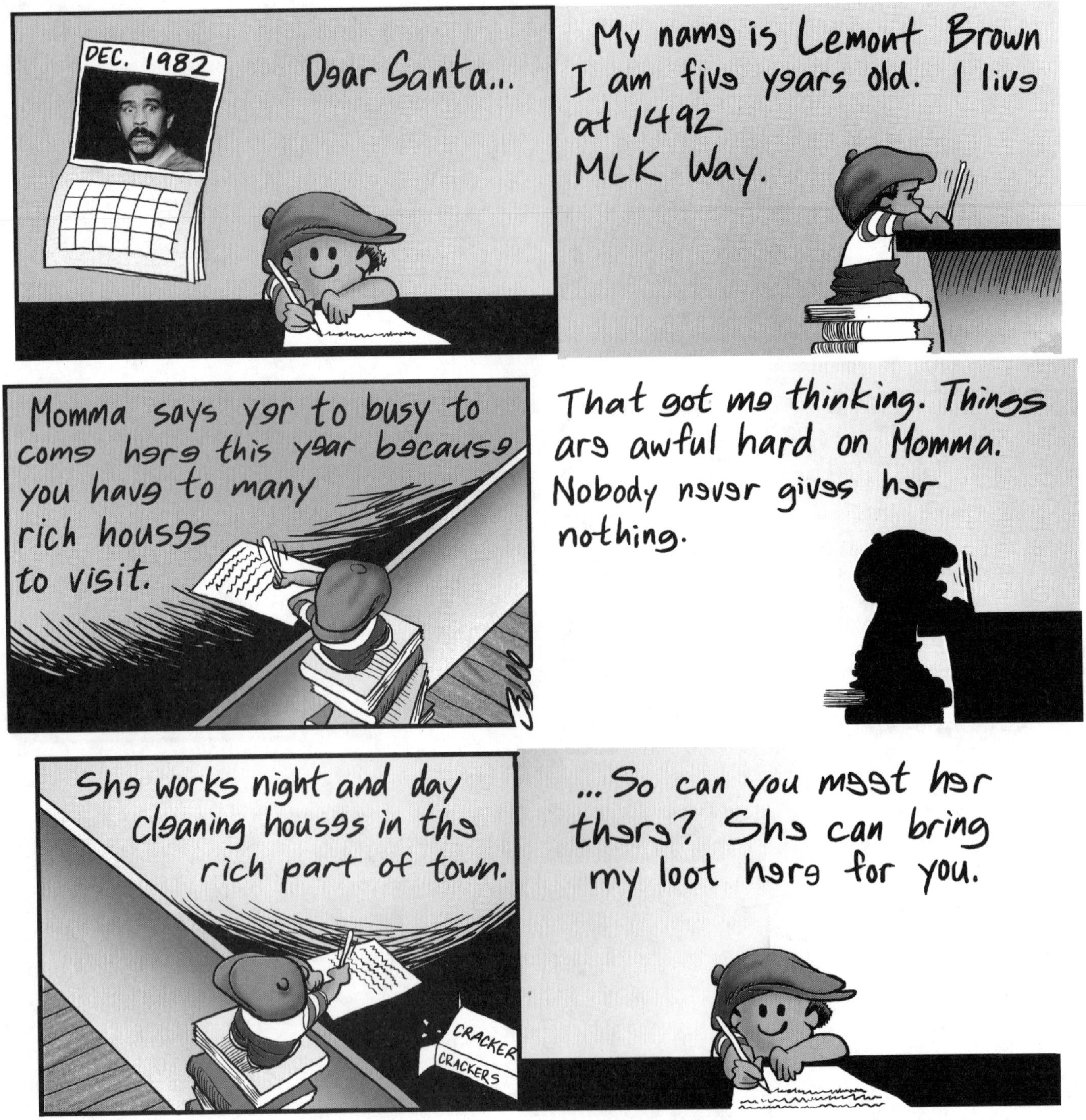
DEC. 1982
Dear Santa...
My name is Lemont Brown I am five years old. I live at 1492 MLK Way.
Momma says yer to busy to come here this year because you have to many rich houses to visit.
That got me thinking. Things are awful hard on Momma. Nobody never gives her nothing.
She works night and day cleaning houses in the rich part of town.
CRACKER
CRACKERS
...So can you meet her there? She can bring my loot here for you.

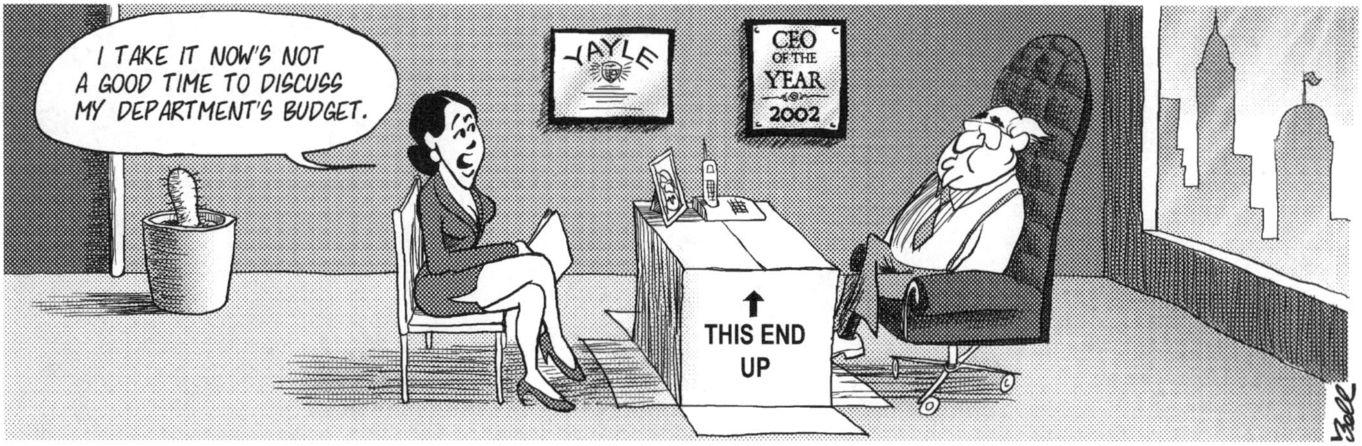
I TAKE IT NOW'S NOT A GOOD TIME TO DISCUSS MY DEPARTMENT'S BUDGET.
YAYLE
CEO OF THE YEAR 2002
THIS END UP

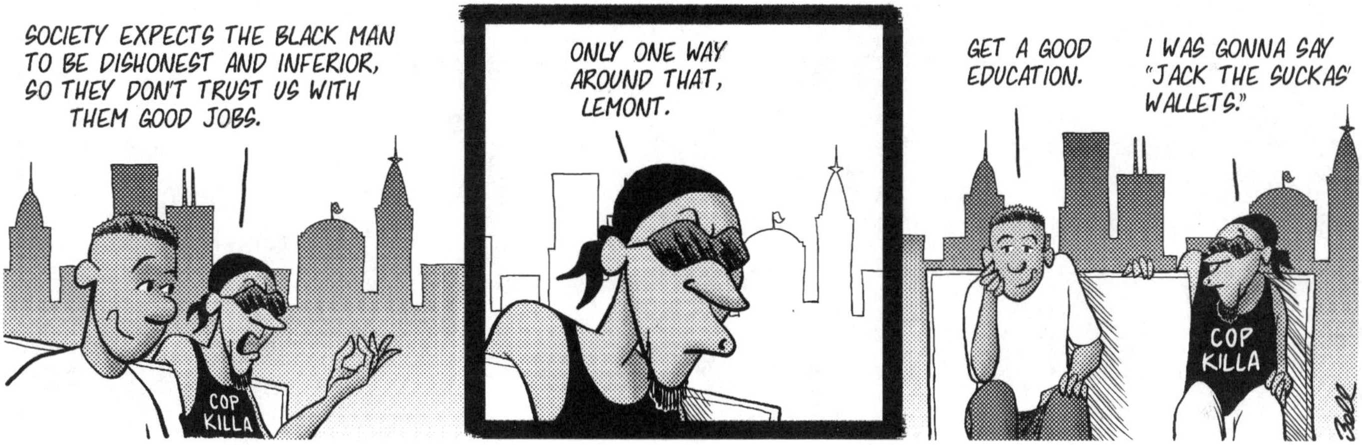
SOCIETY EXPECTS THE BLACK MAN TO BE DISHONEST AND INFERIOR, SO THEY DON'T TRUST US WITH THEM GOOD JOBS.
COP KILLA
ONLY ONE WAY AROUND THAT, LEMONT.
GET A GOOD EDUCATION.
I WAS GONNA SAY "JACK THE SUCKAS' WALLETS."
COP KILLA

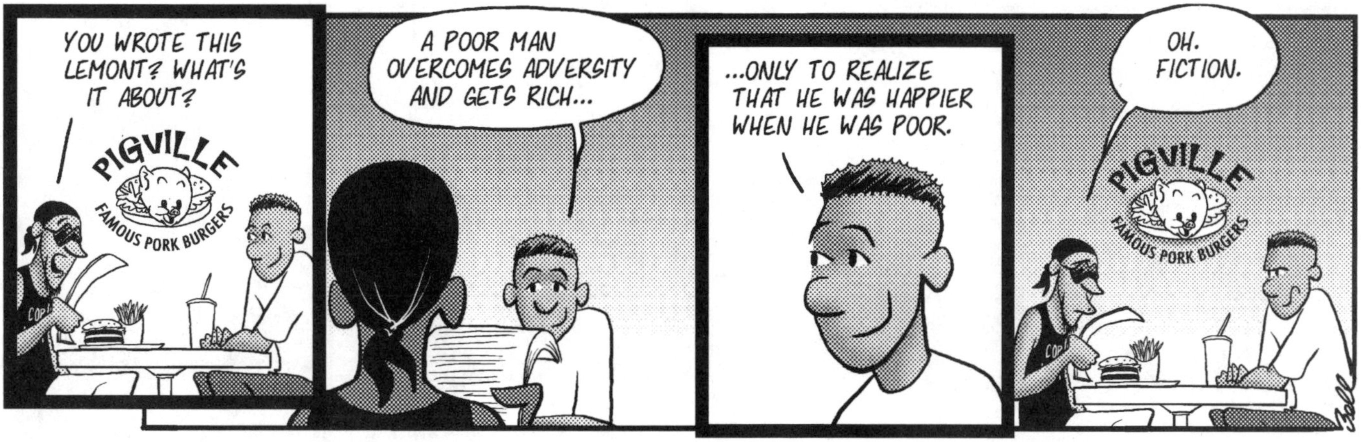
YOU WROTE THIS LEMONT? WHAT'S IT ABOUT?
PIGVILLE FAMOUS PORK BURGERS
A POOR MAN OVERCOMES ADVERSITY AND GETS RICH...
...ONLY TO REALIZE THAT HE WAS HAPPIER WHEN HE WAS POOR.
OH. FICTION.
PIGVILLE FAMOUS PORK BURGERS

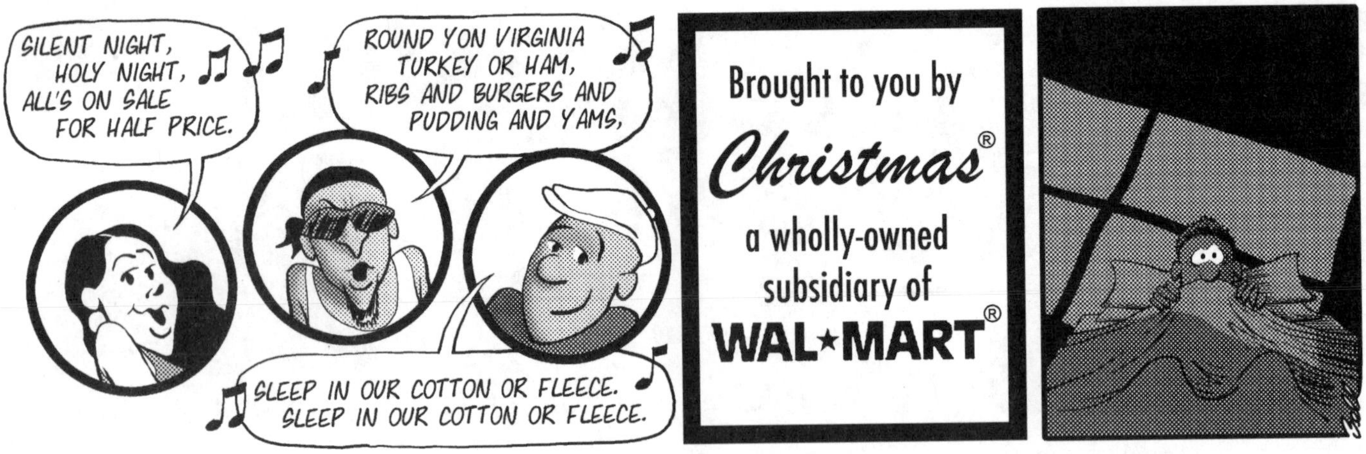
SILENT NIGHT, HOLY NIGHT, ALL'S ON SALE FOR HALF PRICE.
ROUND YON VIRGINIA TURKEY OR HAM, RIBS AND BURGERS AND PUDDING AND YAMS,
SLEEP IN OUR COTTON OR FLEECE. SLEEP IN OUR COTTON OR FLEECE.
Brought to you by Christmas® a wholly-owned subsidiary of WAL★MART®

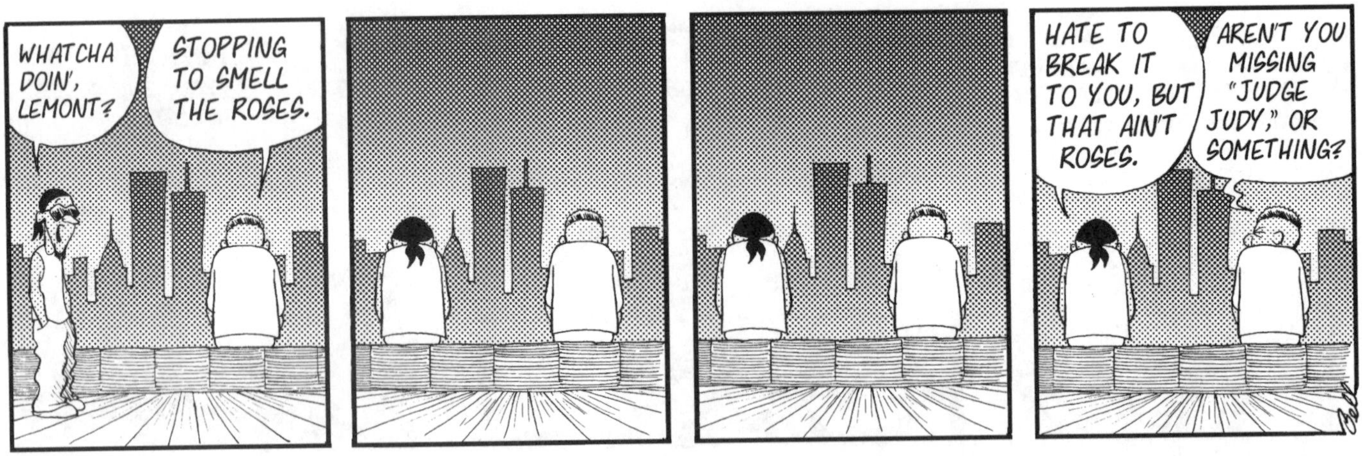
WHATCHA DOIN', LEMONT?
STOPPING TO SMELL THE ROSES.
HATE TO BREAK IT TO YOU, BUT THAT AIN'T ROSES.
AREN'T YOU MISSING "JUDGE JUDY," OR SOMETHING?

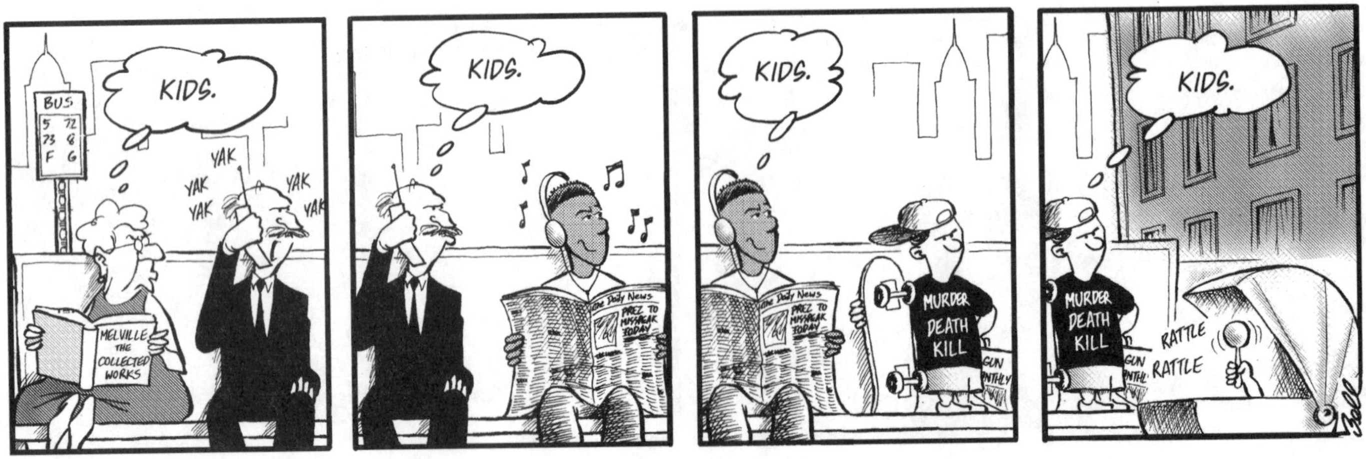
BUS
5 72
73 8
F G
KIDS.
YAK
YAK
YAK
YAK
YAK
MELVILLE THE COLLECTED WORKS
KIDS.
The Daily News
PREZ TO MISSPEAK TODAY
KIDS.
MURDER DEATH KILL
KIDS.
RATTLE
RATTLE

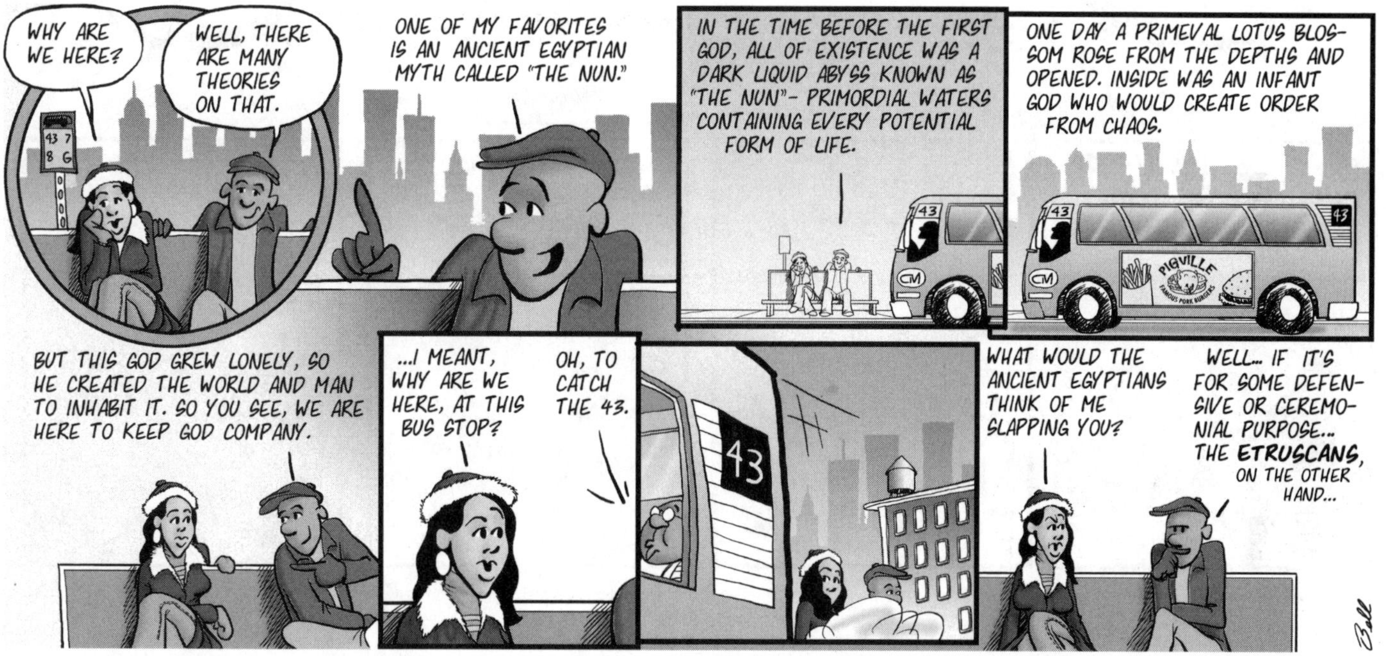
WHY ARE WE HERE?
WELL, THERE ARE MANY THEORIES ON THAT.
ONE OF MY FAVORITES IS AN ANCIENT EGYPTIAN MYTH CALLED "THE NUN."
IN THE TIME BEFORE THE FIRST GOD, ALL OF EXISTENCE WAS A DARK LIQUID ABYSS KNOWN AS "THE NUN"– PRIMORDIAL WATERS CONTAINING EVERY POTENTIAL FORM OF LIFE.
ONE DAY A PRIMEVAL LOTUS BLOSSOM ROSE FROM THE DEPTHS AND OPENED. INSIDE WAS AN INFANT GOD WHO WOULD CREATE ORDER FROM CHAOS.
PIGVILLE
FAMOUS PORK BURGERS
BUT THIS GOD GREW LONELY, SO HE CREATED THE WORLD AND MAN TO INHABIT IT. SO YOU SEE, WE ARE HERE TO KEEP GOD COMPANY.
...I MEANT, WHY ARE WE HERE, AT THIS BUS STOP?
OH, TO CATCH THE 43.
43
WHAT WOULD THE ANCIENT EGYPTIANS THINK OF ME SLAPPING YOU?
WELL... IF IT'S FOR SOME DEFENSIVE OR CEREMONIAL PURPOSE... THE ETRUSCANS, ON THE OTHER HAND...

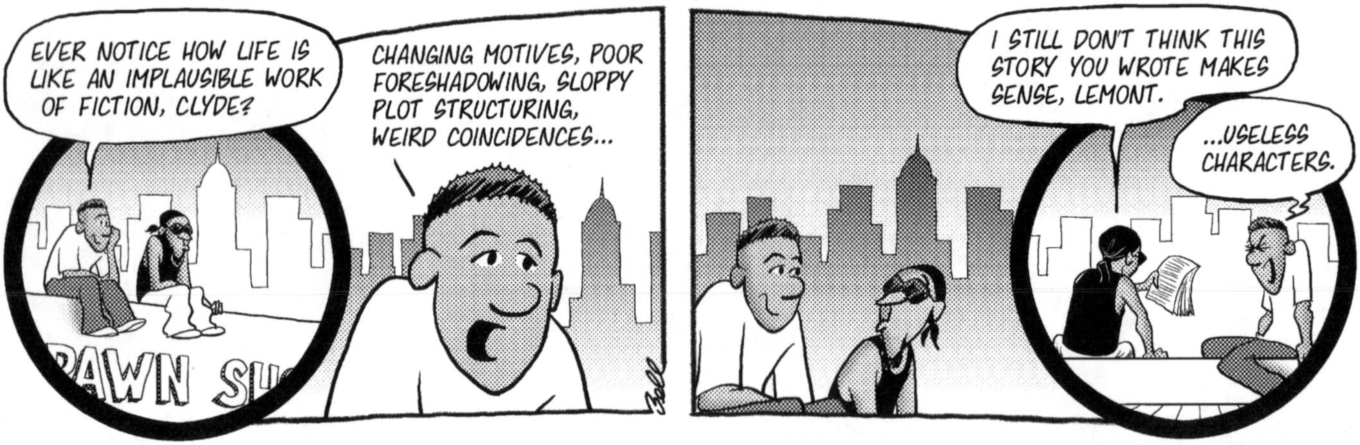
EVER NOTICE HOW LIFE IS LIKE AN IMPLAUSIBLE WORK OF FICTION, CLYDE?
CHANGING MOTIVES, POOR FORESHADOWING, SLOPPY PLOT STRUCTURING, WEIRD COINCIDENCES...
I STILL DON'T THINK THIS STORY YOU WROTE MAKES SENSE, LEMONT.
...USELESS CHARACTERS.

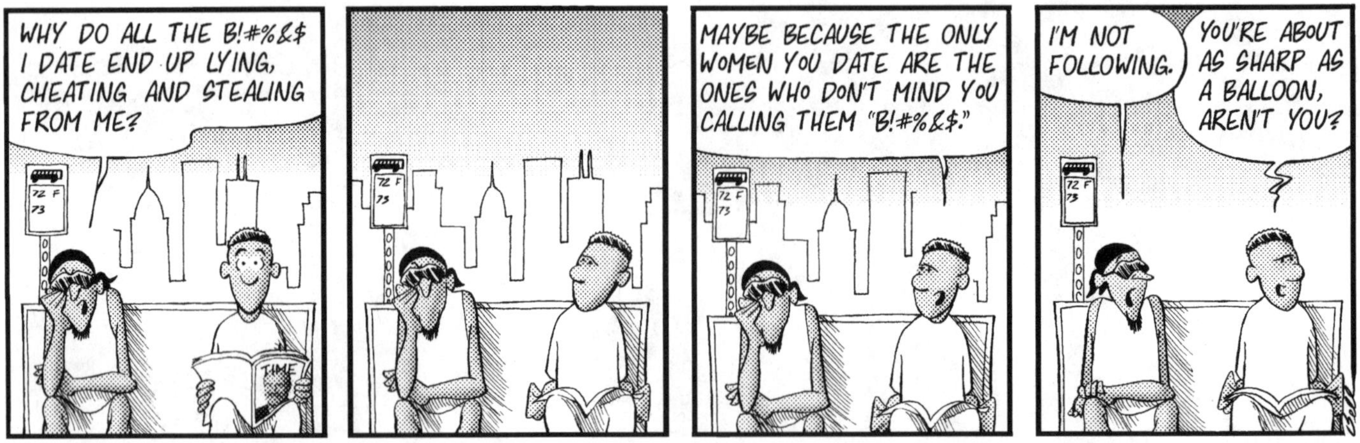
WHY DO ALL THE B!#%&$ I DATE END UP LYING, CHEATING AND STEALING FROM ME?
TIME
MAYBE BECAUSE THE ONLY WOMEN YOU DATE ARE THE ONES WHO DON'T MIND YOU CALLING THEM "B!#%&$."
I'M NOT FOLLOWING.
YOU'RE ABOUT AS SHARP AS A BALLOON, AREN'T YOU?

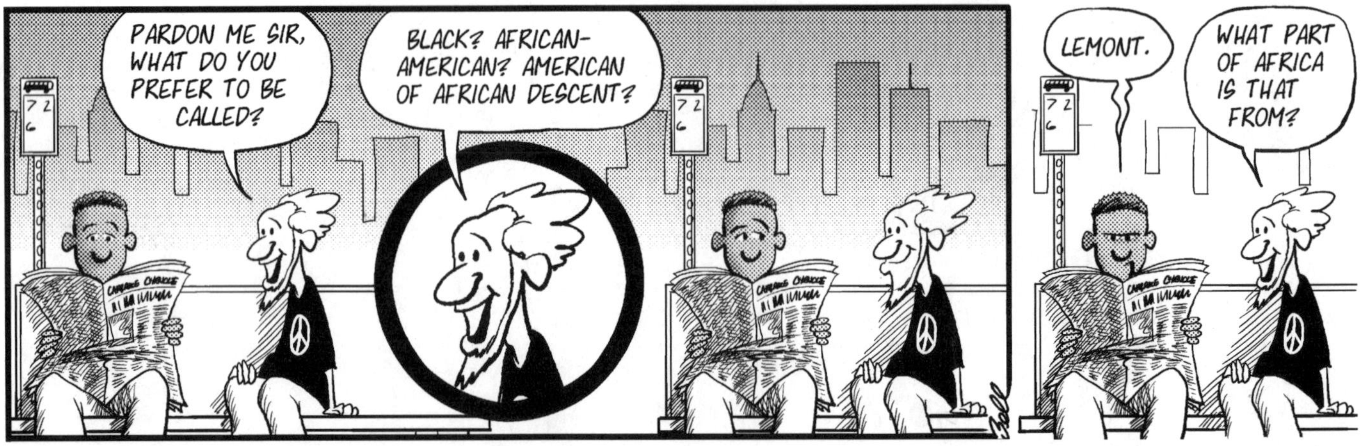
PARDON ME SIR, WHAT DO YOU PREFER TO BE CALLED?
BLACK? AFRICAN-AMERICAN? AMERICAN OF AFRICAN DESCENT?
LEMONT.
WHAT PART OF AFRICA IS THAT FROM?

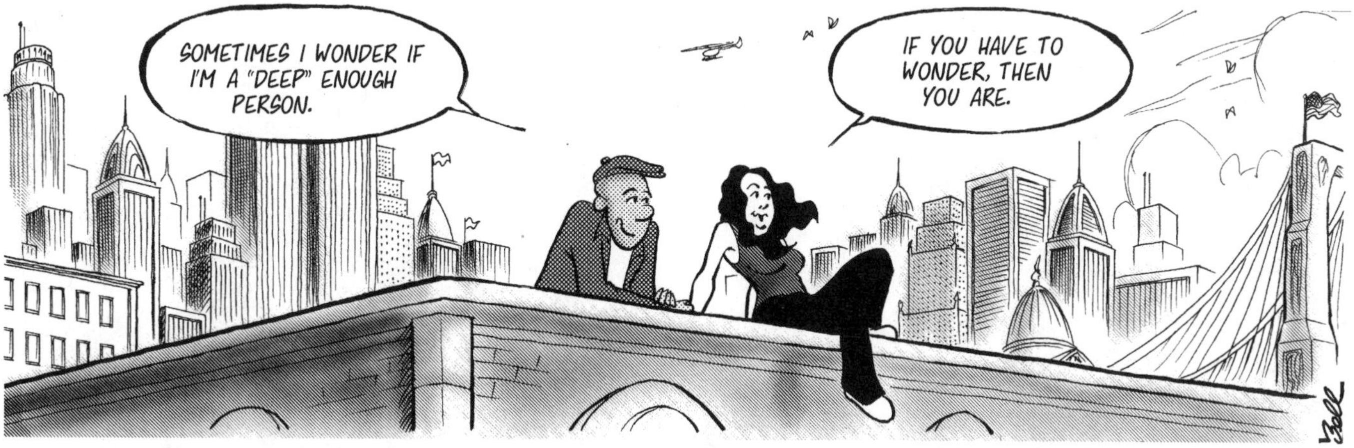
SOMETIMES I WONDER IF I'M A "DEEP" ENOUGH PERSON.
IF YOU HAVE TO WONDER, THEN YOU ARE.

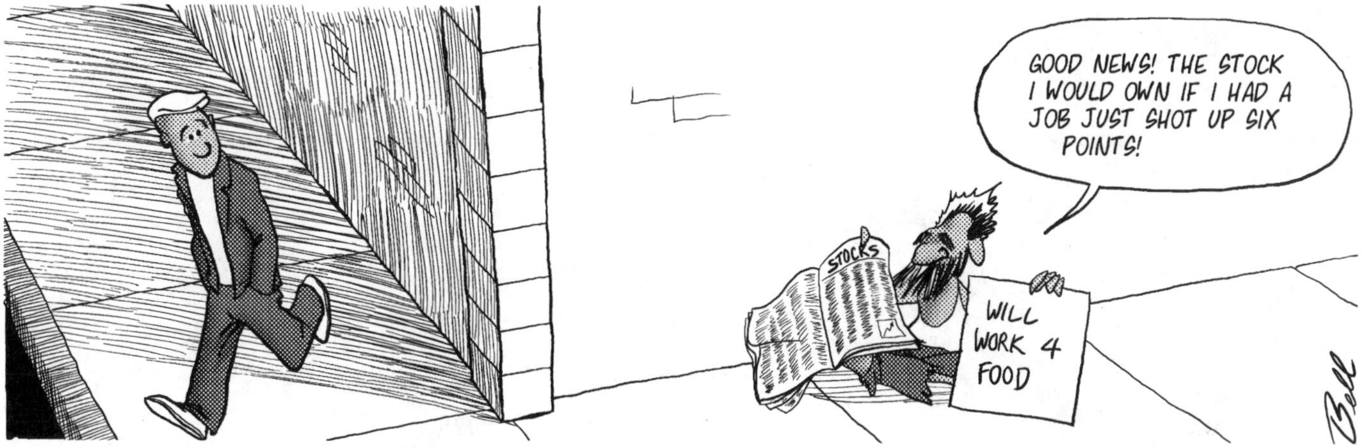
GOOD NEWS! THE STOCK I WOULD OWN IF I HAD A JOB JUST SHOT UP SIX POINTS!
STOCKS
WILL WORK 4 FOOD

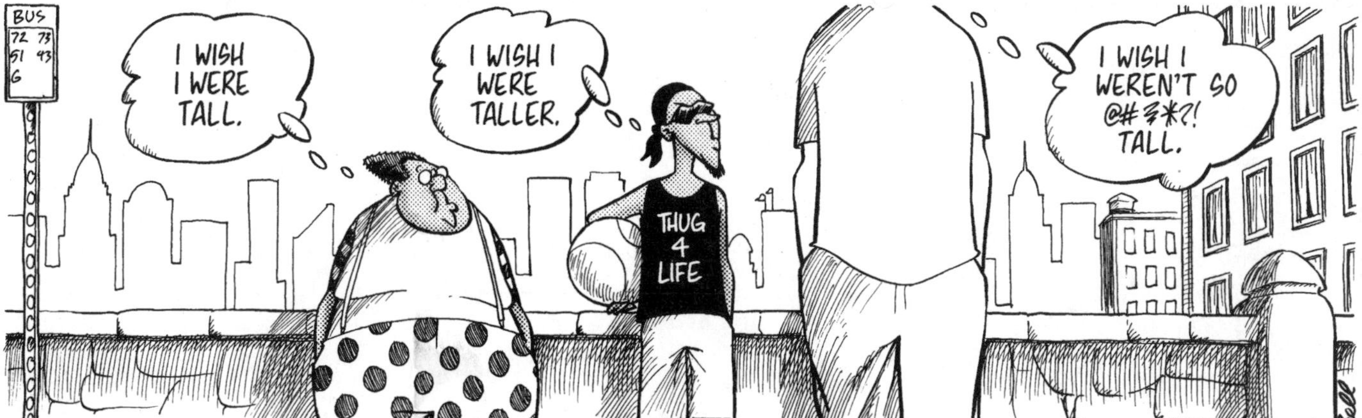
I WISH I WERE TALL.
I WISH I WERE TALLER.
THUG 4 LIFE
I WISH I WEREN'T SO @#*?! TALL.

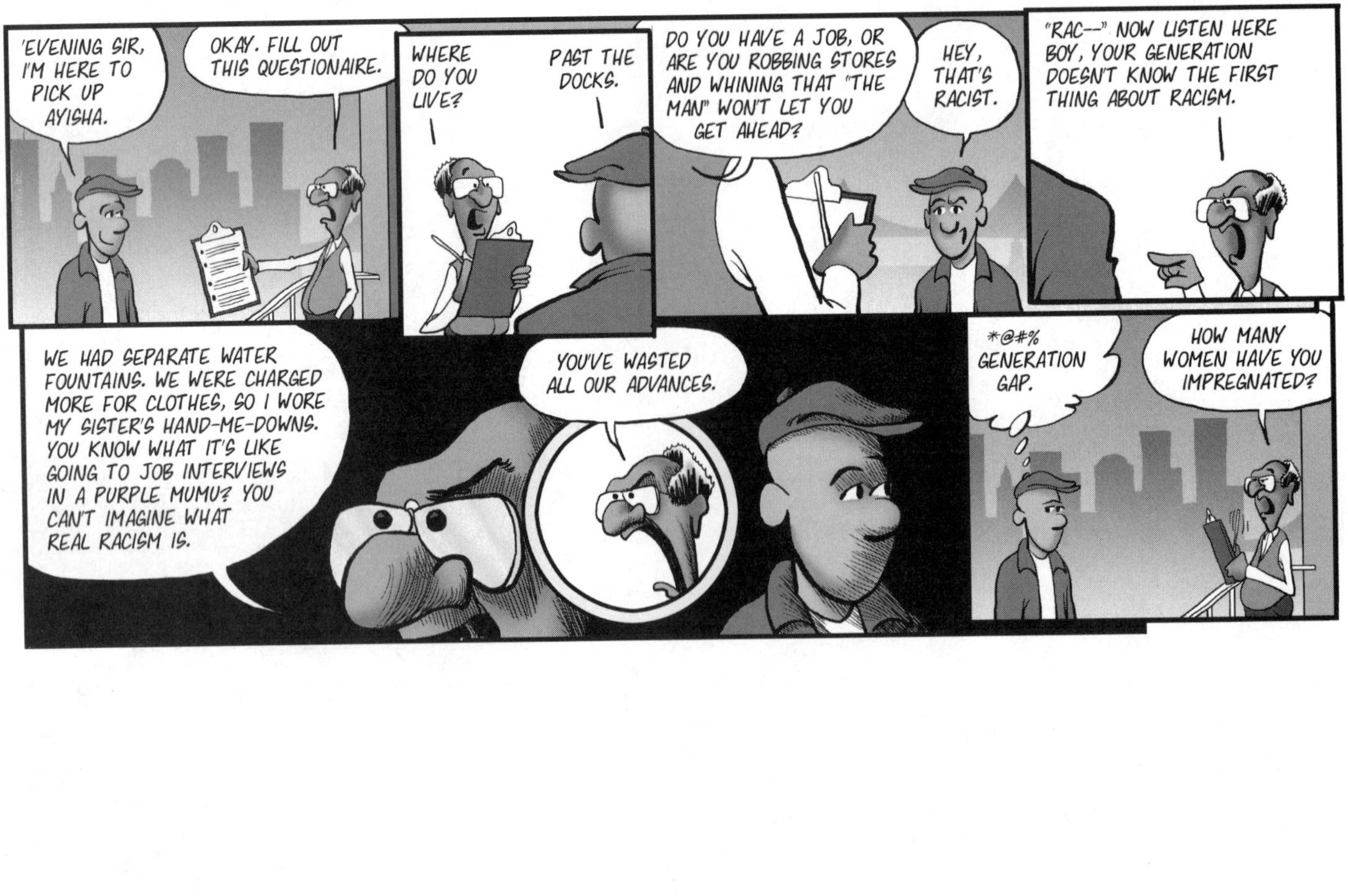
'EVENING SIR, I'M HERE TO PICK UP AYISHA.
OKAY. FILL OUT THIS QUESTIONAIRE.
WHERE DO YOU LIVE?
PAST THE DOCKS.
DO YOU HAVE A JOB, OR ARE YOU ROBBING STORES AND WHINING THAT "THE MAN" WON'T LET YOU GET AHEAD?
HEY, THAT'S RACIST.
"RAC--" NOW LISTEN HERE BOY, YOUR GENERATION DOESN'T KNOW THE FIRST THING ABOUT RACISM.
WE HAD SEPARATE WATER FOUNTAINS. WE WERE CHARGED MORE FOR CLOTHES, SO I WORE MY SISTER'S HAND-ME-DOWNS. YOU KNOW WHAT IT'S LIKE GOING TO JOB INTERVIEWS IN A PURPLE MUMU? YOU CAN'T IMAGINE WHAT REAL RACISM IS.
YOU'VE WASTED ALL OUR ADVANCES.
*@#% GENERATION GAP.
HOW MANY WOMEN HAVE YOU IMPREGNATED?

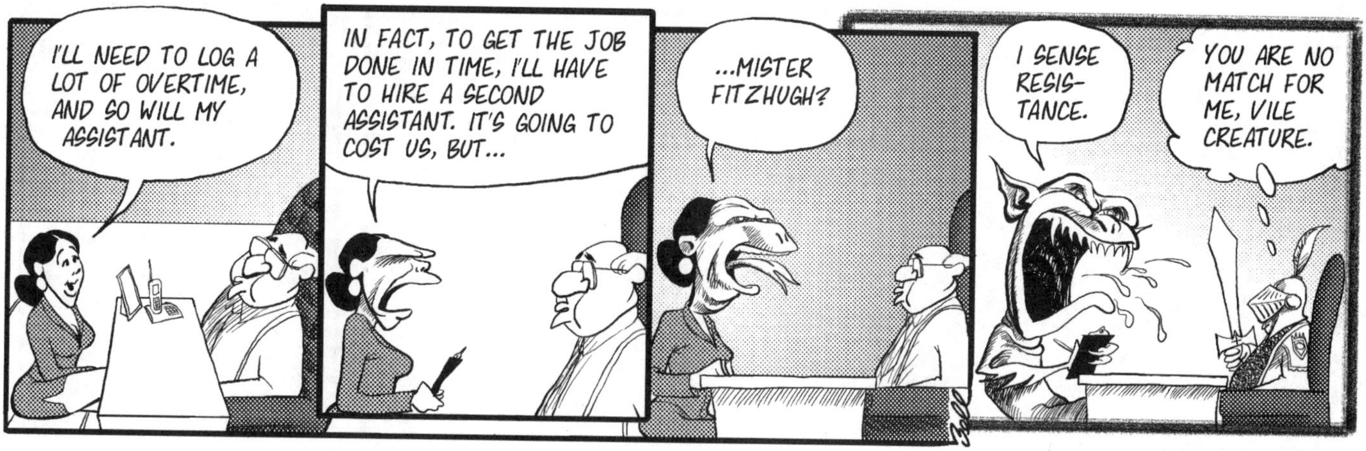
I'LL NEED TO LOG A LOT OF OVERTIME, AND SO WILL MY ASSISTANT.
IN FACT, TO GET THE JOB DONE IN TIME, I'LL HAVE TO HIRE A SECOND ASSISTANT. IT'S GOING TO COST US, BUT...
...MISTER FITZHUGH?
I SENSE RESIS-TANCE.
YOU ARE NO MATCH FOR ME, VILE CREATURE.

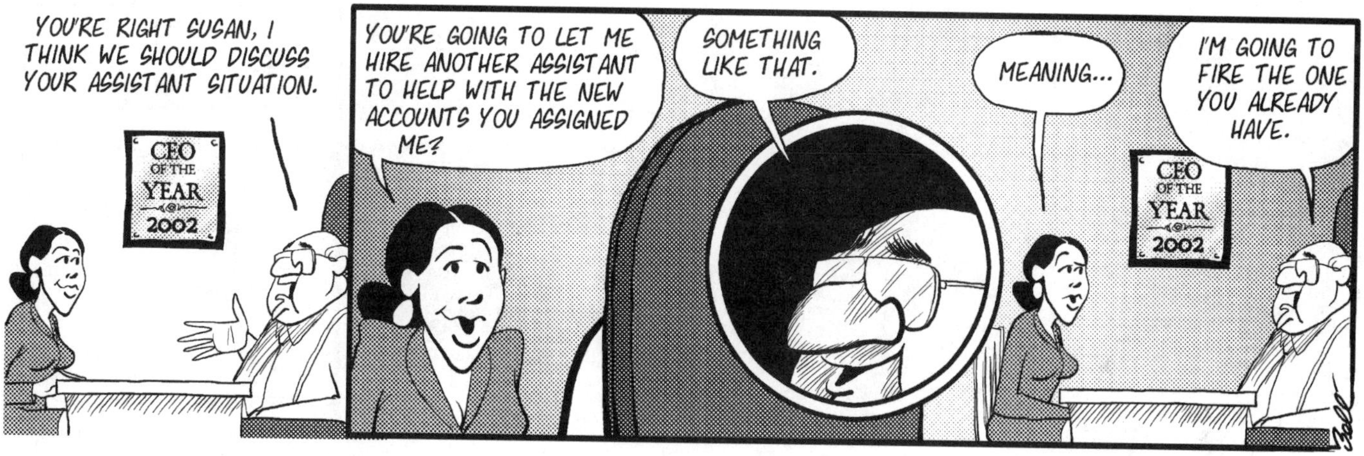
YOU'RE RIGHT SUSAN, I THINK WE SHOULD DISCUSS YOUR ASSISTANT SITUATION.
CEO OF THE YEAR 2002
YOU'RE GOING TO LET ME HIRE ANOTHER ASSISTANT TO HELP WITH THE NEW ACCOUNTS YOU ASSIGNED ME?
SOMETHING LIKE THAT.
MEANING...
I'M GOING TO FIRE THE ONE YOU ALREADY HAVE.
CEO OF THE YEAR 2002

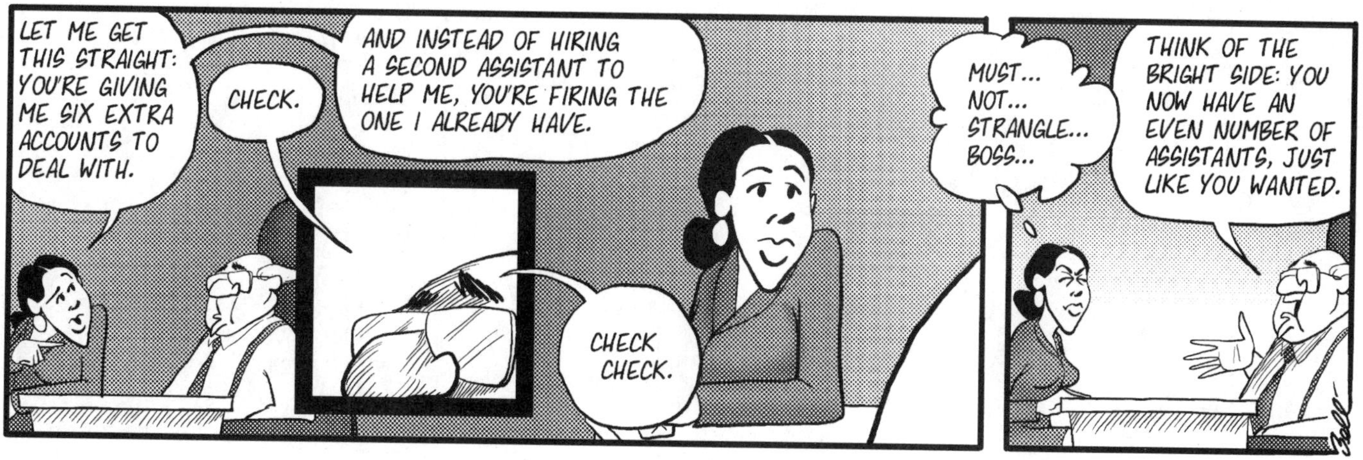
LET ME GET THIS STRAIGHT: YOU'RE GIVING ME SIX EXTRA ACCOUNTS TO DEAL WITH.
CHECK.
AND INSTEAD OF HIRING A SECOND ASSISTANT TO HELP ME, YOU'RE FIRING THE ONE I ALREADY HAVE.
CHECK CHECK.
MUST... NOT... STRANGLE... BOSS...
THINK OF THE BRIGHT SIDE: YOU NOW HAVE AN EVEN NUMBER OF ASSISTANTS, JUST LIKE YOU WANTED.

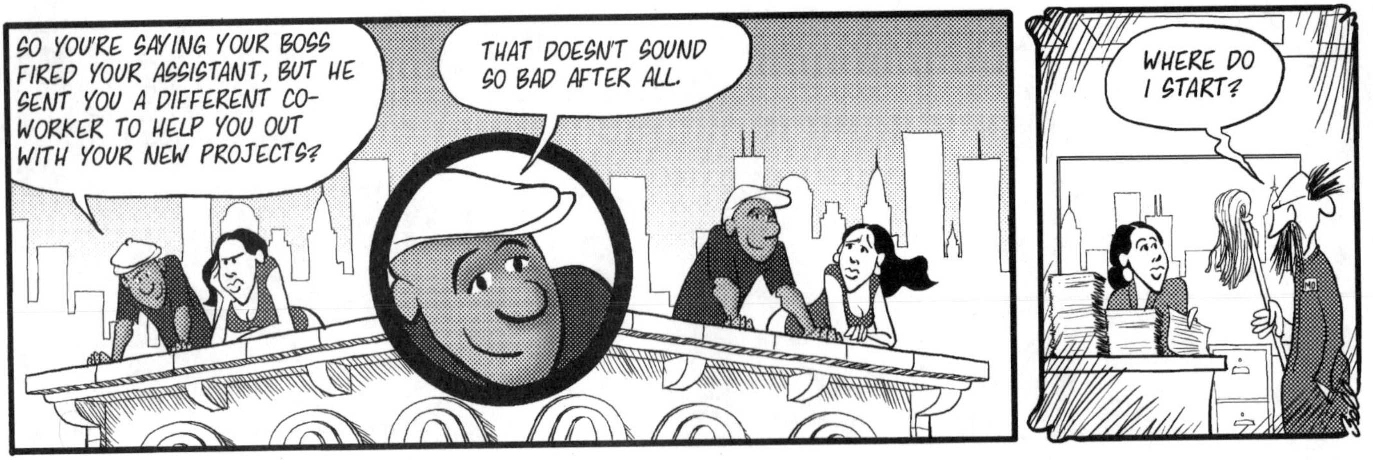
SO YOU'RE SAYING YOUR BOSS FIRED YOUR ASSISTANT, BUT HE SENT YOU A DIFFERENT CO-WORKER TO HELP YOU OUT WITH YOUR NEW PROJECTS?
THAT DOESN'T SOUND SO BAD AFTER ALL.
WHERE DO I START?

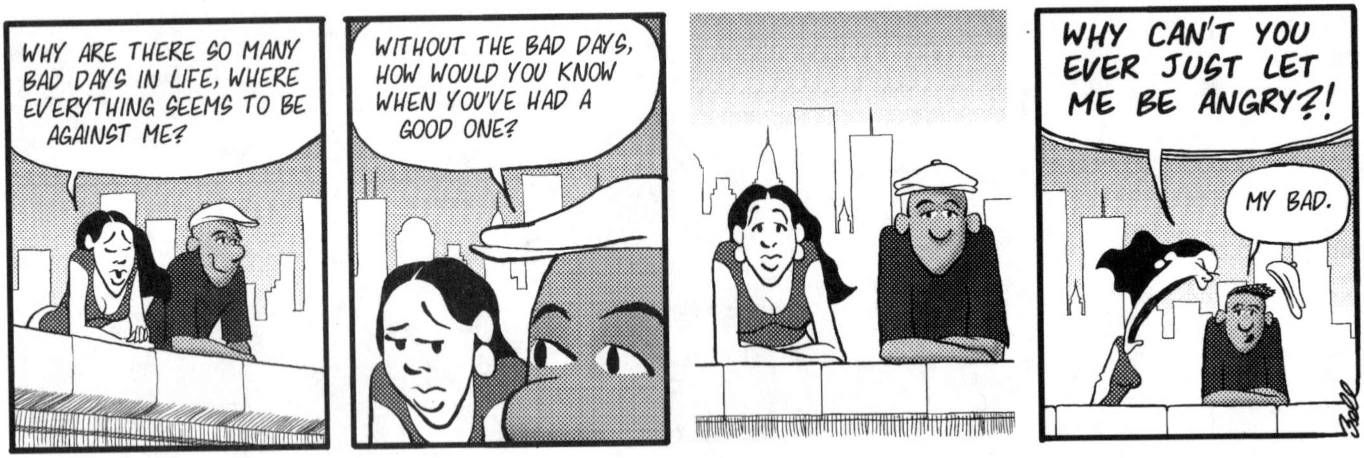
WHY ARE THERE SO MANY BAD DAYS IN LIFE, WHERE EVERYTHING SEEMS TO BE AGAINST ME?
WITHOUT THE BAD DAYS, HOW WOULD YOU KNOW WHEN YOU'VE HAD A GOOD ONE?
WHY CAN'T YOU EVER JUST LET ME BE ANGRY?!
MY BAD.

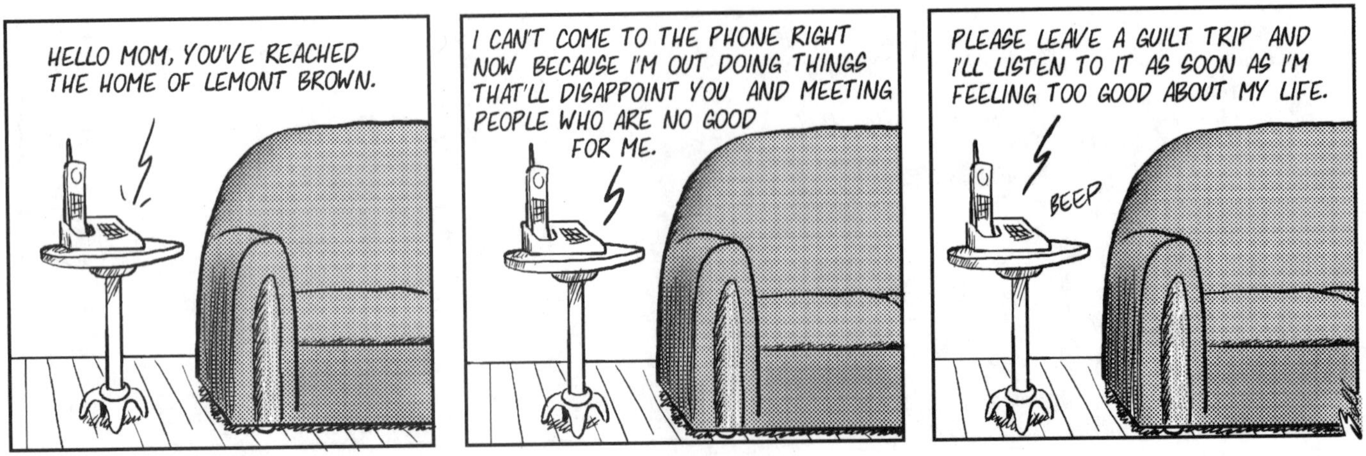
HELLO MOM, YOU'VE REACHED THE HOME OF LEMONT BROWN.
I CAN'T COME TO THE PHONE RIGHT NOW BECAUSE I'M OUT DOING THINGS THAT'LL DISAPPOINT YOU AND MEETING PEOPLE WHO ARE NO GOOD FOR ME.
PLEASE LEAVE A GUILT TRIP AND I'LL LISTEN TO IT AS SOON AS I'M FEELING TOO GOOD ABOUT MY LIFE.
BEEP

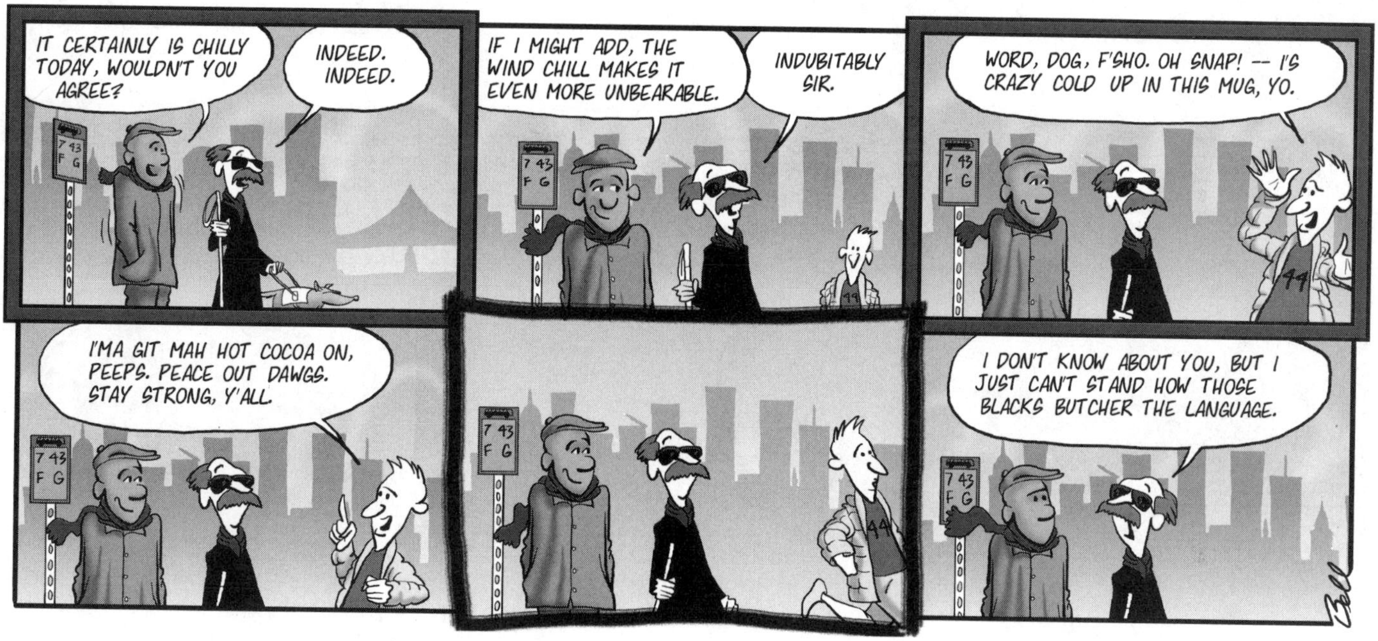

IT CERTAINLY IS CHILLY TODAY, WOULDN'T YOU AGREE?
INDEED. INDEED.
IF I MIGHT ADD, THE WIND CHILL MAKES IT EVEN MORE UNBEARABLE.
INDUBITABLY SIR.
WORD, DOG, F'SHO. OH SNAP! -- I'S CRAZY COLD UP IN THIS MUG, YO.
I'MA GIT MAH HOT COCOA ON, PEEPS. PEACE OUT DAWGS. STAY STRONG, Y'ALL.
I DON'T KNOW ABOUT YOU, BUT I JUST CAN'T STAND HOW THOSE BLACKS BUTCHER THE LANGUAGE.

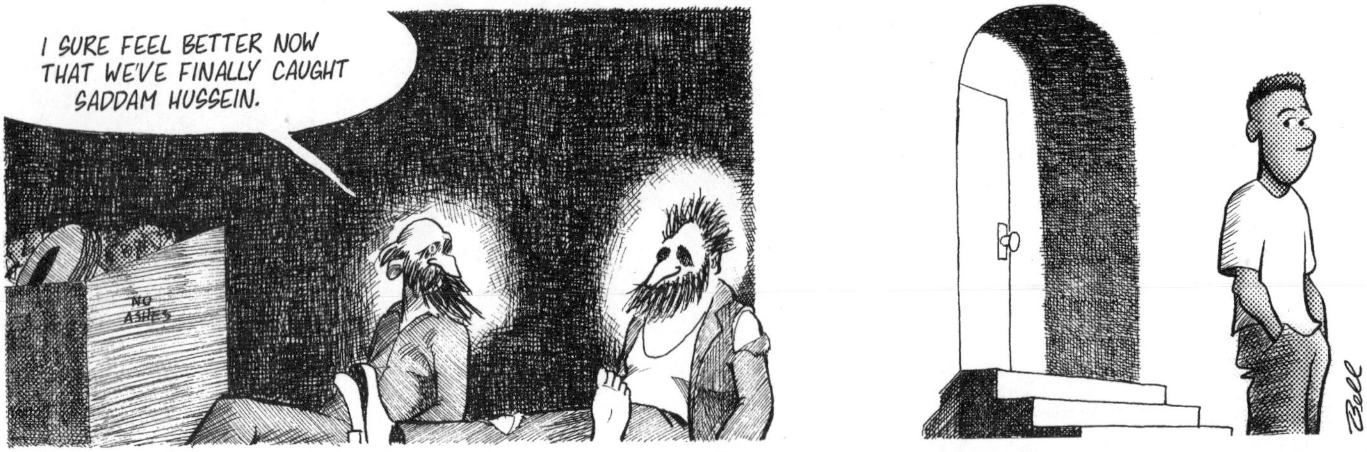

I SURE FEEL BETTER NOW THAT WE'VE FINALLY CAUGHT SADDAM HUSSEIN.
NO ASHES

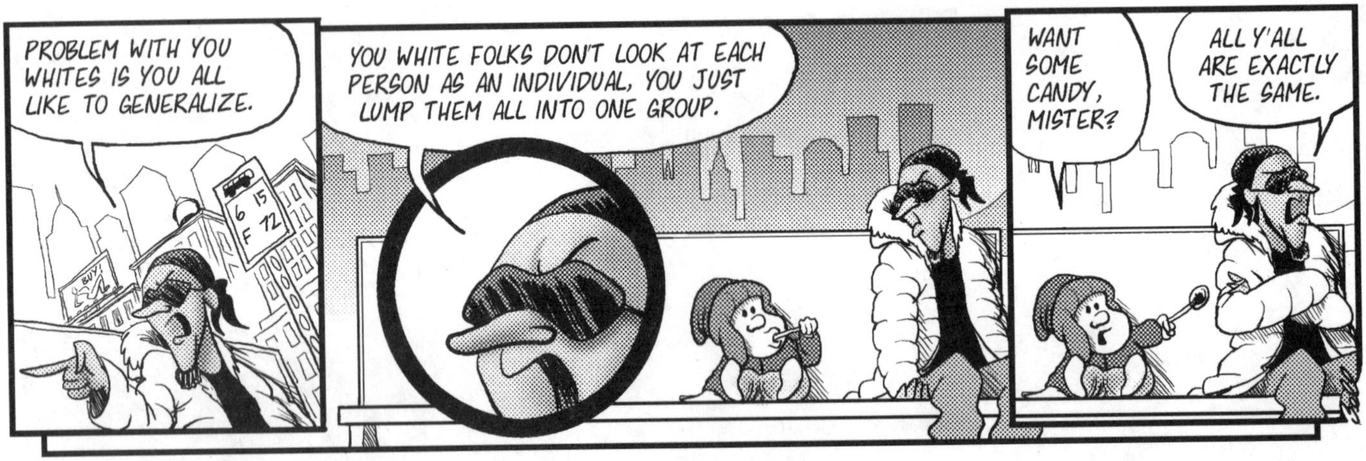

PROBLEM WITH YOU WHITES IS YOU ALL LIKE TO GENERALIZE.
YOU WHITE FOLKS DON'T LOOK AT EACH PERSON AS AN INDIVIDUAL, YOU JUST LUMP THEM ALL INTO ONE GROUP.
WANT SOME CANDY, MISTER?
ALL Y'ALL ARE EXACTLY THE SAME.

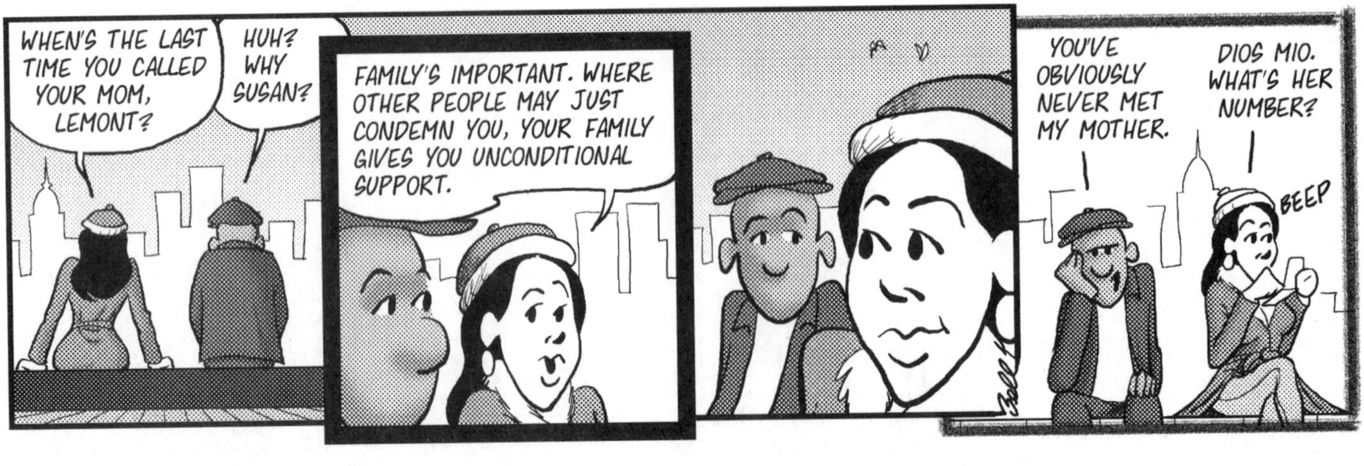

WHEN'S THE LAST TIME YOU CALLED YOUR MOM, LEMONT?
HUH? WHY SUSAN?
FAMILY'S IMPORTANT. WHERE OTHER PEOPLE MAY JUST CONDEMN YOU, YOUR FAMILY GIVES YOU UNCONDITIONAL SUPPORT.
YOU'VE OBVIOUSLY NEVER MET MY MOTHER.
DIOS MIO. WHAT'S HER NUMBER?
BEEP

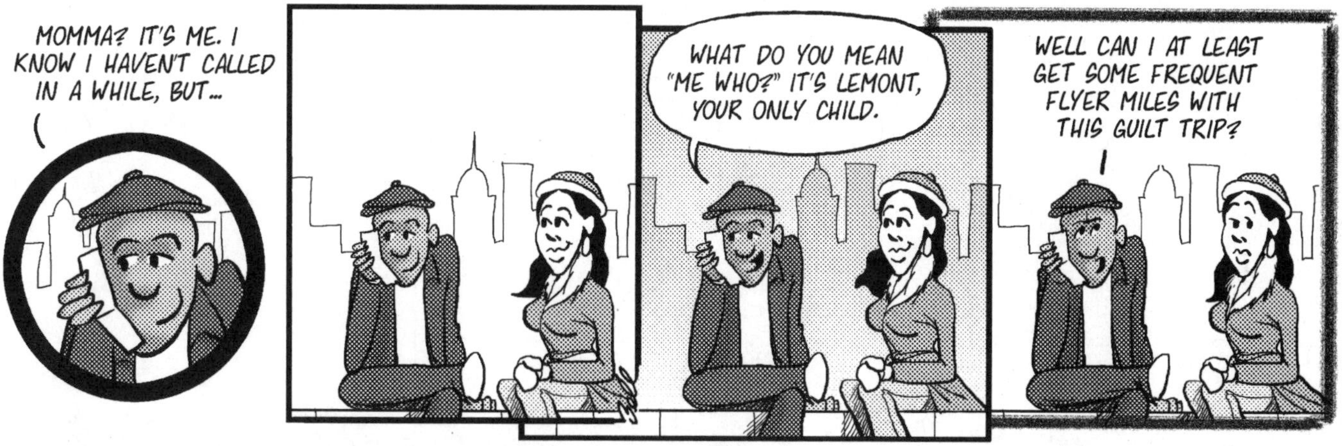
MOMMA? IT'S ME. I KNOW I HAVEN'T CALLED IN A WHILE, BUT...
WHAT DO YOU MEAN "ME WHO?" IT'S LEMONT, YOUR ONLY CHILD.
WELL CAN I AT LEAST GET SOME FREQUENT FLYER MILES WITH THIS GUILT TRIP?

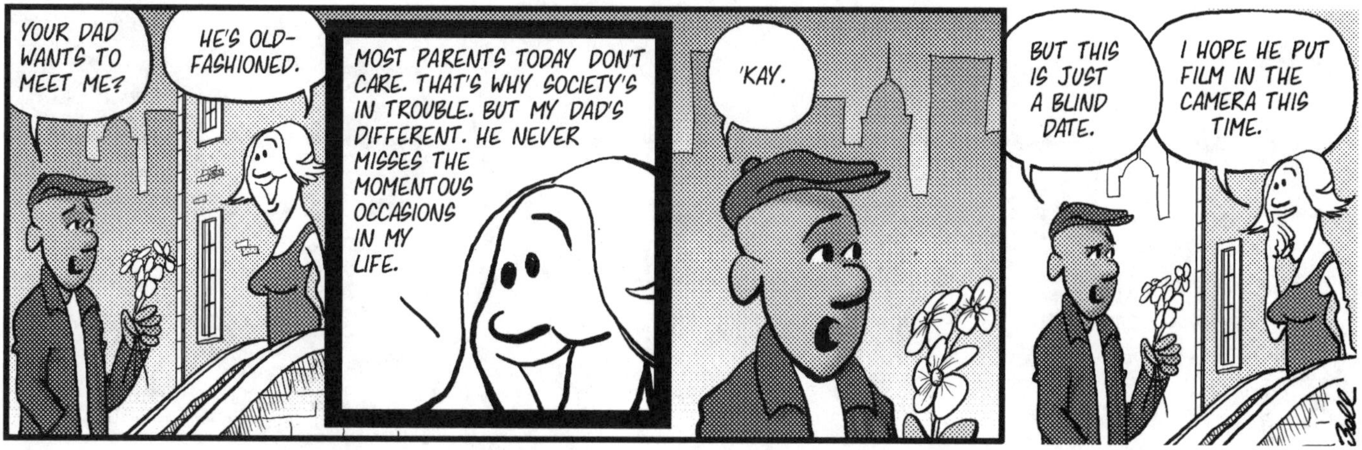
YOUR DAD WANTS TO MEET ME?
HE'S OLD-FASHIONED.
MOST PARENTS TODAY DON'T CARE. THAT'S WHY SOCIETY'S IN TROUBLE. BUT MY DAD'S DIFFERENT. HE NEVER MISSES THE MOMENTOUS OCCASIONS IN MY LIFE.
'KAY.
BUT THIS IS JUST A BLIND DATE.
I HOPE HE PUT FILM IN THE CAMERA THIS TIME.

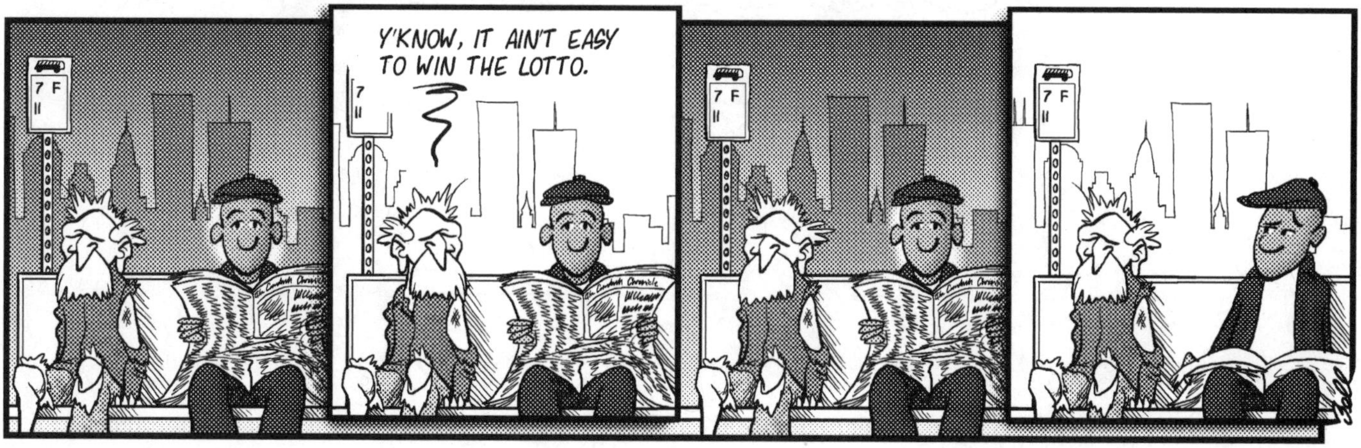
Y'KNOW, IT AIN'T EASY TO WIN THE LOTTO.

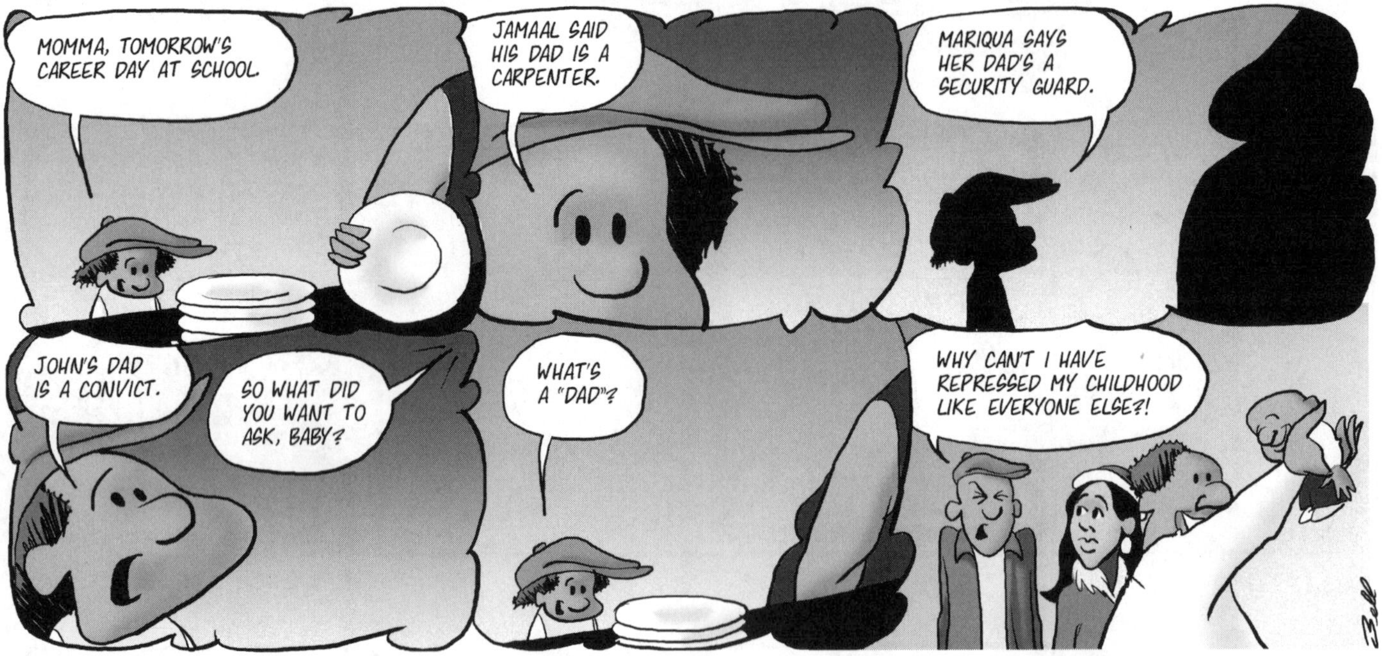
MOMMA, TOMORROW'S CAREER DAY AT SCHOOL.
JAMAAL SAID HIS DAD IS A CARPENTER.
MARIQUA SAYS HER DAD'S A SECURITY GUARD.
JOHN'S DAD IS A CONVICT.
SO WHAT DID YOU WANT TO ASK, BABY?
WHAT'S A "DAD"?
WHY CAN'T I HAVE REPRESSED MY CHILDHOOD LIKE EVERYONE ELSE?!

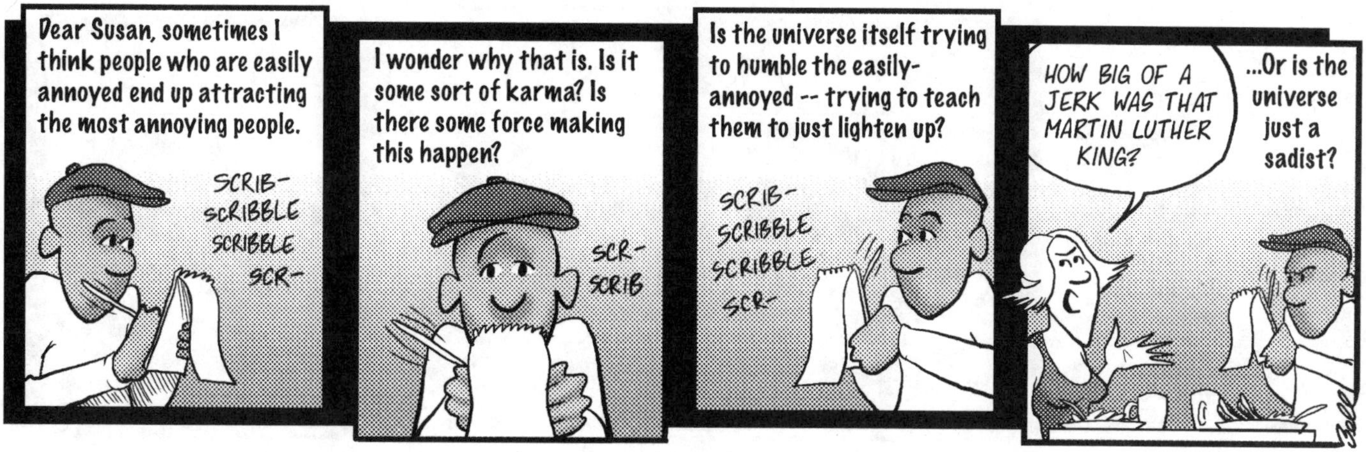
Dear Susan, sometimes I think people who are easily annoyed end up attracting the most annoying people.
SCRIB- SCRIBBLE SCRIBBLE SCR-
I wonder why that is. Is it some sort of karma? Is there some force making this happen?
SCR- SCRIB
Is the universe itself trying to humble the easily-annoyed -- trying to teach them to just lighten up?
SCRIB- SCRIBBLE SCRIBBLE SCR-
HOW BIG OF A JERK WAS THAT MARTIN LUTHER KING?
...Or is the universe just a sadist?

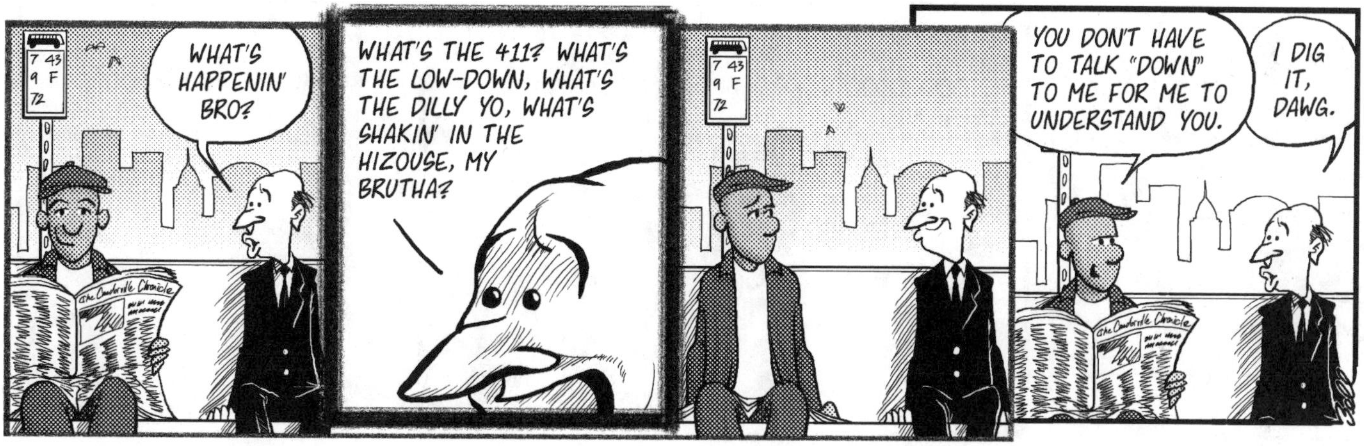
WHAT'S HAPPENIN' BRO?
WHAT'S THE 411? WHAT'S THE LOW-DOWN, WHAT'S THE DILLY YO, WHAT'S SHAKIN' IN THE HIZOUSE, MY BRUTHA?
YOU DON'T HAVE TO TALK "DOWN" TO ME FOR ME TO UNDERSTAND YOU.
I DIG IT, DAWG.

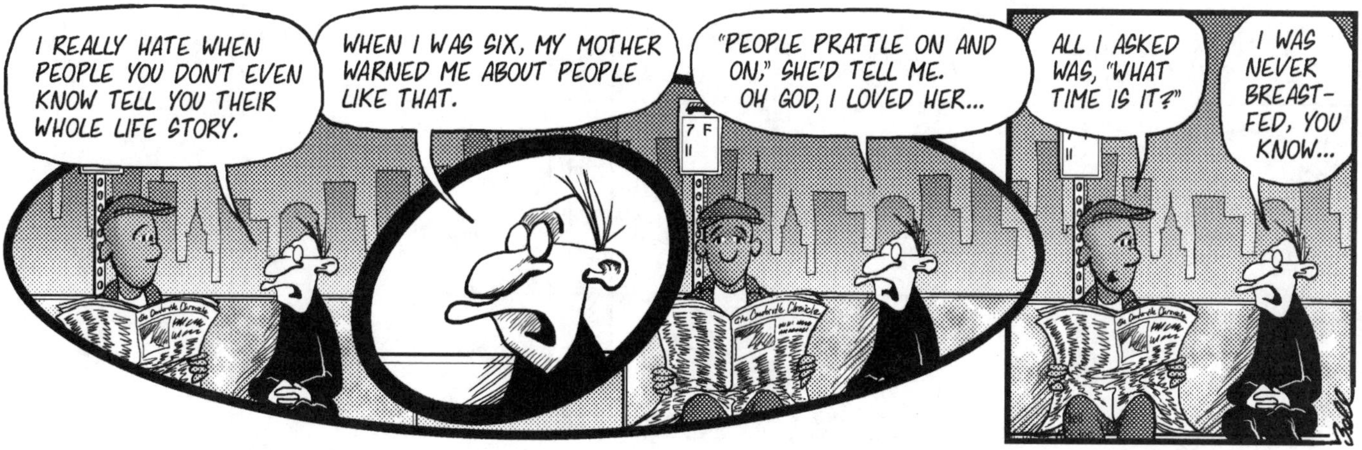
I REALLY HATE WHEN PEOPLE YOU DON'T EVEN KNOW TELL YOU THEIR WHOLE LIFE STORY.
WHEN I WAS SIX, MY MOTHER WARNED ME ABOUT PEOPLE LIKE THAT.
"PEOPLE PRATTLE ON AND ON," SHE'D TELL ME. OH GOD, I LOVED HER...
ALL I ASKED WAS, "WHAT TIME IS IT?"
I WAS NEVER BREAST-FED, YOU KNOW...

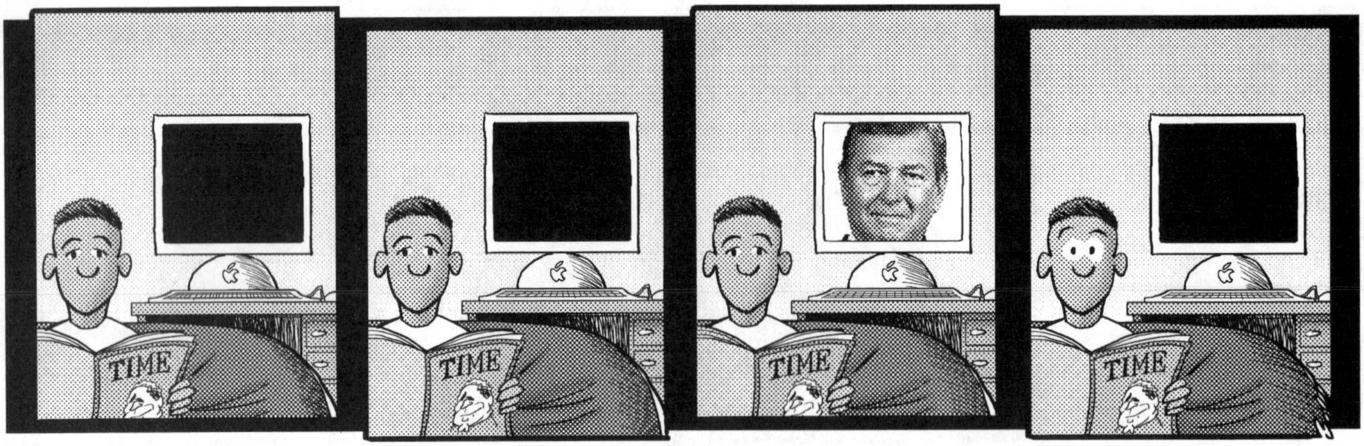
TIME
TIME
TIME
TIME

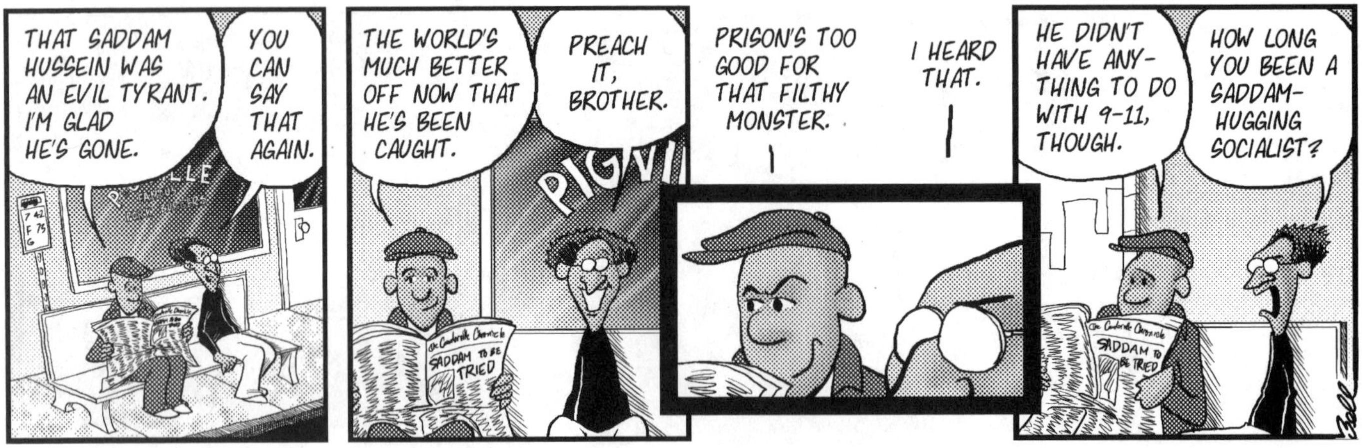
THAT SADDAM HUSSEIN WAS AN EVIL TYRANT. I'M GLAD HE'S GONE.
YOU CAN SAY THAT AGAIN.
THE WORLD'S MUCH BETTER OFF NOW THAT HE'S BEEN CAUGHT.
PREACH IT, BROTHER.
SADDAM TO BE TRIED
PRISON'S TOO GOOD FOR THAT FILTHY MONSTER.
I HEARD THAT.
HE DIDN'T HAVE ANYTHING TO DO WITH 9-11, THOUGH.
HOW LONG YOU BEEN A SADDAM-HUGGING SOCIALIST?
SADDAM TO BE TRIED

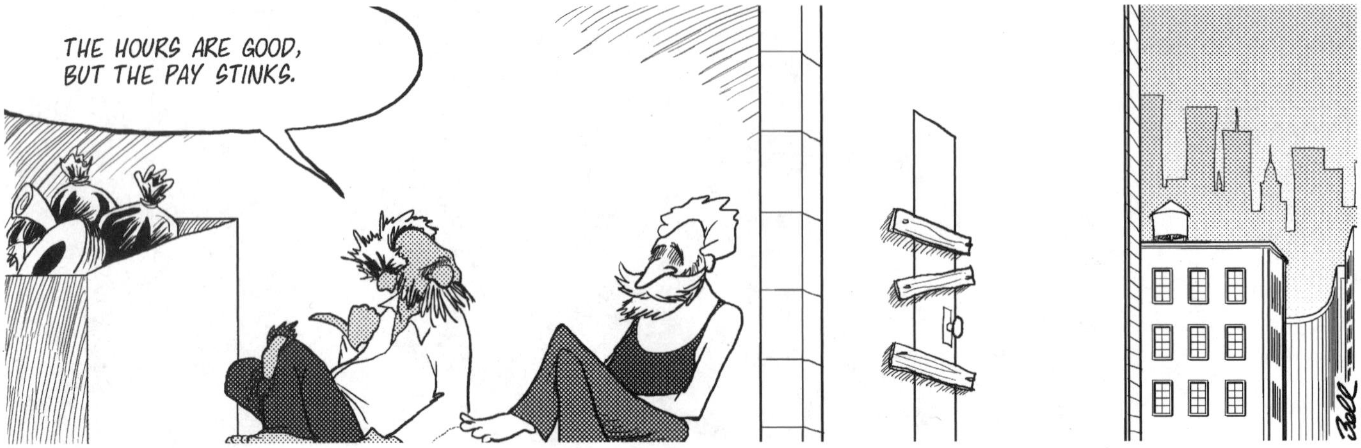
THE HOURS ARE GOOD, BUT THE PAY STINKS.

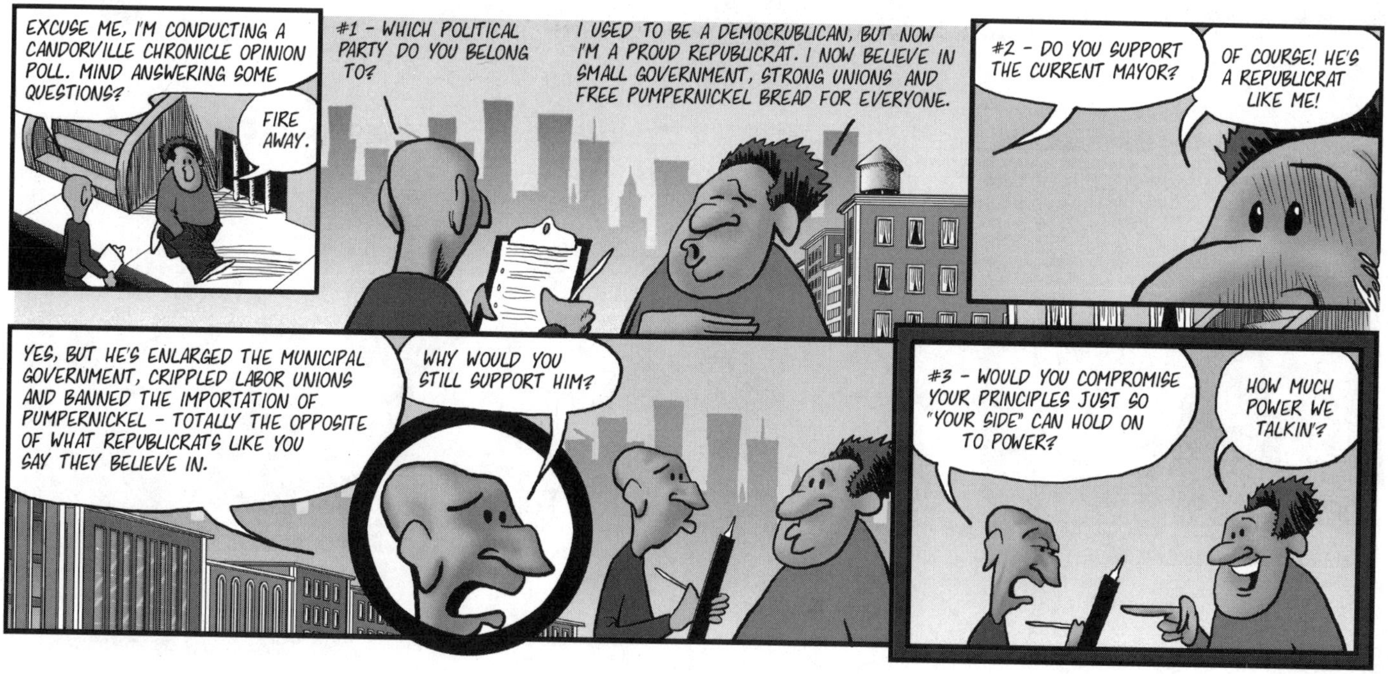
EXCUSE ME, I'M CONDUCTING A CANDORVILLE CHRONICLE OPINION POLL. MIND ANSWERING SOME QUESTIONS?
FIRE AWAY.
#1 - WHICH POLITICAL PARTY DO YOU BELONG TO?
I USED TO BE A DEMOCRUBLICAN, BUT NOW I'M A PROUD REPUBLICRAT. I NOW BELIEVE IN SMALL GOVERNMENT, STRONG UNIONS AND FREE PUMPERNICKEL BREAD FOR EVERYONE.
#2 - DO YOU SUPPORT THE CURRENT MAYOR?
OF COURSE! HE'S A REPUBLICRAT LIKE ME!
YES, BUT HE'S ENLARGED THE MUNICIPAL GOVERNMENT, CRIPPLED LABOR UNIONS AND BANNED THE IMPORTATION OF PUMPERNICKEL - TOTALLY THE OPPOSITE OF WHAT REPUBLICRATS LIKE YOU SAY THEY BELIEVE IN.
WHY WOULD YOU STILL SUPPORT HIM?
#3 - WOULD YOU COMPROMISE YOUR PRINCIPLES JUST SO "YOUR SIDE" CAN HOLD ON TO POWER?
HOW MUCH POWER WE TALKIN'?

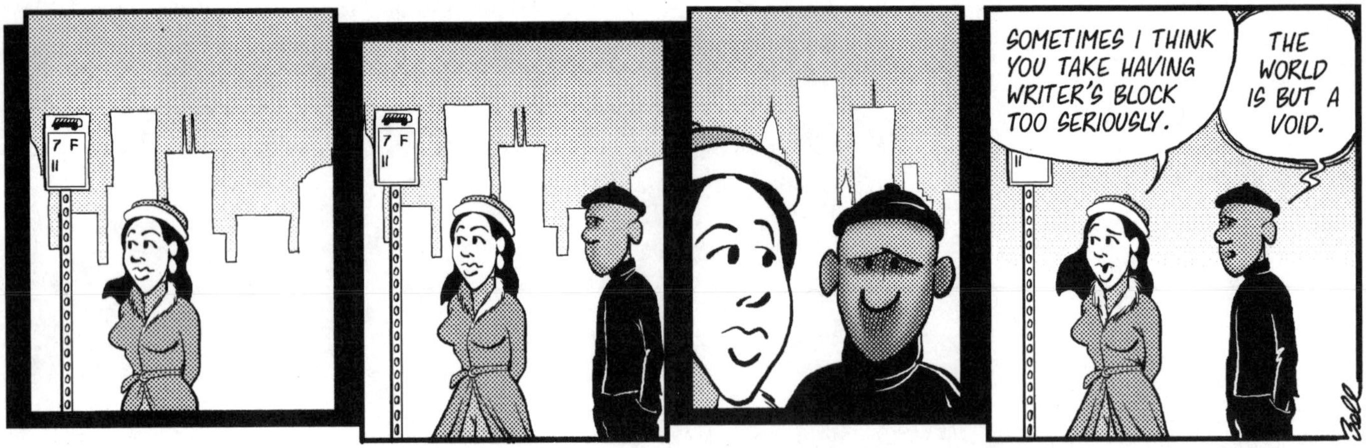
7 F
SOMETIMES I THINK YOU TAKE HAVING WRITER'S BLOCK TOO SERIOUSLY.
THE WORLD IS BUT A VOID.

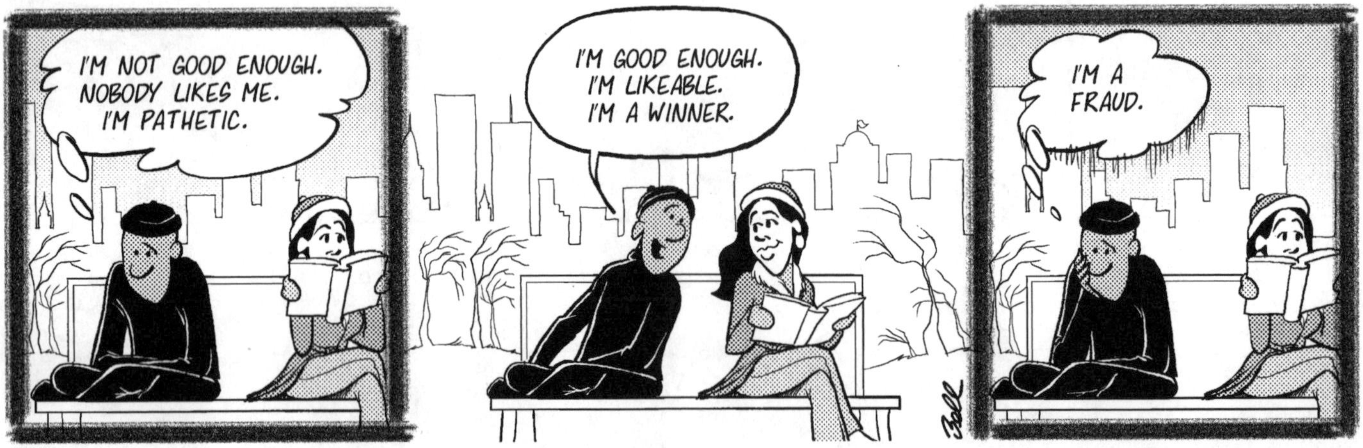
I'M NOT GOOD ENOUGH. NOBODY LIKES ME. I'M PATHETIC.
I'M GOOD ENOUGH. I'M LIKEABLE. I'M A WINNER.
I'M A FRAUD.

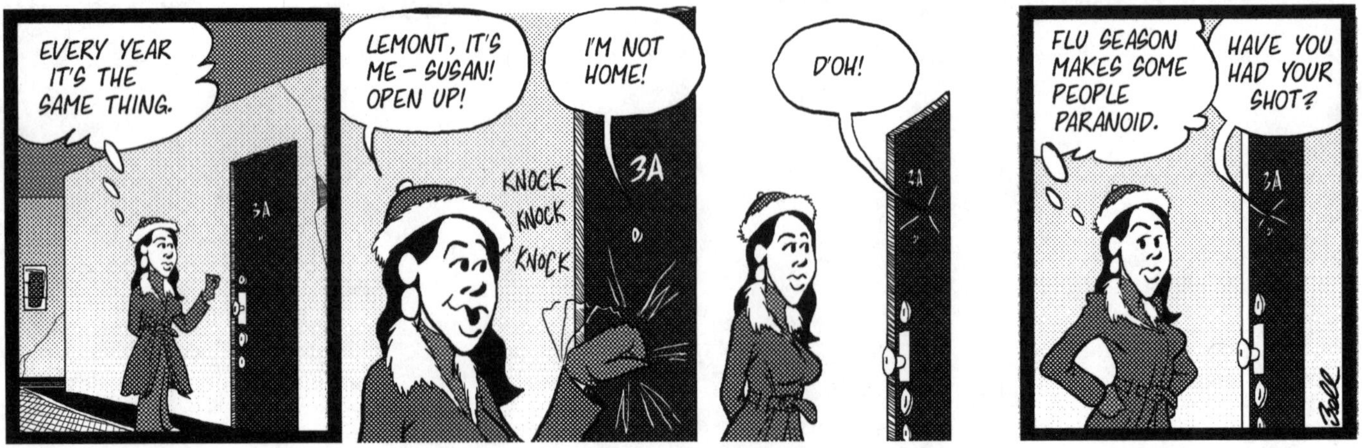
EVERY YEAR IT'S THE SAME THING.
3A
LEMONT, IT'S ME – SUSAN! OPEN UP!
KNOCK KNOCK KNOCK
I'M NOT HOME!
D'OH!
FLU SEASON MAKES SOME PEOPLE PARANOID.
HAVE YOU HAD YOUR SHOT?

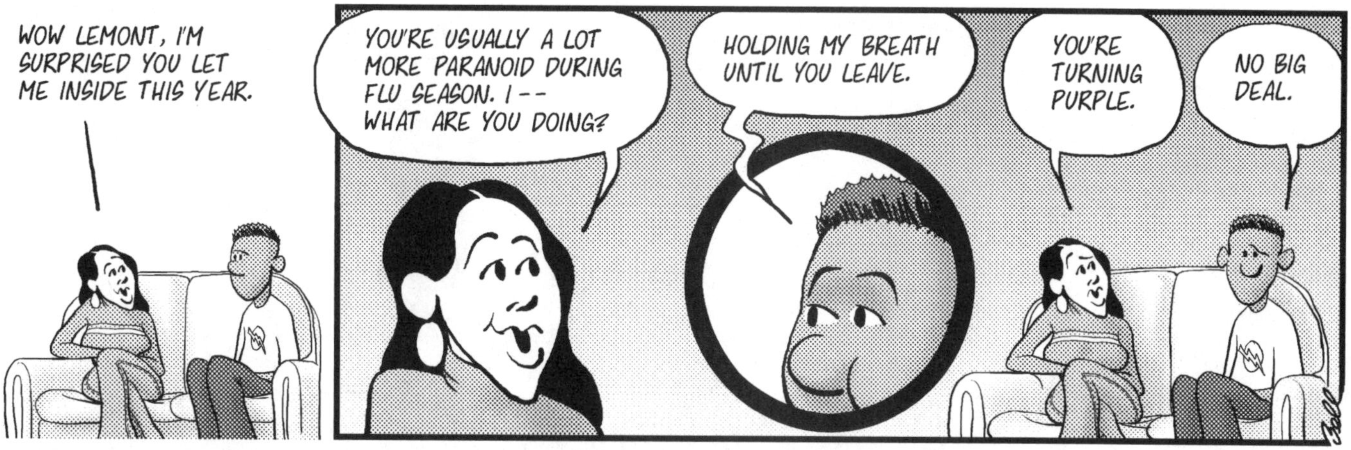
WOW LEMONT, I'M SURPRISED YOU LET ME INSIDE THIS YEAR.
YOU'RE USUALLY A LOT MORE PARANOID DURING FLU SEASON. I -- WHAT ARE YOU DOING?
HOLDING MY BREATH UNTIL YOU LEAVE.
YOU'RE TURNING PURPLE.
NO BIG DEAL.

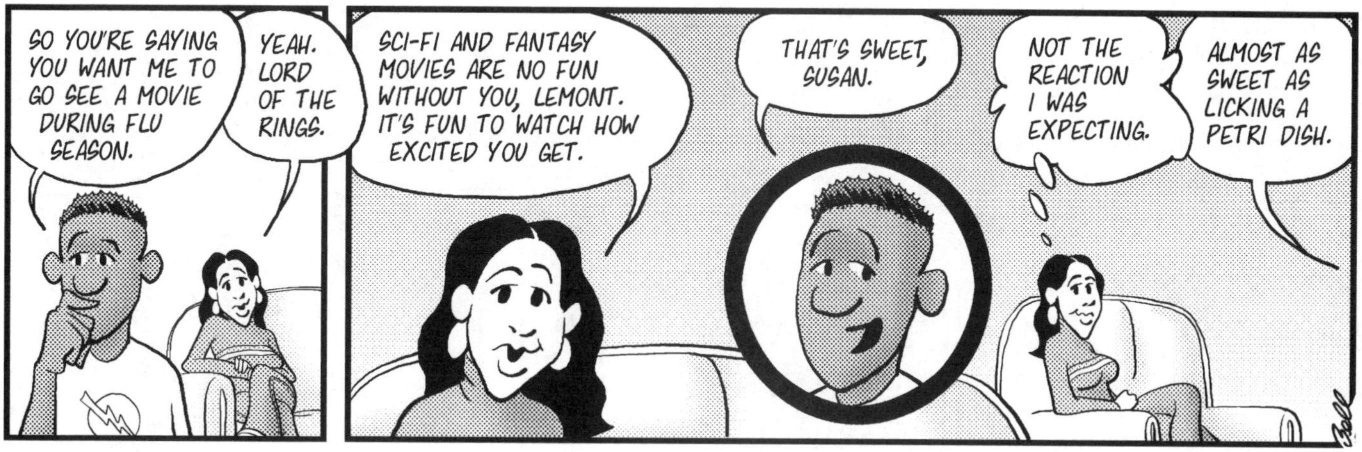
SO YOU'RE SAYING YOU WANT ME TO GO SEE A MOVIE DURING FLU SEASON.
YEAH. LORD OF THE RINGS.
SCI-FI AND FANTASY MOVIES ARE NO FUN WITHOUT YOU, LEMONT. IT'S FUN TO WATCH HOW EXCITED YOU GET.
THAT'S SWEET, SUSAN.
NOT THE REACTION I WAS EXPECTING.
ALMOST AS SWEET AS LICKING A PETRI DISH.

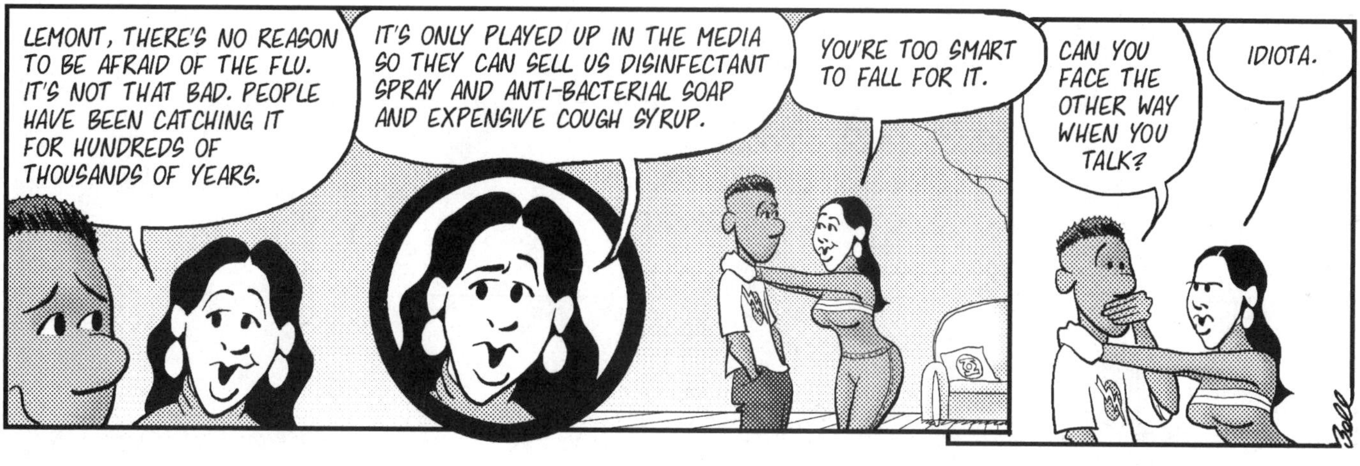
LEMONT, THERE'S NO REASON TO BE AFRAID OF THE FLU. IT'S NOT THAT BAD. PEOPLE HAVE BEEN CATCHING IT FOR HUNDREDS OF THOUSANDS OF YEARS.
IT'S ONLY PLAYED UP IN THE MEDIA SO THEY CAN SELL US DISINFECTANT SPRAY AND ANTI-BACTERIAL SOAP AND EXPENSIVE COUGH SYRUP.
YOU'RE TOO SMART TO FALL FOR IT.
CAN YOU FACE THE OTHER WAY WHEN YOU TALK?
IDIOTA.

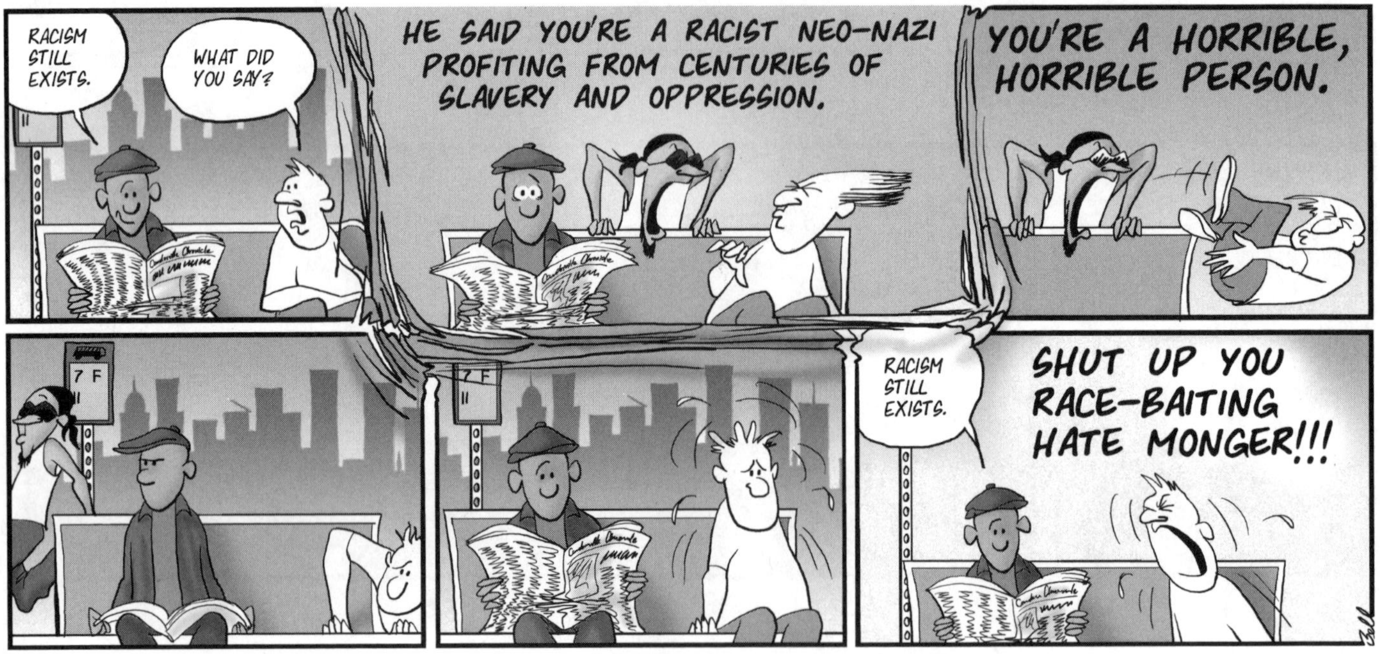
RACISM STILL EXISTS.
WHAT DID YOU SAY?
HE SAID YOU'RE A RACIST NEO-NAZI PROFITING FROM CENTURIES OF SLAVERY AND OPPRESSION.
YOU'RE A HORRIBLE, HORRIBLE PERSON.
7 F
7 F
RACISM STILL EXISTS.
SHUT UP YOU RACE-BAITING HATE MONGER!!!

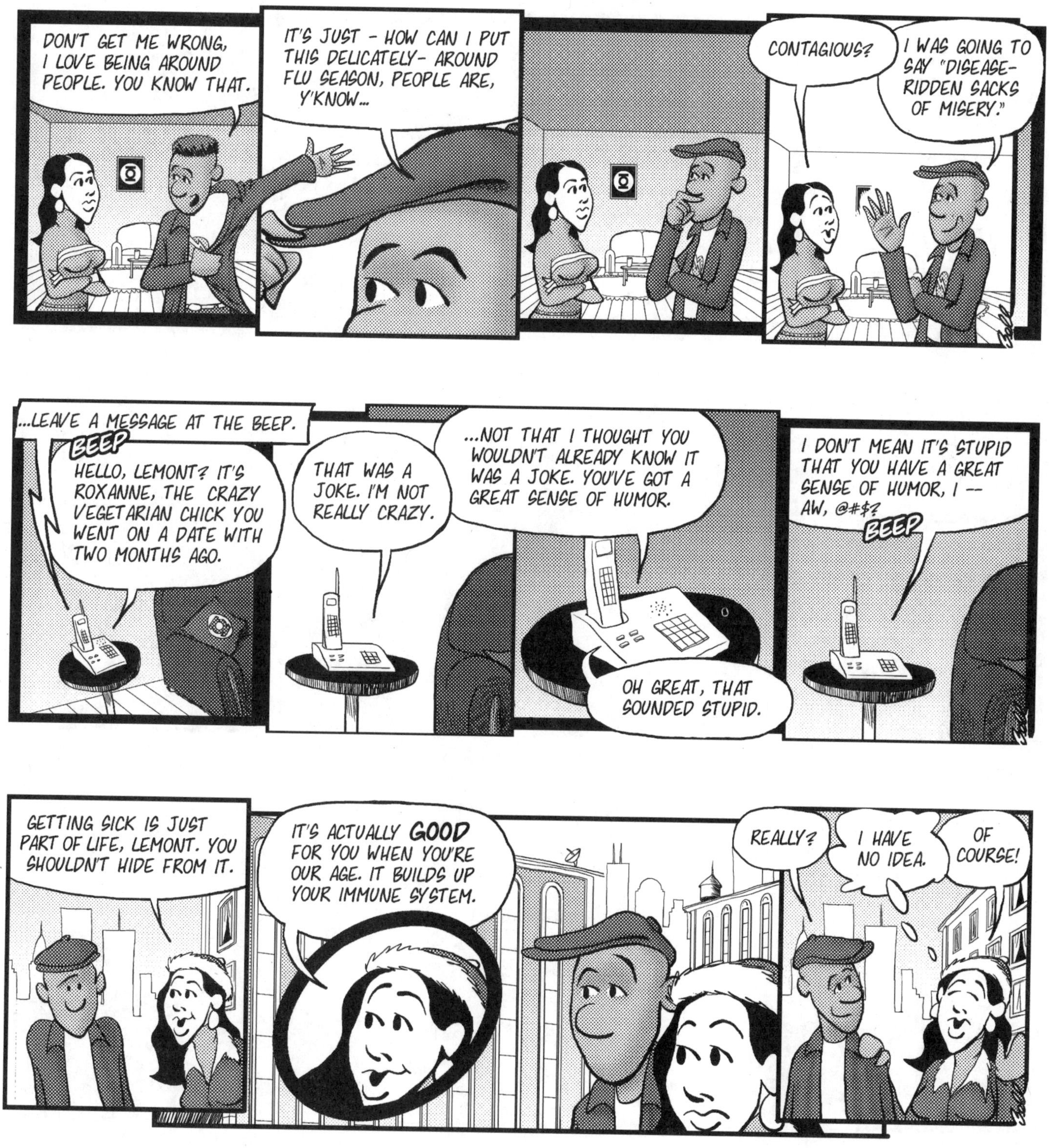
DON'T GET ME WRONG, I LOVE BEING AROUND PEOPLE. YOU KNOW THAT.
IT'S JUST - HOW CAN I PUT THIS DELICATELY- AROUND FLU SEASON, PEOPLE ARE, Y'KNOW...
CONTAGIOUS?
I WAS GOING TO SAY "DISEASE-RIDDEN SACKS OF MISERY."
...LEAVE A MESSAGE AT THE BEEP.
BEEP
HELLO, LEMONT? IT'S ROXANNE, THE CRAZY VEGETARIAN CHICK YOU WENT ON A DATE WITH TWO MONTHS AGO.
THAT WAS A JOKE. I'M NOT REALLY CRAZY.
...NOT THAT I THOUGHT YOU WOULDN'T ALREADY KNOW IT WAS A JOKE. YOU'VE GOT A GREAT SENSE OF HUMOR.
OH GREAT, THAT SOUNDED STUPID.
I DON'T MEAN IT'S STUPID THAT YOU HAVE A GREAT SENSE OF HUMOR, I -- AW, @#$?
BEEP
GETTING SICK IS JUST PART OF LIFE, LEMONT. YOU SHOULDN'T HIDE FROM IT.
IT'S ACTUALLY **GOOD** FOR YOU WHEN YOU'RE OUR AGE. IT BUILDS UP YOUR IMMUNE SYSTEM.
REALLY?
I HAVE NO IDEA.
OF COURSE!

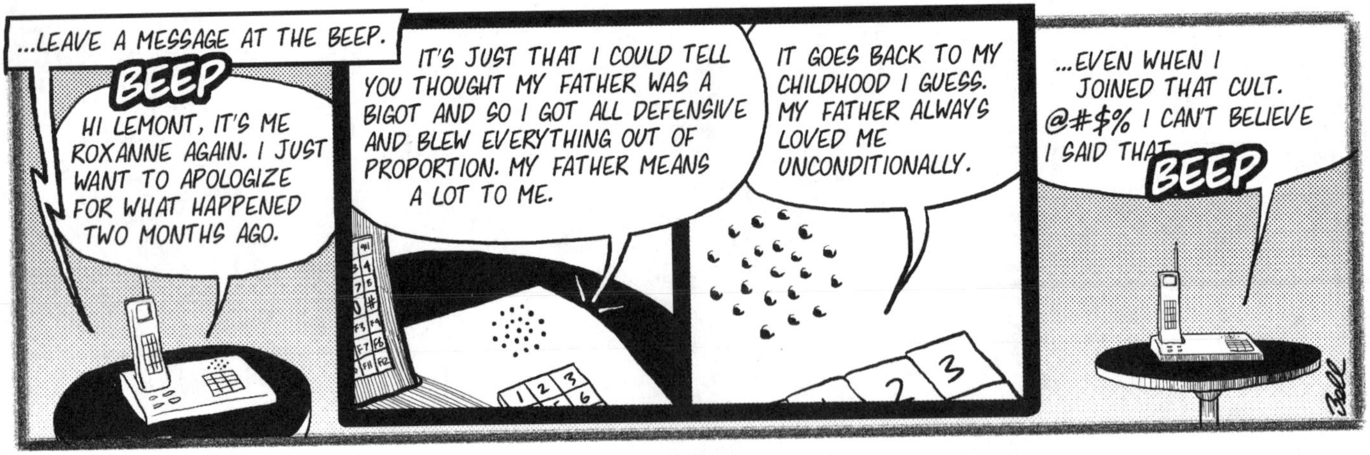
...LEAVE A MESSAGE AT THE BEEP.
BEEP
HI LEMONT, IT'S ME ROXANNE AGAIN. I JUST WANT TO APOLOGIZE FOR WHAT HAPPENED TWO MONTHS AGO.
IT'S JUST THAT I COULD TELL YOU THOUGHT MY FATHER WAS A BIGOT AND SO I GOT ALL DEFENSIVE AND BLEW EVERYTHING OUT OF PROPORTION. MY FATHER MEANS A LOT TO ME.
IT GOES BACK TO MY CHILDHOOD I GUESS. MY FATHER ALWAYS LOVED ME UNCONDITIONALLY.
...EVEN WHEN I JOINED THAT CULT. @#$% I CAN'T BELIEVE I SAID THAT
BEEP

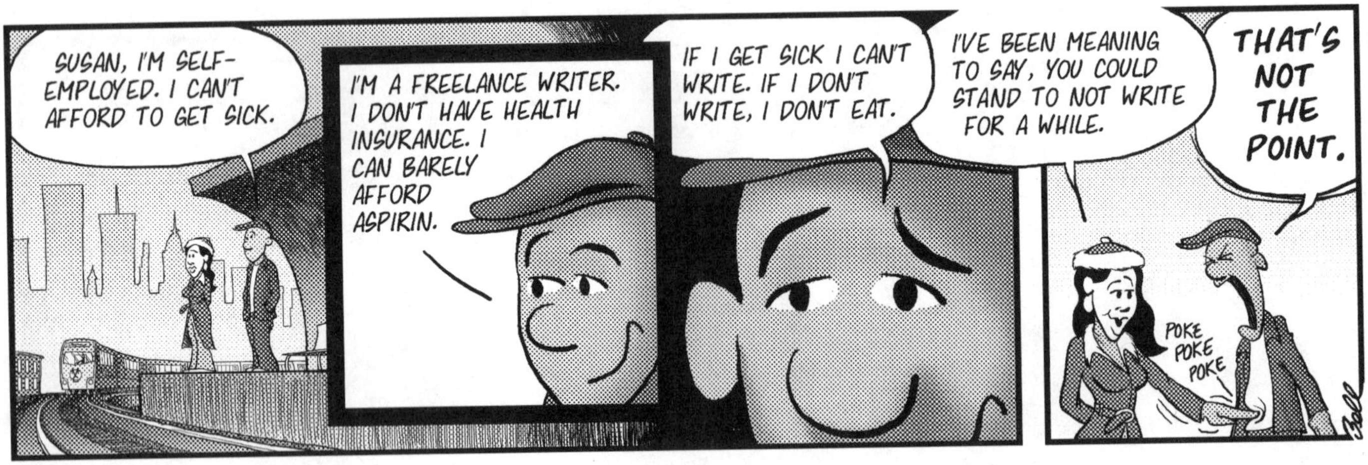
SUSAN, I'M SELF-EMPLOYED. I CAN'T AFFORD TO GET SICK.
I'M A FREELANCE WRITER. I DON'T HAVE HEALTH INSURANCE. I CAN BARELY AFFORD ASPIRIN.
IF I GET SICK I CAN'T WRITE. IF I DON'T WRITE, I DON'T EAT.
I'VE BEEN MEANING TO SAY, YOU COULD STAND TO NOT WRITE FOR A WHILE.
THAT'S NOT THE POINT.
POKE POKE POKE

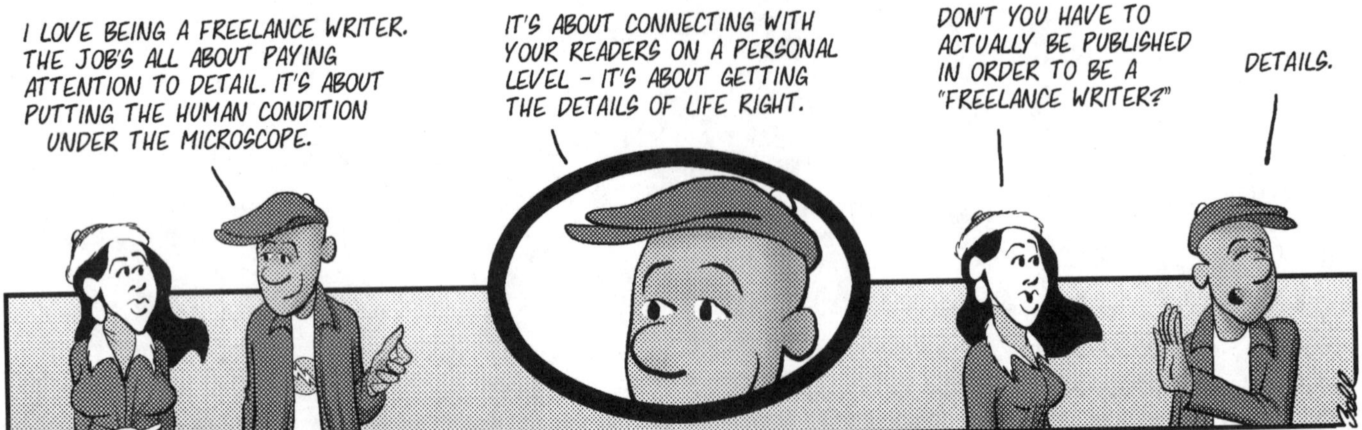
I LOVE BEING A FREELANCE WRITER. THE JOB'S ALL ABOUT PAYING ATTENTION TO DETAIL. IT'S ABOUT PUTTING THE HUMAN CONDITION UNDER THE MICROSCOPE.
IT'S ABOUT CONNECTING WITH YOUR READERS ON A PERSONAL LEVEL - IT'S ABOUT GETTING THE DETAILS OF LIFE RIGHT.
DON'T YOU HAVE TO ACTUALLY BE PUBLISHED IN ORDER TO BE A "FREELANCE WRITER?"
DETAILS.

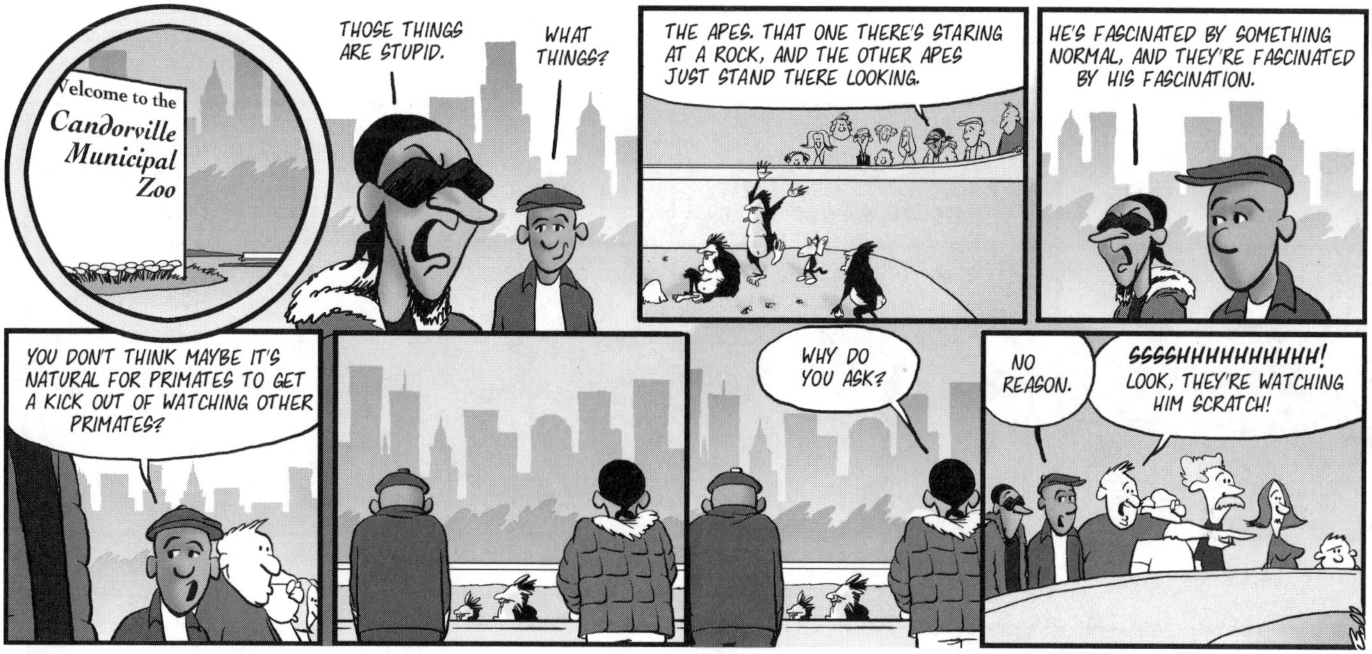

Welcome to the
Candorville
Municipal
Zoo
THOSE THINGS ARE STUPID.
WHAT THINGS?
THE APES. THAT ONE THERE'S STARING AT A ROCK, AND THE OTHER APES JUST STAND THERE LOOKING.
HE'S FASCINATED BY SOMETHING NORMAL, AND THEY'RE FASCINATED BY HIS FASCINATION.
YOU DON'T THINK MAYBE IT'S NATURAL FOR PRIMATES TO GET A KICK OUT OF WATCHING OTHER PRIMATES?
WHY DO YOU ASK?
NO REASON.
SSSSHHHHHHHHHH! LOOK, THEY'RE WATCHING HIM SCRATCH!

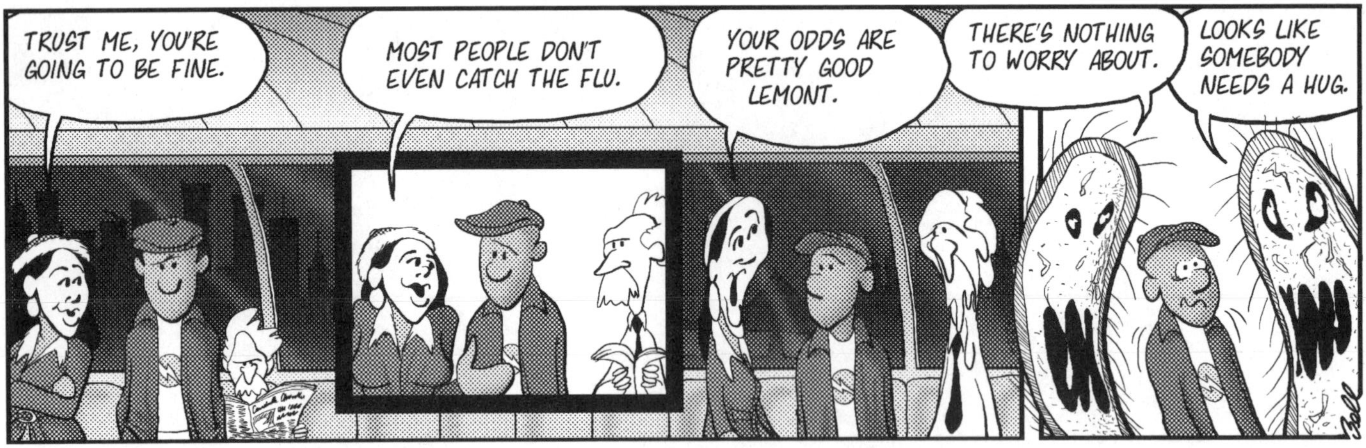
TRUST ME, YOU'RE GOING TO BE FINE.
MOST PEOPLE DON'T EVEN CATCH THE FLU.
YOUR ODDS ARE PRETTY GOOD LEMONT.
THERE'S NOTHING TO WORRY ABOUT.
LOOKS LIKE SOMEBODY NEEDS A HUG.

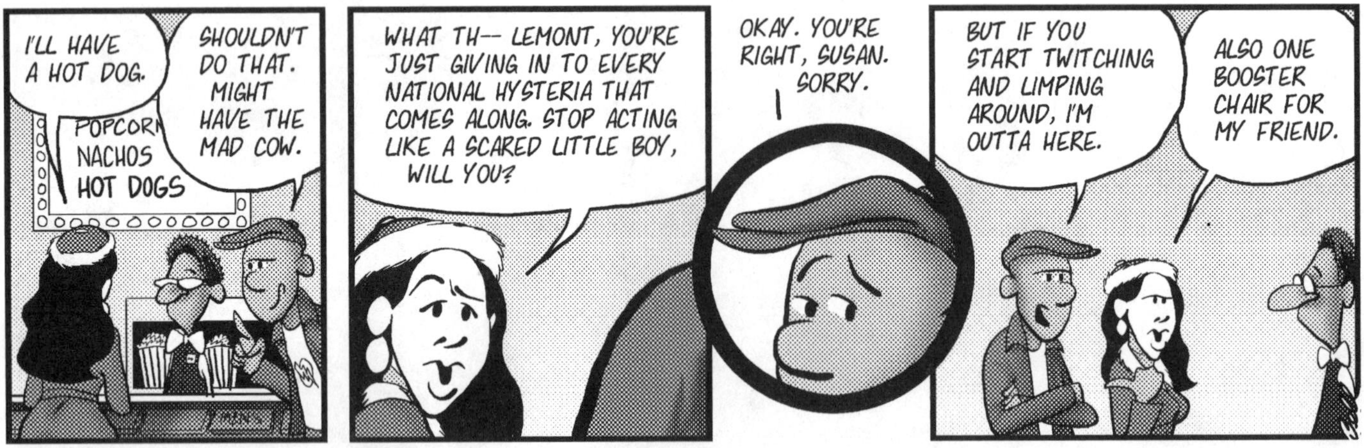
I'LL HAVE A HOT DOG.
SHOULDN'T DO THAT. MIGHT HAVE THE MAD COW.
POPCOR
NACHOS
HOT DOGS
WHAT TH-- LEMONT, YOU'RE JUST GIVING IN TO EVERY NATIONAL HYSTERIA THAT COMES ALONG. STOP ACTING LIKE A SCARED LITTLE BOY, WILL YOU?
OKAY. YOU'RE RIGHT, SUSAN. SORRY.
BUT IF YOU START TWITCHING AND LIMPING AROUND, I'M OUTTA HERE.
ALSO ONE BOOSTER CHAIR FOR MY FRIEND.

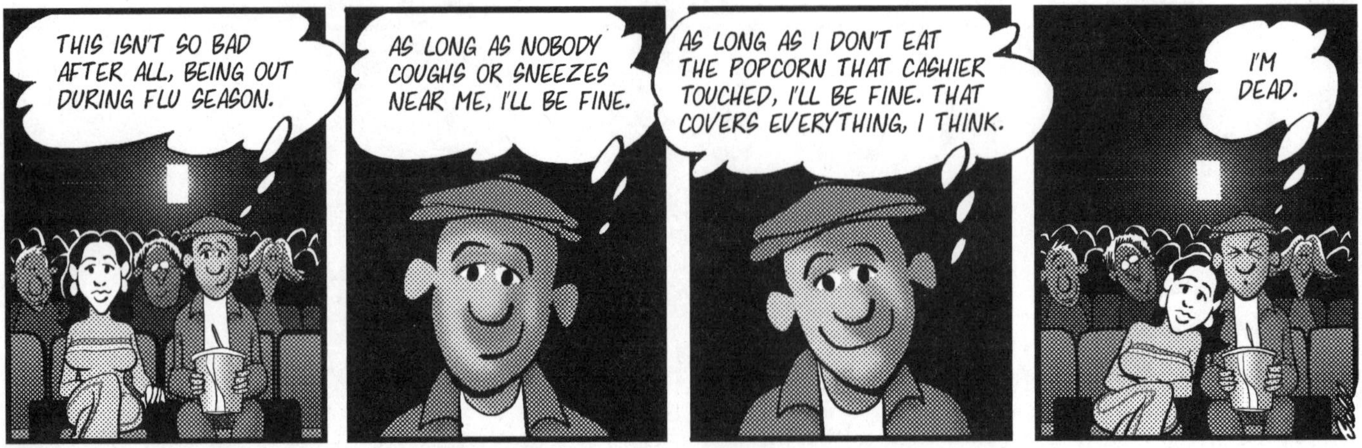
THIS ISN'T SO BAD AFTER ALL, BEING OUT DURING FLU SEASON.
AS LONG AS NOBODY COUGHS OR SNEEZES NEAR ME, I'LL BE FINE.
AS LONG AS I DON'T EAT THE POPCORN THAT CASHIER TOUCHED, I'LL BE FINE. THAT COVERS EVERYTHING, I THINK.
I'M DEAD.

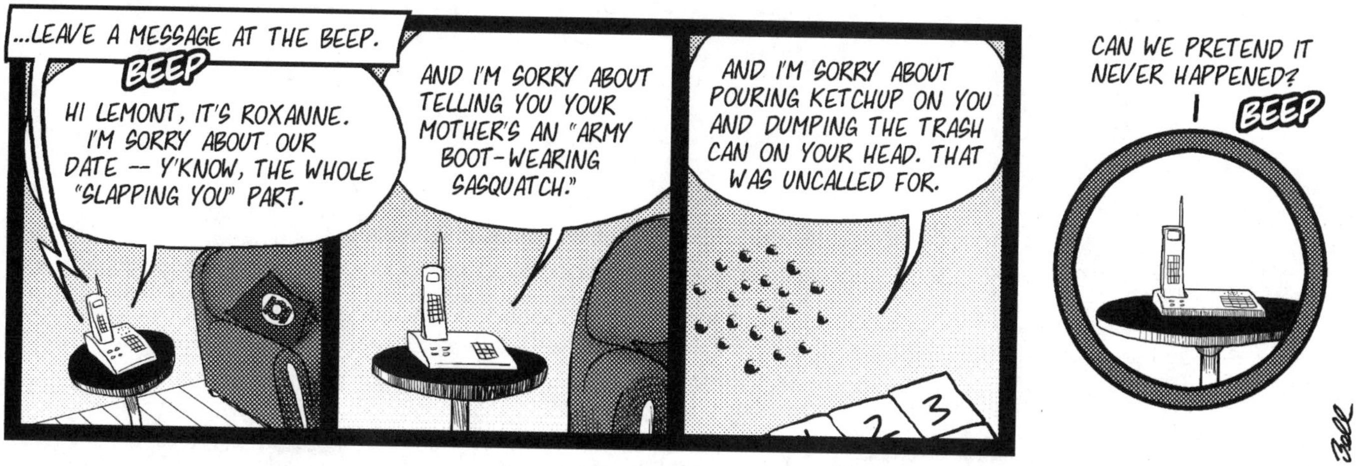
...LEAVE A MESSAGE AT THE BEEP.
BEEP
HI LEMONT, IT'S ROXANNE. I'M SORRY ABOUT OUR DATE -- Y'KNOW, THE WHOLE "SLAPPING YOU" PART.
AND I'M SORRY ABOUT TELLING YOU YOUR MOTHER'S AN "ARMY BOOT-WEARING SASQUATCH."
AND I'M SORRY ABOUT POURING KETCHUP ON YOU AND DUMPING THE TRASH CAN ON YOUR HEAD. THAT WAS UNCALLED FOR.
CAN WE PRETEND IT NEVER HAPPENED?
BEEP

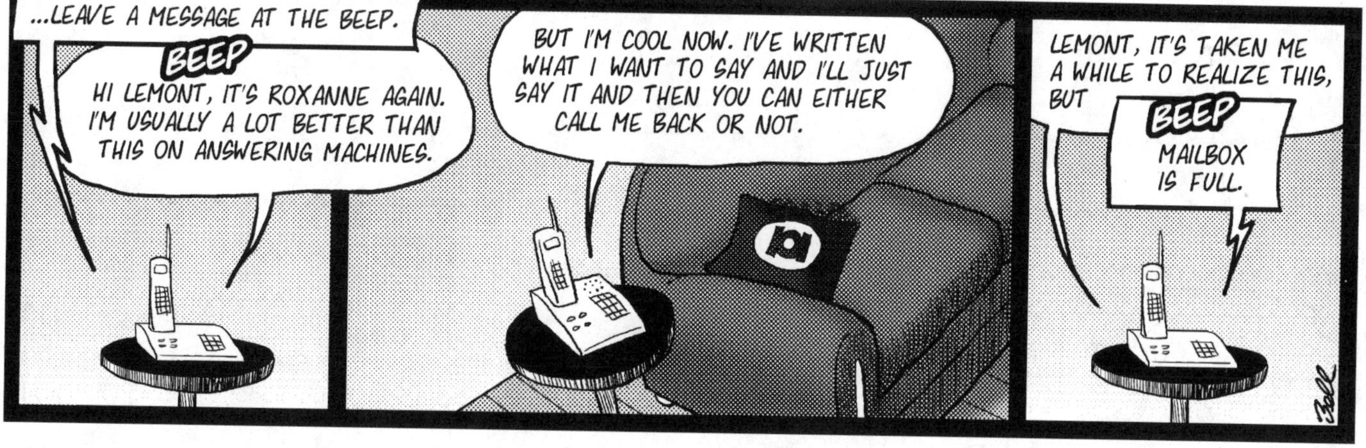
...LEAVE A MESSAGE AT THE BEEP.
BEEP
HI LEMONT, IT'S ROXANNE AGAIN. I'M USUALLY A LOT BETTER THAN THIS ON ANSWERING MACHINES.
BUT I'M COOL NOW. I'VE WRITTEN WHAT I WANT TO SAY AND I'LL JUST SAY IT AND THEN YOU CAN EITHER CALL ME BACK OR NOT.
LEMONT, IT'S TAKEN ME A WHILE TO REALIZE THIS, BUT
BEEP
MAILBOX IS FULL.

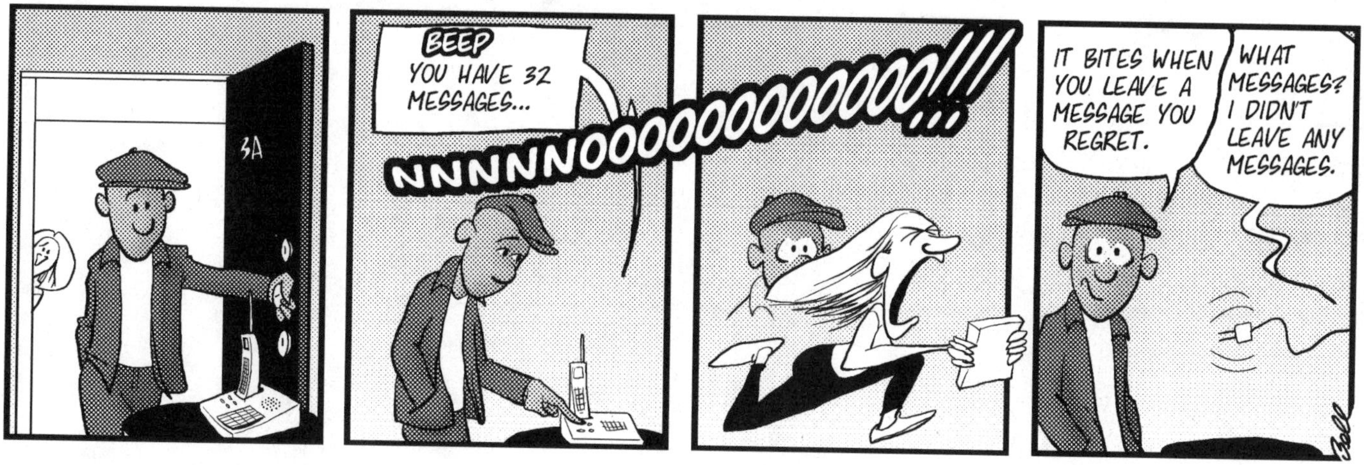
3A
BEEP
YOU HAVE 32 MESSAGES...
NNNNNOOOOOOOOOOOOOO!!!...
IT BITES WHEN YOU LEAVE A MESSAGE YOU REGRET.
WHAT MESSAGES? I DIDN'T LEAVE ANY MESSAGES.

YOUR POLITICAL PARTY IS NOTHING BUT A BUNCH OF WHINERS.
ALL YOU PEOPLE DO IS ATTACK YOUR OPPONENTS AND DISMISS THEM AS UNPATRIOTIC NINCOMPOOPS. WHINER.
WELL, YOU'RE "WHINING" WHEN YOU COMPLAIN ABOUT OUR LEGITIMATE EXPRESSION OF GRIEVANCES.
YOUR "LEGITMATE EXPRESSION" IS JUST A WHINY DIATRIBE THAT MARGINALIZES MY POINT OF VIEW AND BELITTLES MY INTELLIGENCE.
AND YOUR RESPONSE TO MY VIEWS IS JUST A WHINY ATTEMPT TO DISMISS THEM AS AN IDEOLOGICAL "DIATRIBE."
STOP ATTACKING ME.
I'M NOT ATTACKING YOU, YOU'RE ATTACKING ME.
POLITICS IS GETTING TOO WHINY.
WHINER.
YOU'RE NOT BEING FAIR.

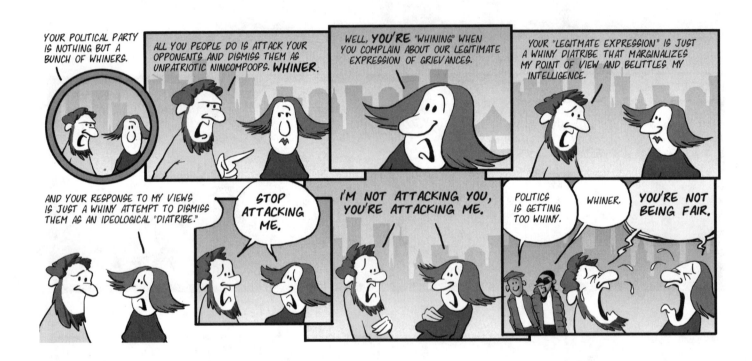

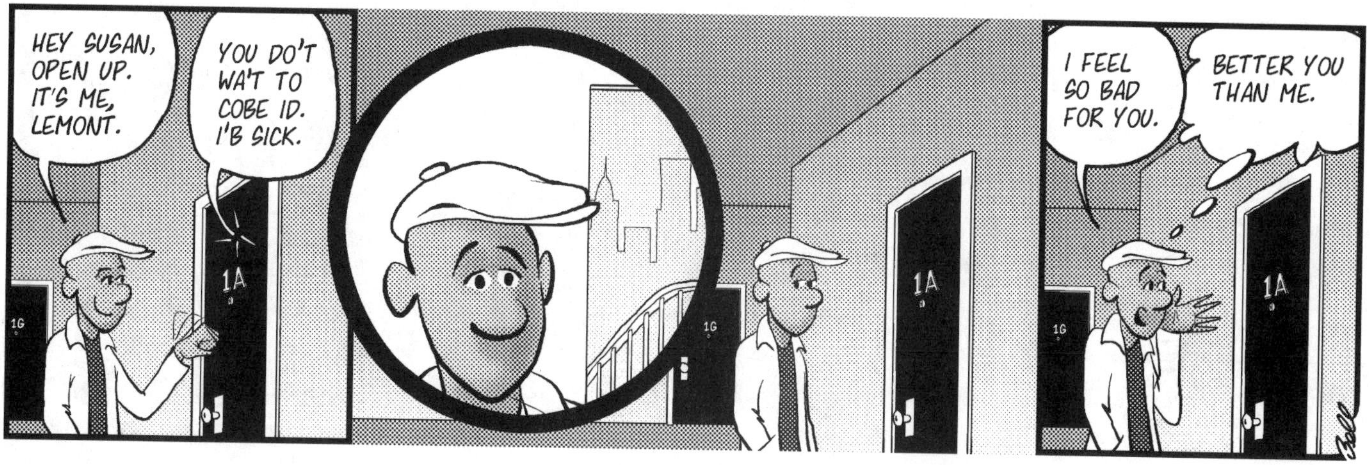
HEY SUSAN, OPEN UP. IT'S ME, LEMONT.
YOU DO'T WA'T TO COBE ID. I'B SICK.
1A
1G
I FEEL SO BAD FOR YOU.
BETTER YOU THAN ME.

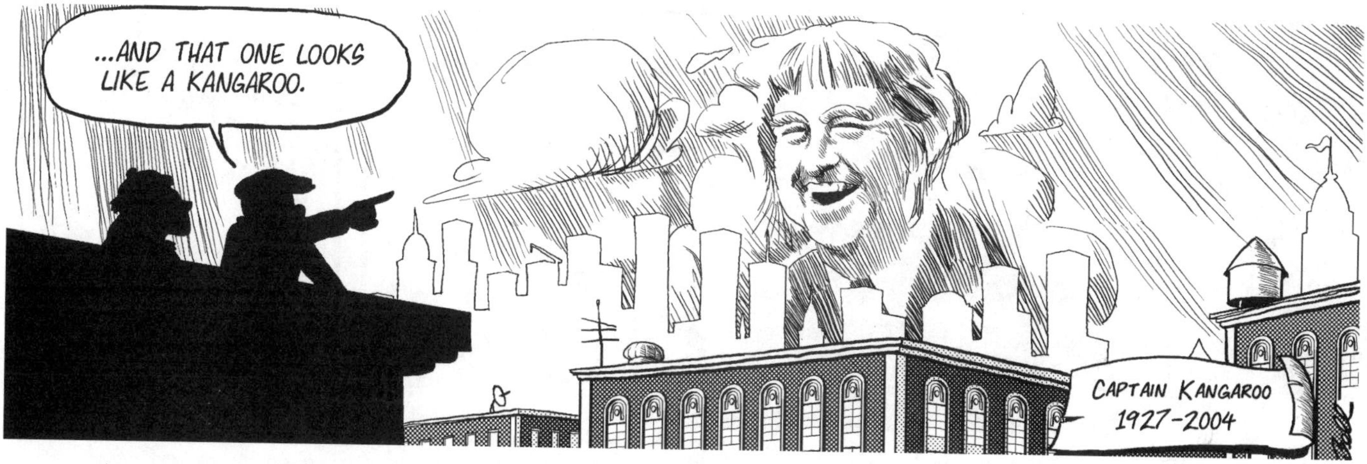
...AND THAT ONE LOOKS LIKE A KANGAROO.
CAPTAIN KANGAROO 1927–2004

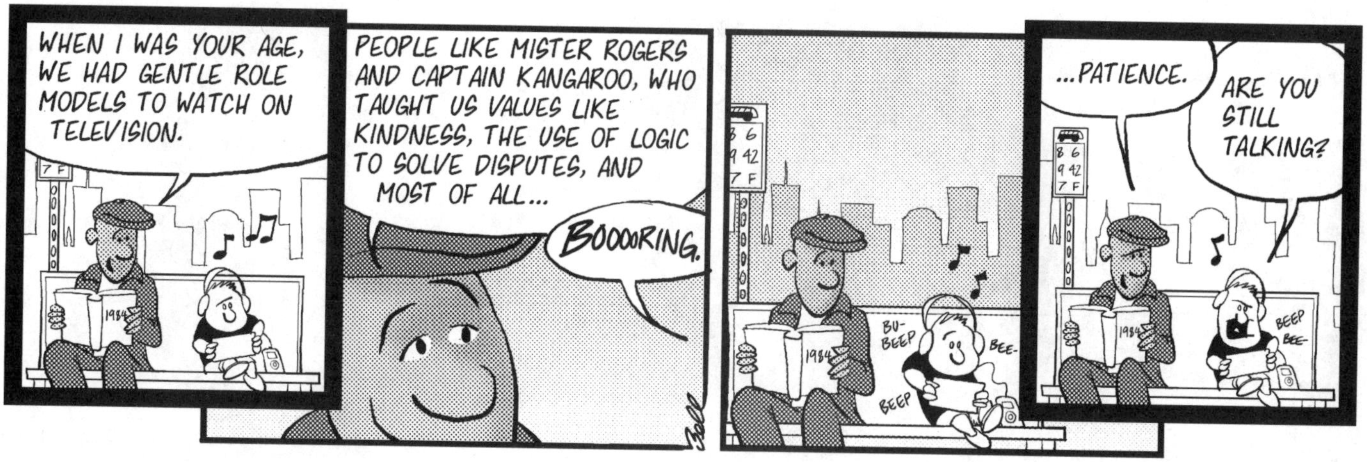
WHEN I WAS YOUR AGE, WE HAD GENTLE ROLE MODELS TO WATCH ON TELEVISION.
1984
PEOPLE LIKE MISTER ROGERS AND CAPTAIN KANGAROO, WHO TAUGHT US VALUES LIKE KINDNESS, THE USE OF LOGIC TO SOLVE DISPUTES, AND MOST OF ALL...
BOOOORING.
BU-BEEP
BEE-
BEEP
...PATIENCE.
ARE YOU STILL TALKING?
BEEP BEE-

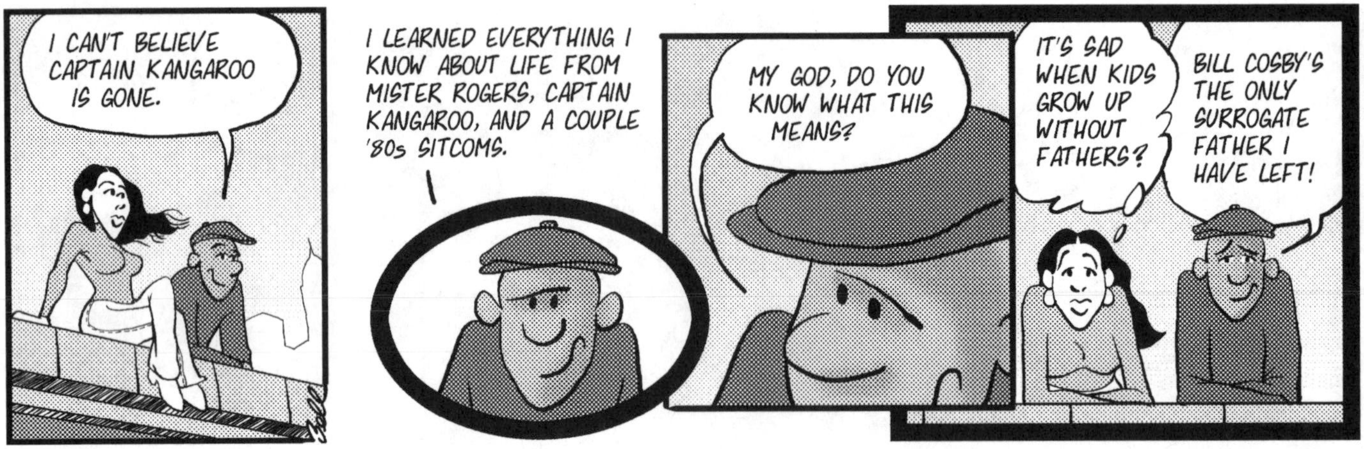
I CAN'T BELIEVE CAPTAIN KANGAROO IS GONE.
I LEARNED EVERYTHING I KNOW ABOUT LIFE FROM MISTER ROGERS, CAPTAIN KANGAROO, AND A COUPLE '80s SITCOMS.
MY GOD, DO YOU KNOW WHAT THIS MEANS?
IT'S SAD WHEN KIDS GROW UP WITHOUT FATHERS?
BILL COSBY'S THE ONLY SURROGATE FATHER I HAVE LEFT!

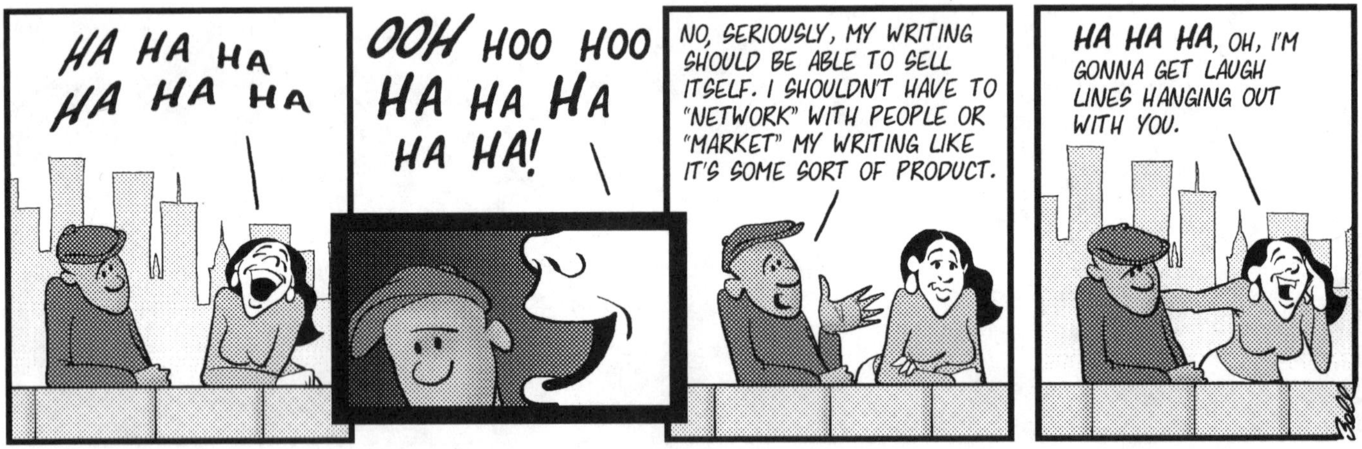
HA HA HA HA HA HA
OOH HOO HOO HA HA HA HA HA!
NO, SERIOUSLY, MY WRITING SHOULD BE ABLE TO SELL ITSELF. I SHOULDN'T HAVE TO "NETWORK" WITH PEOPLE OR "MARKET" MY WRITING LIKE IT'S SOME SORT OF PRODUCT.
HA HA HA, OH, I'M GONNA GET LAUGH LINES HANGING OUT WITH YOU.

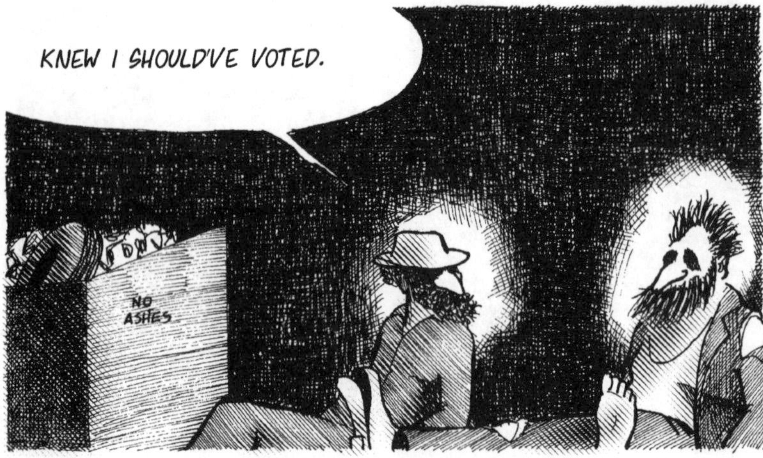
KNEW I SHOULD'VE VOTED.
NO ASHES

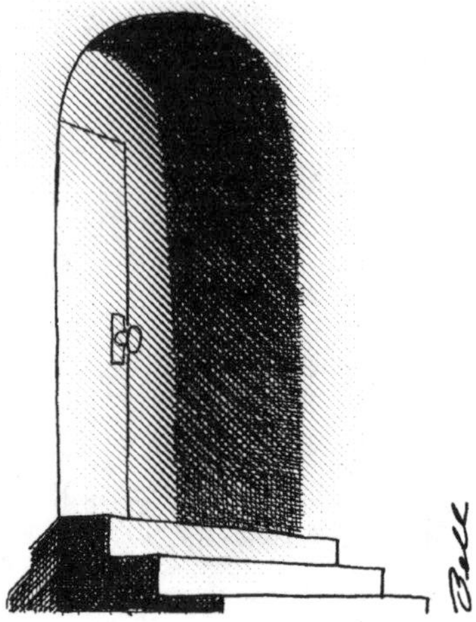

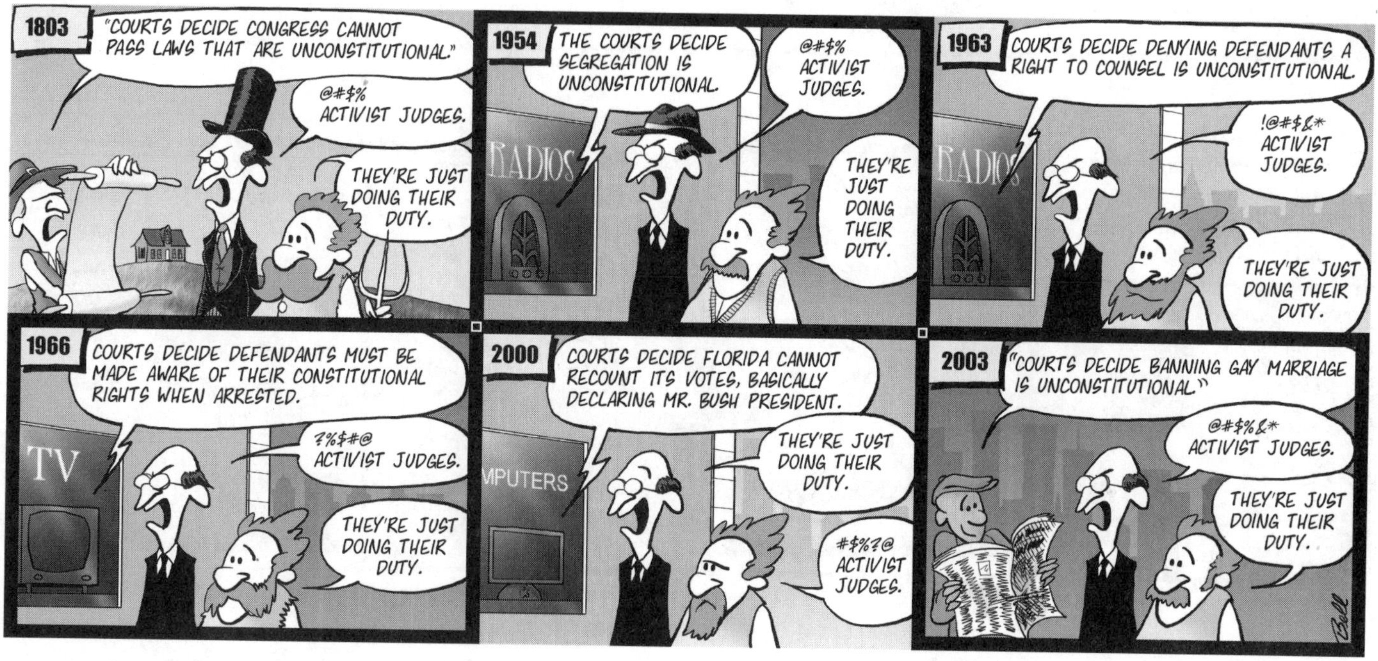

1803
"COURTS DECIDE CONGRESS CANNOT PASS LAWS THAT ARE UNCONSTITUTIONAL."
@#$% ACTIVIST JUDGES.
THEY'RE JUST DOING THEIR DUTY.
1954
THE COURTS DECIDE SEGREGATION IS UNCONSTITUTIONAL.
@#$% ACTIVIST JUDGES.
THEY'RE JUST DOING THEIR DUTY.
RADIOS
1963
COURTS DECIDE DENYING DEFENDANTS A RIGHT TO COUNSEL IS UNCONSTITUTIONAL.
!@#$&* ACTIVIST JUDGES.
THEY'RE JUST DOING THEIR DUTY.
RADIOS
1966
COURTS DECIDE DEFENDANTS MUST BE MADE AWARE OF THEIR CONSTITUTIONAL RIGHTS WHEN ARRESTED.
?%$#@ ACTIVIST JUDGES.
THEY'RE JUST DOING THEIR DUTY.
TV
2000
COURTS DECIDE FLORIDA CANNOT RECOUNT ITS VOTES, BASICALLY DECLARING MR. BUSH PRESIDENT.
THEY'RE JUST DOING THEIR DUTY.
#$%?@ ACTIVIST JUDGES.
MPUTERS
2003
"COURTS DECIDE BANNING GAY MARRIAGE IS UNCONSTITUTIONAL."
@#$%&* ACTIVIST JUDGES.
THEY'RE JUST DOING THEIR DUTY.
Bell

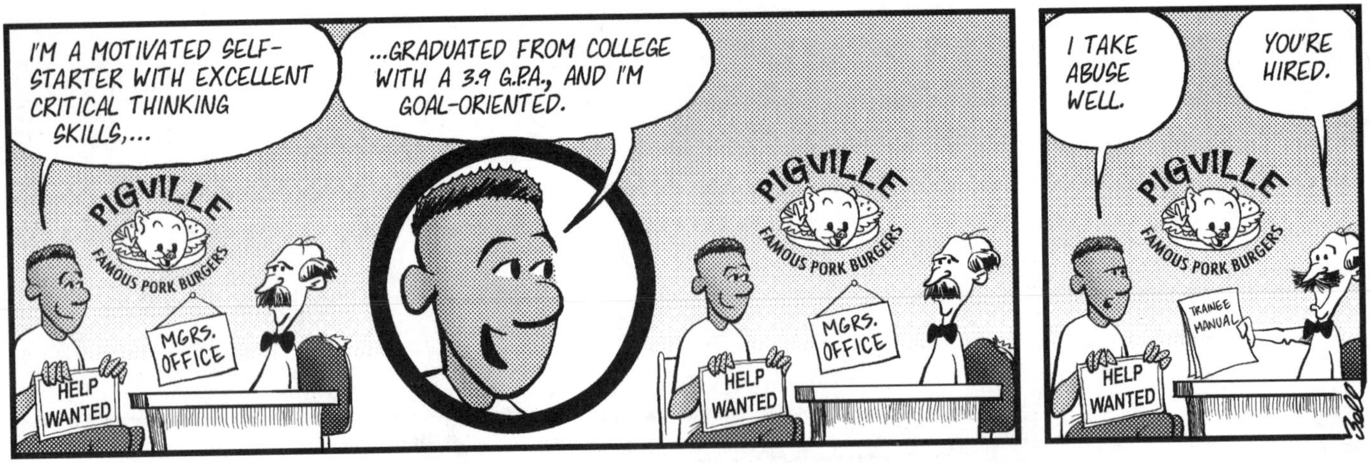
I'M A MOTIVATED SELF-STARTER WITH EXCELLENT CRITICAL THINKING SKILLS,...
PIGVILLE
FAMOUS PORK BURGERS
MGRS. OFFICE
HELP WANTED
...GRADUATED FROM COLLEGE WITH A 3.9 G.P.A., AND I'M GOAL-ORIENTED.
I TAKE ABUSE WELL.
YOU'RE HIRED.
TRAINEE MANUAL

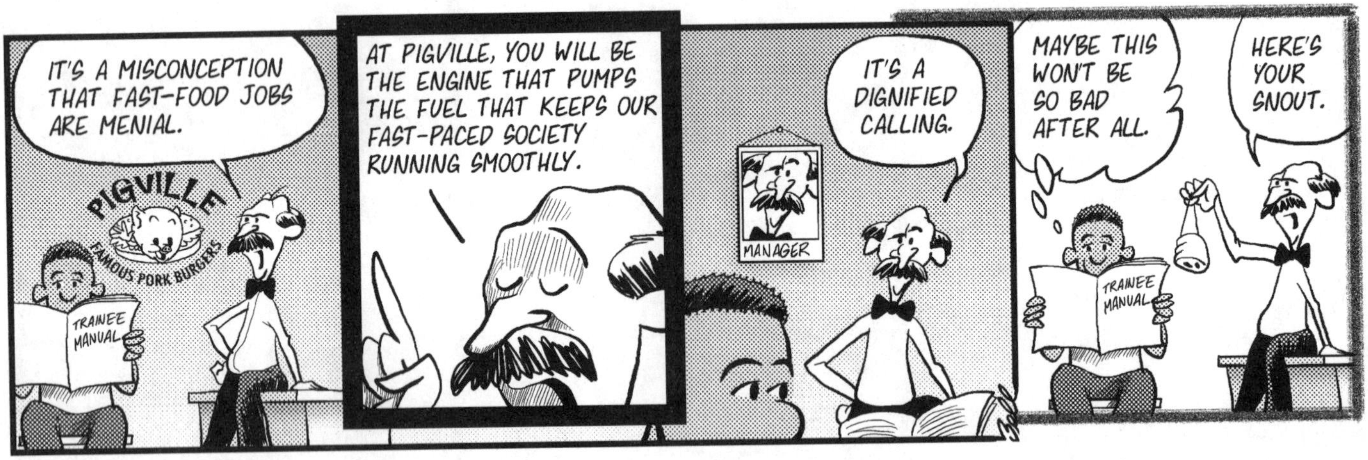
IT'S A MISCONCEPTION THAT FAST-FOOD JOBS ARE MENIAL.
PIGVILLE
FAMOUS PORK BURGERS
TRAINEE MANUAL
AT PIGVILLE, YOU WILL BE THE ENGINE THAT PUMPS THE FUEL THAT KEEPS OUR FAST-PACED SOCIETY RUNNING SMOOTHLY.
MANAGER
IT'S A DIGNIFIED CALLING.
MAYBE THIS WON'T BE SO BAD AFTER ALL.
HERE'S YOUR SNOUT.

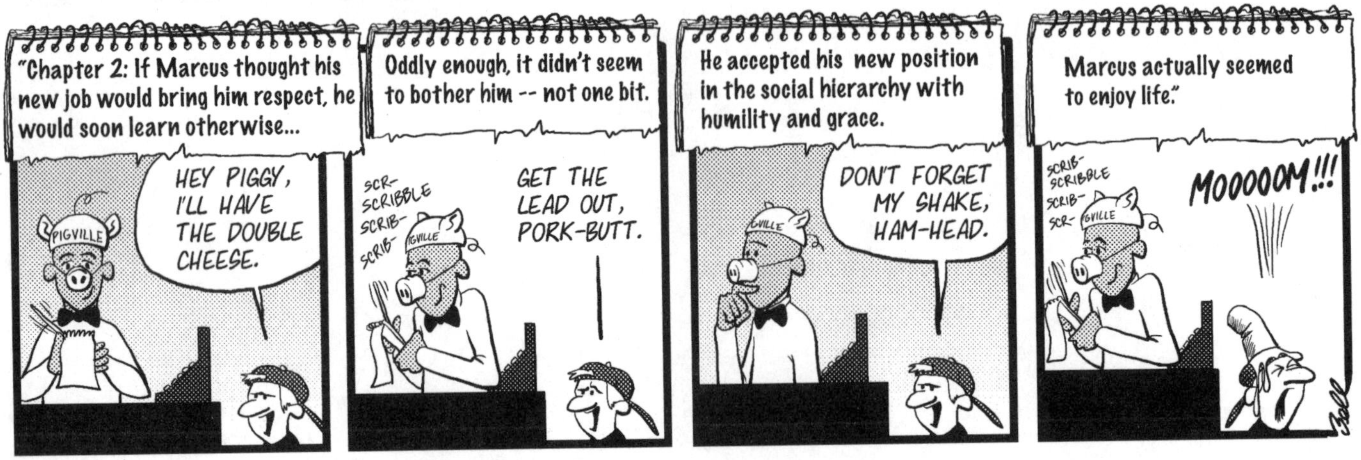
"Chapter 2: If Marcus thought his new job would bring him respect, he would soon learn otherwise...
HEY PIGGY, I'LL HAVE THE DOUBLE CHEESE.
PIGVILLE
Oddly enough, it didn't seem to bother him -- not one bit.
SCR- SCRIBBLE SCRIB- SCRIB-
GET THE LEAD OUT, PORK-BUTT.
He accepted his new position in the social hierarchy with humility and grace.
DON'T FORGET MY SHAKE, HAM-HEAD.
Marcus actually seemed to enjoy life."
SCRIB- SCRIBBLE SCRIB- SCR-
MOOOOOM!!!

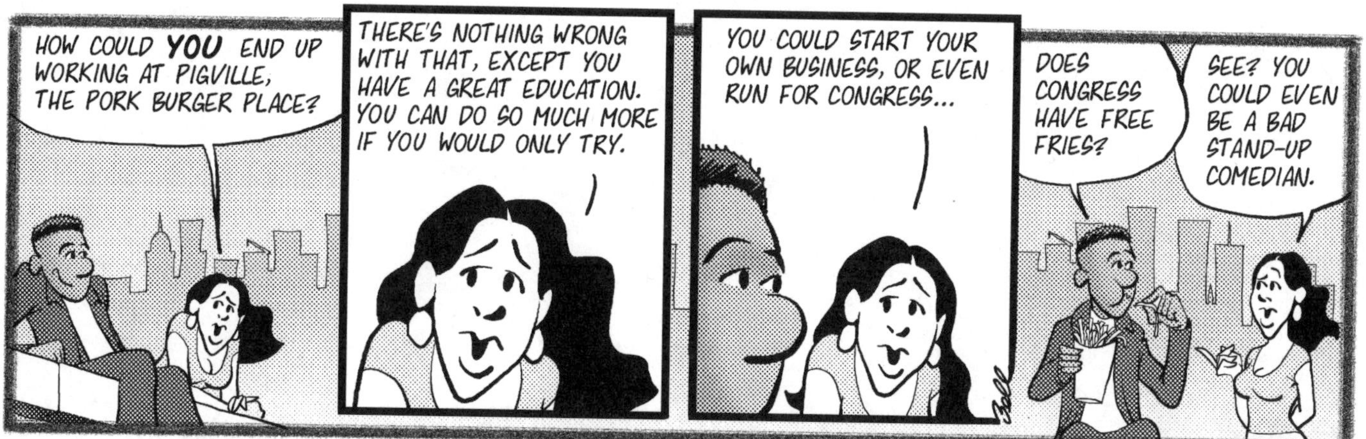
HOW COULD **YOU** END UP WORKING AT PIGVILLE, THE PORK BURGER PLACE?
THERE'S NOTHING WRONG WITH THAT, EXCEPT YOU HAVE A GREAT EDUCATION. YOU CAN DO SO MUCH MORE IF YOU WOULD ONLY TRY.
YOU COULD START YOUR OWN BUSINESS, OR EVEN RUN FOR CONGRESS...
DOES CONGRESS HAVE FREE FRIES?
SEE? YOU COULD EVEN BE A BAD STAND-UP COMEDIAN.

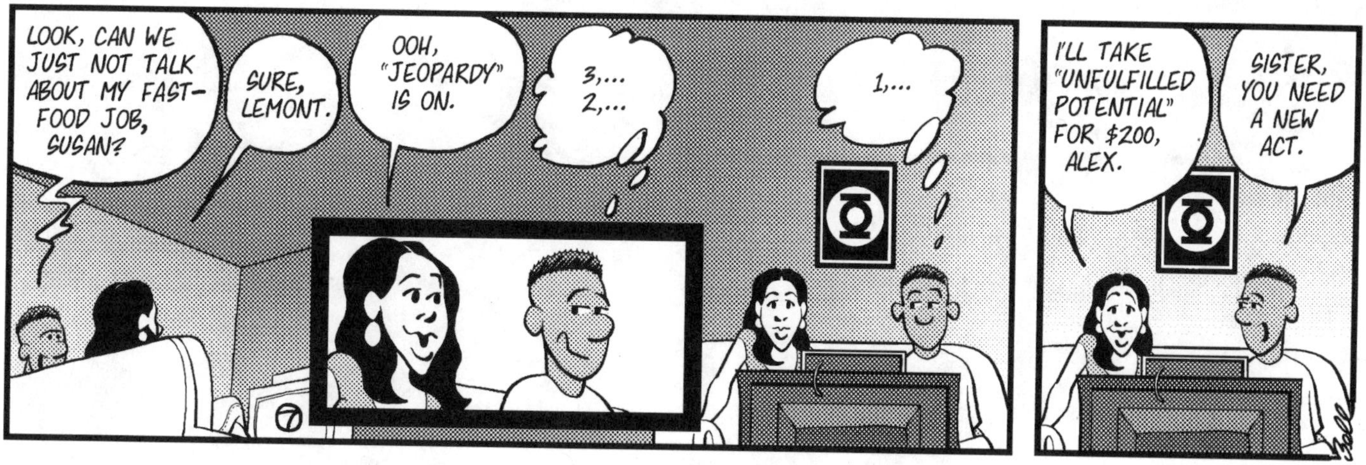
LOOK, CAN WE JUST NOT TALK ABOUT MY FAST-FOOD JOB, SUSAN?
SURE, LEMONT.
OOH, "JEOPARDY" IS ON.
3,... 2,...
1,...
I'LL TAKE "UNFULFILLED POTENTIAL" FOR $200, ALEX.
SISTER, YOU NEED A NEW ACT.

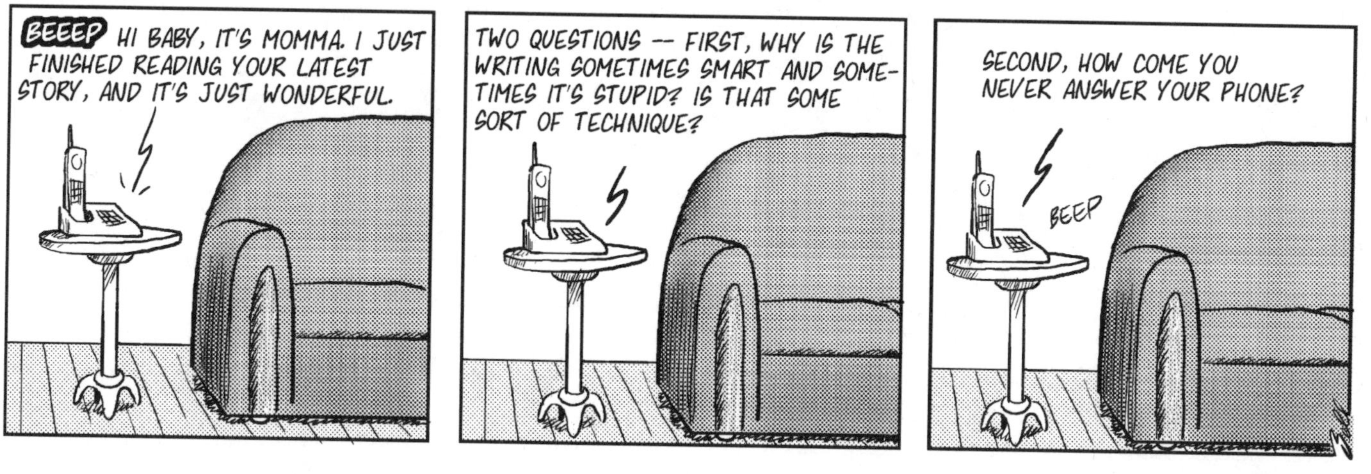
BEEEP HI BABY, IT'S MOMMA. I JUST FINISHED READING YOUR LATEST STORY, AND IT'S JUST WONDERFUL.
TWO QUESTIONS -- FIRST, WHY IS THE WRITING SOMETIMES SMART AND SOMETIMES IT'S STUPID? IS THAT SOME SORT OF TECHNIQUE?
SECOND, HOW COME YOU NEVER ANSWER YOUR PHONE?
BEEP

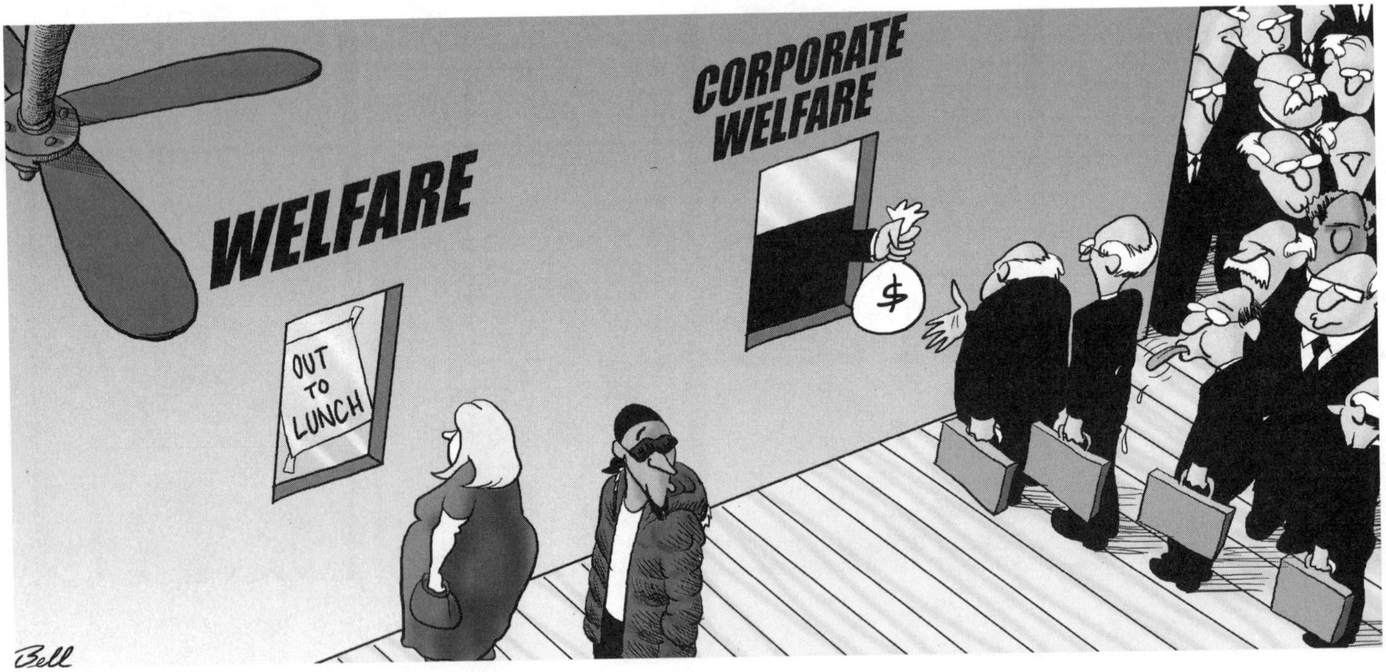
WELFARE
OUT TO LUNCH
CORPORATE WELFARE
$
Bell

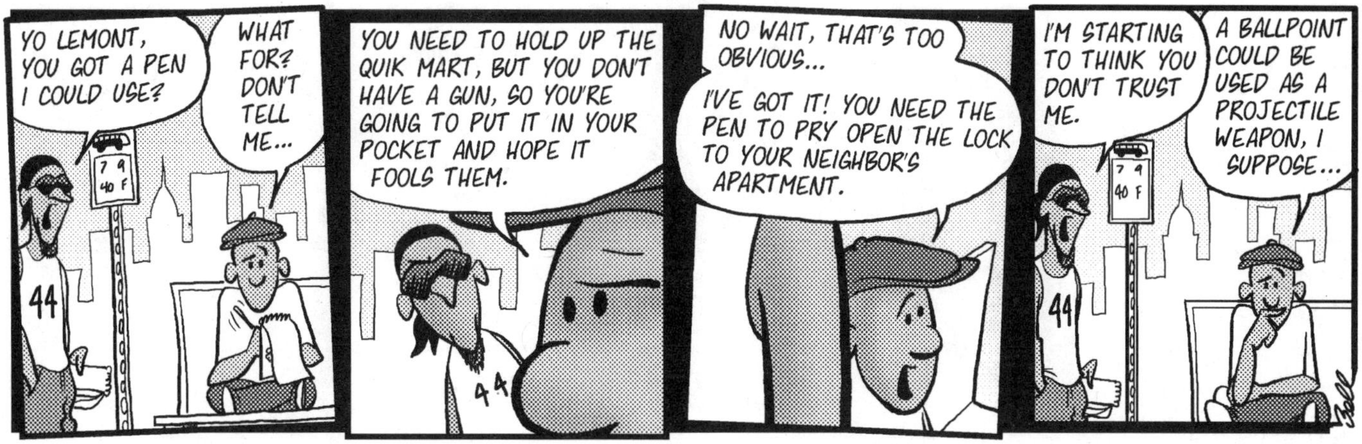
YO LEMONT, YOU GOT A PEN I COULD USE?
WHAT FOR? DON'T TELL ME...
7 9
40 F
44
YOU NEED TO HOLD UP THE QUIK MART, BUT YOU DON'T HAVE A GUN, SO YOU'RE GOING TO PUT IT IN YOUR POCKET AND HOPE IT FOOLS THEM.
44
NO WAIT, THAT'S TOO OBVIOUS...
I'VE GOT IT! YOU NEED THE PEN TO PRY OPEN THE LOCK TO YOUR NEIGHBOR'S APARTMENT.
I'M STARTING TO THINK YOU DON'T TRUST ME.
A BALLPOINT COULD BE USED AS A PROJECTILE WEAPON, I SUPPOSE...
7 9
40 F
44

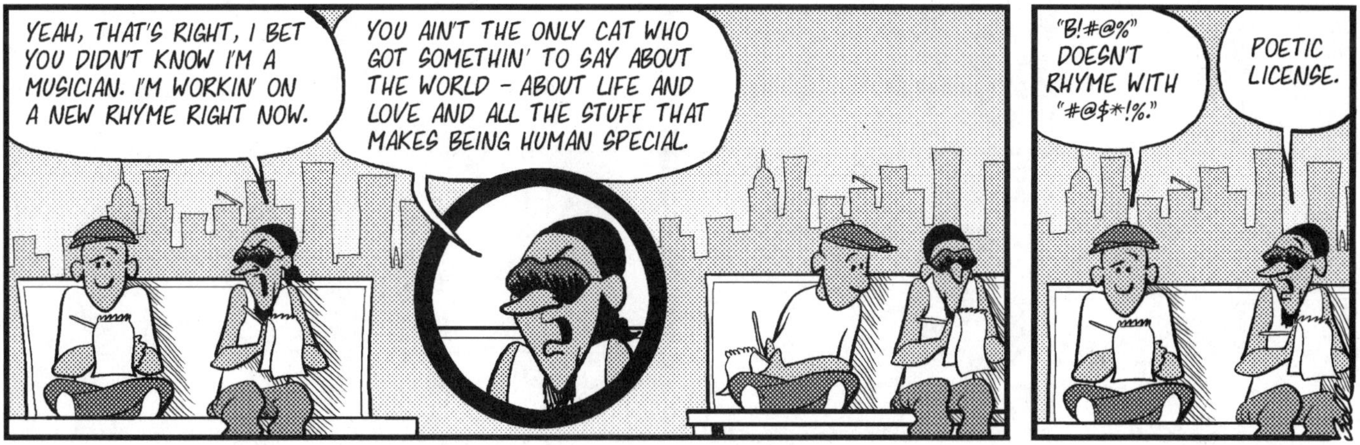
YEAH, THAT'S RIGHT, I BET YOU DIDN'T KNOW I'M A MUSICIAN. I'M WORKIN' ON A NEW RHYME RIGHT NOW.
YOU AIN'T THE ONLY CAT WHO GOT SOMETHIN' TO SAY ABOUT THE WORLD – ABOUT LIFE AND LOVE AND ALL THE STUFF THAT MAKES BEING HUMAN SPECIAL.
"B!#@%" DOESN'T RHYME WITH "#@$*!%."
POETIC LICENSE.

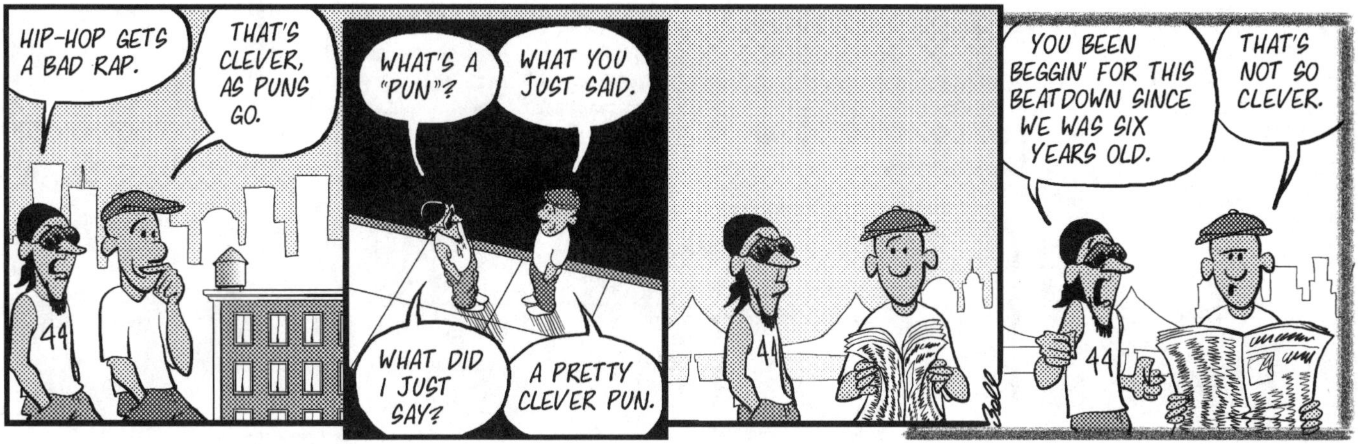
HIP-HOP GETS A BAD RAP.
THAT'S CLEVER, AS PUNS GO.
44
WHAT'S A "PUN"?
WHAT YOU JUST SAID.
WHAT DID I JUST SAY?
A PRETTY CLEVER PUN.
44
YOU BEEN BEGGIN' FOR THIS BEATDOWN SINCE WE WAS SIX YEARS OLD.
THAT'S NOT SO CLEVER.
44

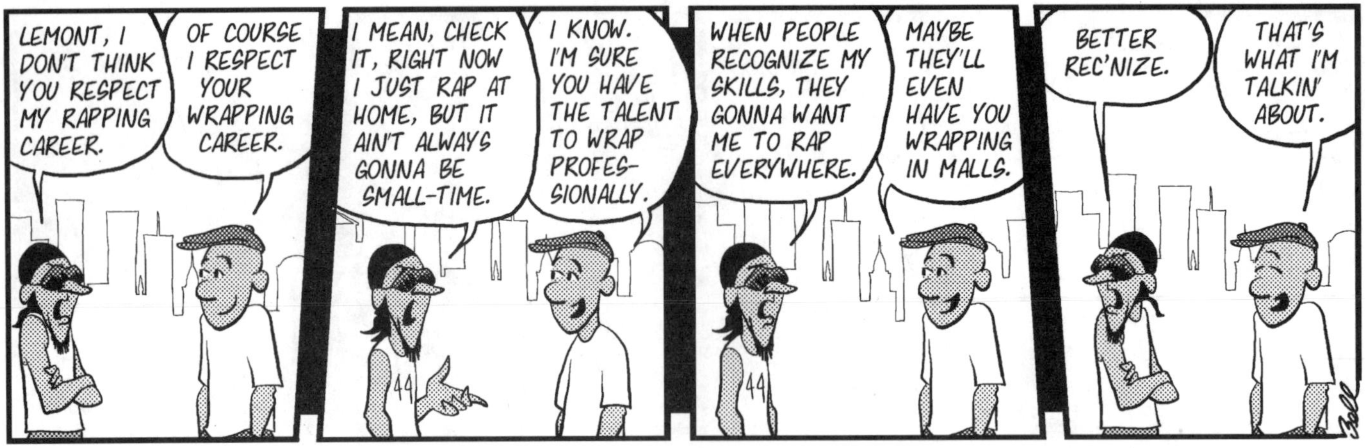
LEMONT, I DON'T THINK YOU RESPECT MY RAPPING CAREER.
OF COURSE I RESPECT YOUR WRAPPING CAREER.
I MEAN, CHECK IT, RIGHT NOW I JUST RAP AT HOME, BUT IT AIN'T ALWAYS GONNA BE SMALL-TIME.
I KNOW. I'M SURE YOU HAVE THE TALENT TO WRAP PROFES-SIONALLY.
WHEN PEOPLE RECOGNIZE MY SKILLS, THEY GONNA WANT ME TO RAP EVERYWHERE.
MAYBE THEY'LL EVEN HAVE YOU WRAPPING IN MALLS.
BETTER REC'NIZE.
THAT'S WHAT I'M TALKIN' ABOUT.

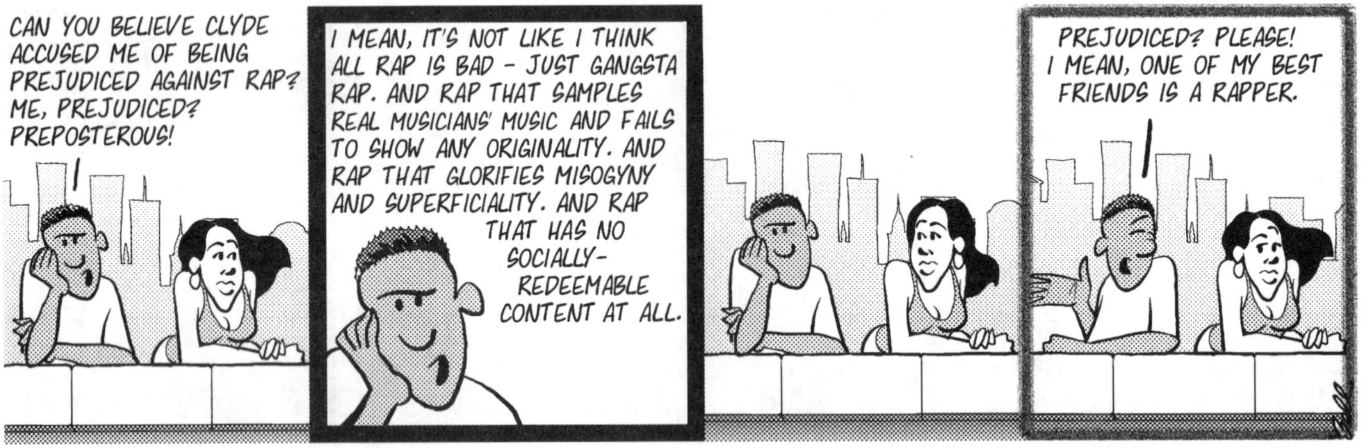
CAN YOU BELIEVE CLYDE ACCUSED ME OF BEING PREJUDICED AGAINST RAP? ME, PREJUDICED? PREPOSTEROUS!
I MEAN, IT'S NOT LIKE I THINK ALL RAP IS BAD - JUST GANGSTA RAP. AND RAP THAT SAMPLES REAL MUSICIANS' MUSIC AND FAILS TO SHOW ANY ORIGINALITY. AND RAP THAT GLORIFIES MISOGYNY AND SUPERFICIALITY. AND RAP THAT HAS NO SOCIALLY-REDEEMABLE CONTENT AT ALL.
PREJUDICED? PLEASE! I MEAN, ONE OF MY BEST FRIENDS IS A RAPPER.

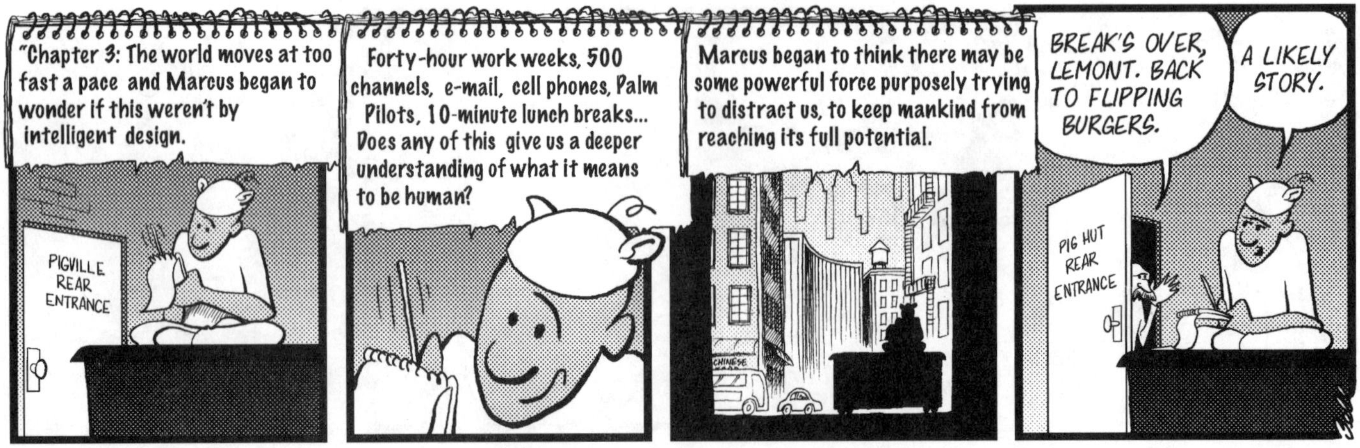
"Chapter 3: The world moves at too fast a pace and Marcus began to wonder if this weren't by intelligent design.
PIGVILLE REAR ENTRANCE
Forty-hour work weeks, 500 channels, e-mail, cell phones, Palm Pilots, 10-minute lunch breaks... Does any of this give us a deeper understanding of what it means to be human?
Marcus began to think there may be some powerful force purposely trying to distract us, to keep mankind from reaching its full potential.
BREAK'S OVER, LEMONT. BACK TO FLIPPING BURGERS.
A LIKELY STORY.
PIG HUT REAR ENTRANCE

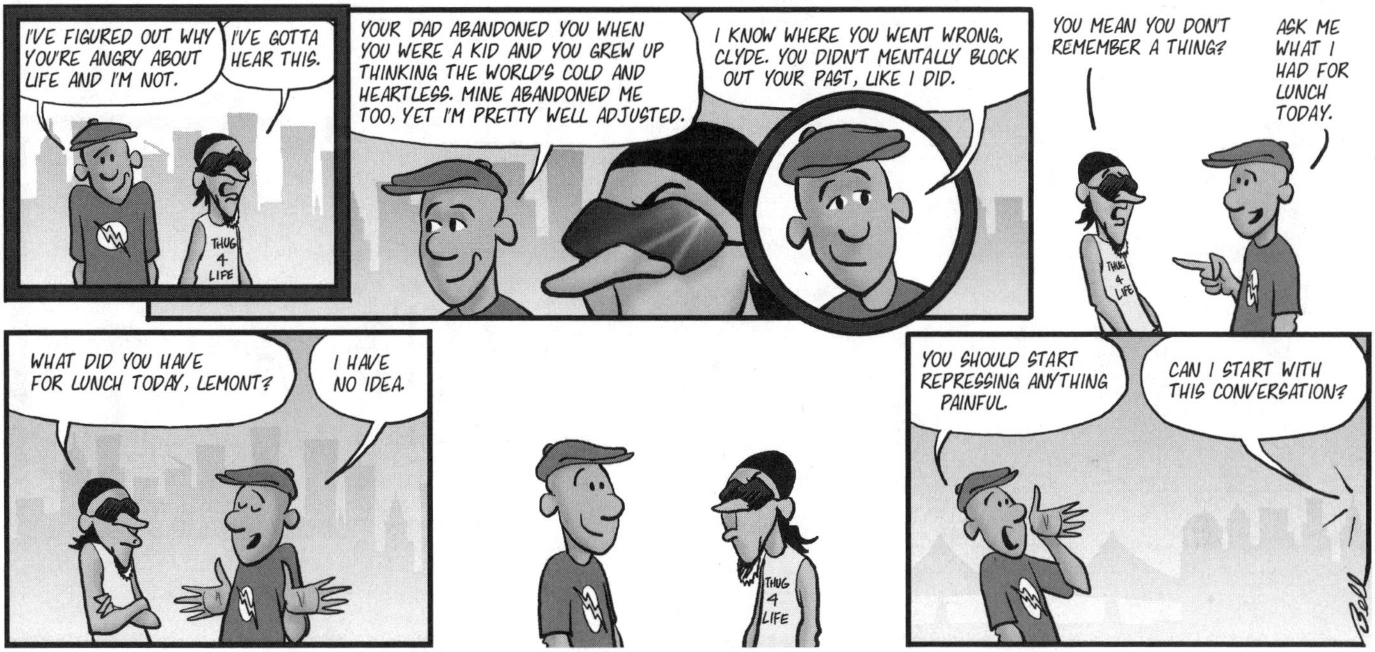
I'VE FIGURED OUT WHY YOU'RE ANGRY ABOUT LIFE AND I'M NOT.
I'VE GOTTA HEAR THIS.
YOUR DAD ABANDONED YOU WHEN YOU WERE A KID AND YOU GREW UP THINKING THE WORLD'S COLD AND HEARTLESS. MINE ABANDONED ME TOO, YET I'M PRETTY WELL ADJUSTED.
I KNOW WHERE YOU WENT WRONG, CLYDE. YOU DIDN'T MENTALLY BLOCK OUT YOUR PAST, LIKE I DID.
YOU MEAN YOU DON'T REMEMBER A THING?
ASK ME WHAT I HAD FOR LUNCH TODAY.
THUG 4 LIFE
WHAT DID YOU HAVE FOR LUNCH TODAY, LEMONT?
I HAVE NO IDEA.
YOU SHOULD START REPRESSING ANYTHING PAINFUL.
CAN I START WITH THIS CONVERSATION?
Bell

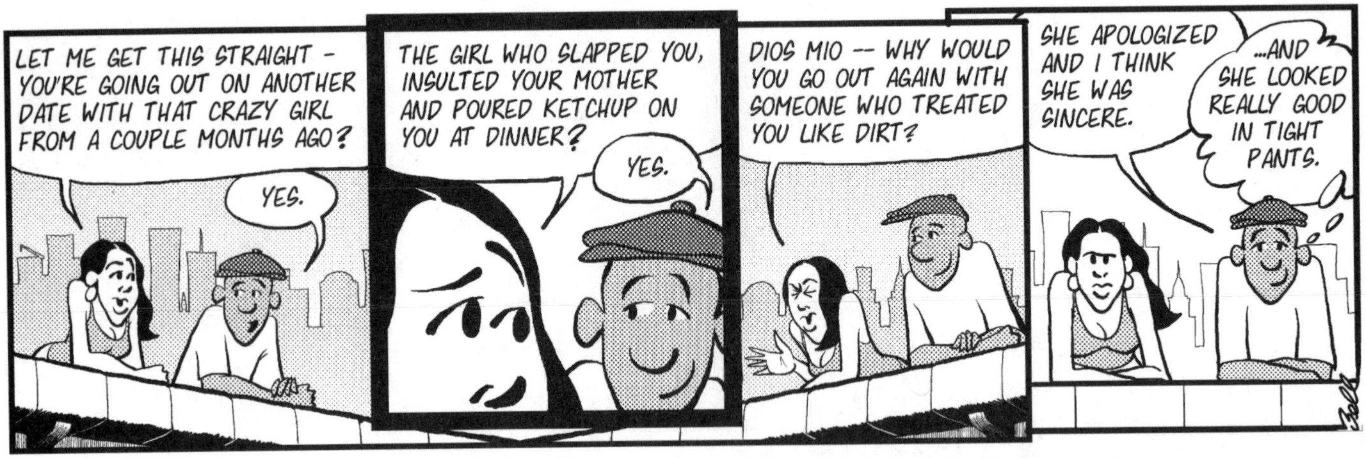
LET ME GET THIS STRAIGHT - YOU'RE GOING OUT ON ANOTHER DATE WITH THAT CRAZY GIRL FROM A COUPLE MONTHS AGO?
YES.
THE GIRL WHO SLAPPED YOU, INSULTED YOUR MOTHER AND POURED KETCHUP ON YOU AT DINNER?
YES.
DIOS MIO -- WHY WOULD YOU GO OUT AGAIN WITH SOMEONE WHO TREATED YOU LIKE DIRT?
SHE APOLOGIZED AND I THINK SHE WAS SINCERE.
...AND SHE LOOKED REALLY GOOD IN TIGHT PANTS.

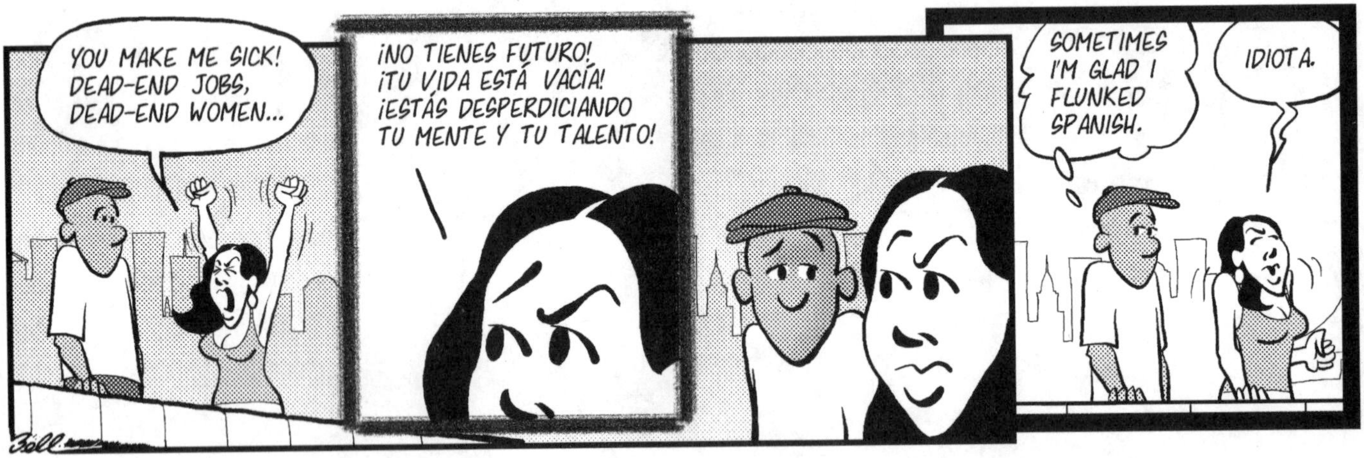
YOU MAKE ME SICK! DEAD-END JOBS, DEAD-END WOMEN...
¡NO TIENES FUTURO! ¡TU VIDA ESTÁ VACÍA! ¡ESTÁS DESPERDICIANDO TU MENTE Y TU TALENTO!
SOMETIMES I'M GLAD I FLUNKED SPANISH.
IDIOTA.

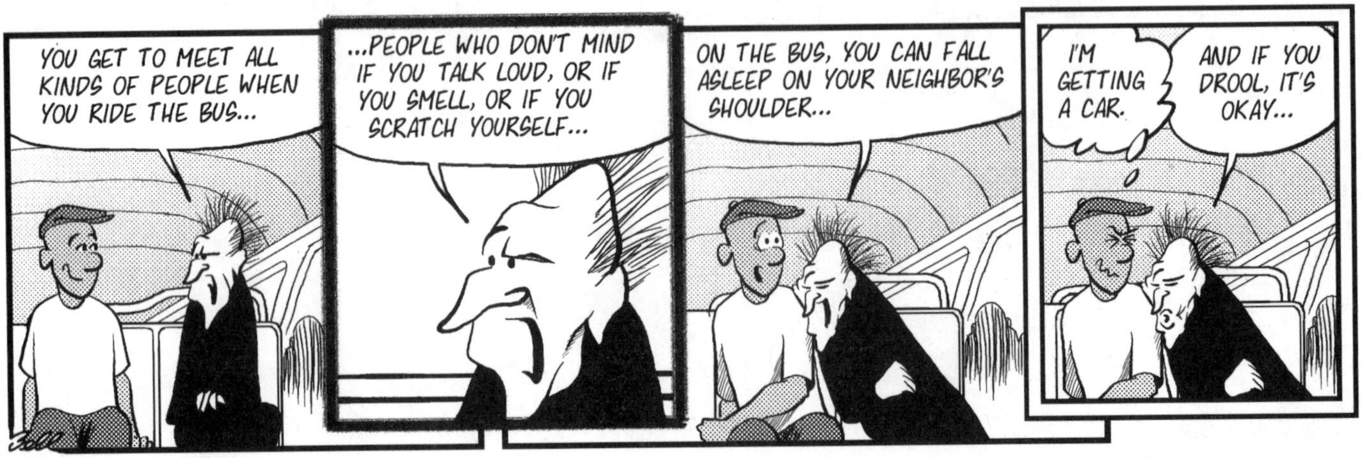
YOU GET TO MEET ALL KINDS OF PEOPLE WHEN YOU RIDE THE BUS...
...PEOPLE WHO DON'T MIND IF YOU TALK LOUD, OR IF YOU SMELL, OR IF YOU SCRATCH YOURSELF...
ON THE BUS, YOU CAN FALL ASLEEP ON YOUR NEIGHBOR'S SHOULDER...
AND IF YOU DROOL, IT'S OKAY...
I'M GETTING A CAR.

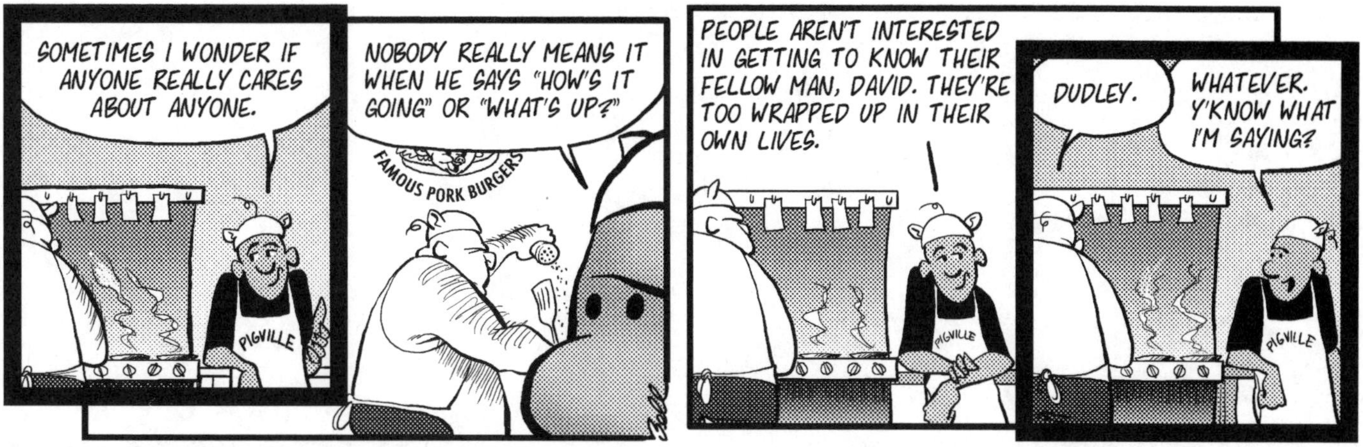
SOMETIMES I WONDER IF ANYONE REALLY CARES ABOUT ANYONE.
NOBODY REALLY MEANS IT WHEN HE SAYS "HOW'S IT GOING" OR "WHAT'S UP?"
FAMOUS PORK BURGERS
PIGVILLE
PEOPLE AREN'T INTERESTED IN GETTING TO KNOW THEIR FELLOW MAN, DAVID. THEY'RE TOO WRAPPED UP IN THEIR OWN LIVES.
DUDLEY.
WHATEVER. Y'KNOW WHAT I'M SAYING?

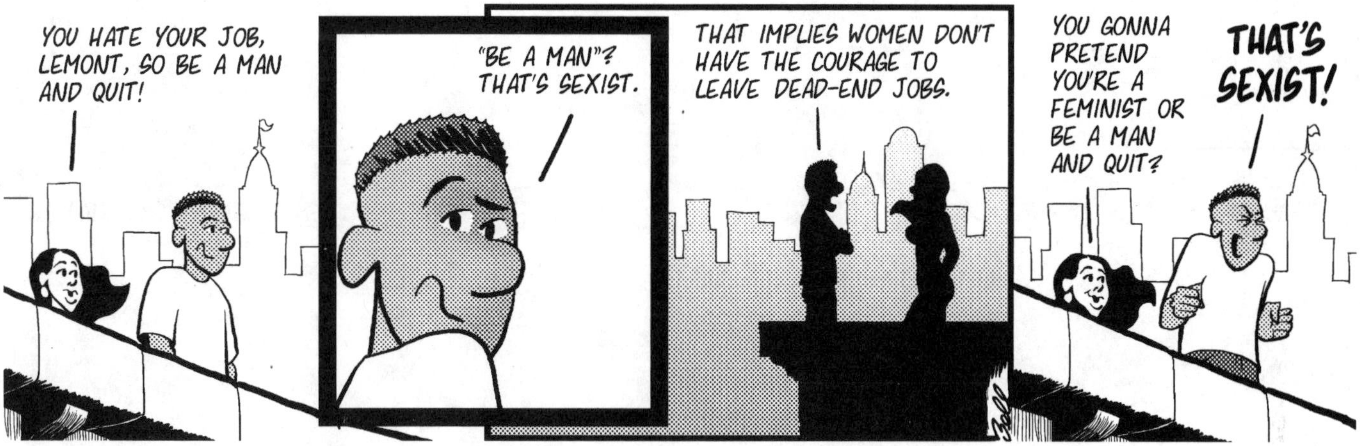
YOU HATE YOUR JOB, LEMONT, SO BE A MAN AND QUIT!
"BE A MAN"? THAT'S SEXIST.
THAT IMPLIES WOMEN DON'T HAVE THE COURAGE TO LEAVE DEAD-END JOBS.
YOU GONNA PRETEND YOU'RE A FEMINIST OR BE A MAN AND QUIT?
THAT'S SEXIST!

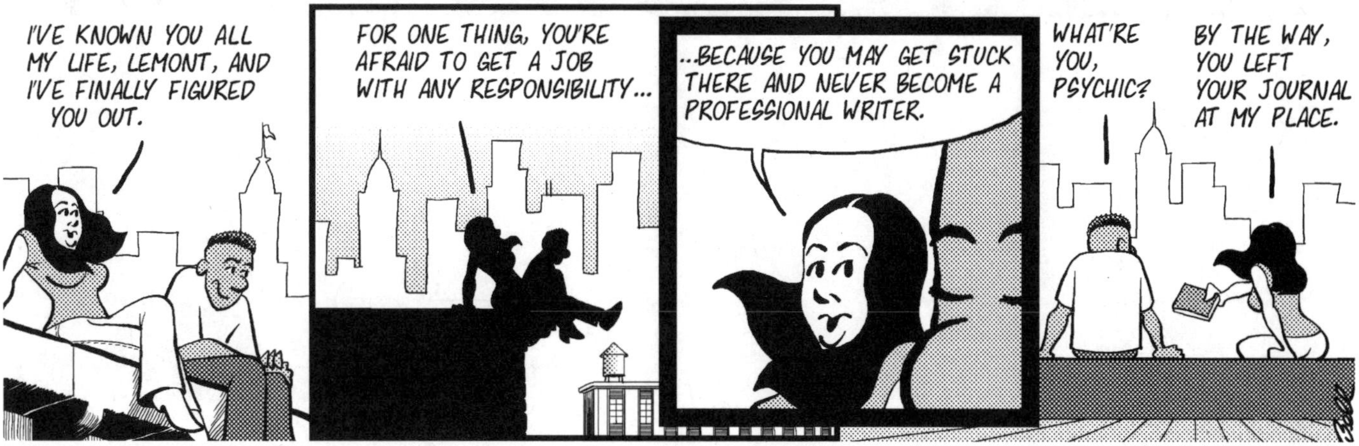
I'VE KNOWN YOU ALL MY LIFE, LEMONT, AND I'VE FINALLY FIGURED YOU OUT.
FOR ONE THING, YOU'RE AFRAID TO GET A JOB WITH ANY RESPONSIBILITY...
...BECAUSE YOU MAY GET STUCK THERE AND NEVER BECOME A PROFESSIONAL WRITER.
WHAT'RE YOU, PSYCHIC?
BY THE WAY, YOU LEFT YOUR JOURNAL AT MY PLACE.

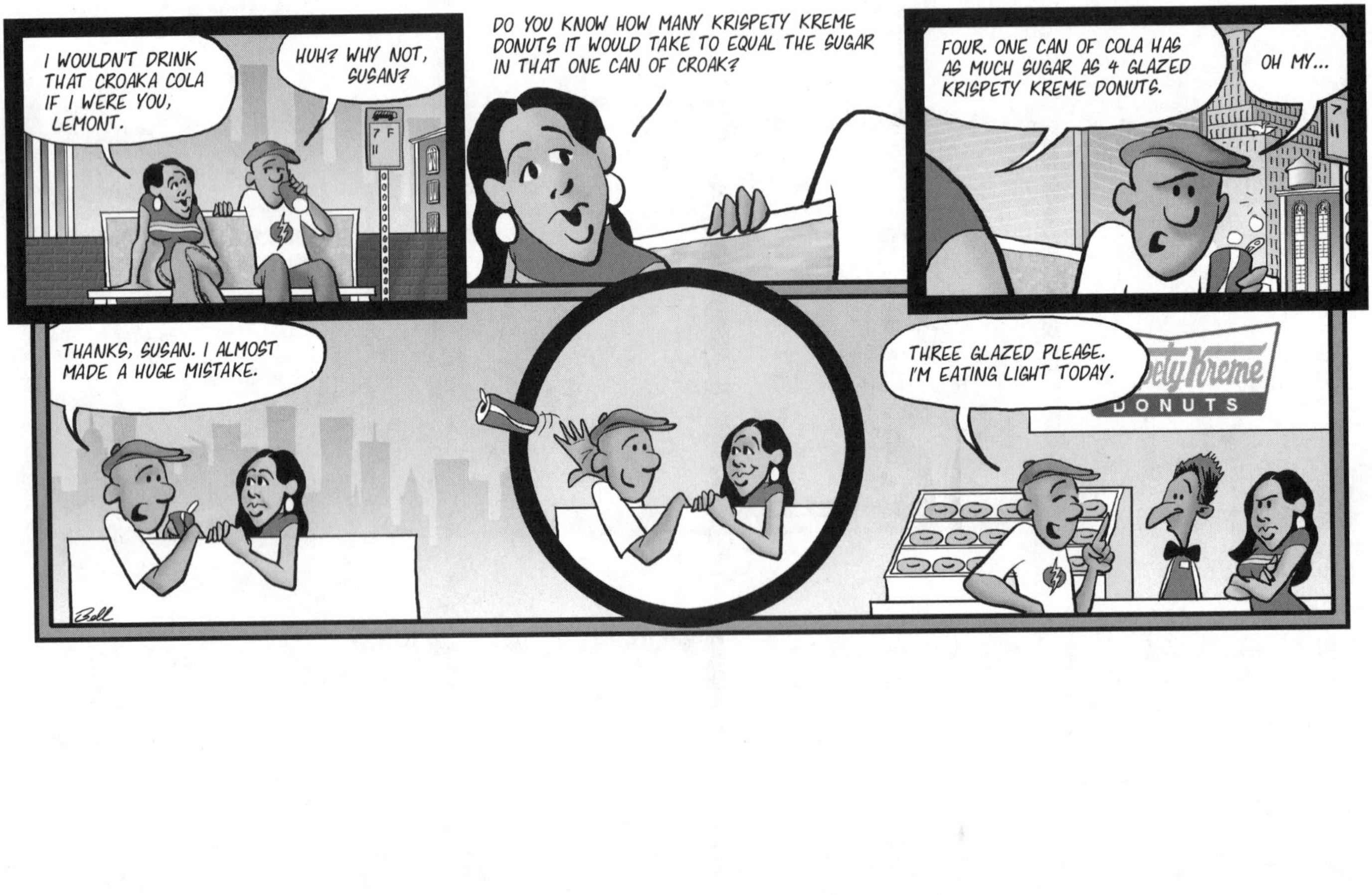
I WOULDN'T DRINK THAT CROAKA COLA IF I WERE YOU, LEMONT.
HUH? WHY NOT, SUSAN?
DO YOU KNOW HOW MANY KRISPETY KREME DONUTS IT WOULD TAKE TO EQUAL THE SUGAR IN THAT ONE CAN OF CROAK?
FOUR. ONE CAN OF COLA HAS AS MUCH SUGAR AS 4 GLAZED KRISPETY KREME DONUTS.
OH MY...
THANKS, SUSAN. I ALMOST MADE A HUGE MISTAKE.
THREE GLAZED PLEASE. I'M EATING LIGHT TODAY.
DONUTS

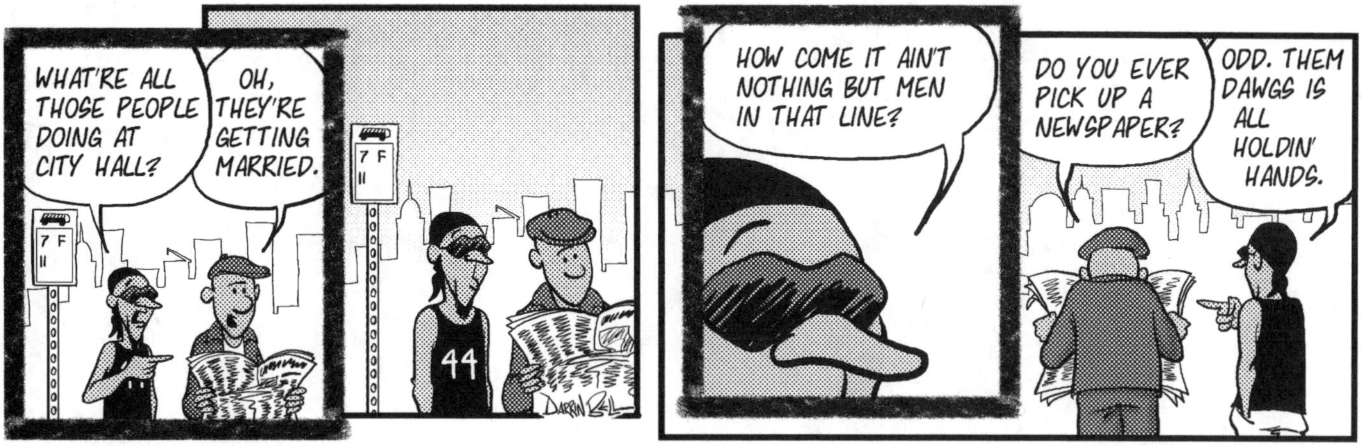
WHAT'RE ALL THOSE PEOPLE DOING AT CITY HALL?
OH, THEY'RE GETTING MARRIED.
HOW COME IT AIN'T NOTHING BUT MEN IN THAT LINE?
DO YOU EVER PICK UP A NEWSPAPER?
ODD. THEM DAWGS IS ALL HOLDIN' HANDS.
DARRIN BELL

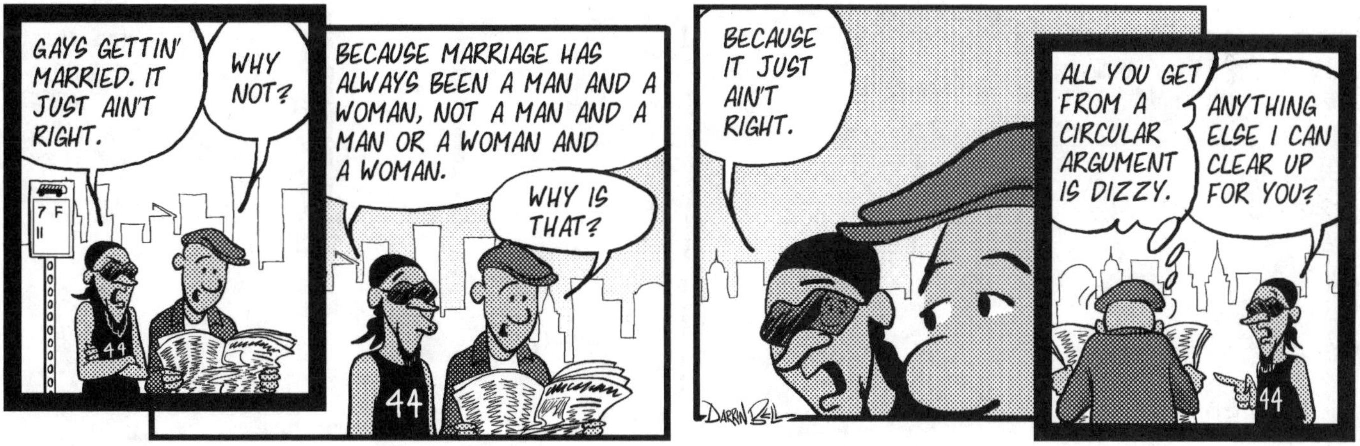
GAYS GETTIN' MARRIED. IT JUST AIN'T RIGHT.
WHY NOT?
BECAUSE MARRIAGE HAS ALWAYS BEEN A MAN AND A WOMAN, NOT A MAN AND A MAN OR A WOMAN AND A WOMAN.
WHY IS THAT?
BECAUSE IT JUST AIN'T RIGHT.
ALL YOU GET FROM A CIRCULAR ARGUMENT IS DIZZY.
ANYTHING ELSE I CAN CLEAR UP FOR YOU?
DARRIN BELL

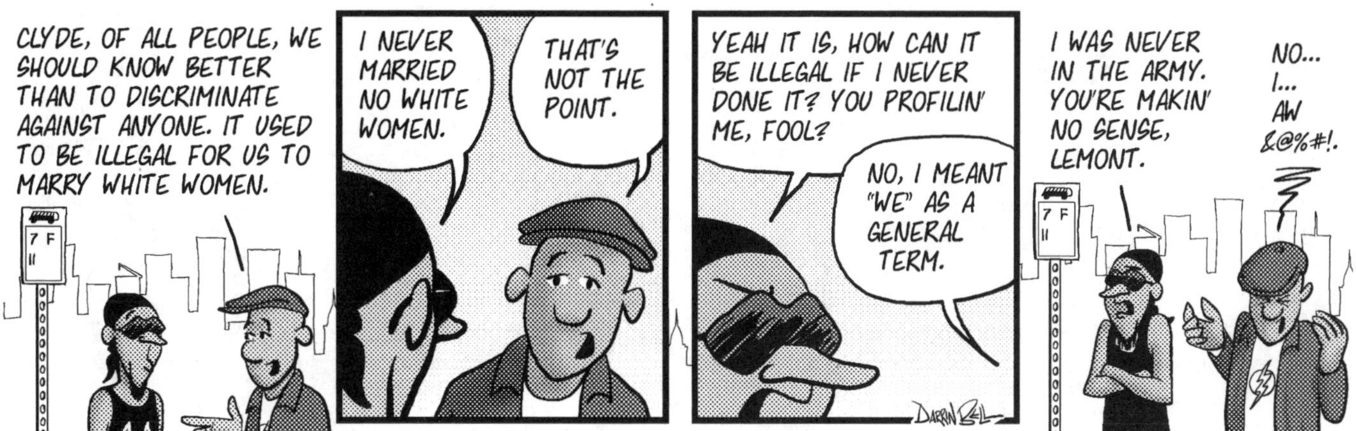
CLYDE, OF ALL PEOPLE, WE SHOULD KNOW BETTER THAN TO DISCRIMINATE AGAINST ANYONE. IT USED TO BE ILLEGAL FOR US TO MARRY WHITE WOMEN.
I NEVER MARRIED NO WHITE WOMEN.
THAT'S NOT THE POINT.
YEAH IT IS, HOW CAN IT BE ILLEGAL IF I NEVER DONE IT? YOU PROFILIN' ME, FOOL?
NO, I MEANT "WE" AS A GENERAL TERM.
I WAS NEVER IN THE ARMY. YOU'RE MAKIN' NO SENSE, LEMONT.
NO... I... AW &@%#!.
DARRIN BELL

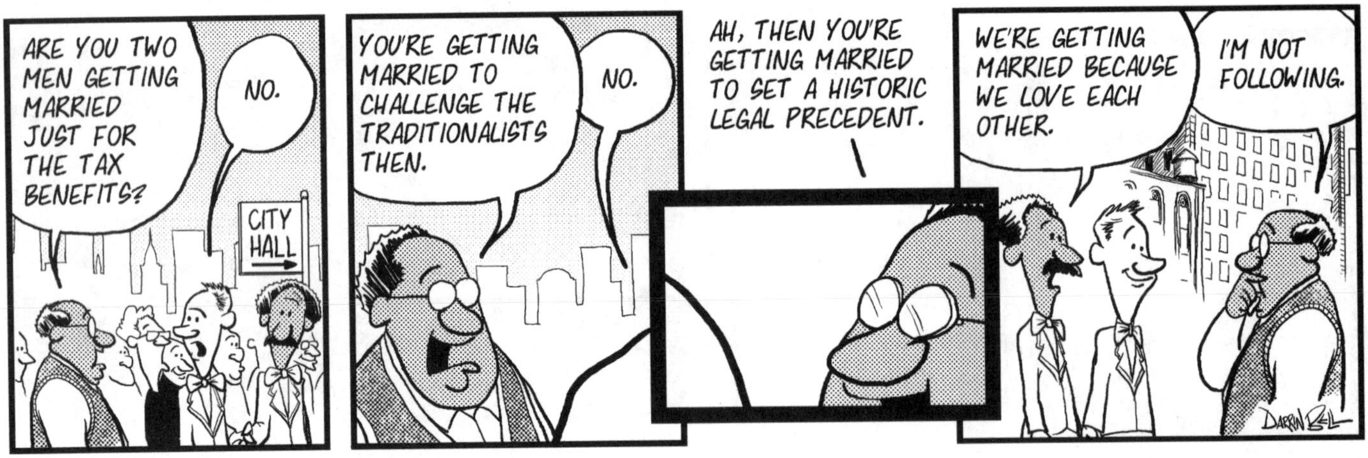
ARE YOU TWO MEN GETTING MARRIED JUST FOR THE TAX BENEFITS?
NO.
CITY HALL
YOU'RE GETTING MARRIED TO CHALLENGE THE TRADITIONALISTS THEN.
NO.
AH, THEN YOU'RE GETTING MARRIED TO SET A HISTORIC LEGAL PRECEDENT.
WE'RE GETTING MARRIED BECAUSE WE LOVE EACH OTHER.
I'M NOT FOLLOWING.
DARRIN BELL

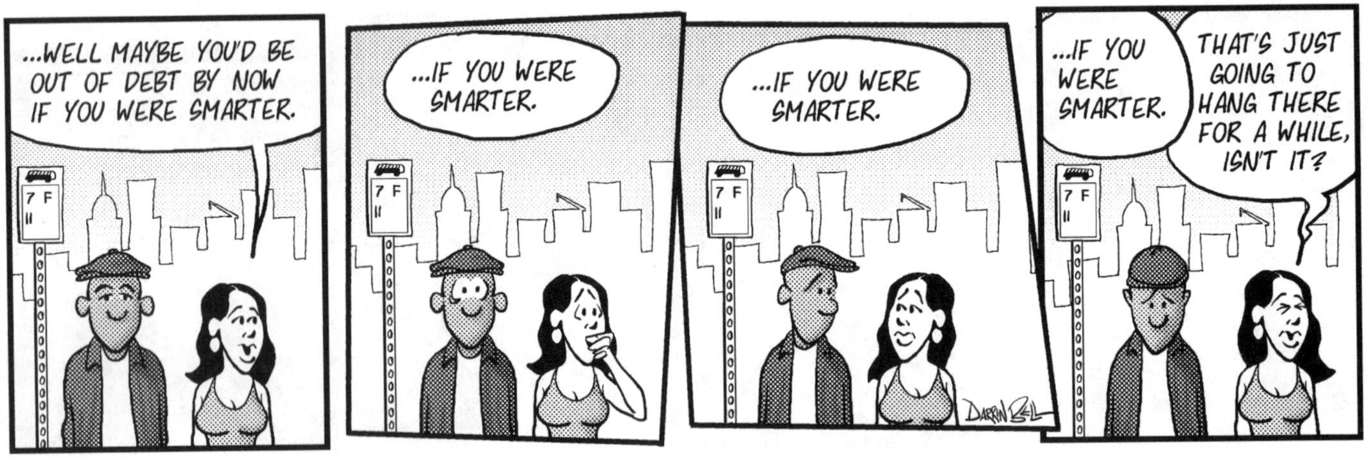
...WELL MAYBE YOU'D BE OUT OF DEBT BY NOW IF YOU WERE SMARTER.
...IF YOU WERE SMARTER.
...IF YOU WERE SMARTER.
DARRIN BELL
...IF YOU WERE SMARTER.
THAT'S JUST GOING TO HANG THERE FOR A WHILE, ISN'T IT?

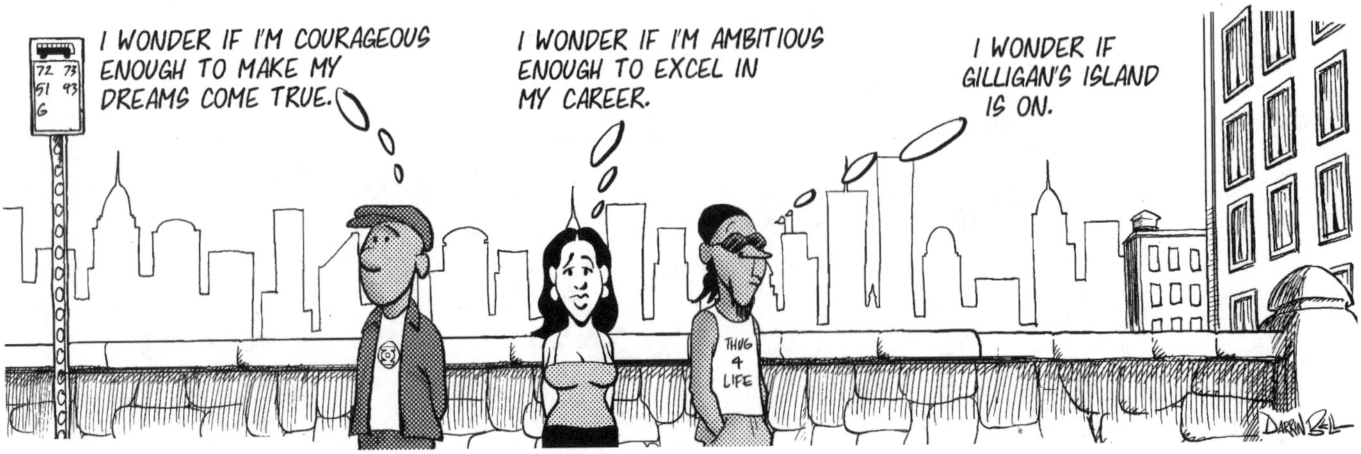
72 73
51 43
G
I WONDER IF I'M COURAGEOUS ENOUGH TO MAKE MY DREAMS COME TRUE.
I WONDER IF I'M AMBITIOUS ENOUGH TO EXCEL IN MY CAREER.
I WONDER IF GILLIGAN'S ISLAND IS ON.
THUG 4 LIFE
DARRIN BELL

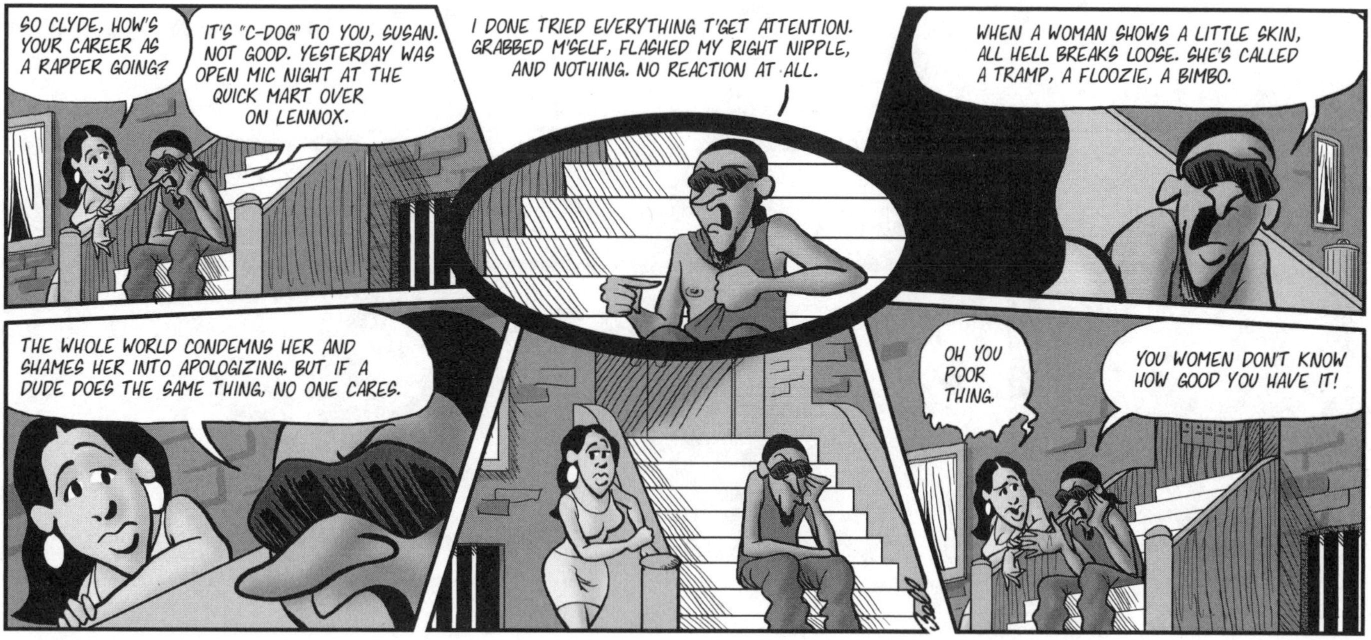

SO CLYDE, HOW'S YOUR CAREER AS A RAPPER GOING?
IT'S "C-DOG" TO YOU, SUSAN. NOT GOOD. YESTERDAY WAS OPEN MIC NIGHT AT THE QUICK MART OVER ON LENNOX.
I DONE TRIED EVERYTHING T'GET ATTENTION. GRABBED M'SELF, FLASHED MY RIGHT NIPPLE, AND NOTHING. NO REACTION AT ALL.
WHEN A WOMAN SHOWS A LITTLE SKIN, ALL HELL BREAKS LOOSE. SHE'S CALLED A TRAMP, A FLOOZIE, A BIMBO.
THE WHOLE WORLD CONDEMNS HER AND SHAMES HER INTO APOLOGIZING. BUT IF A DUDE DOES THE SAME THING, NO ONE CARES.
OH YOU POOR THING.
YOU WOMEN DON'T KNOW HOW GOOD YOU HAVE IT!

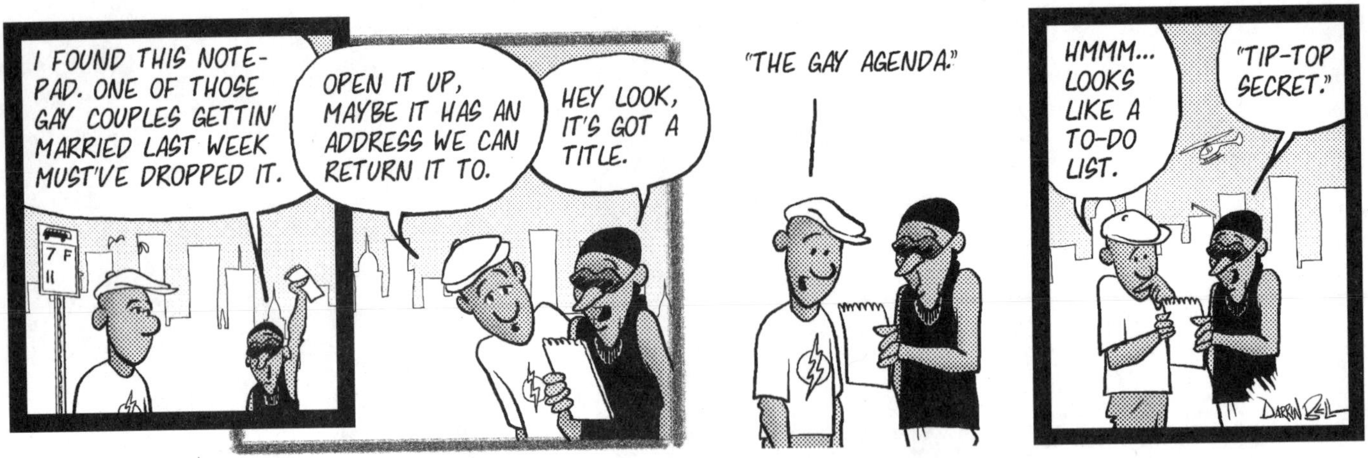
I FOUND THIS NOTE-PAD. ONE OF THOSE GAY COUPLES GETTIN' MARRIED LAST WEEK MUST'VE DROPPED IT.
7 F
11
OPEN IT UP, MAYBE IT HAS AN ADDRESS WE CAN RETURN IT TO.
HEY LOOK, IT'S GOT A TITLE.
"THE GAY AGENDA."
HMMM... LOOKS LIKE A TO-DO LIST.
"TIP-TOP SECRET."

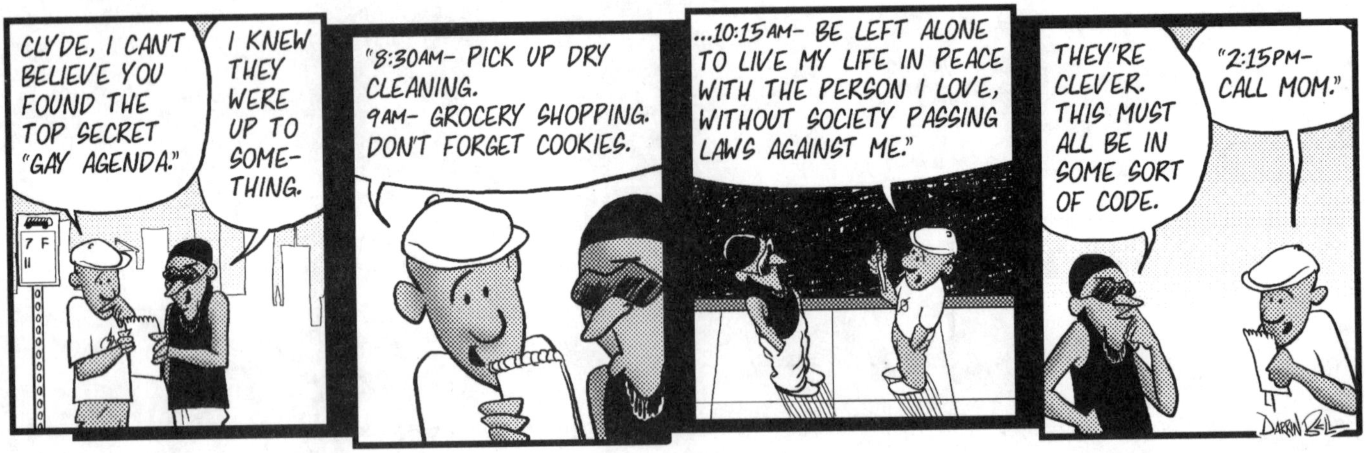
CLYDE, I CAN'T BELIEVE YOU FOUND THE TOP SECRET "GAY AGENDA."
I KNEW THEY WERE UP TO SOME-THING.
7 F
11
"8:30AM- PICK UP DRY CLEANING.
9AM- GROCERY SHOPPING. DON'T FORGET COOKIES.
...10:15AM- BE LEFT ALONE TO LIVE MY LIFE IN PEACE WITH THE PERSON I LOVE, WITHOUT SOCIETY PASSING LAWS AGAINST ME."
THEY'RE CLEVER. THIS MUST ALL BE IN SOME SORT OF CODE.
"2:15PM- CALL MOM."

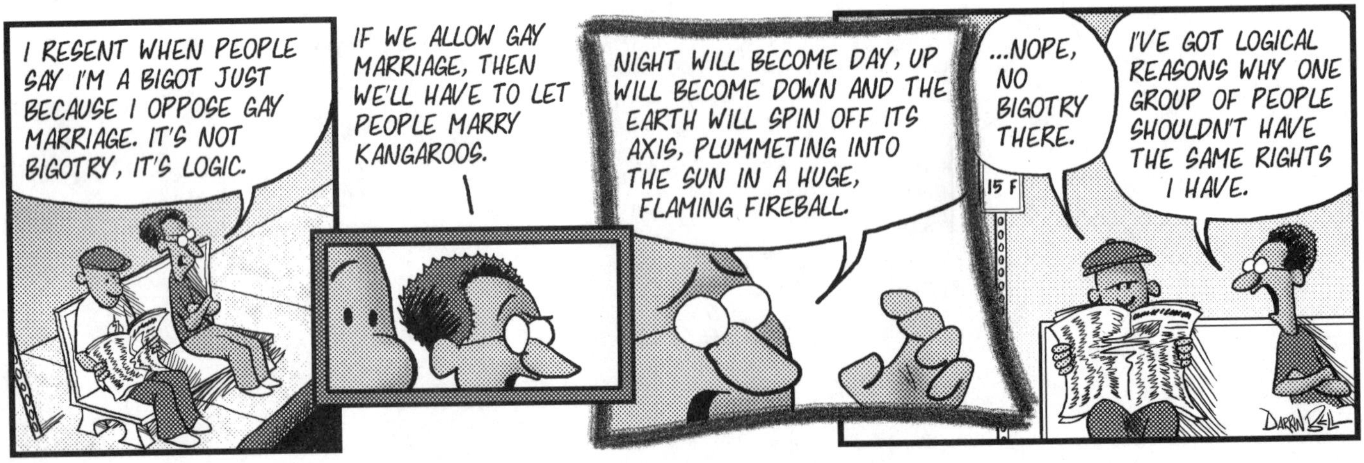
I RESENT WHEN PEOPLE SAY I'M A BIGOT JUST BECAUSE I OPPOSE GAY MARRIAGE. IT'S NOT BIGOTRY, IT'S LOGIC.
IF WE ALLOW GAY MARRIAGE, THEN WE'LL HAVE TO LET PEOPLE MARRY KANGAROOS.
NIGHT WILL BECOME DAY, UP WILL BECOME DOWN AND THE EARTH WILL SPIN OFF ITS AXIS, PLUMMETING INTO THE SUN IN A HUGE, FLAMING FIREBALL.
...NOPE, NO BIGOTRY THERE.
I'VE GOT LOGICAL REASONS WHY ONE GROUP OF PEOPLE SHOULDN'T HAVE THE SAME RIGHTS I HAVE.
15 F

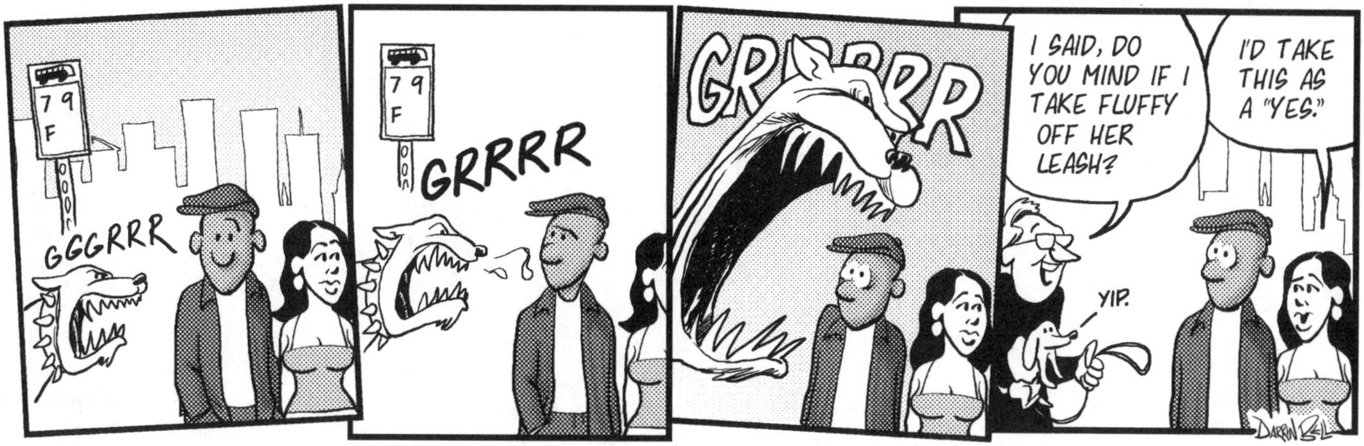
GGGRRR
GRRRR
GRRRRR
I SAID, DO YOU MIND IF I TAKE FLUFFY OFF HER LEASH?
YIP.
I'D TAKE THIS AS A "YES."
DARRIN BELL

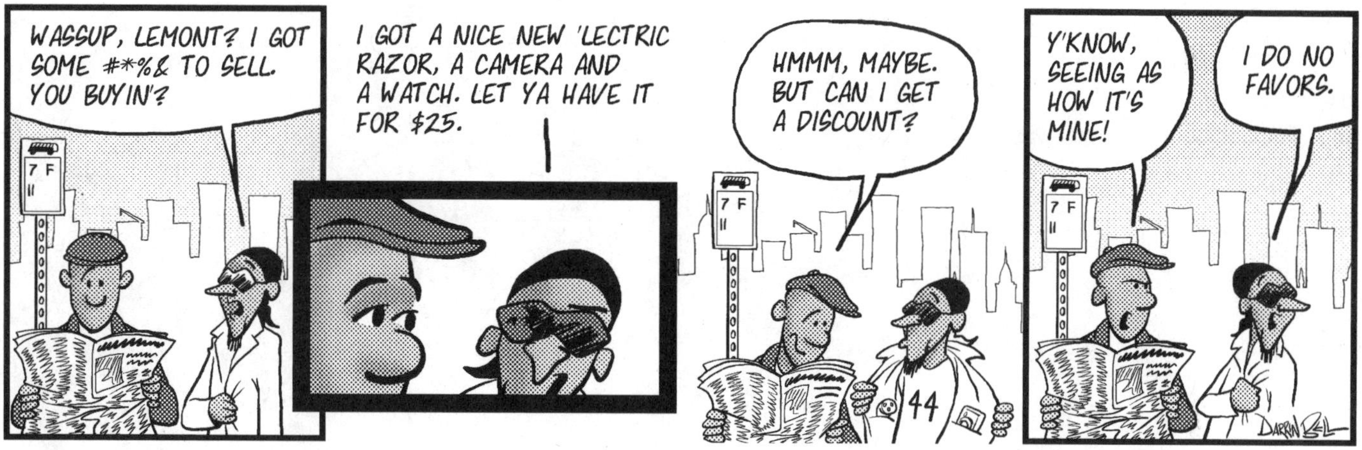
WASSUP, LEMONT? I GOT SOME #*%& TO SELL. YOU BUYIN'?
I GOT A NICE NEW 'LECTRIC RAZOR, A CAMERA AND A WATCH. LET YA HAVE IT FOR $25.
HMMM, MAYBE. BUT CAN I GET A DISCOUNT?
44
Y'KNOW, SEEING AS HOW IT'S MINE!
I DO NO FAVORS.
DARRIN BELL

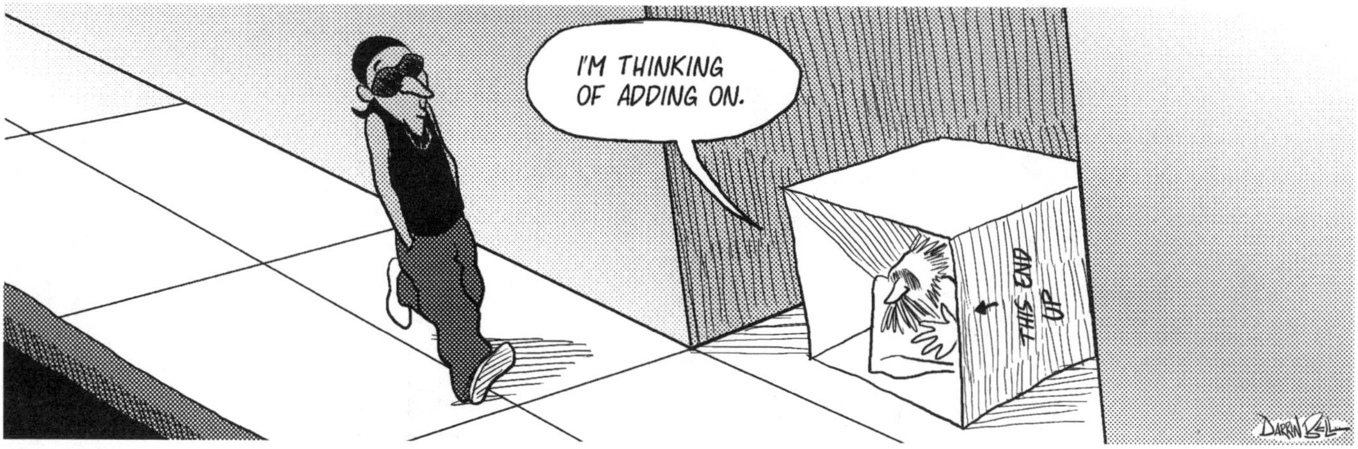
I'M THINKING OF ADDING ON.
THIS END UP
DARRIN BELL

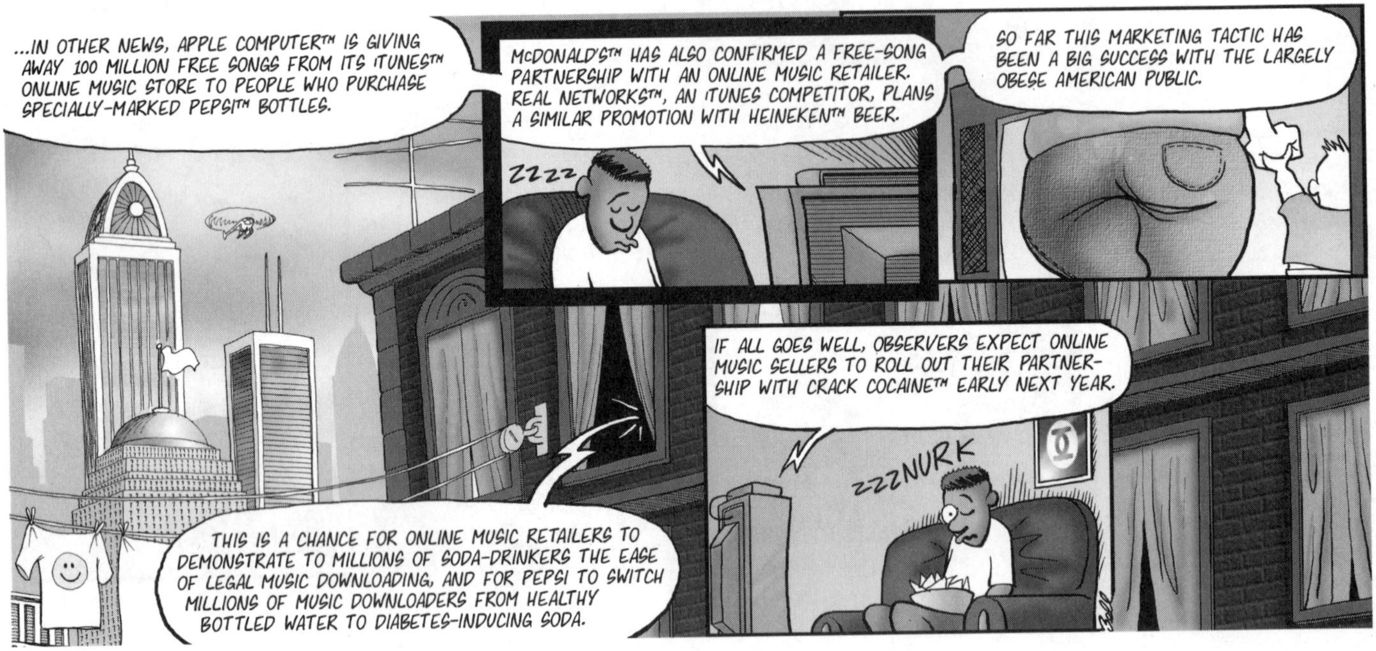
...IN OTHER NEWS, APPLE COMPUTER™ IS GIVING AWAY 100 MILLION FREE SONGS FROM ITS ITUNES™ ONLINE MUSIC STORE TO PEOPLE WHO PURCHASE SPECIALLY-MARKED PEPSI™ BOTTLES.
MCDONALD'S™ HAS ALSO CONFIRMED A FREE-SONG PARTNERSHIP WITH AN ONLINE MUSIC RETAILER. REAL NETWORKS™, AN ITUNES COMPETITOR, PLANS A SIMILAR PROMOTION WITH HEINEKEN™ BEER.
ZZZZ
SO FAR THIS MARKETING TACTIC HAS BEEN A BIG SUCCESS WITH THE LARGELY OBESE AMERICAN PUBLIC.
THIS IS A CHANCE FOR ONLINE MUSIC RETAILERS TO DEMONSTRATE TO MILLIONS OF SODA-DRINKERS THE EASE OF LEGAL MUSIC DOWNLOADING, AND FOR PEPSI TO SWITCH MILLIONS OF MUSIC DOWNLOADERS FROM HEALTHY BOTTLED WATER TO DIABETES-INDUCING SODA.
IF ALL GOES WELL, OBSERVERS EXPECT ONLINE MUSIC SELLERS TO ROLL OUT THEIR PARTNERSHIP WITH CRACK COCAINE™ EARLY NEXT YEAR.
ZZZNURK

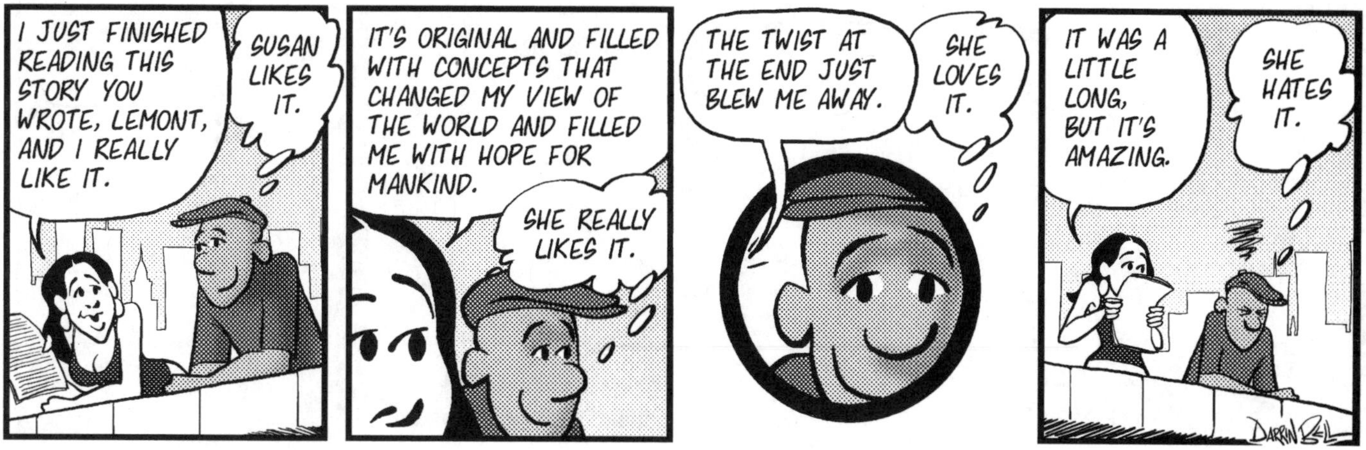
I JUST FINISHED READING THIS STORY YOU WROTE, LEMONT, AND I REALLY LIKE IT.
SUSAN LIKES IT.
IT'S ORIGINAL AND FILLED WITH CONCEPTS THAT CHANGED MY VIEW OF THE WORLD AND FILLED ME WITH HOPE FOR MANKIND.
SHE REALLY LIKES IT.
THE TWIST AT THE END JUST BLEW ME AWAY.
SHE LOVES IT.
IT WAS A LITTLE LONG, BUT IT'S AMAZING.
SHE HATES IT.
DARRIN BELL

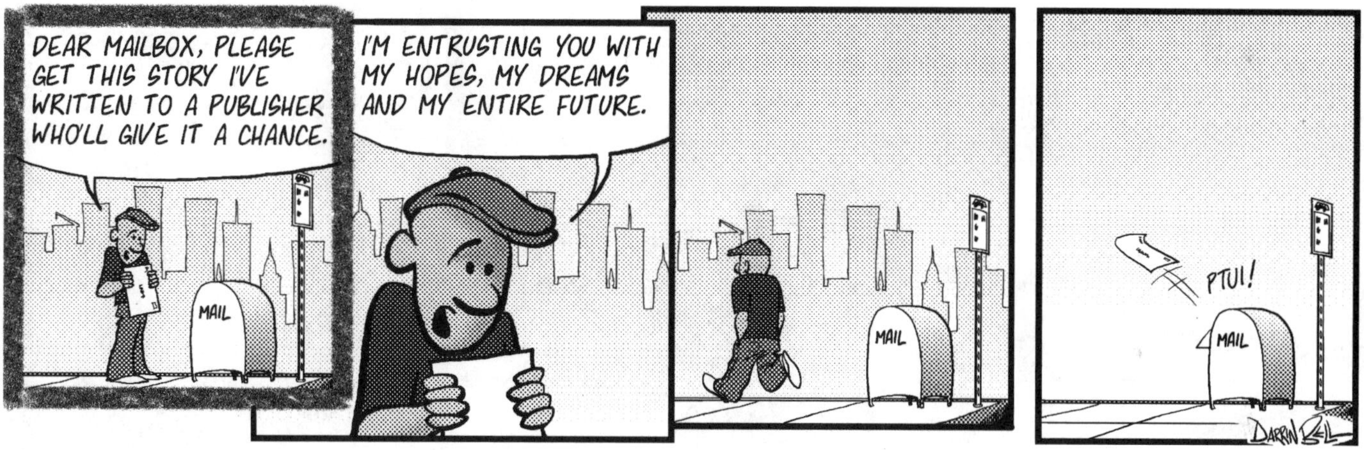
DEAR MAILBOX, PLEASE GET THIS STORY I'VE WRITTEN TO A PUBLISHER WHO'LL GIVE IT A CHANCE.
MAIL
I'M ENTRUSTING YOU WITH MY HOPES, MY DREAMS AND MY ENTIRE FUTURE.
MAIL
PTUI!
MAIL
DARRIN BELL

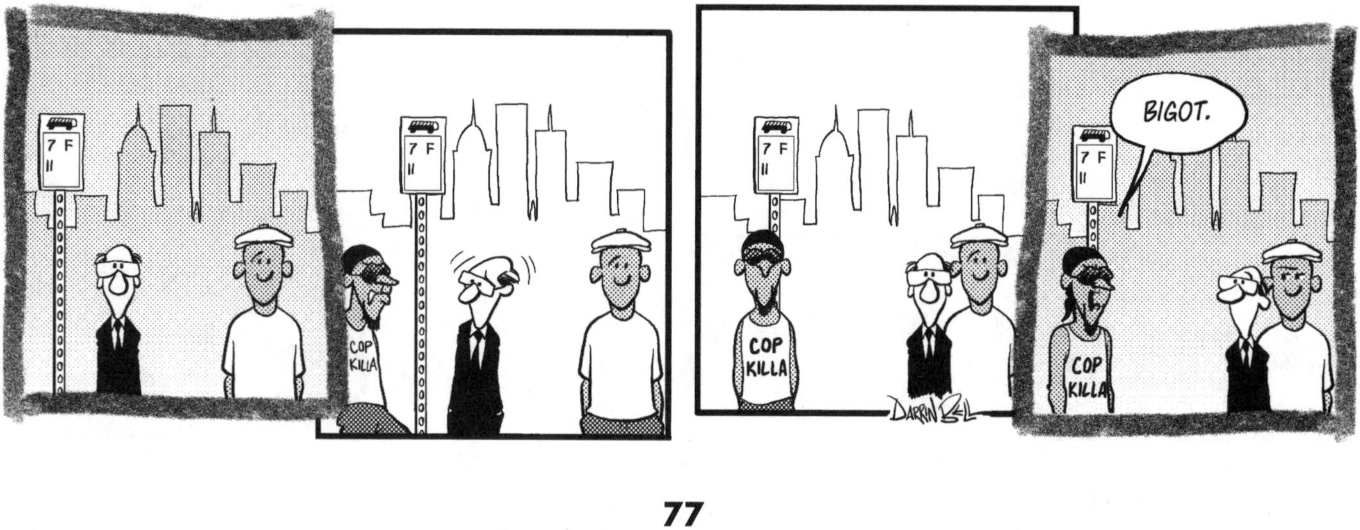
COP KILLA
COP KILLA
DARRIN BELL
BIGOT.
COP KILLA

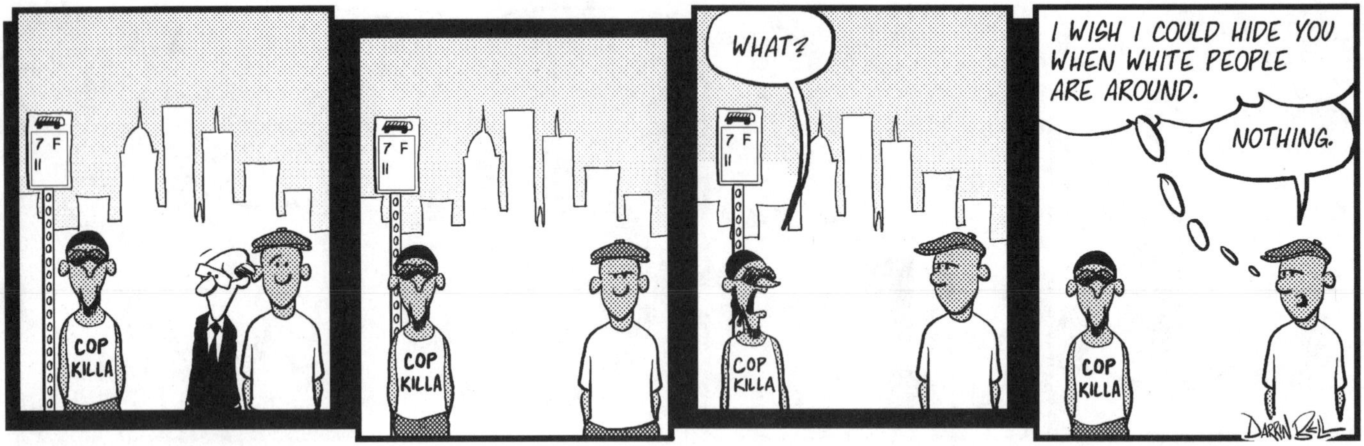
COP KILLA
WHAT?
I WISH I COULD HIDE YOU WHEN WHITE PEOPLE ARE AROUND.
NOTHING.
DARRIN BELL

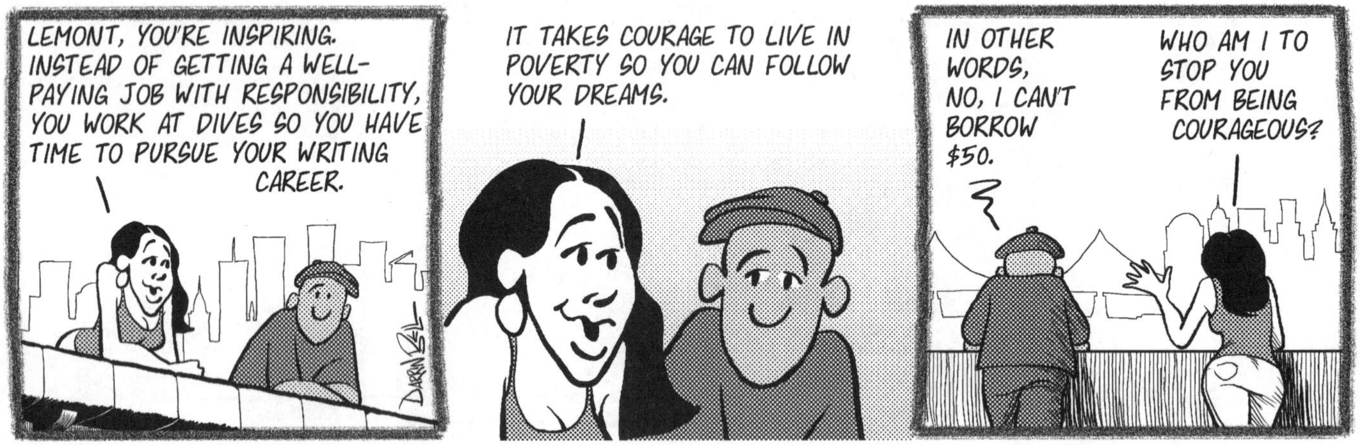
LEMONT, YOU'RE INSPIRING. INSTEAD OF GETTING A WELL-PAYING JOB WITH RESPONSIBILITY, YOU WORK AT DIVES SO YOU HAVE TIME TO PURSUE YOUR WRITING CAREER.
IT TAKES COURAGE TO LIVE IN POVERTY SO YOU CAN FOLLOW YOUR DREAMS.
IN OTHER WORDS, NO, I CAN'T BORROW $50.
WHO AM I TO STOP YOU FROM BEING COURAGEOUS?
DARRIN BELL

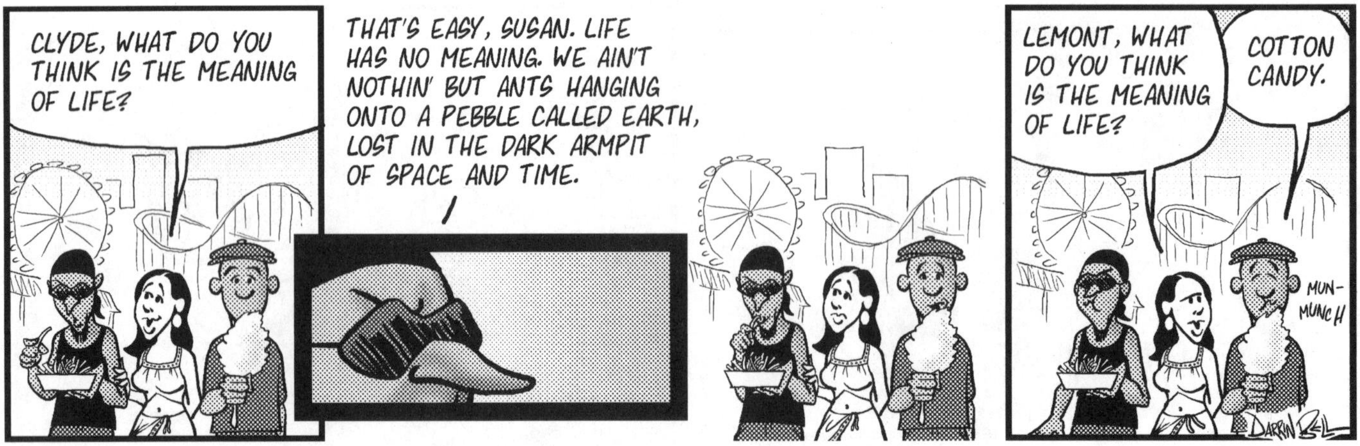
CLYDE, WHAT DO YOU THINK IS THE MEANING OF LIFE?
THAT'S EASY, SUSAN. LIFE HAS NO MEANING. WE AIN'T NOTHIN' BUT ANTS HANGING ONTO A PEBBLE CALLED EARTH, LOST IN THE DARK ARMPIT OF SPACE AND TIME.
LEMONT, WHAT DO YOU THINK IS THE MEANING OF LIFE?
COTTON CANDY.
MUN-MUNCH
DARRIN BELL

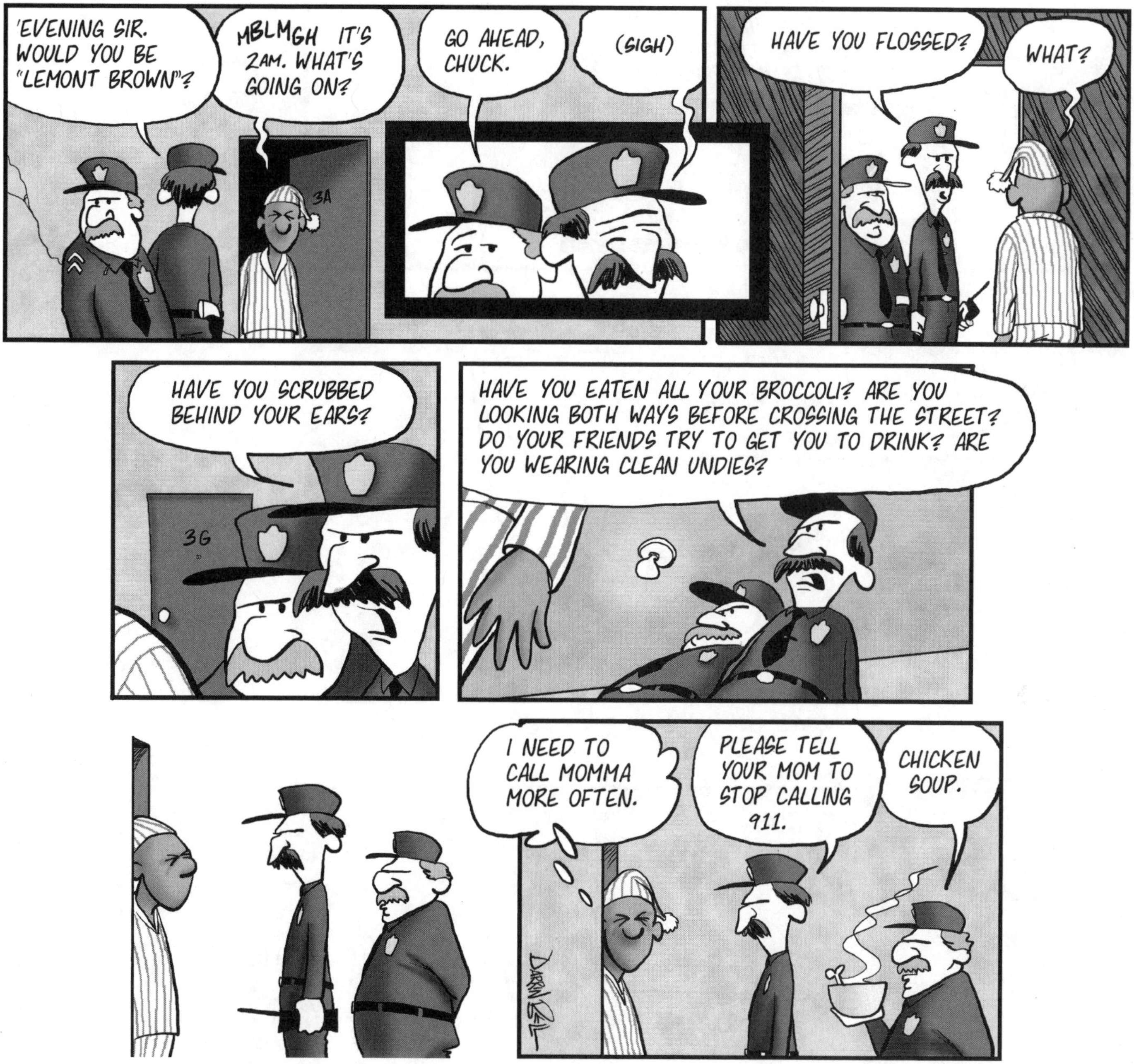

'EVENING SIR. WOULD YOU BE "LEMONT BROWN"?
MBLMGH IT'S 2AM. WHAT'S GOING ON?
3A
GO AHEAD, CHUCK.
(SIGH)
HAVE YOU FLOSSED?
WHAT?
HAVE YOU SCRUBBED BEHIND YOUR EARS?
3G
HAVE YOU EATEN ALL YOUR BROCCOLI? ARE YOU LOOKING BOTH WAYS BEFORE CROSSING THE STREET? DO YOUR FRIENDS TRY TO GET YOU TO DRINK? ARE YOU WEARING CLEAN UNDIES?
I NEED TO CALL MOMMA MORE OFTEN.
PLEASE TELL YOUR MOM TO STOP CALLING 911.
CHICKEN SOUP.
DARRIN BELL

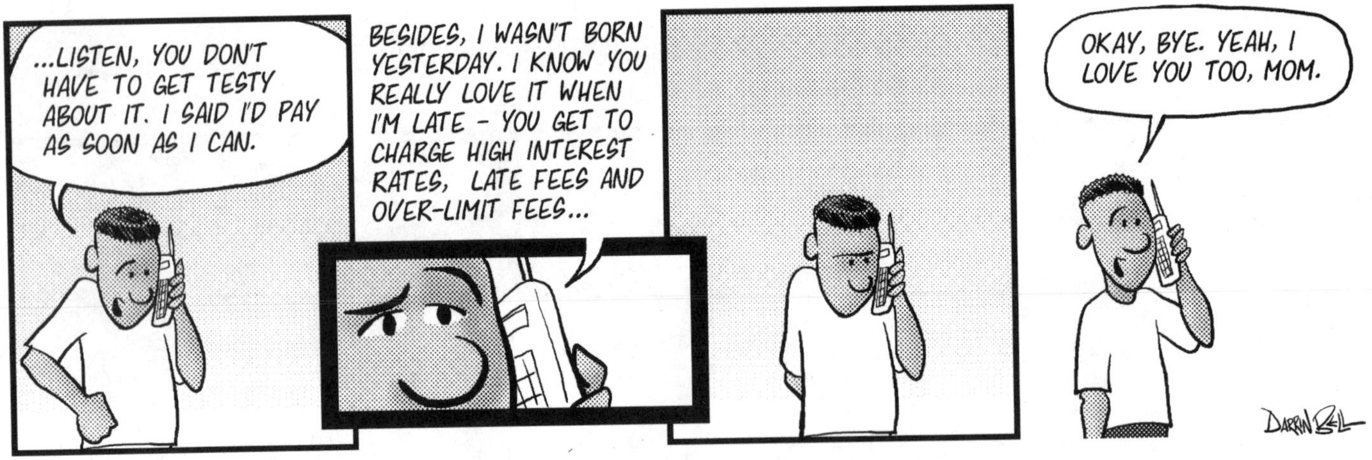
...LISTEN, YOU DON'T HAVE TO GET TESTY ABOUT IT. I SAID I'D PAY AS SOON AS I CAN.
BESIDES, I WASN'T BORN YESTERDAY. I KNOW YOU REALLY LOVE IT WHEN I'M LATE - YOU GET TO CHARGE HIGH INTEREST RATES, LATE FEES AND OVER-LIMIT FEES...
OKAY, BYE. YEAH, I LOVE YOU TOO, MOM.
DARRIN BELL

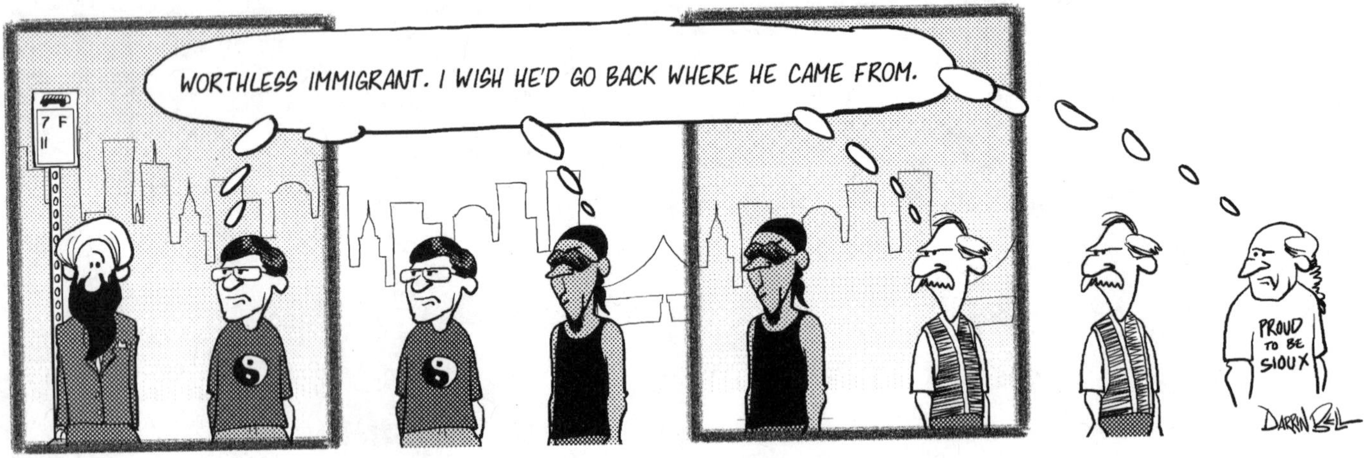
7 F
WORTHLESS IMMIGRANT. I WISH HE'D GO BACK WHERE HE CAME FROM.
PROUD TO BE SIOUX
DARRIN BELL

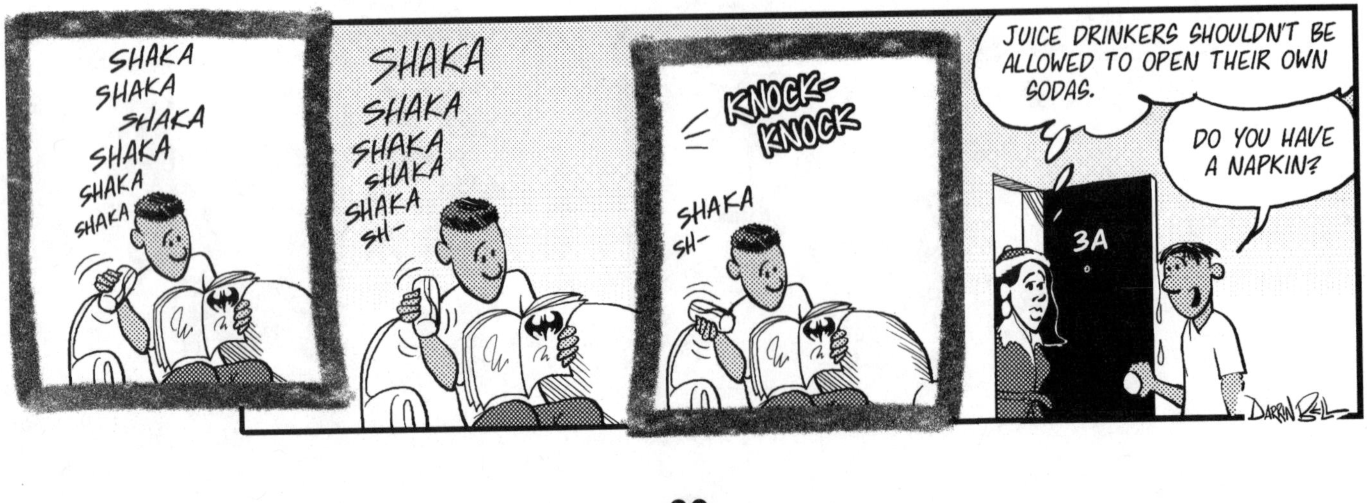
SHAKA SHAKA SHAKA SHAKA SHAKA SHAKA
SHAKA SHAKA SHAKA SHAKA SHAKA SH-
KNOCK-KNOCK
SHAKA SH-
JUICE DRINKERS SHOULDN'T BE ALLOWED TO OPEN THEIR OWN SODAS.
DO YOU HAVE A NAPKIN?
3A
DARRIN BELL

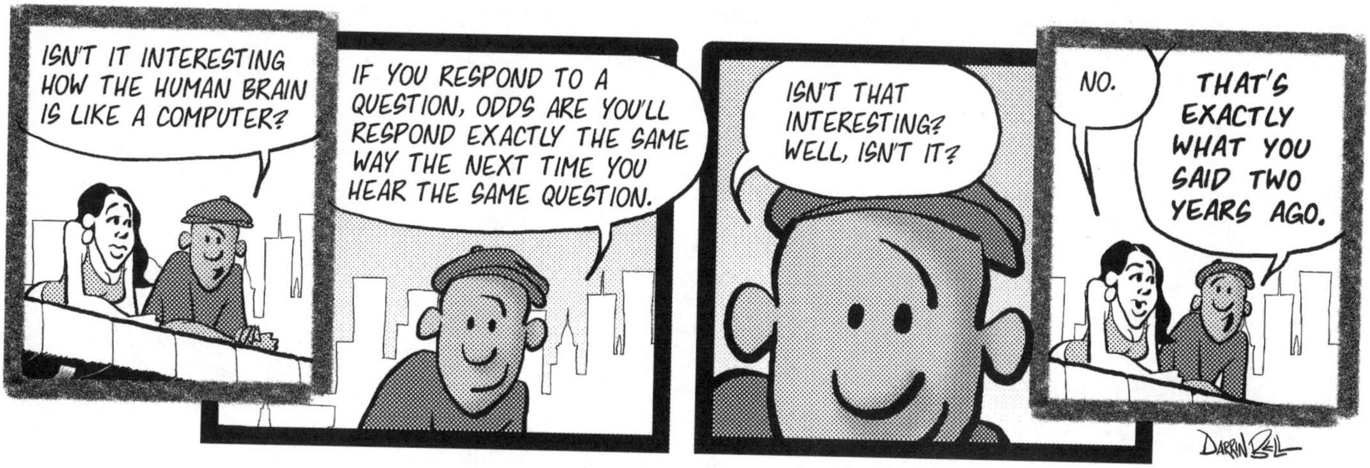
ISN'T IT INTERESTING HOW THE HUMAN BRAIN IS LIKE A COMPUTER?
IF YOU RESPOND TO A QUESTION, ODDS ARE YOU'LL RESPOND EXACTLY THE SAME WAY THE NEXT TIME YOU HEAR THE SAME QUESTION.
ISN'T THAT INTERESTING? WELL, ISN'T IT?
NO.
THAT'S EXACTLY WHAT YOU SAID TWO YEARS AGO.
DARRIN BELL

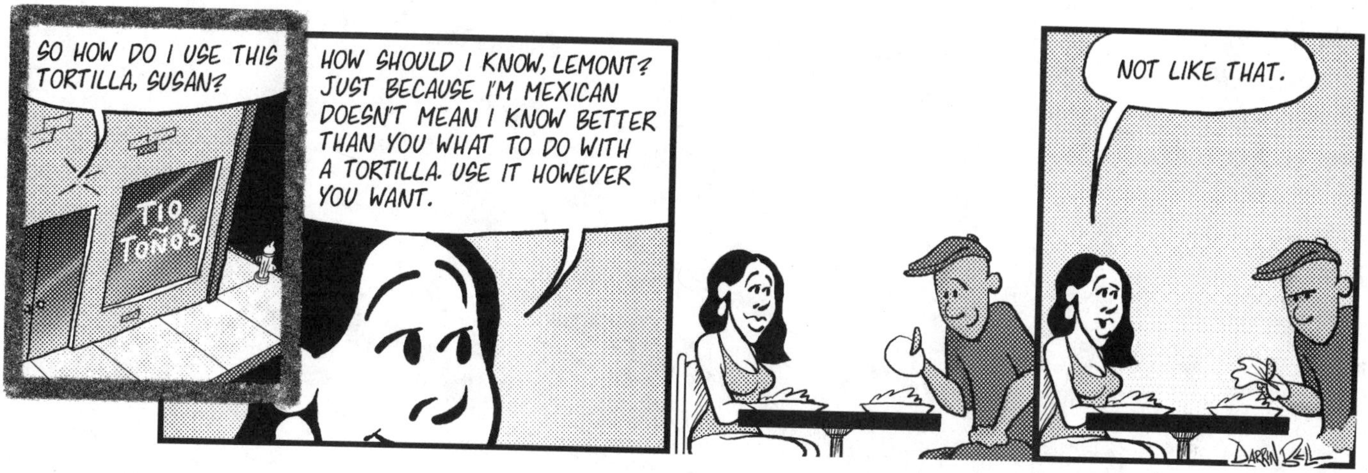
SO HOW DO I USE THIS TORTILLA, SUSAN?
TIO TOÑO'S
HOW SHOULD I KNOW, LEMONT? JUST BECAUSE I'M MEXICAN DOESN'T MEAN I KNOW BETTER THAN YOU WHAT TO DO WITH A TORTILLA. USE IT HOWEVER YOU WANT.
NOT LIKE THAT.
DARRIN BELL

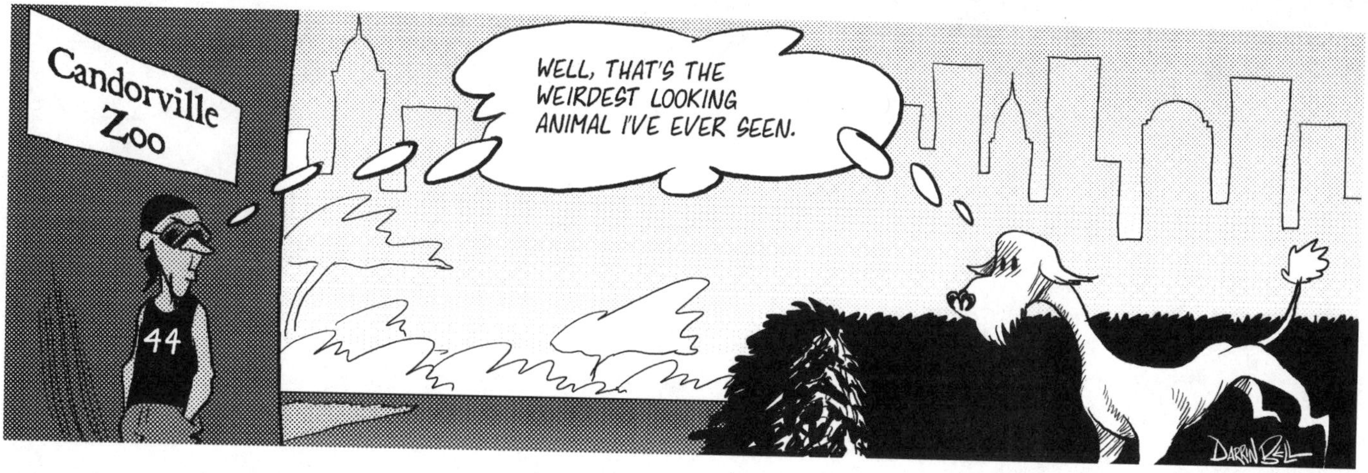
Candorville Zoo
WELL, THAT'S THE WEIRDEST LOOKING ANIMAL I'VE EVER SEEN.
44
DARRIN BELL

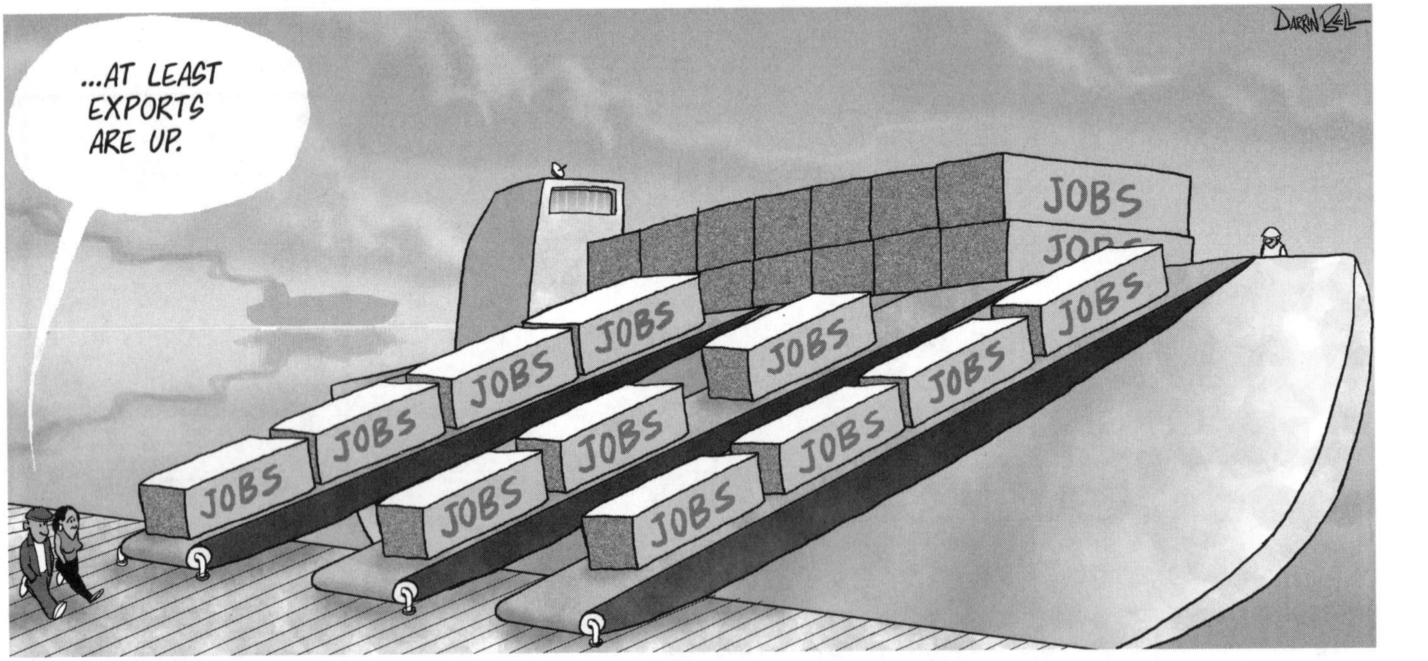
...AT LEAST EXPORTS ARE UP.
JOBS
JOBS
JOBS
JOBS
JOBS
JOBS
JOBS
JOBS
JOBS
JOBS
JOBS
JOBS
JOBS
DARRIN BELL

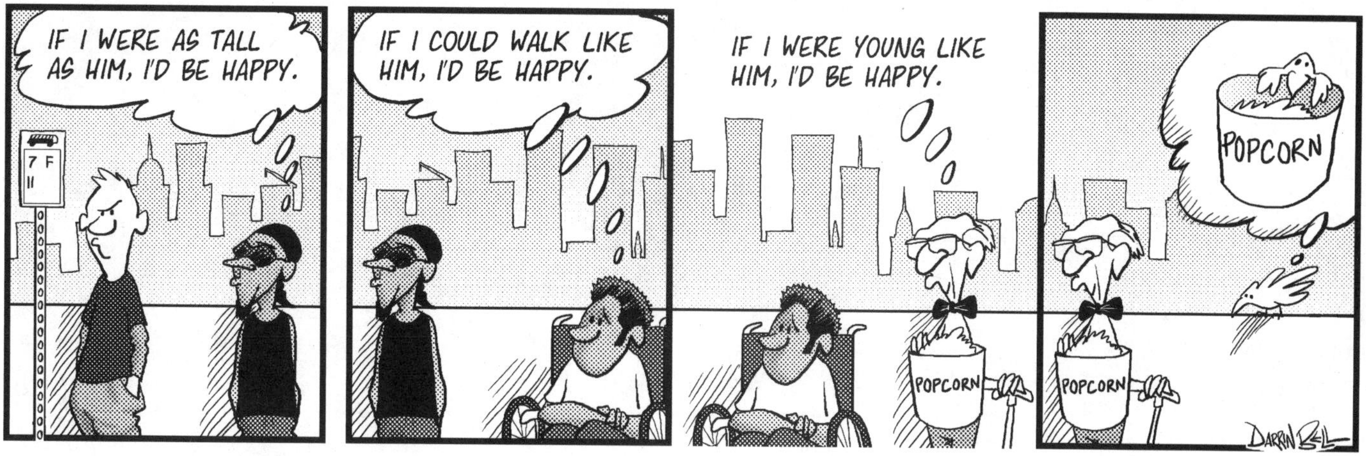
IF I WERE AS TALL AS HIM, I'D BE HAPPY.
IF I COULD WALK LIKE HIM, I'D BE HAPPY.
IF I WERE YOUNG LIKE HIM, I'D BE HAPPY.
POPCORN
POPCORN
POPCORN
POPCORN
DARRIN BELL

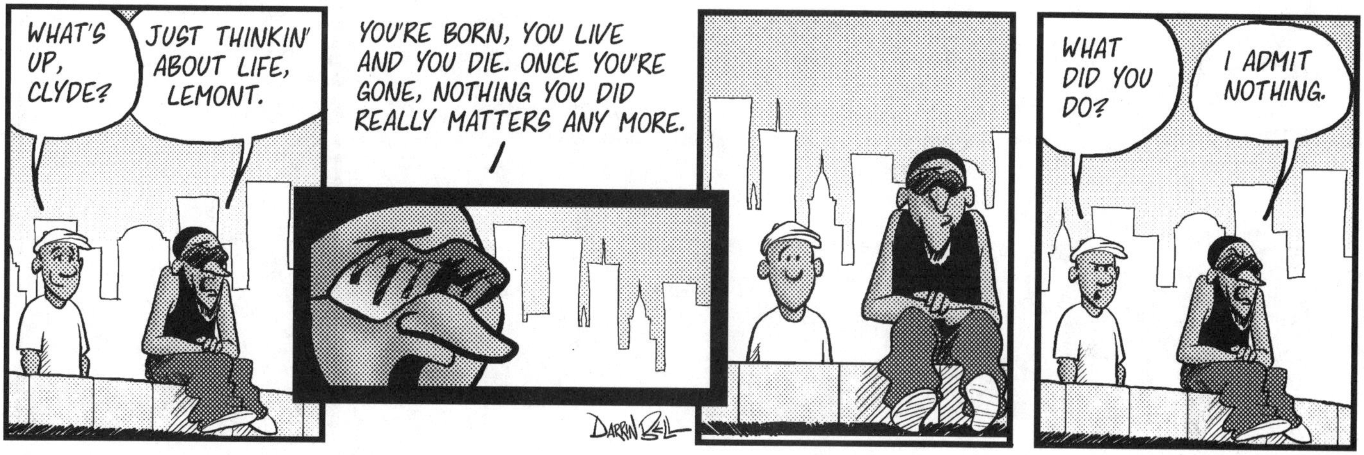
WHAT'S UP, CLYDE?
JUST THINKIN' ABOUT LIFE, LEMONT.
YOU'RE BORN, YOU LIVE AND YOU DIE. ONCE YOU'RE GONE, NOTHING YOU DID REALLY MATTERS ANY MORE.
WHAT DID YOU DO?
I ADMIT NOTHING.
DARRIN BELL

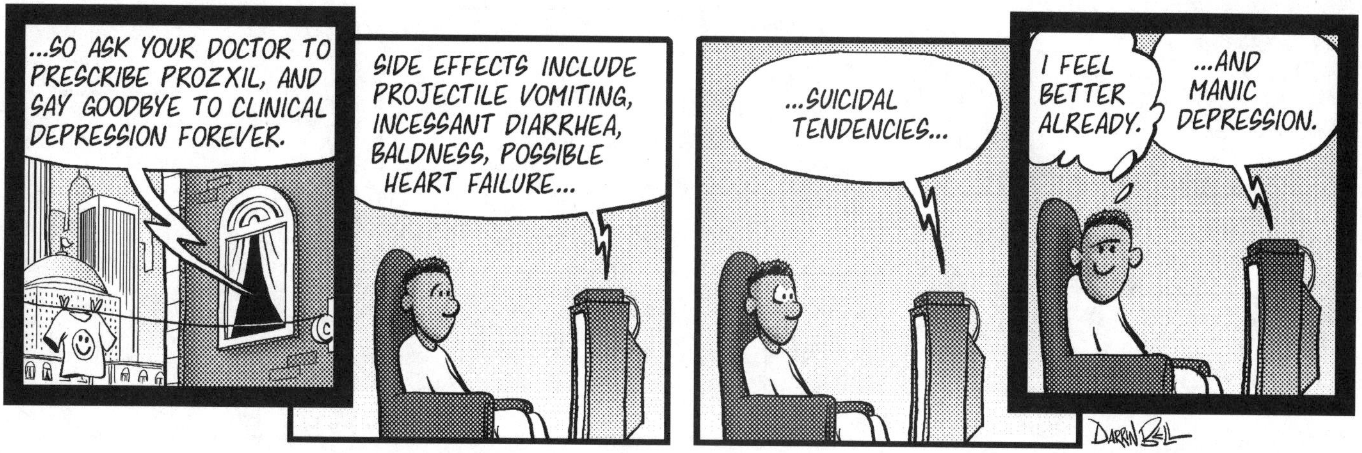
...SO ASK YOUR DOCTOR TO PRESCRIBE PROZXIL, AND SAY GOODBYE TO CLINICAL DEPRESSION FOREVER.
SIDE EFFECTS INCLUDE PROJECTILE VOMITING, INCESSANT DIARRHEA, BALDNESS, POSSIBLE HEART FAILURE...
...SUICIDAL TENDENCIES...
I FEEL BETTER ALREADY.
...AND MANIC DEPRESSION.
DARRIN BELL

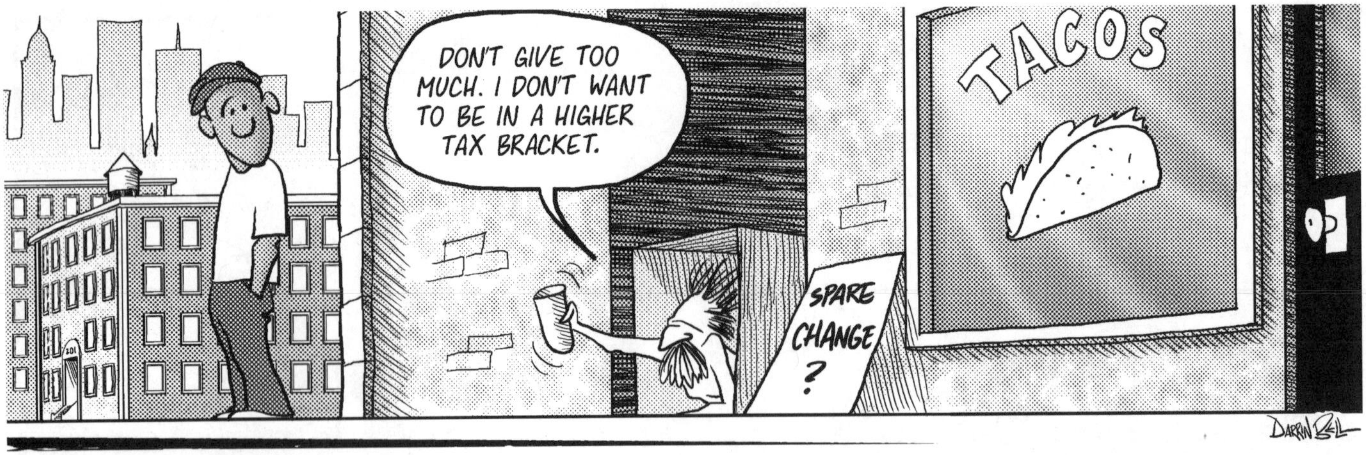
DON'T GIVE TOO MUCH. I DON'T WANT TO BE IN A HIGHER TAX BRACKET.
TACOS
SPARE CHANGE ?
DARRIN BELL

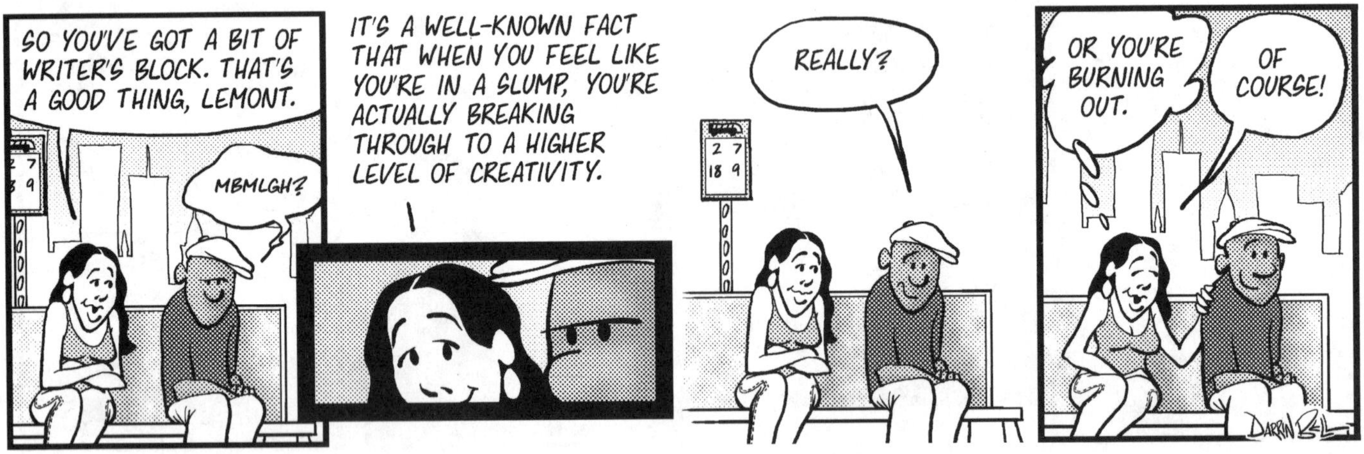
SO YOU'VE GOT A BIT OF WRITER'S BLOCK. THAT'S A GOOD THING, LEMONT.
MBMLGH?
IT'S A WELL-KNOWN FACT THAT WHEN YOU FEEL LIKE YOU'RE IN A SLUMP, YOU'RE ACTUALLY BREAKING THROUGH TO A HIGHER LEVEL OF CREATIVITY.
REALLY?
OR YOU'RE BURNING OUT.
OF COURSE!
DARRIN BELL

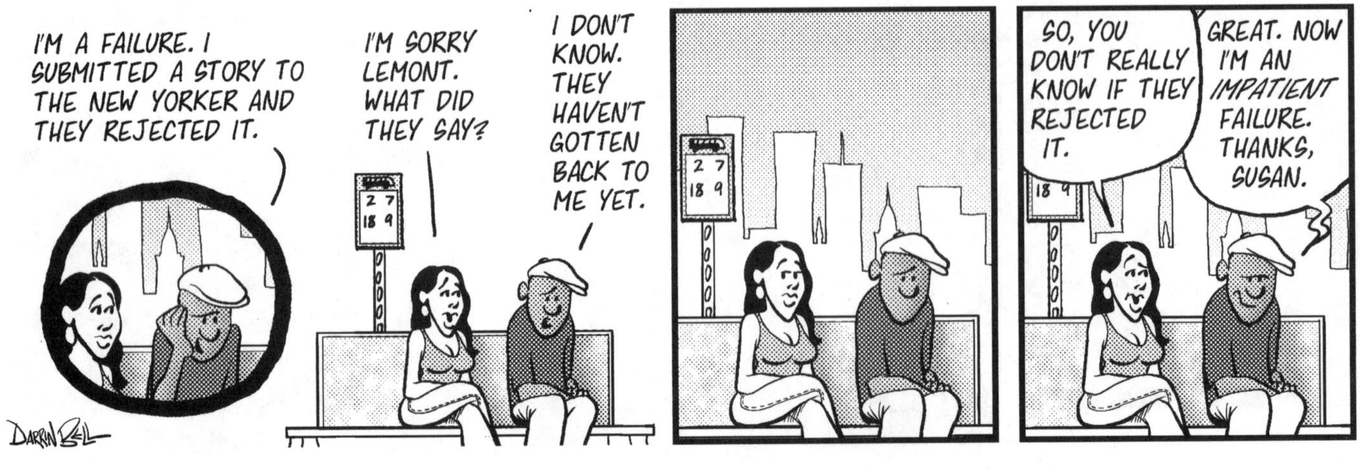
I'M A FAILURE. I SUBMITTED A STORY TO THE NEW YORKER AND THEY REJECTED IT.
I'M SORRY LEMONT. WHAT DID THEY SAY?
I DON'T KNOW. THEY HAVEN'T GOTTEN BACK TO ME YET.
SO, YOU DON'T REALLY KNOW IF THEY REJECTED IT.
GREAT. NOW I'M AN *IMPATIENT* FAILURE. THANKS, SUSAN.
DARRIN BELL

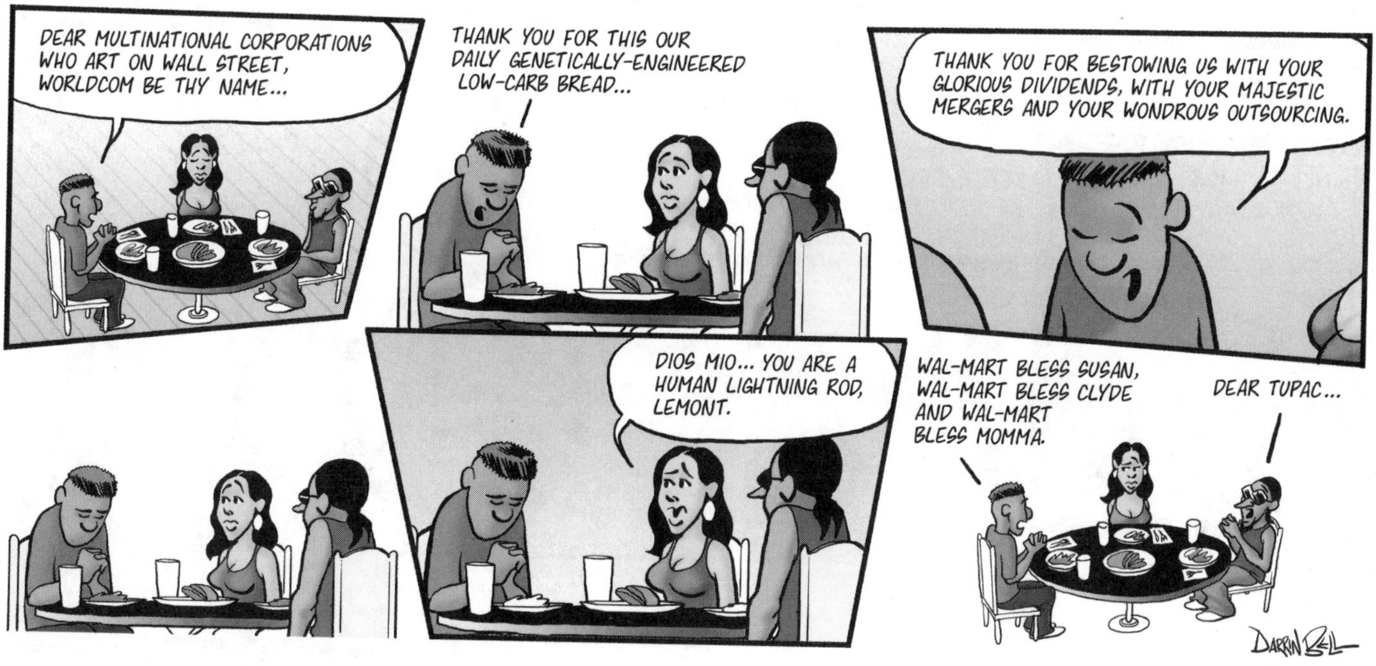
DEAR MULTINATIONAL CORPORATIONS WHO ART ON WALL STREET, WORLDCOM BE THY NAME...
THANK YOU FOR THIS OUR DAILY GENETICALLY-ENGINEERED LOW-CARB BREAD...
THANK YOU FOR BESTOWING US WITH YOUR GLORIOUS DIVIDENDS, WITH YOUR MAJESTIC MERGERS AND YOUR WONDROUS OUTSOURCING.
DIOS MIO... YOU ARE A HUMAN LIGHTNING ROD, LEMONT.
WAL-MART BLESS SUSAN, WAL-MART BLESS CLYDE AND WAL-MART BLESS MOMMA.
DEAR TUPAC...
DARRIN BELL

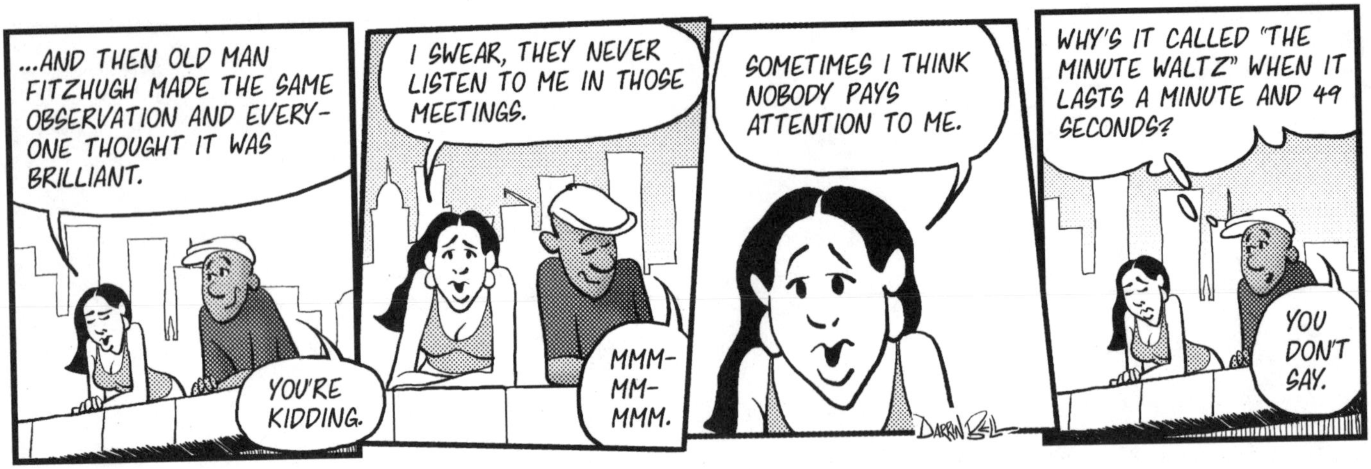
...AND THEN OLD MAN FITZHUGH MADE THE SAME OBSERVATION AND EVERY-ONE THOUGHT IT WAS BRILLIANT.
YOU'RE KIDDING.
I SWEAR, THEY NEVER LISTEN TO ME IN THOSE MEETINGS.
MMM-MM-MMM.
SOMETIMES I THINK NOBODY PAYS ATTENTION TO ME.
WHY'S IT CALLED "THE MINUTE WALTZ" WHEN IT LASTS A MINUTE AND 49 SECONDS?
YOU DON'T SAY.

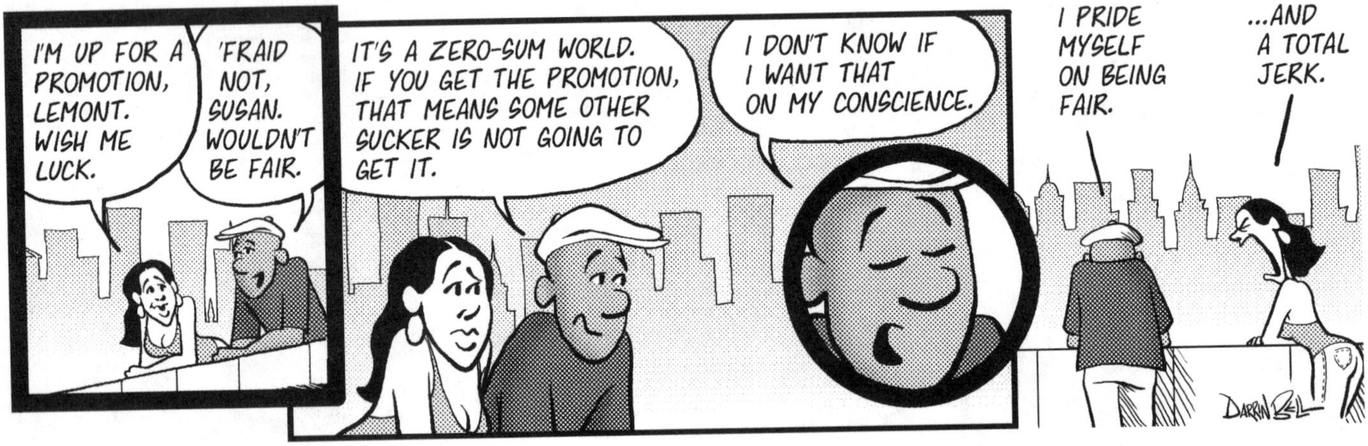
I'M UP FOR A PROMOTION, LEMONT. WISH ME LUCK.
'FRAID NOT, SUSAN. WOULDN'T BE FAIR.
IT'S A ZERO-SUM WORLD. IF YOU GET THE PROMOTION, THAT MEANS SOME OTHER SUCKER IS NOT GOING TO GET IT.
I DON'T KNOW IF I WANT THAT ON MY CONSCIENCE.
I PRIDE MYSELF ON BEING FAIR.
...AND A TOTAL JERK.

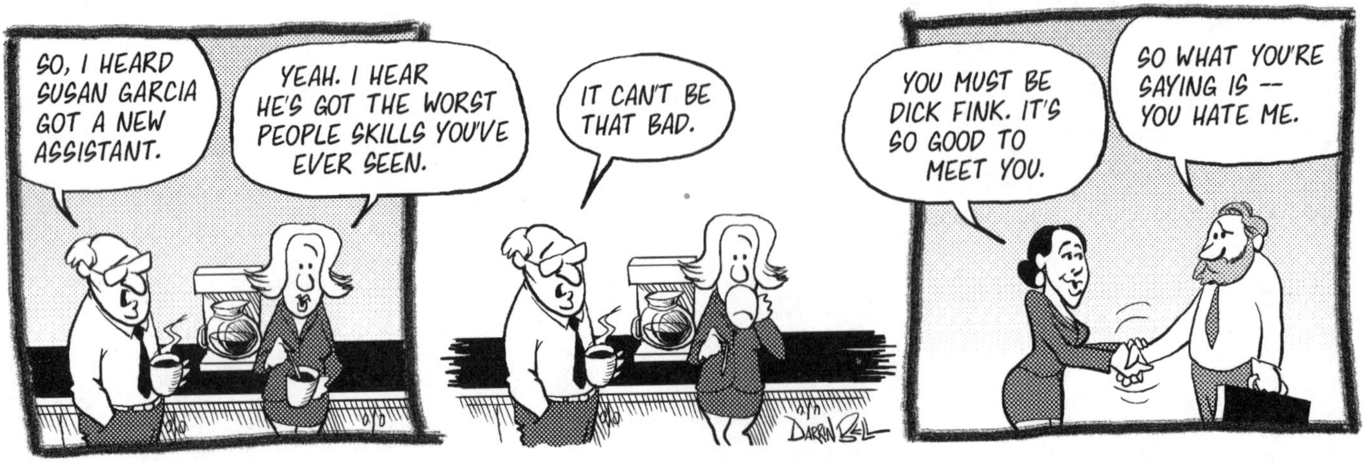
SO, I HEARD SUSAN GARCIA GOT A NEW ASSISTANT.
YEAH. I HEAR HE'S GOT THE WORST PEOPLE SKILLS YOU'VE EVER SEEN.
IT CAN'T BE THAT BAD.
YOU MUST BE DICK FINK. IT'S SO GOOD TO MEET YOU.
SO WHAT YOU'RE SAYING IS -- YOU HATE ME.

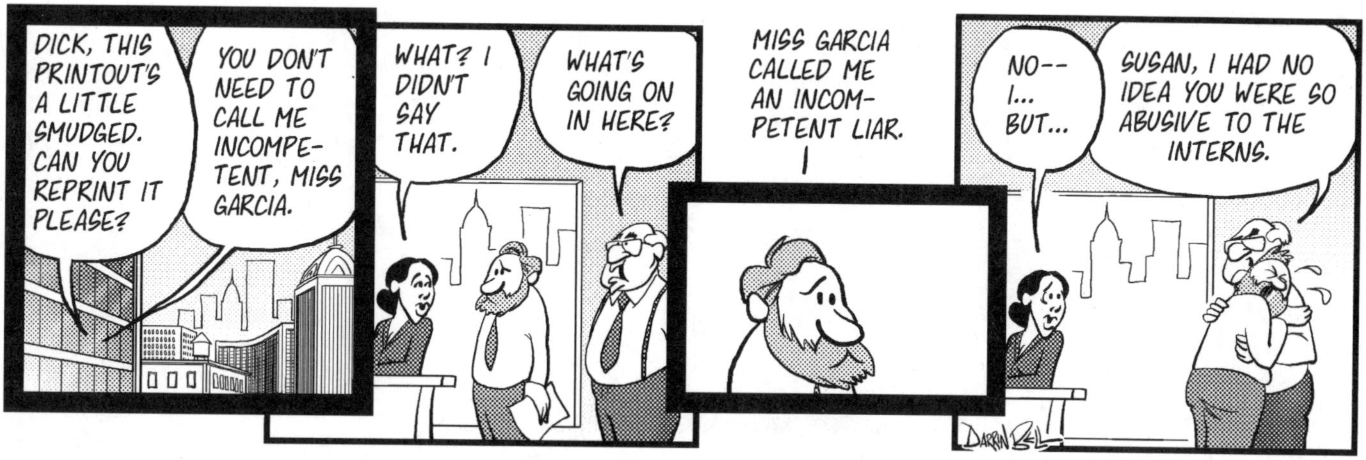
DICK, THIS PRINTOUT'S A LITTLE SMUDGED. CAN YOU REPRINT IT PLEASE?
YOU DON'T NEED TO CALL ME INCOMPETENT, MISS GARCIA.
WHAT? I DIDN'T SAY THAT.
WHAT'S GOING ON IN HERE?
MISS GARCIA CALLED ME AN INCOMPETENT LIAR.
NO-- I... BUT...
SUSAN, I HAD NO IDEA YOU WERE SO ABUSIVE TO THE INTERNS.
DARRIN BELL

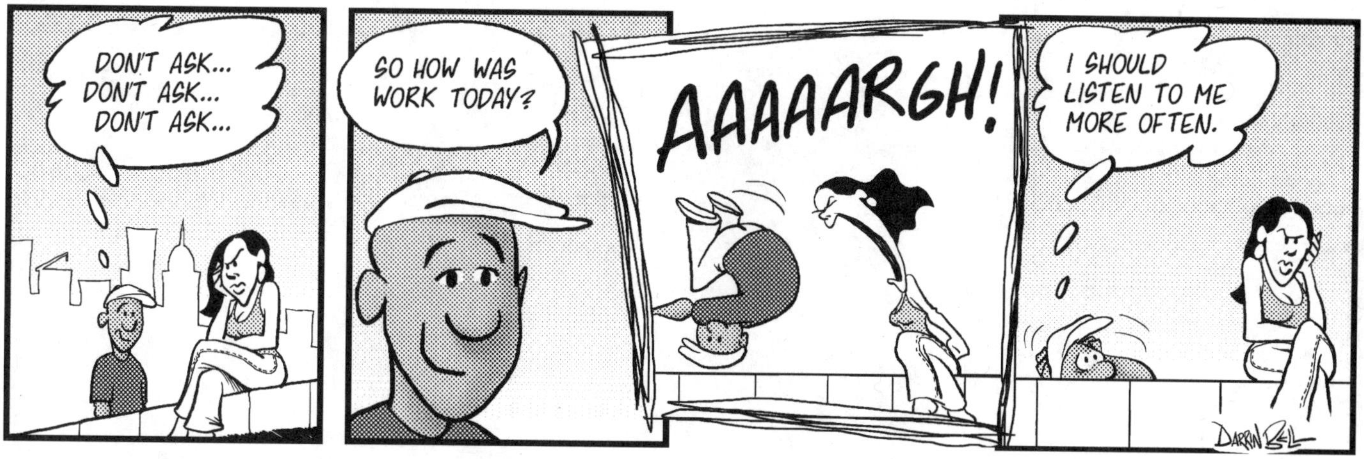
DON'T ASK... DON'T ASK... DON'T ASK...
SO HOW WAS WORK TODAY?
AAAAARGH!
I SHOULD LISTEN TO ME MORE OFTEN.
DARRIN BELL

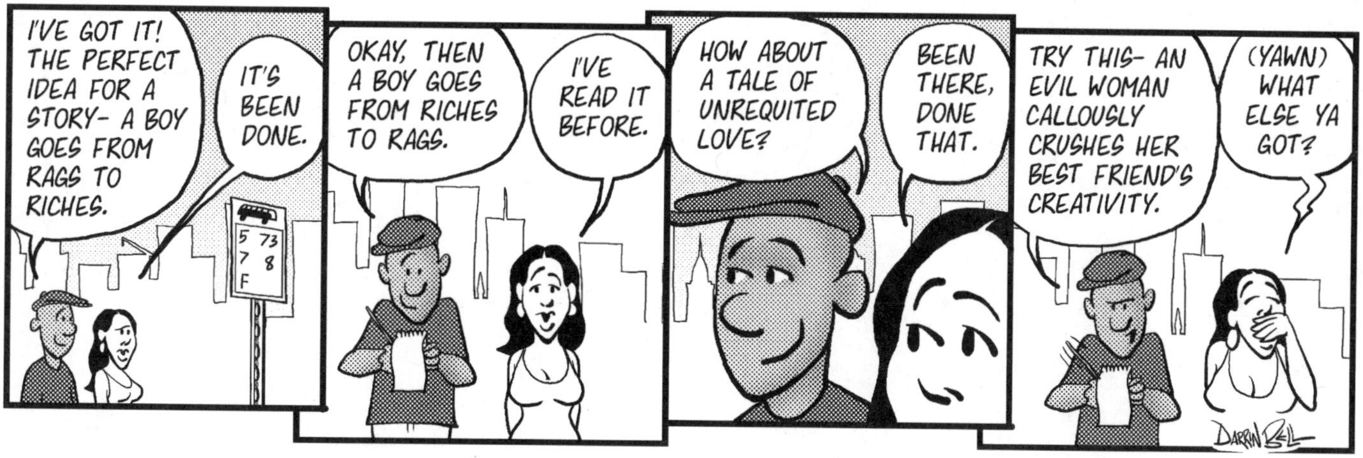
I'VE GOT IT! THE PERFECT IDEA FOR A STORY- A BOY GOES FROM RAGS TO RICHES.
IT'S BEEN DONE.
5 73
7 8
F
OKAY, THEN A BOY GOES FROM RICHES TO RAGS.
I'VE READ IT BEFORE.
HOW ABOUT A TALE OF UNREQUITED LOVE?
BEEN THERE, DONE THAT.
TRY THIS- AN EVIL WOMAN CALLOUSLY CRUSHES HER BEST FRIEND'S CREATIVITY.
(YAWN) WHAT ELSE YA GOT?
DARRIN BELL

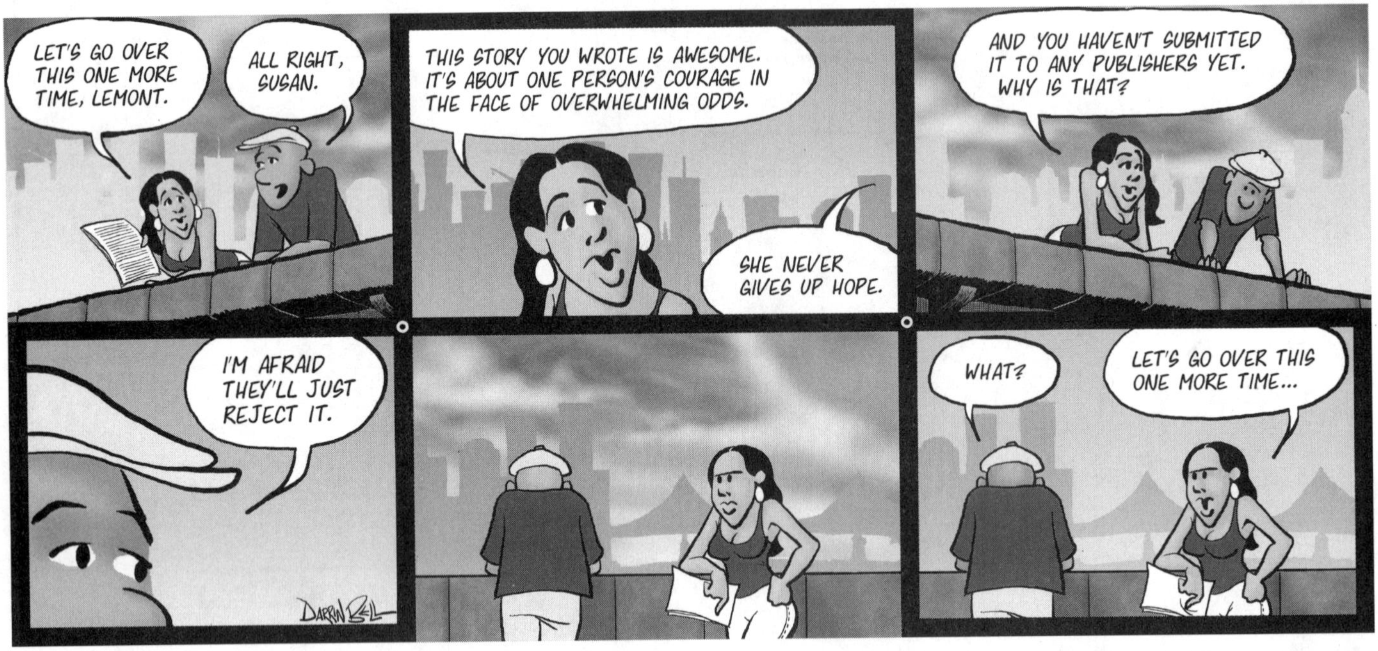
LET'S GO OVER THIS ONE MORE TIME, LEMONT.
ALL RIGHT, SUSAN.
THIS STORY YOU WROTE IS AWESOME. IT'S ABOUT ONE PERSON'S COURAGE IN THE FACE OF OVERWHELMING ODDS.
SHE NEVER GIVES UP HOPE.
AND YOU HAVEN'T SUBMITTED IT TO ANY PUBLISHERS YET. WHY IS THAT?
I'M AFRAID THEY'LL JUST REJECT IT.
DARRIN BELL
WHAT?
LET'S GO OVER THIS ONE MORE TIME...

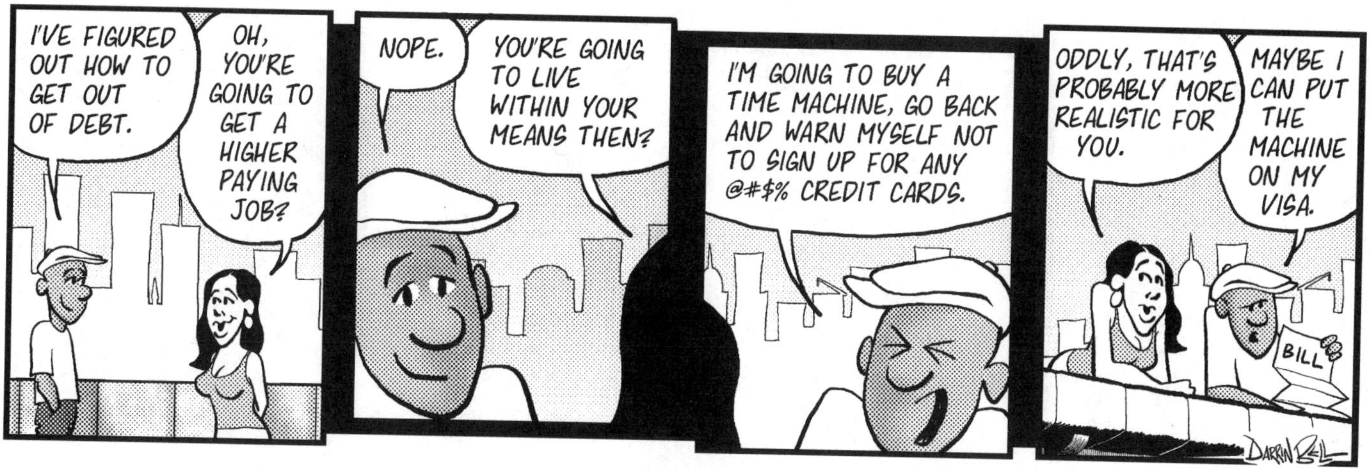
I'VE FIGURED OUT HOW TO GET OUT OF DEBT.
OH, YOU'RE GOING TO GET A HIGHER PAYING JOB?
NOPE.
YOU'RE GOING TO LIVE WITHIN YOUR MEANS THEN?
I'M GOING TO BUY A TIME MACHINE, GO BACK AND WARN MYSELF NOT TO SIGN UP FOR ANY @#$% CREDIT CARDS.
ODDLY, THAT'S PROBABLY MORE REALISTIC FOR YOU.
MAYBE I CAN PUT THE MACHINE ON MY VISA.
BILL
DARRIN BELL

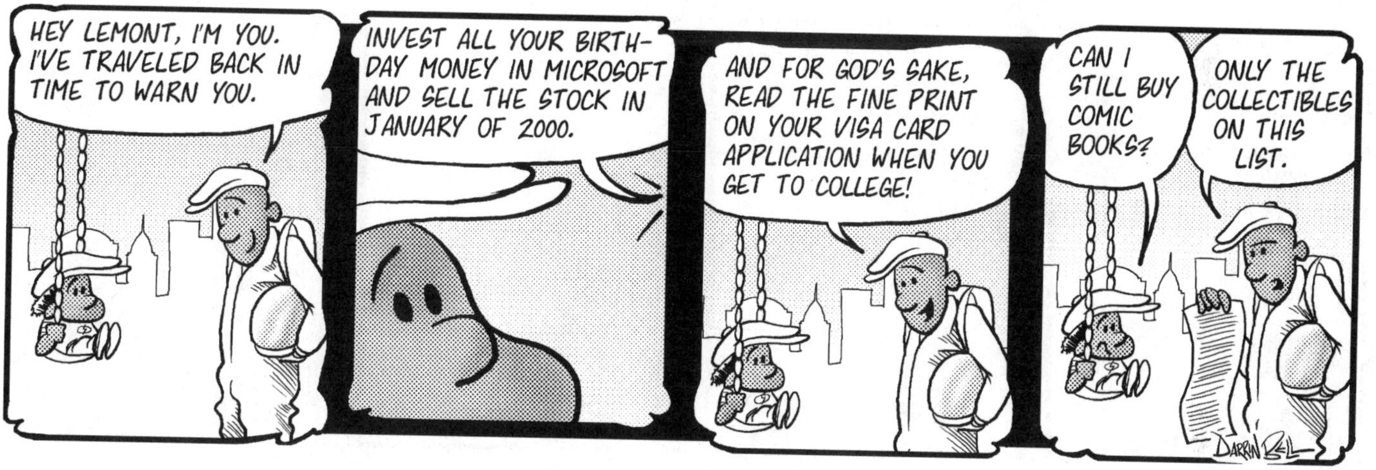
HEY LEMONT, I'M YOU. I'VE TRAVELED BACK IN TIME TO WARN YOU.
INVEST ALL YOUR BIRTH-DAY MONEY IN MICROSOFT AND SELL THE STOCK IN JANUARY OF 2000.
AND FOR GOD'S SAKE, READ THE FINE PRINT ON YOUR VISA CARD APPLICATION WHEN YOU GET TO COLLEGE!
CAN I STILL BUY COMIC BOOKS?
ONLY THE COLLECTIBLES ON THIS LIST.
DARRIN BELL

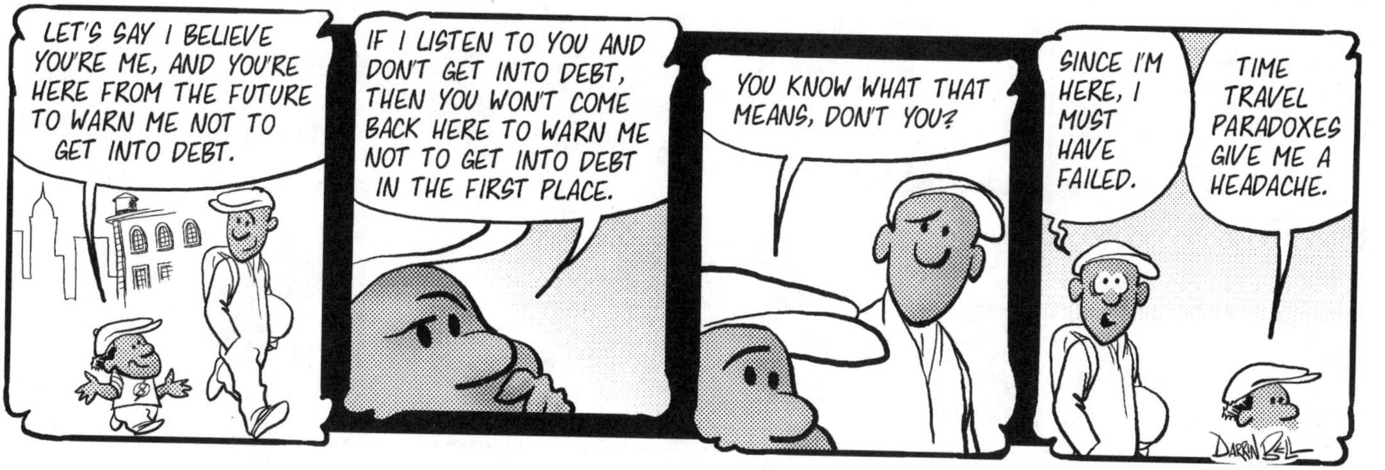
LET'S SAY I BELIEVE YOU'RE ME, AND YOU'RE HERE FROM THE FUTURE TO WARN ME NOT TO GET INTO DEBT.
IF I LISTEN TO YOU AND DON'T GET INTO DEBT, THEN YOU WON'T COME BACK HERE TO WARN ME NOT TO GET INTO DEBT IN THE FIRST PLACE.
YOU KNOW WHAT THAT MEANS, DON'T YOU?
SINCE I'M HERE, I MUST HAVE FAILED.
TIME TRAVEL PARADOXES GIVE ME A HEADACHE.
DARRIN BELL

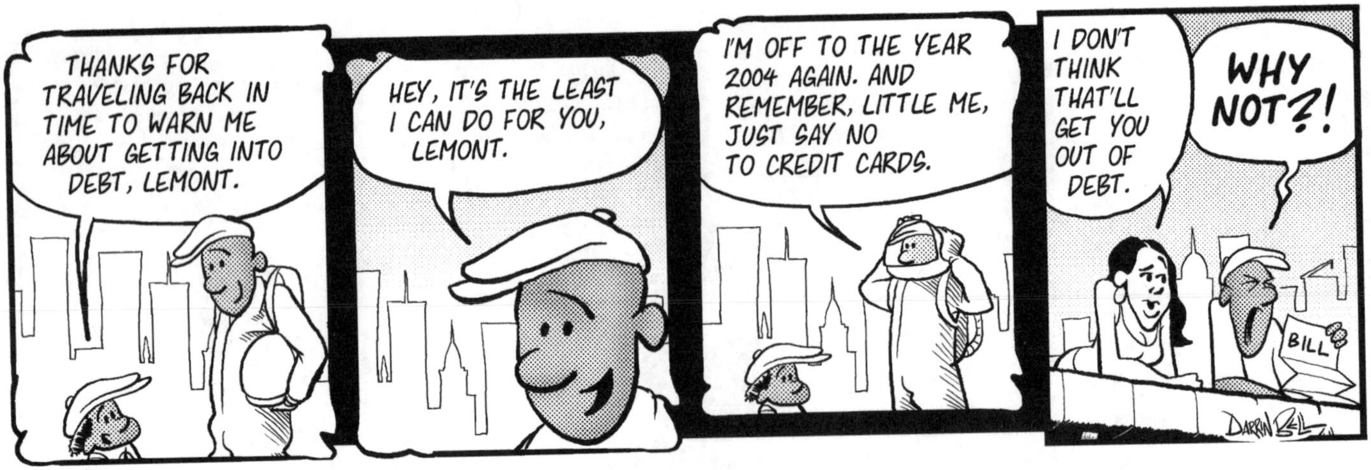
THANKS FOR TRAVELING BACK IN TIME TO WARN ME ABOUT GETTING INTO DEBT, LEMONT.
HEY, IT'S THE LEAST I CAN DO FOR YOU, LEMONT.
I'M OFF TO THE YEAR 2004 AGAIN. AND REMEMBER, LITTLE ME, JUST SAY NO TO CREDIT CARDS.
I DON'T THINK THAT'LL GET YOU OUT OF DEBT.
WHY NOT?!
BILL
DARRIN BELL

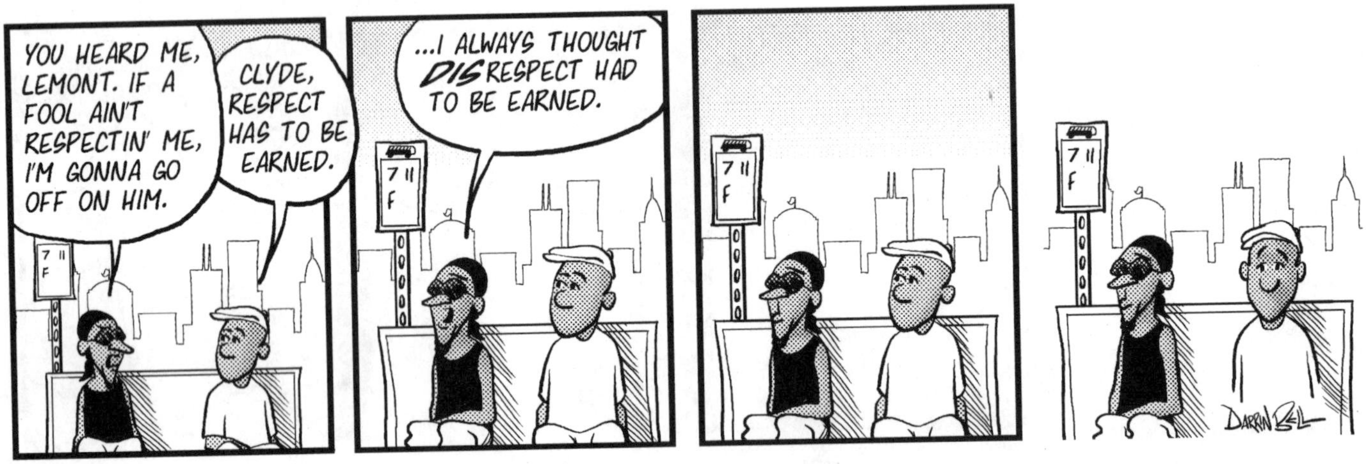
YOU HEARD ME, LEMONT. IF A FOOL AIN'T RESPECTIN' ME, I'M GONNA GO OFF ON HIM.
CLYDE, RESPECT HAS TO BE EARNED.
...I ALWAYS THOUGHT DISRESPECT HAD TO BE EARNED.
DARRIN BELL

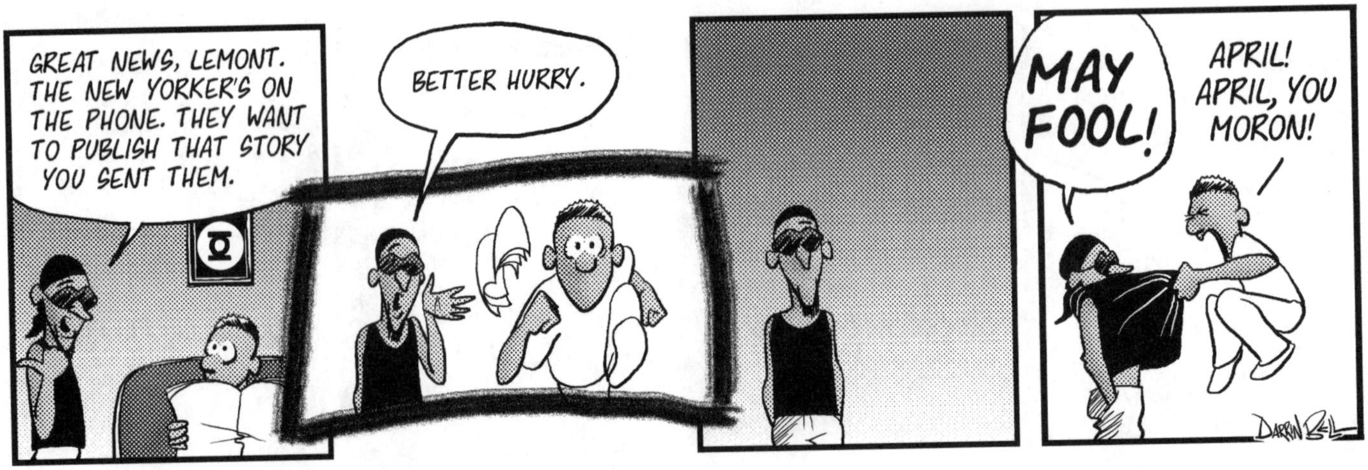
GREAT NEWS, LEMONT. THE NEW YORKER'S ON THE PHONE. THEY WANT TO PUBLISH THAT STORY YOU SENT THEM.
BETTER HURRY.
MAY FOOL!
APRIL! APRIL, YOU MORON!
DARRIN BELL

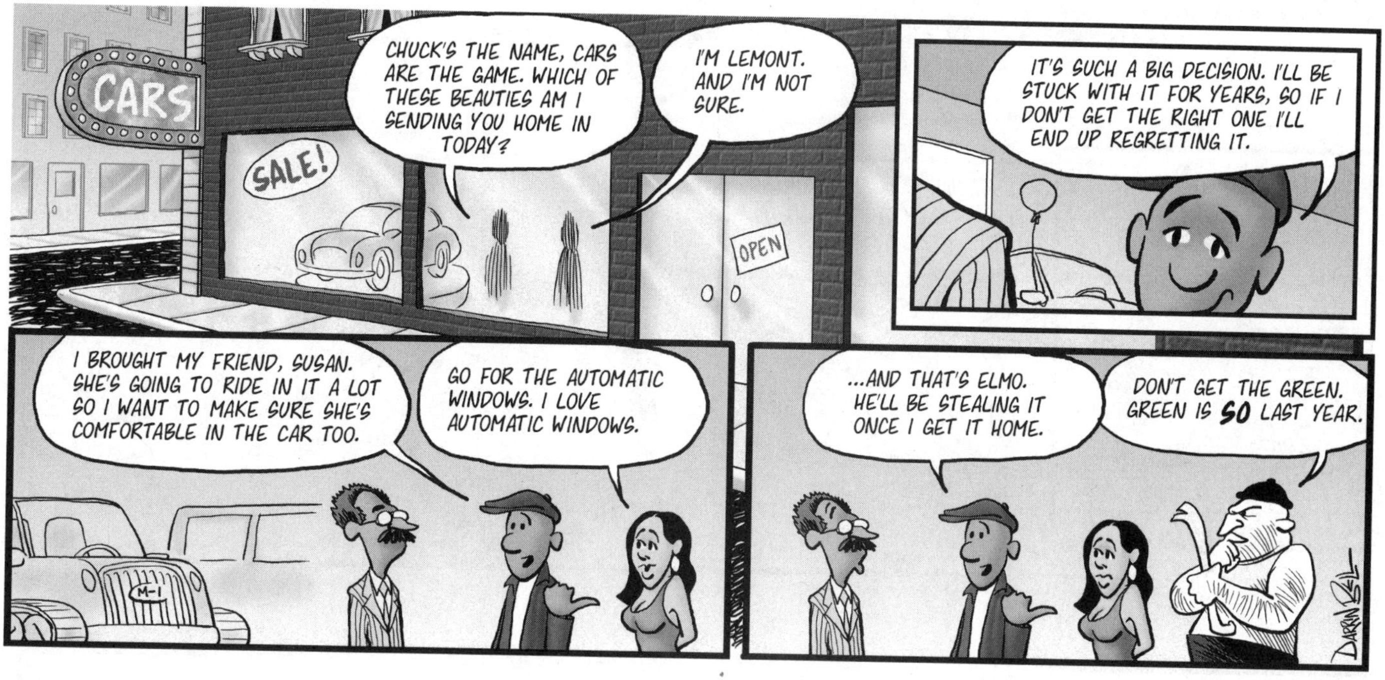
CARS
SALE!
OPEN
CHUCK'S THE NAME, CARS ARE THE GAME. WHICH OF THESE BEAUTIES AM I SENDING YOU HOME IN TODAY?
I'M LEMONT. AND I'M NOT SURE.
IT'S SUCH A BIG DECISION. I'LL BE STUCK WITH IT FOR YEARS, SO IF I DON'T GET THE RIGHT ONE I'LL END UP REGRETTING IT.
I BROUGHT MY FRIEND, SUSAN. SHE'S GOING TO RIDE IN IT A LOT SO I WANT TO MAKE SURE SHE'S COMFORTABLE IN THE CAR TOO.
GO FOR THE AUTOMATIC WINDOWS. I LOVE AUTOMATIC WINDOWS.
M-1
...AND THAT'S ELMO. HE'LL BE STEALING IT ONCE I GET IT HOME.
DON'T GET THE GREEN. GREEN IS **SO** LAST YEAR.
DARRIN BELL

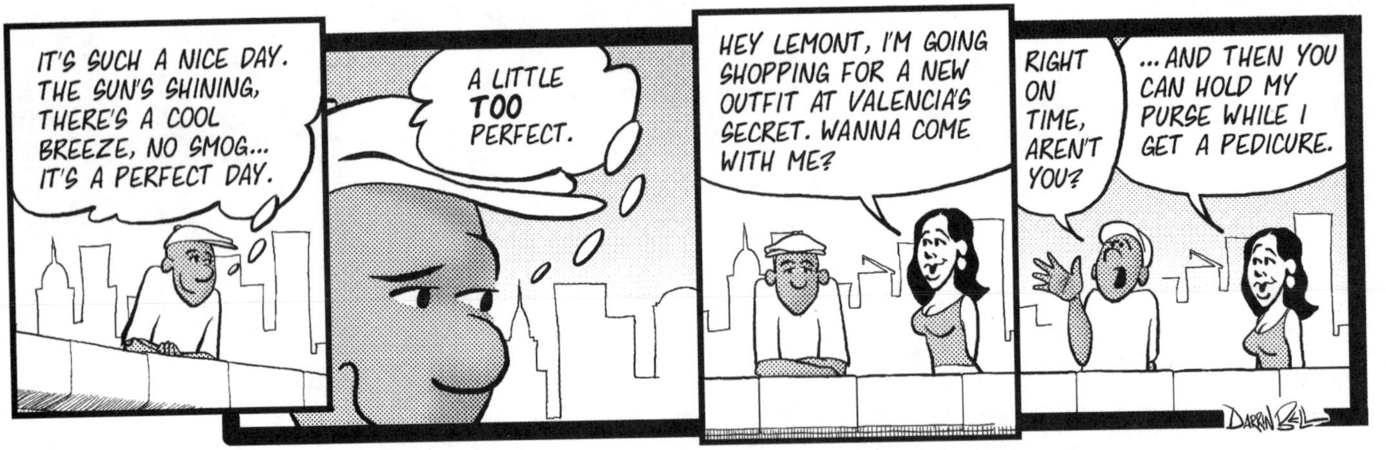
IT'S SUCH A NICE DAY. THE SUN'S SHINING, THERE'S A COOL BREEZE, NO SMOG... IT'S A PERFECT DAY.
A LITTLE **TOO** PERFECT.
HEY LEMONT, I'M GOING SHOPPING FOR A NEW OUTFIT AT VALENCIA'S SECRET. WANNA COME WITH ME?
RIGHT ON TIME, AREN'T YOU?
...AND THEN YOU CAN HOLD MY PURSE WHILE I GET A PEDICURE.
DARRIN BELL

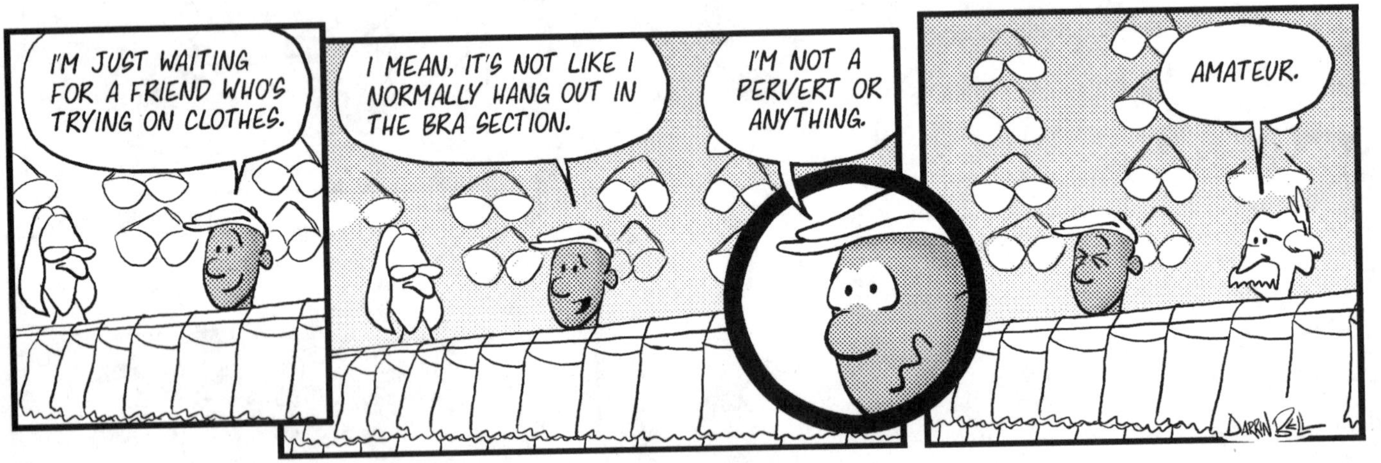
I'M JUST WAITING FOR A FRIEND WHO'S TRYING ON CLOTHES.
I MEAN, IT'S NOT LIKE I NORMALLY HANG OUT IN THE BRA SECTION.
I'M NOT A PERVERT OR ANYTHING.
AMATEUR.
DARRIN BELL

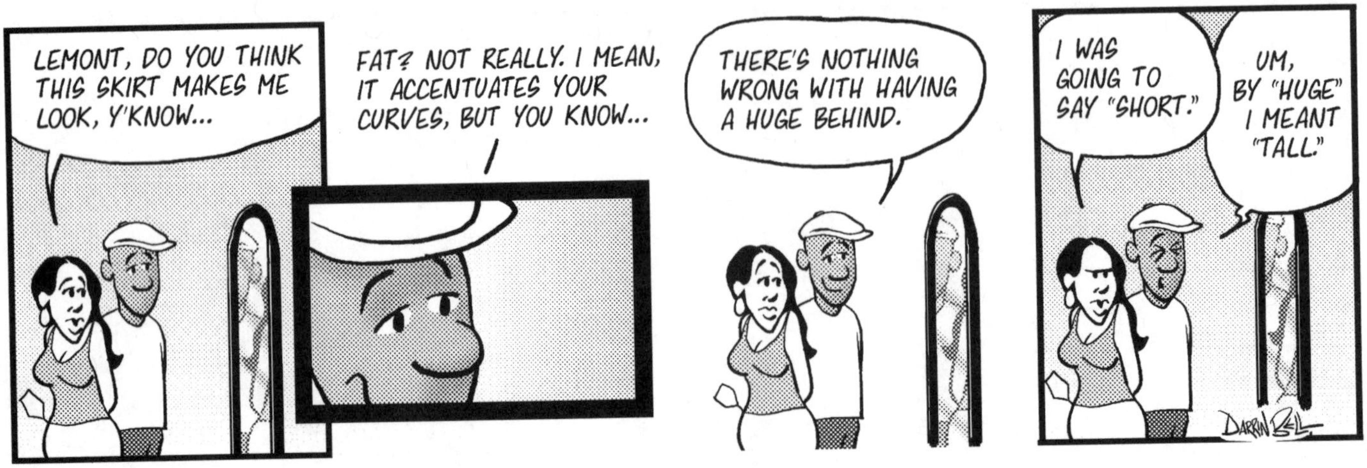
LEMONT, DO YOU THINK THIS SKIRT MAKES ME LOOK, Y'KNOW...
FAT? NOT REALLY. I MEAN, IT ACCENTUATES YOUR CURVES, BUT YOU KNOW...
THERE'S NOTHING WRONG WITH HAVING A HUGE BEHIND.
I WAS GOING TO SAY "SHORT."
UM, BY "HUGE" I MEANT "TALL."
DARRIN BELL

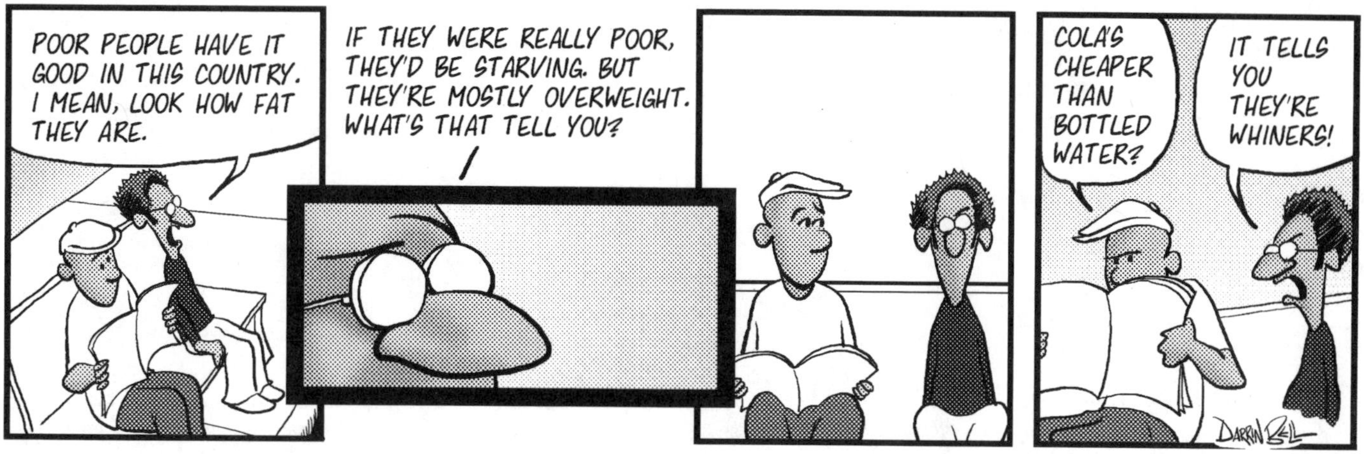
POOR PEOPLE HAVE IT GOOD IN THIS COUNTRY. I MEAN, LOOK HOW FAT THEY ARE.
IF THEY WERE REALLY POOR, THEY'D BE STARVING. BUT THEY'RE MOSTLY OVERWEIGHT. WHAT'S THAT TELL YOU?
COLA'S CHEAPER THAN BOTTLED WATER?
IT TELLS YOU THEY'RE WHINERS!
DARRIN BELL

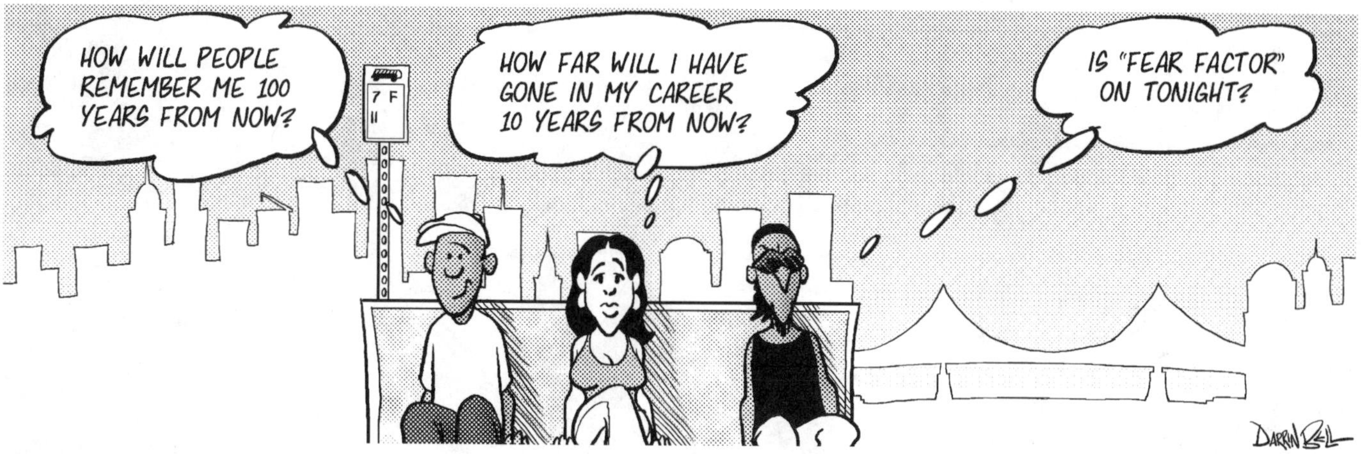
HOW WILL PEOPLE REMEMBER ME 100 YEARS FROM NOW?
7 F
HOW FAR WILL I HAVE GONE IN MY CAREER 10 YEARS FROM NOW?
IS "FEAR FACTOR" ON TONIGHT?
DARRIN BELL

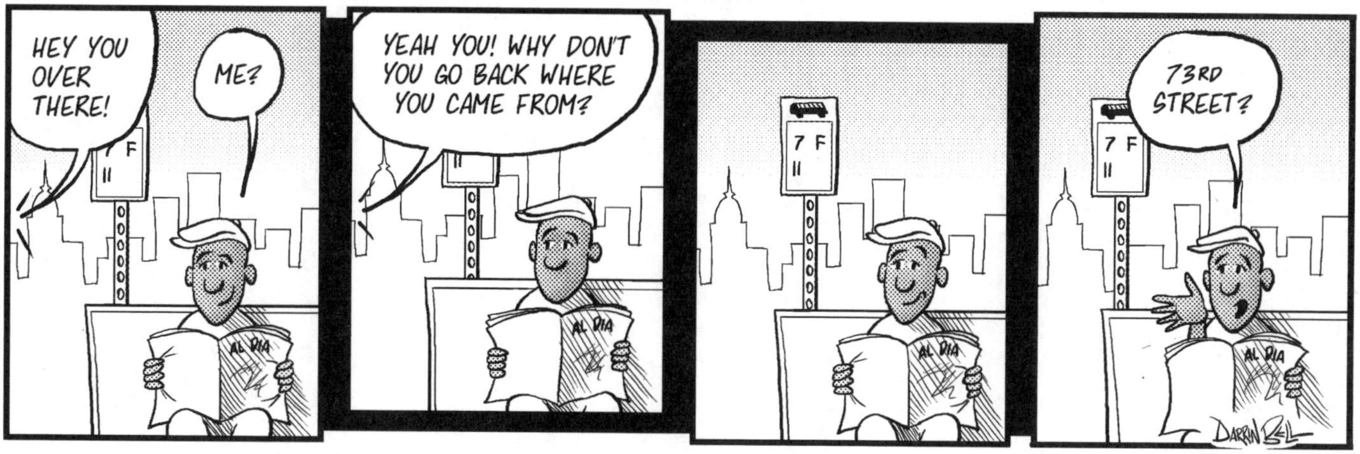
HEY YOU OVER THERE!
ME?
YEAH YOU! WHY DON'T YOU GO BACK WHERE YOU CAME FROM?
73RD STREET?
AL DIA
DARRIN BELL

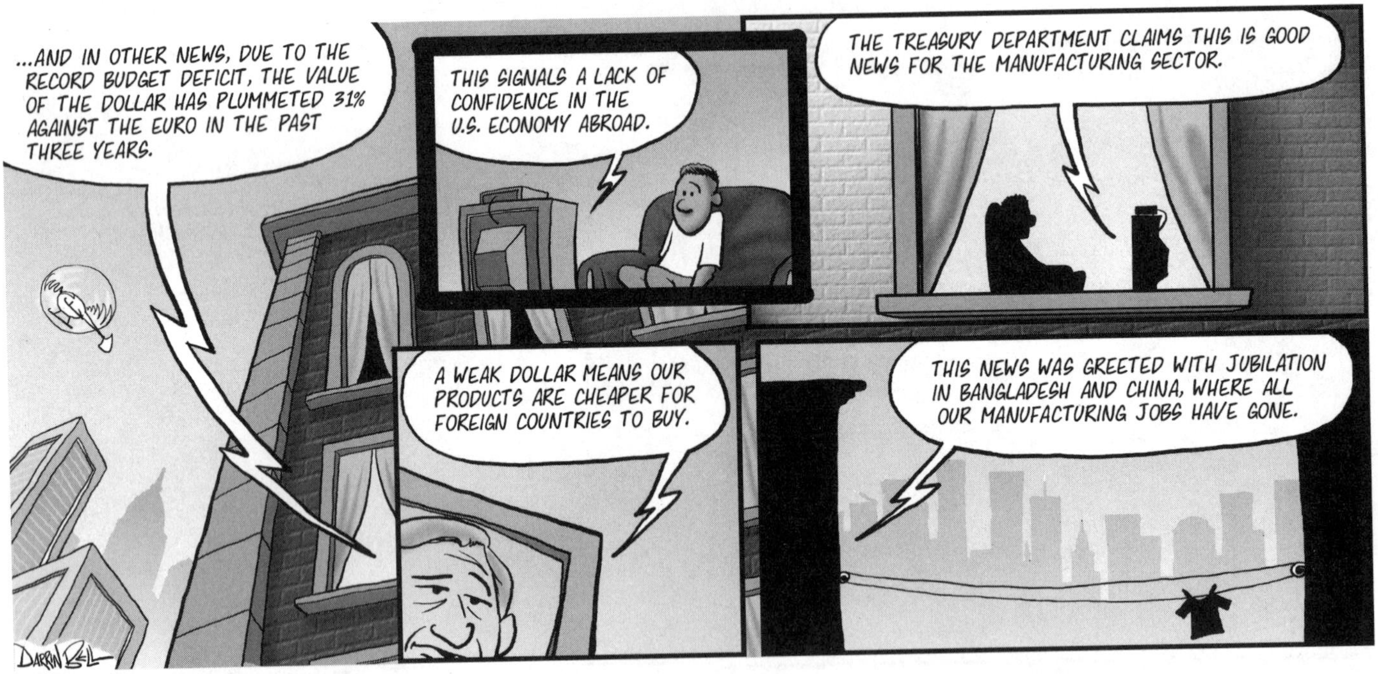
...AND IN OTHER NEWS, DUE TO THE RECORD BUDGET DEFICIT, THE VALUE OF THE DOLLAR HAS PLUMMETED 31% AGAINST THE EURO IN THE PAST THREE YEARS.
THIS SIGNALS A LACK OF CONFIDENCE IN THE U.S. ECONOMY ABROAD.
THE TREASURY DEPARTMENT CLAIMS THIS IS GOOD NEWS FOR THE MANUFACTURING SECTOR.
A WEAK DOLLAR MEANS OUR PRODUCTS ARE CHEAPER FOR FOREIGN COUNTRIES TO BUY.
THIS NEWS WAS GREETED WITH JUBILATION IN BANGLADESH AND CHINA, WHERE ALL OUR MANUFACTURING JOBS HAVE GONE.
DARRIN BELL

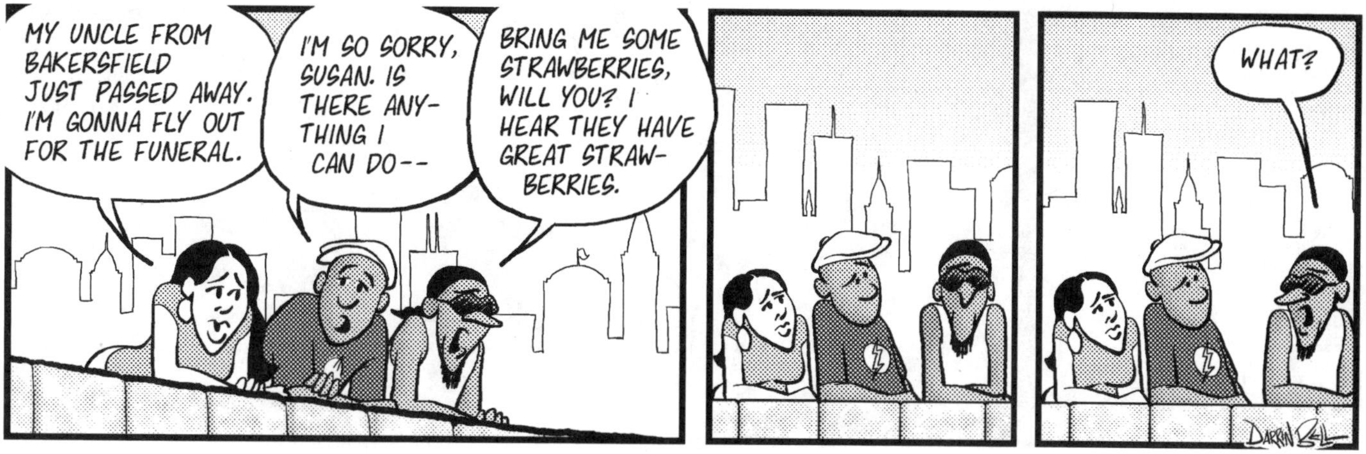
MY UNCLE FROM BAKERSFIELD JUST PASSED AWAY. I'M GONNA FLY OUT FOR THE FUNERAL.
I'M SO SORRY, SUSAN. IS THERE ANY-THING I CAN DO--
BRING ME SOME STRAWBERRIES, WILL YOU? I HEAR THEY HAVE GREAT STRAW-BERRIES.
WHAT?
DARRIN BELL

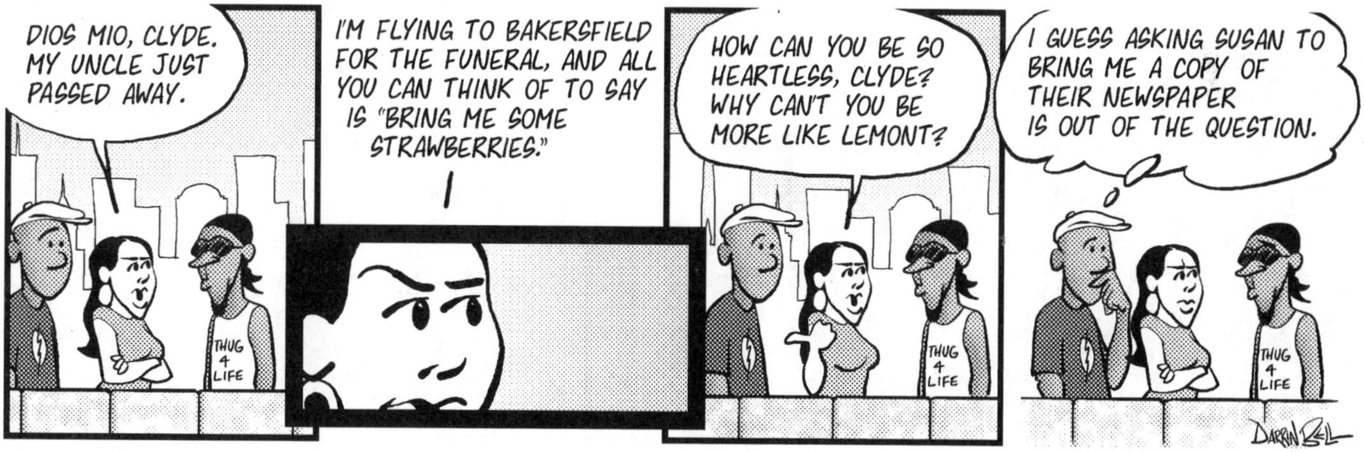
DIOS MIO, CLYDE. MY UNCLE JUST PASSED AWAY.
I'M FLYING TO BAKERSFIELD FOR THE FUNERAL, AND ALL YOU CAN THINK OF TO SAY IS "BRING ME SOME STRAWBERRIES."
HOW CAN YOU BE SO HEARTLESS, CLYDE? WHY CAN'T YOU BE MORE LIKE LEMONT?
I GUESS ASKING SUSAN TO BRING ME A COPY OF THEIR NEWSPAPER IS OUT OF THE QUESTION.
THUG 4 LIFE
DARRIN BELL

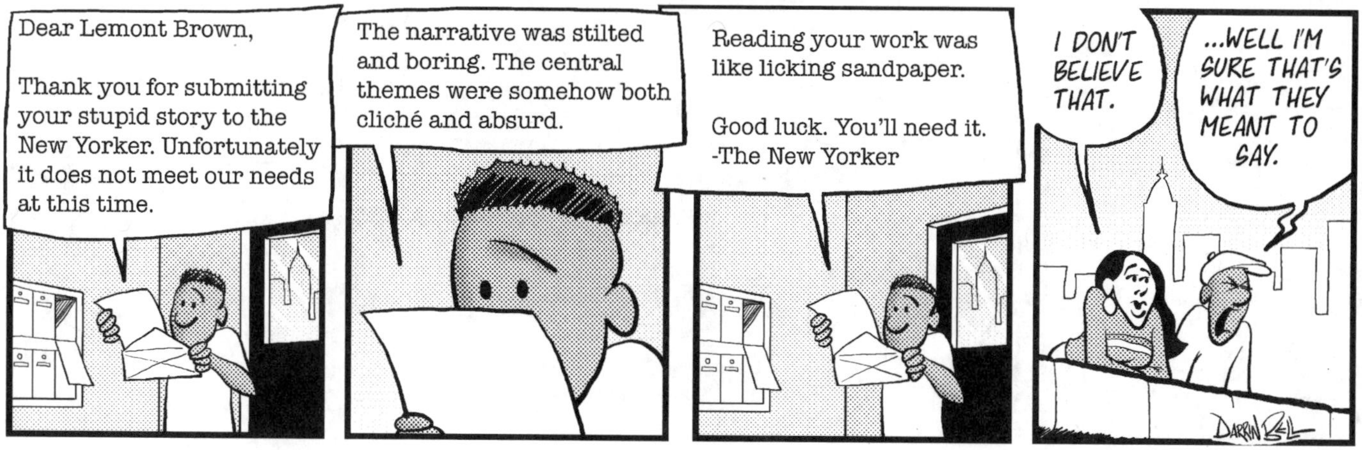
Dear Lemont Brown,
Thank you for submitting your stupid story to the New Yorker. Unfortunately it does not meet our needs at this time.
The narrative was stilted and boring. The central themes were somehow both cliché and absurd.
Reading your work was like licking sandpaper.
Good luck. You'll need it.
-The New Yorker
I DON'T BELIEVE THAT.
...WELL I'M SURE THAT'S WHAT THEY MEANT TO SAY.
DARRIN BELL

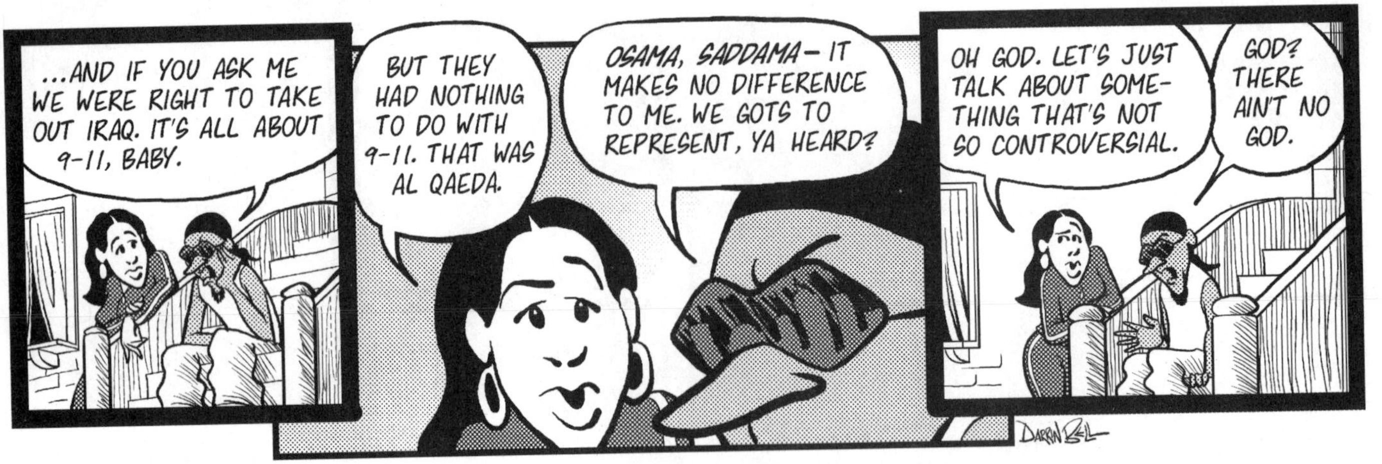
...AND IF YOU ASK ME WE WERE RIGHT TO TAKE OUT IRAQ. IT'S ALL ABOUT 9-11, BABY.
BUT THEY HAD NOTHING TO DO WITH 9-11. THAT WAS AL QAEDA.
OSAMA, SADDAMA— IT MAKES NO DIFFERENCE TO ME. WE GOTS TO REPRESENT, YA HEARD?
OH GOD. LET'S JUST TALK ABOUT SOME-THING THAT'S NOT SO CONTROVERSIAL.
GOD? THERE AIN'T NO GOD.
DARRIN BELL

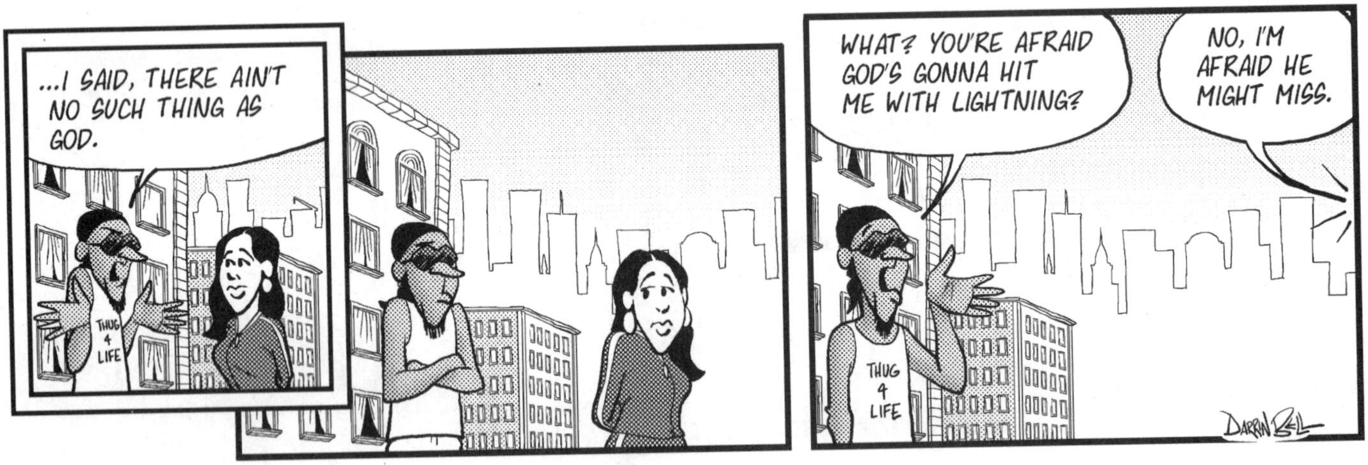
...I SAID, THERE AIN'T NO SUCH THING AS GOD.
THUG 4 LIFE
WHAT? YOU'RE AFRAID GOD'S GONNA HIT ME WITH LIGHTNING?
NO, I'M AFRAID HE MIGHT MISS.
THUG 4 LIFE
DARRIN BELL

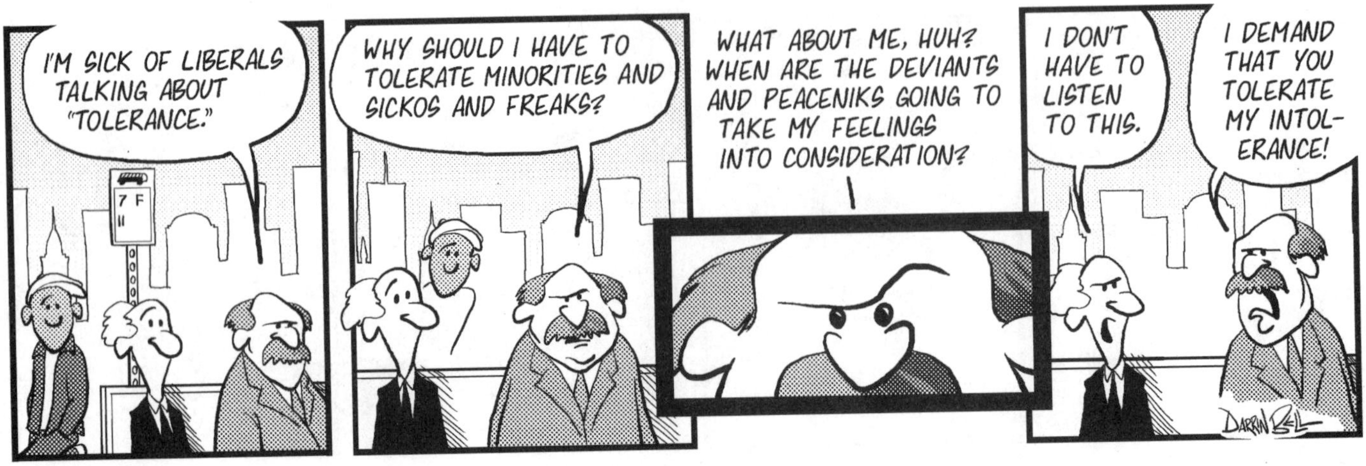
I'M SICK OF LIBERALS TALKING ABOUT "TOLERANCE."
7 F
WHY SHOULD I HAVE TO TOLERATE MINORITIES AND SICKOS AND FREAKS?
WHAT ABOUT ME, HUH? WHEN ARE THE DEVIANTS AND PEACENIKS GOING TO TAKE MY FEELINGS INTO CONSIDERATION?
I DON'T HAVE TO LISTEN TO THIS.
I DEMAND THAT YOU TOLERATE MY INTOL-ERANCE!
DARRIN BELL

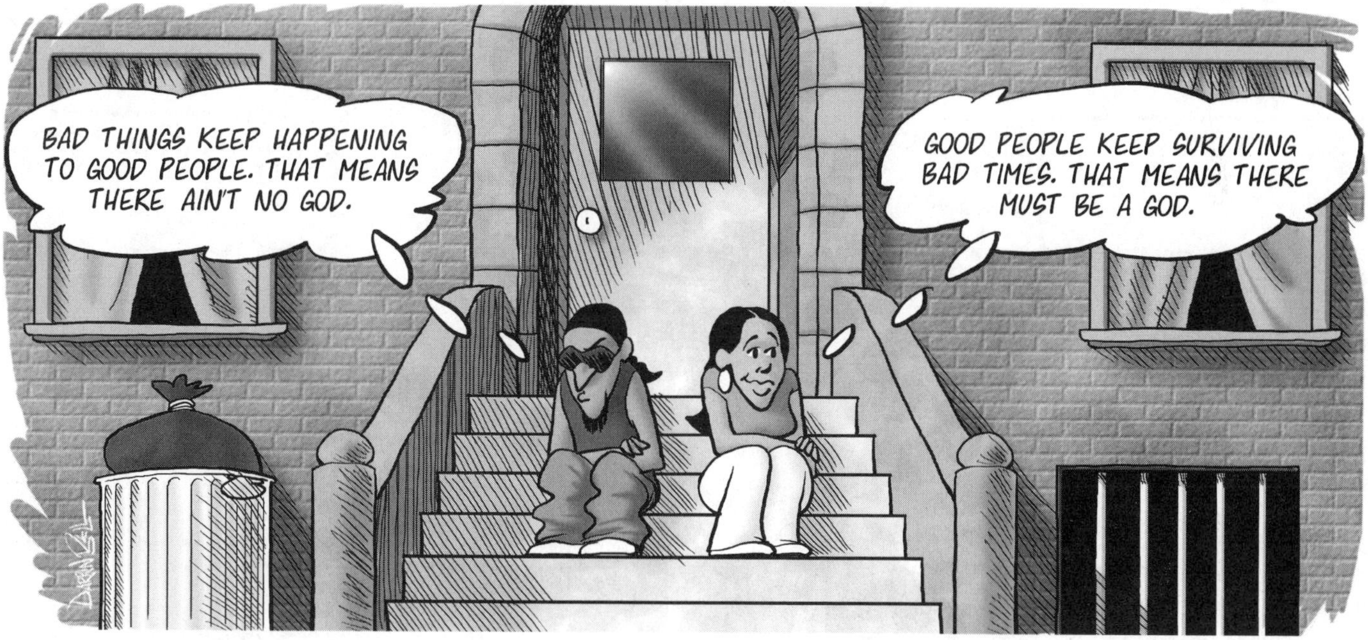
BAD THINGS KEEP HAPPENING TO GOOD PEOPLE. THAT MEANS THERE AIN'T NO GOD.
GOOD PEOPLE KEEP SURVIVING BAD TIMES. THAT MEANS THERE MUST BE A GOD.

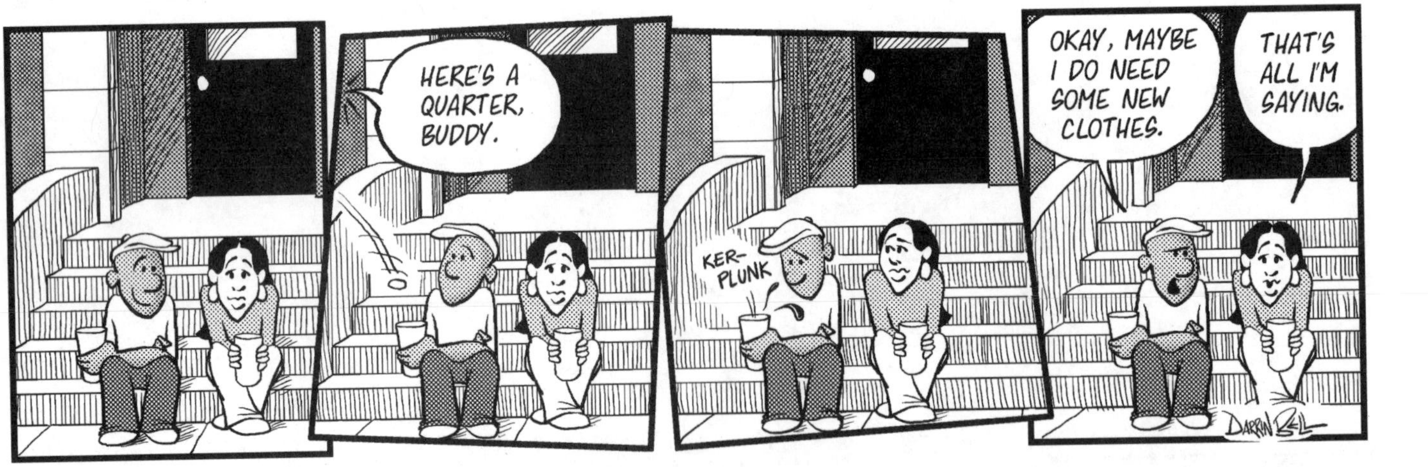
HERE'S A QUARTER, BUDDY.
KER-PLUNK
OKAY, MAYBE I DO NEED SOME NEW CLOTHES.
THAT'S ALL I'M SAYING.
DARRIN BELL

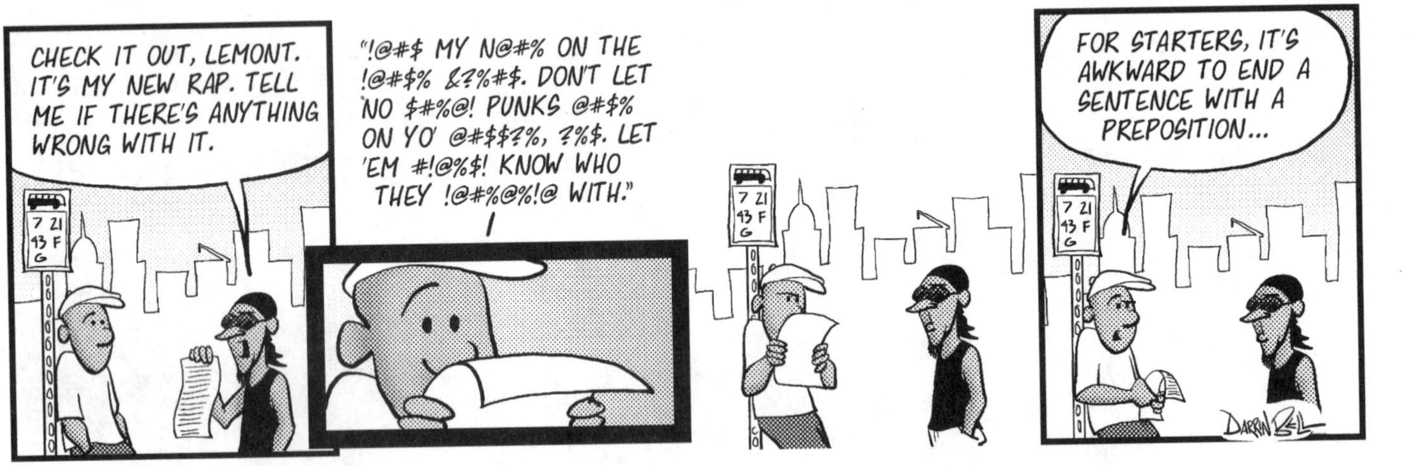
CHECK IT OUT, LEMONT. IT'S MY NEW RAP. TELL ME IF THERE'S ANYTHING WRONG WITH IT.
"!@#$ MY N@#% ON THE !@#$% &?%#$. DON'T LET NO $#%@! PUNKS @#$% ON YO' @#$$?%, ?%$. LET 'EM #!@%$! KNOW WHO THEY !@#%@%!@ WITH."
FOR STARTERS, IT'S AWKWARD TO END A SENTENCE WITH A PREPOSITION...
DARRIN BELL

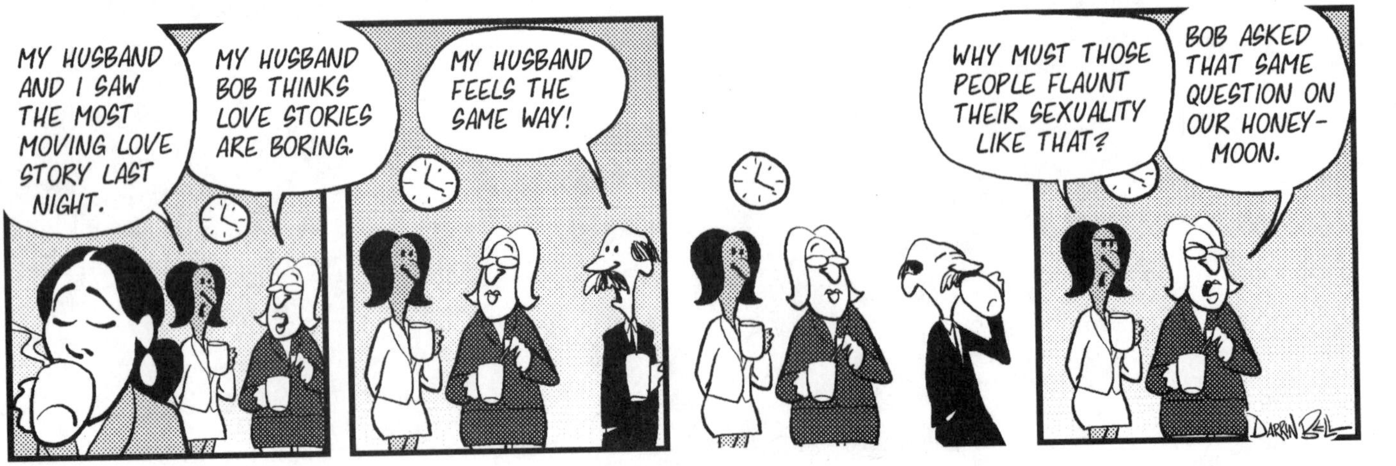
MY HUSBAND AND I SAW THE MOST MOVING LOVE STORY LAST NIGHT.
MY HUSBAND BOB THINKS LOVE STORIES ARE BORING.
MY HUSBAND FEELS THE SAME WAY!
WHY MUST THOSE PEOPLE FLAUNT THEIR SEXUALITY LIKE THAT?
BOB ASKED THAT SAME QUESTION ON OUR HONEY-MOON.
DARRIN BELL

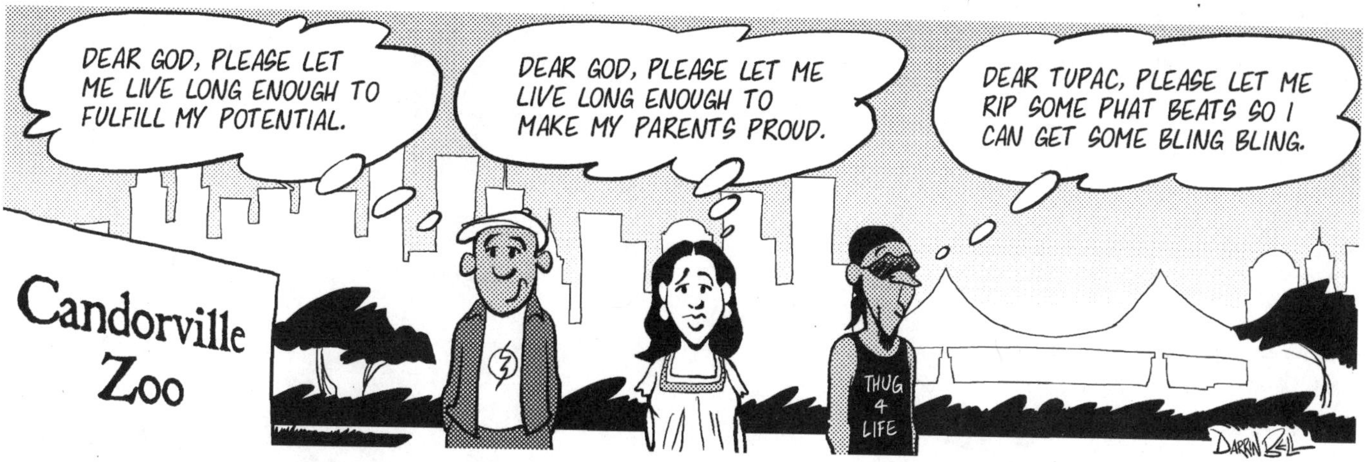
DEAR GOD, PLEASE LET ME LIVE LONG ENOUGH TO FULFILL MY POTENTIAL.
DEAR GOD, PLEASE LET ME LIVE LONG ENOUGH TO MAKE MY PARENTS PROUD.
DEAR TUPAC, PLEASE LET ME RIP SOME PHAT BEATS SO I CAN GET SOME BLING BLING.
Candorville Zoo
THUG 4 LIFE
DARRIN BELL

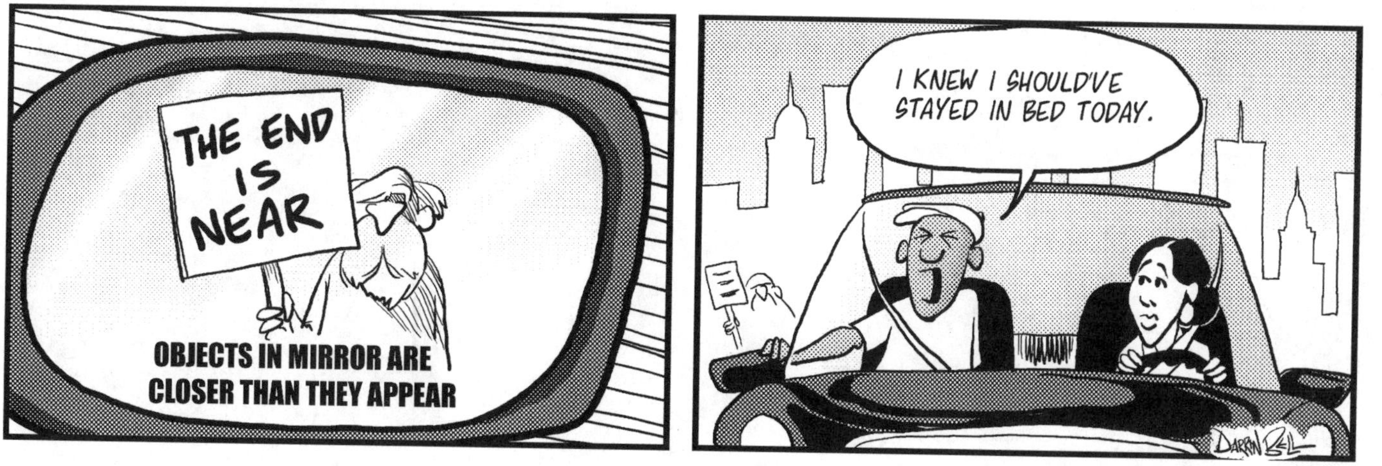
THE END IS NEAR
OBJECTS IN MIRROR ARE CLOSER THAN THEY APPEAR
I KNEW I SHOULD'VE STAYED IN BED TODAY.
DARRIN BELL

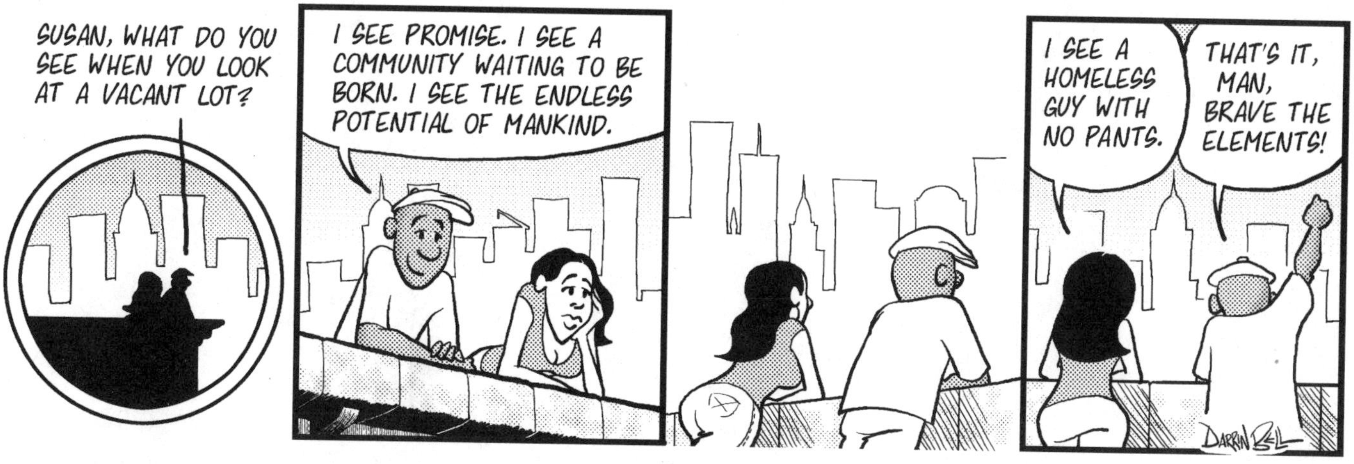
SUSAN, WHAT DO YOU SEE WHEN YOU LOOK AT A VACANT LOT?
I SEE PROMISE. I SEE A COMMUNITY WAITING TO BE BORN. I SEE THE ENDLESS POTENTIAL OF MANKIND.
I SEE A HOMELESS GUY WITH NO PANTS.
THAT'S IT, MAN, BRAVE THE ELEMENTS!
DARRIN BELL

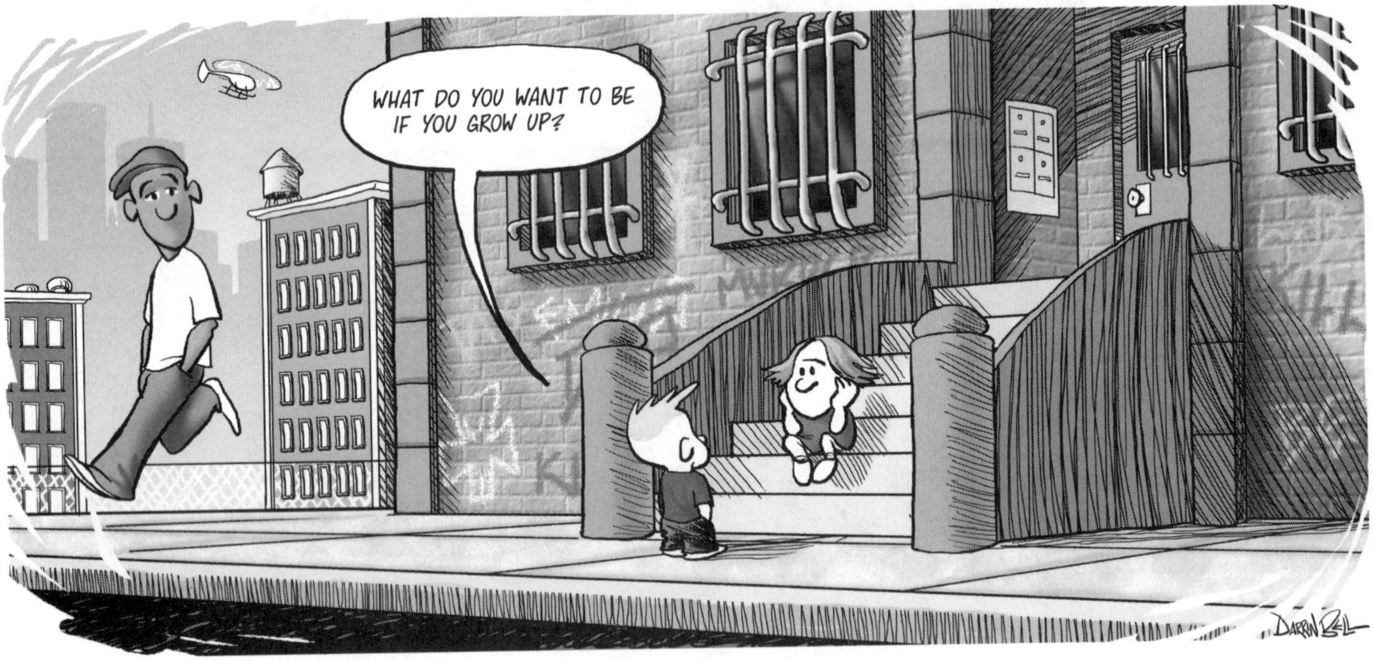
WHAT DO YOU WANT TO BE IF YOU GROW UP?
DARRIN BELL

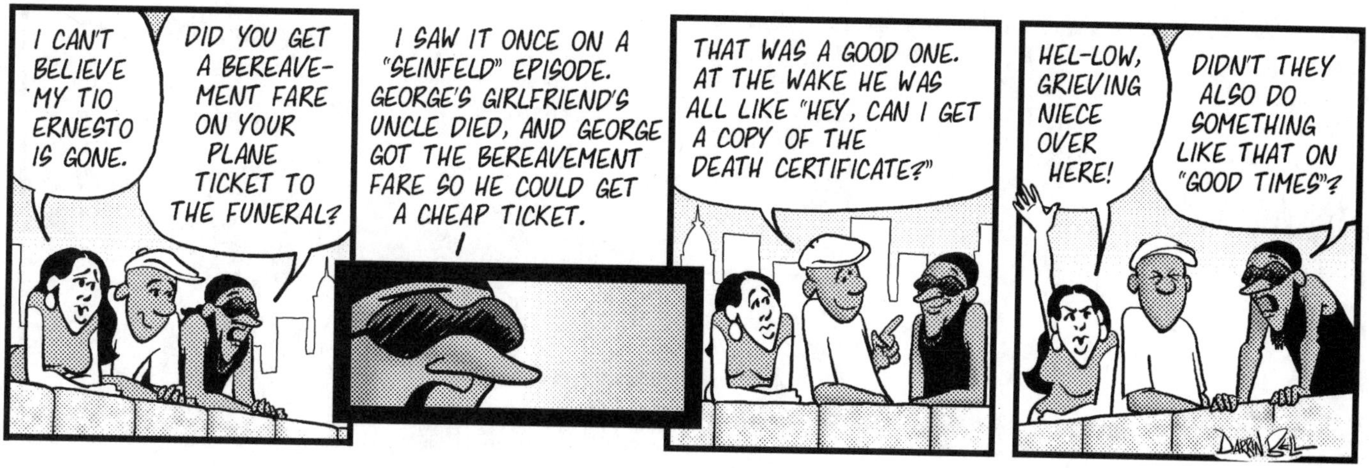
I CAN'T BELIEVE MY TIO ERNESTO IS GONE.
DID YOU GET A BEREAVEMENT FARE ON YOUR PLANE TICKET TO THE FUNERAL?
I SAW IT ONCE ON A "SEINFELD" EPISODE. GEORGE'S GIRLFRIEND'S UNCLE DIED, AND GEORGE GOT THE BEREAVEMENT FARE SO HE COULD GET A CHEAP TICKET.
THAT WAS A GOOD ONE. AT THE WAKE HE WAS ALL LIKE "HEY, CAN I GET A COPY OF THE DEATH CERTIFICATE?"
HEL-LOW, GRIEVING NIECE OVER HERE!
DIDN'T THEY ALSO DO SOMETHING LIKE THAT ON "GOOD TIMES"?
DARRIN BELL

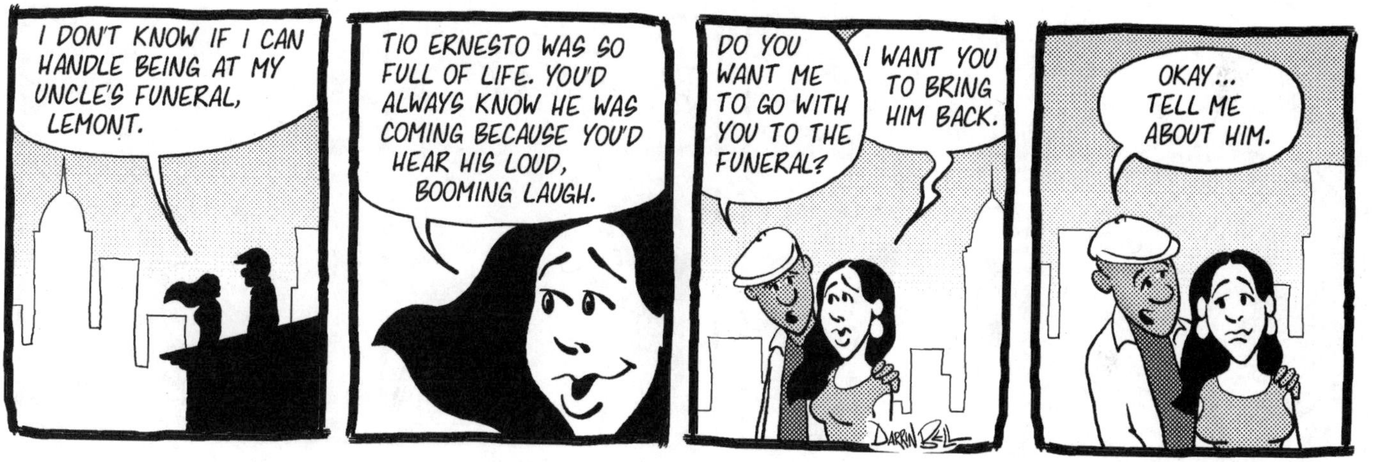
I DON'T KNOW IF I CAN HANDLE BEING AT MY UNCLE'S FUNERAL, LEMONT.
TIO ERNESTO WAS SO FULL OF LIFE. YOU'D ALWAYS KNOW HE WAS COMING BECAUSE YOU'D HEAR HIS LOUD, BOOMING LAUGH.
DO YOU WANT ME TO GO WITH YOU TO THE FUNERAL?
I WANT YOU TO BRING HIM BACK.
DARRIN BELL
OKAY... TELL ME ABOUT HIM.

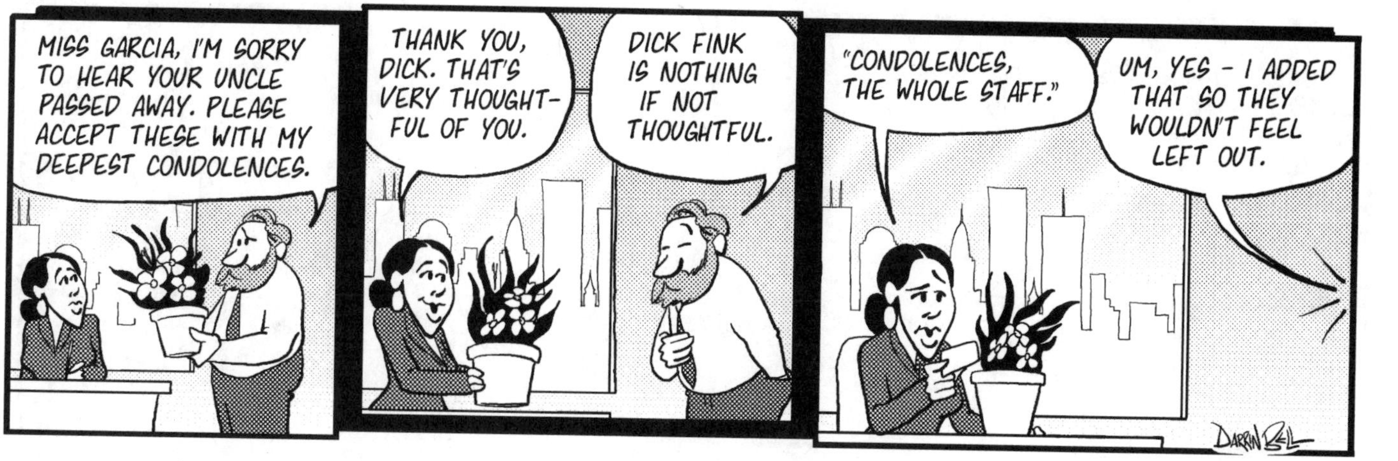
MISS GARCIA, I'M SORRY TO HEAR YOUR UNCLE PASSED AWAY. PLEASE ACCEPT THESE WITH MY DEEPEST CONDOLENCES.
THANK YOU, DICK. THAT'S VERY THOUGHTFUL OF YOU.
DICK FINK IS NOTHING IF NOT THOUGHTFUL.
"CONDOLENCES, THE WHOLE STAFF."
UM, YES - I ADDED THAT SO THEY WOULDN'T FEEL LEFT OUT.
DARRIN BELL

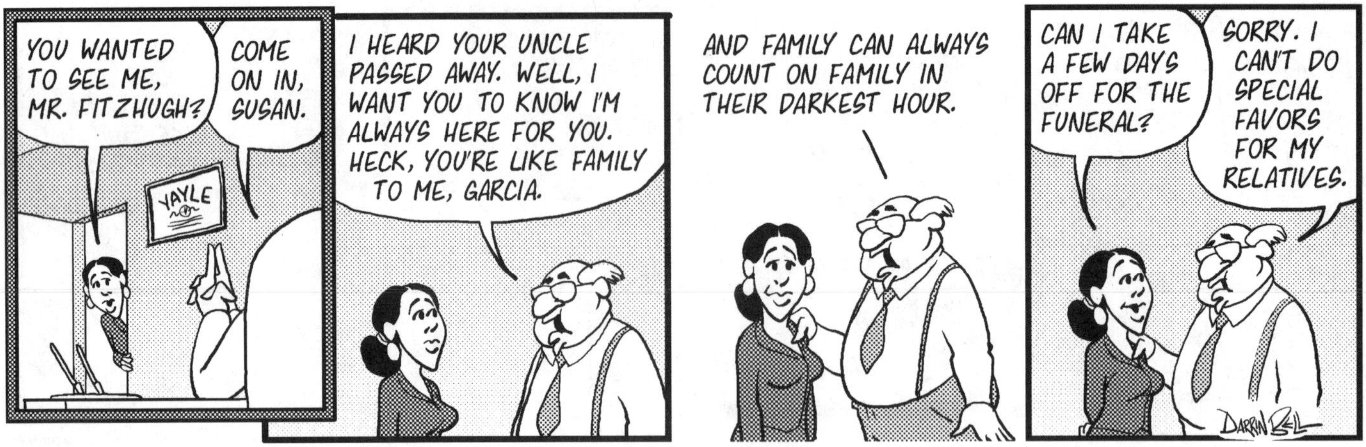
YOU WANTED TO SEE ME, MR. FITZHUGH?
COME ON IN, SUSAN.
YAYLE
I HEARD YOUR UNCLE PASSED AWAY. WELL, I WANT YOU TO KNOW I'M ALWAYS HERE FOR YOU. HECK, YOU'RE LIKE FAMILY TO ME, GARCIA.
AND FAMILY CAN ALWAYS COUNT ON FAMILY IN THEIR DARKEST HOUR.
CAN I TAKE A FEW DAYS OFF FOR THE FUNERAL?
SORRY. I CAN'T DO SPECIAL FAVORS FOR MY RELATIVES.
DARRIN BELL

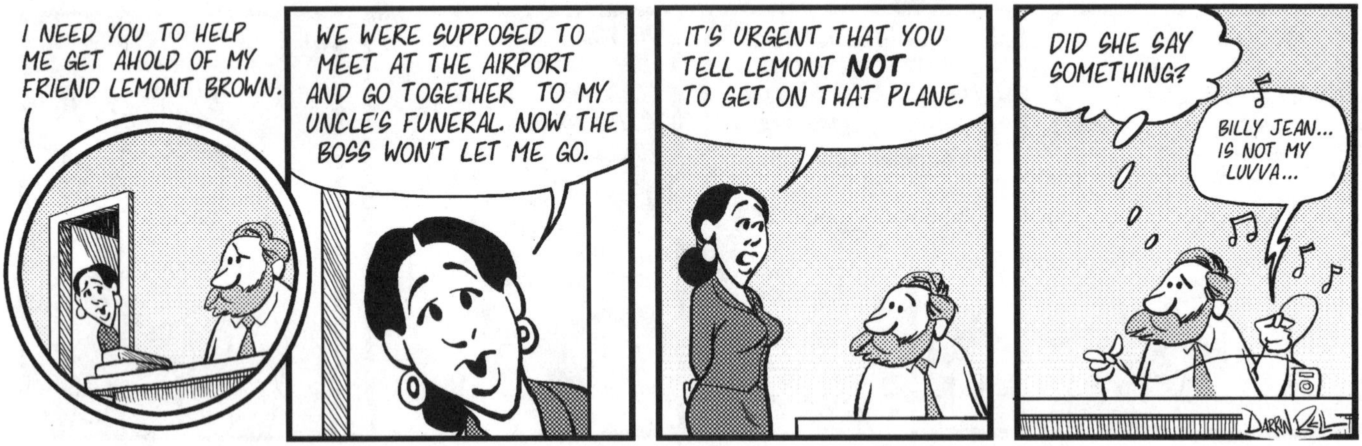
I NEED YOU TO HELP ME GET AHOLD OF MY FRIEND LEMONT BROWN.
WE WERE SUPPOSED TO MEET AT THE AIRPORT AND GO TOGETHER TO MY UNCLE'S FUNERAL. NOW THE BOSS WON'T LET ME GO.
IT'S URGENT THAT YOU TELL LEMONT **NOT** TO GET ON THAT PLANE.
DID SHE SAY SOMETHING?
BILLY JEAN... IS NOT MY LUVVA...
DARRIN BELL

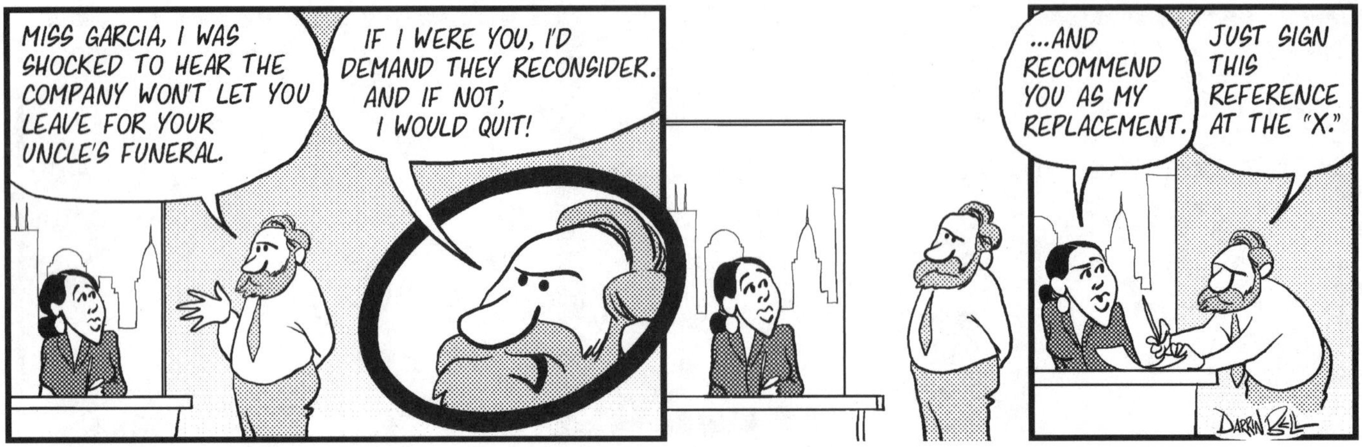
MISS GARCIA, I WAS SHOCKED TO HEAR THE COMPANY WON'T LET YOU LEAVE FOR YOUR UNCLE'S FUNERAL.
IF I WERE YOU, I'D DEMAND THEY RECONSIDER. AND IF NOT, I WOULD QUIT!
...AND RECOMMEND YOU AS MY REPLACEMENT.
JUST SIGN THIS REFERENCE AT THE "X."
DARRIN BELL

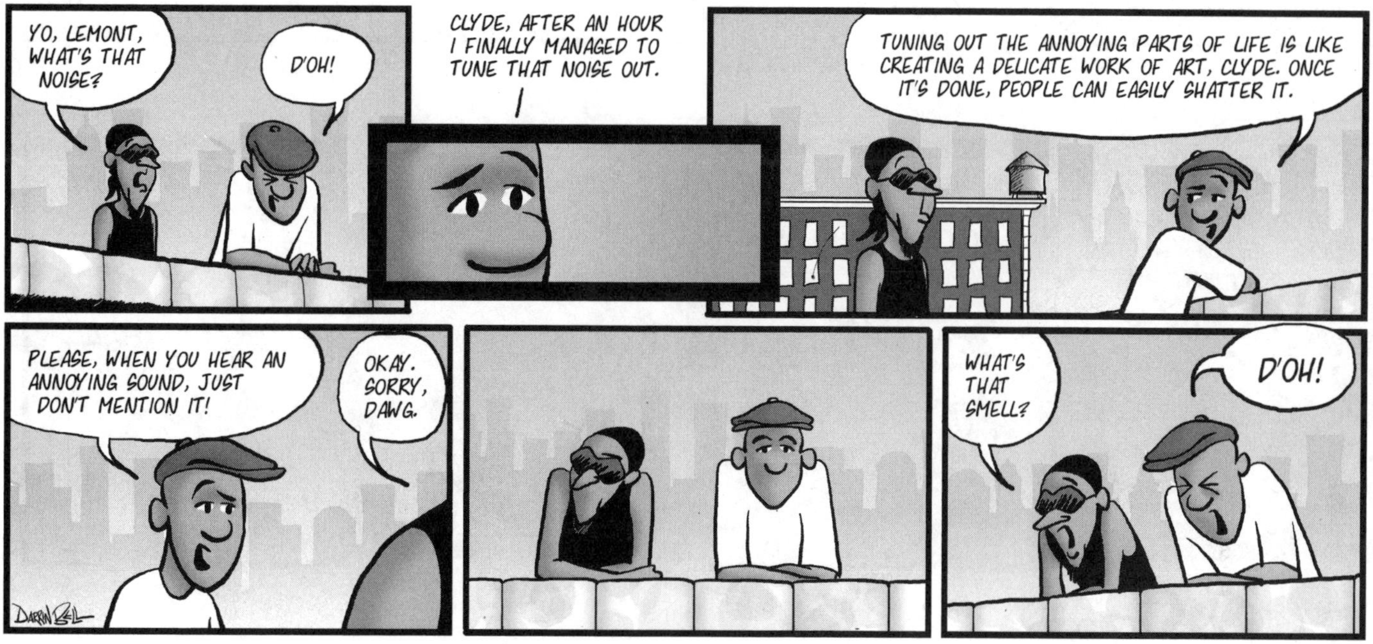
YO, LEMONT, WHAT'S THAT NOISE?
D'OH!
CLYDE, AFTER AN HOUR I FINALLY MANAGED TO TUNE THAT NOISE OUT.
TUNING OUT THE ANNOYING PARTS OF LIFE IS LIKE CREATING A DELICATE WORK OF ART, CLYDE. ONCE IT'S DONE, PEOPLE CAN EASILY SHATTER IT.
PLEASE, WHEN YOU HEAR AN ANNOYING SOUND, JUST DON'T MENTION IT!
OKAY. SORRY, DAWG.
WHAT'S THAT SMELL?
D'OH!
DARRIN BELL

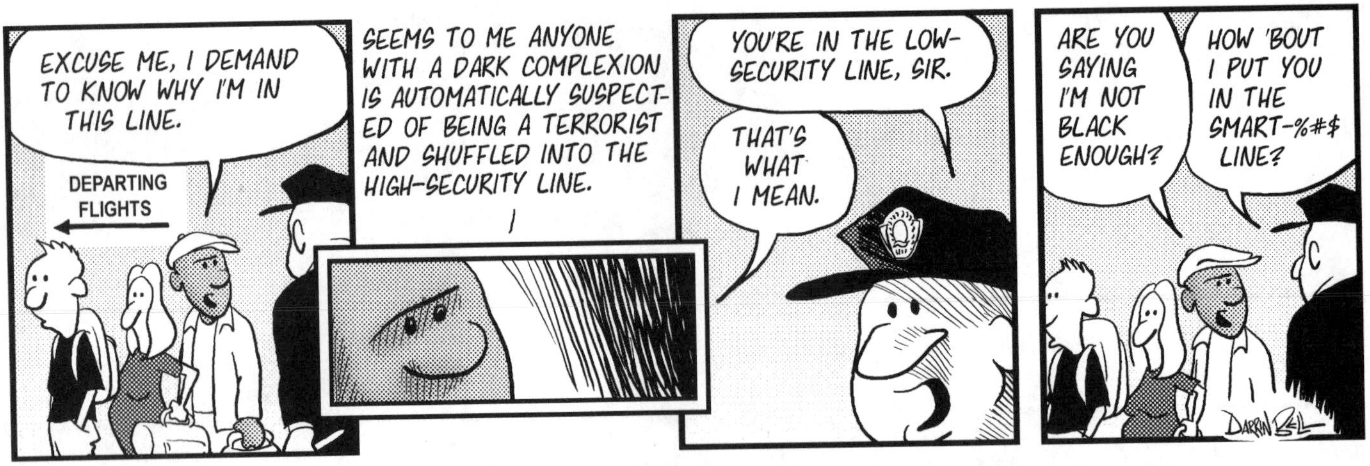
EXCUSE ME, I DEMAND TO KNOW WHY I'M IN THIS LINE.
DEPARTING FLIGHTS
SEEMS TO ME ANYONE WITH A DARK COMPLEXION IS AUTOMATICALLY SUSPECTED OF BEING A TERRORIST AND SHUFFLED INTO THE HIGH-SECURITY LINE.
YOU'RE IN THE LOW-SECURITY LINE, SIR.
THAT'S WHAT I MEAN.
ARE YOU SAYING I'M NOT BLACK ENOUGH?
HOW 'BOUT I PUT YOU IN THE SMART-%#$ LINE?
DARRIN BELL

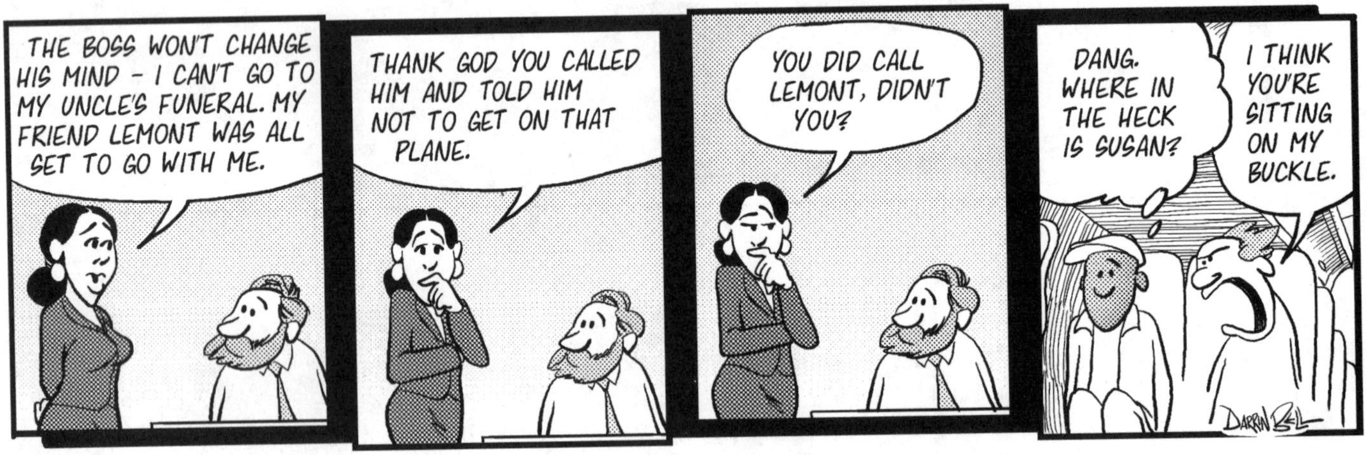
THE BOSS WON'T CHANGE HIS MIND - I CAN'T GO TO MY UNCLE'S FUNERAL. MY FRIEND LEMONT WAS ALL SET TO GO WITH ME.
THANK GOD YOU CALLED HIM AND TOLD HIM NOT TO GET ON THAT PLANE.
YOU DID CALL LEMONT, DIDN'T YOU?
DANG. WHERE IN THE HECK IS SUSAN?
I THINK YOU'RE SITTING ON MY BUCKLE.
DARRIN BELL

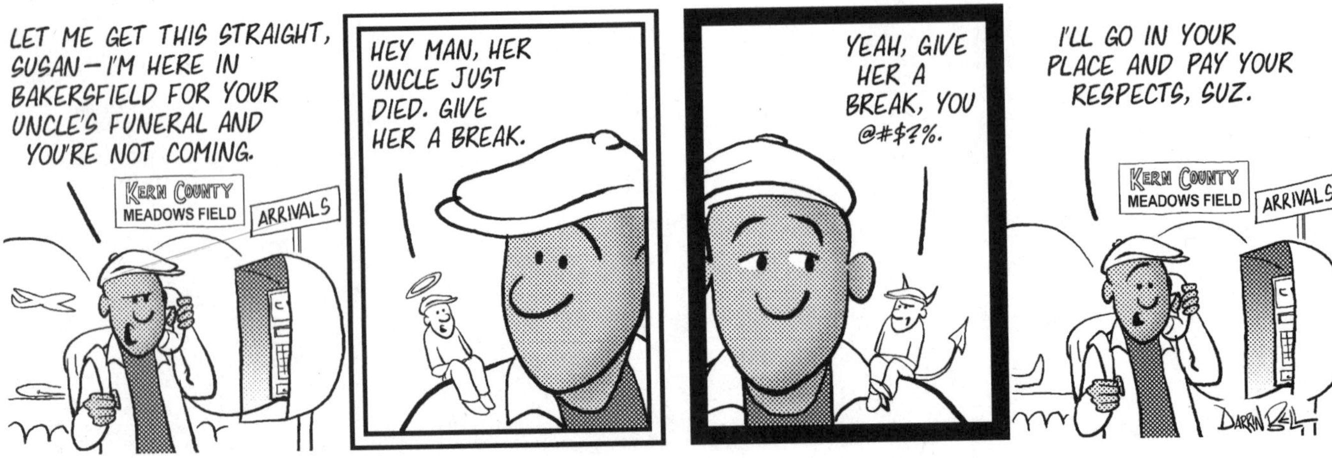
LET ME GET THIS STRAIGHT, SUSAN—I'M HERE IN BAKERSFIELD FOR YOUR UNCLE'S FUNERAL AND YOU'RE NOT COMING.
KERN COUNTY MEADOWS FIELD
ARRIVALS
HEY MAN, HER UNCLE JUST DIED. GIVE HER A BREAK.
YEAH, GIVE HER A BREAK, YOU @#$?%.
I'LL GO IN YOUR PLACE AND PAY YOUR RESPECTS, SUZ.
KERN COUNTY MEADOWS FIELD
ARRIVALS
DARRIN BELL

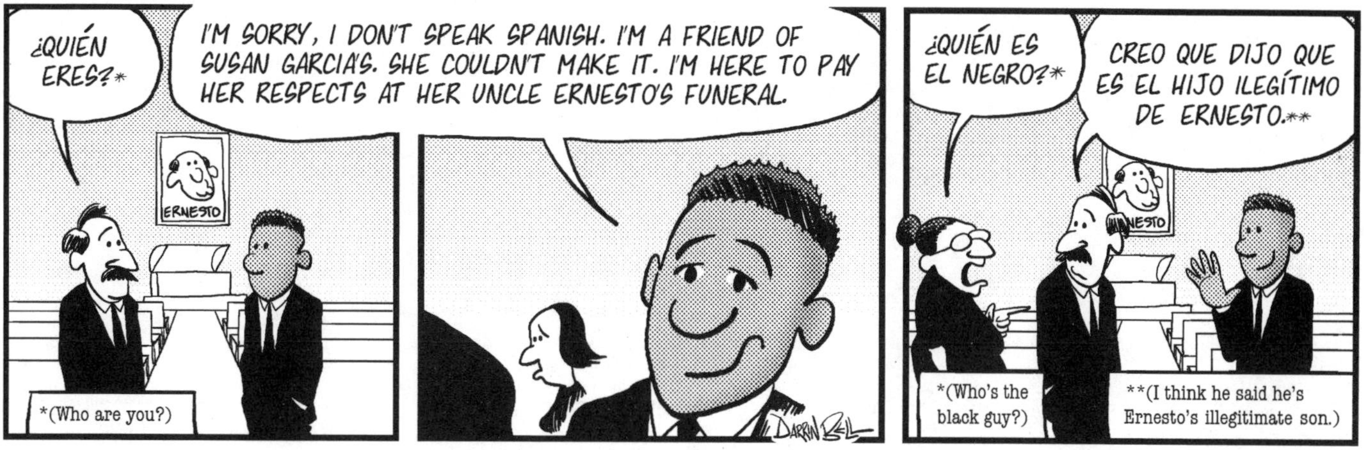
¿QUIÉN ERES?*
I'M SORRY, I DON'T SPEAK SPANISH. I'M A FRIEND OF SUSAN GARCIA'S. SHE COULDN'T MAKE IT. I'M HERE TO PAY HER RESPECTS AT HER UNCLE ERNESTO'S FUNERAL.
ERNESTO
*(Who are you?)
¿QUIÉN ES EL NEGRO?*
CREO QUE DIJO QUE ES EL HIJO ILEGÍTIMO DE ERNESTO.**
*(Who's the black guy?)
**(I think he said he's Ernesto's illegitimate son.)
DARRIN BELL

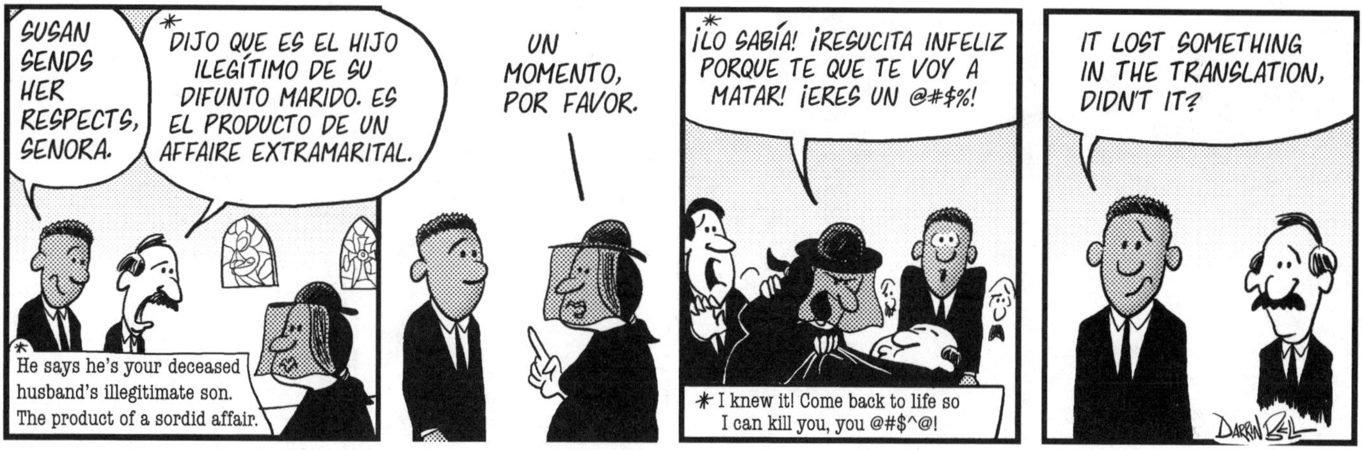
SUSAN SENDS HER RESPECTS, SENORA.
*DIJO QUE ES EL HIJO ILEGÍTIMO DE SU DIFUNTO MARIDO. ES EL PRODUCTO DE UN AFFAIRE EXTRAMARITAL.
*He says he's your deceased husband's illegitimate son. The product of a sordid affair.
UN MOMENTO, POR FAVOR.
*¡LO SABÍA! ¡RESUCITA INFELIZ PORQUE TE QUE TE VOY A MATAR! ¡ERES UN @#$%!
* I knew it! Come back to life so I can kill you, you @#$^@!
IT LOST SOMETHING IN THE TRANSLATION, DIDN'T IT?
DARRIN BELL

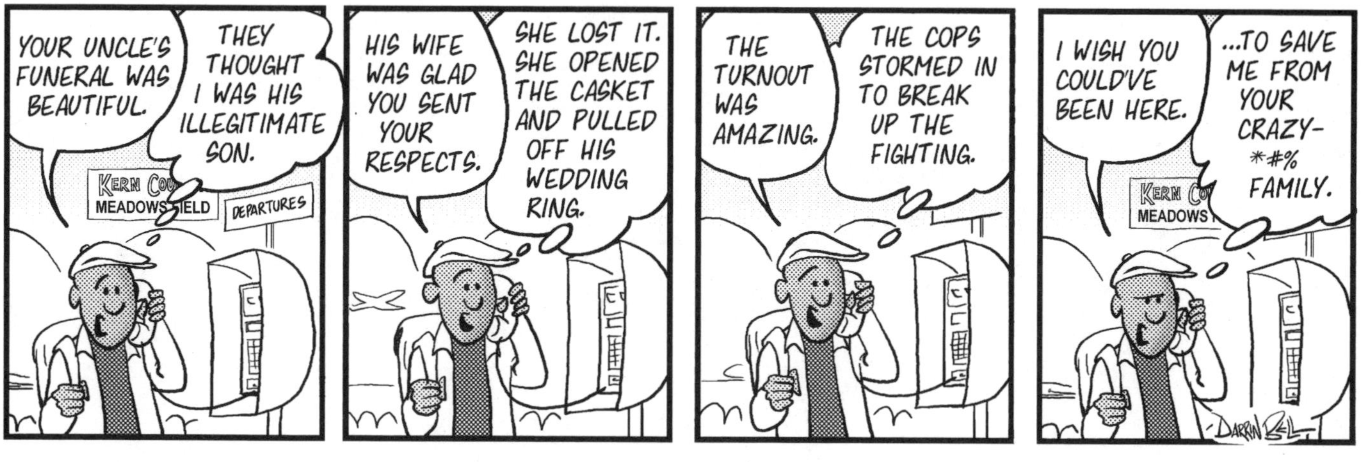
YOUR UNCLE'S FUNERAL WAS BEAUTIFUL.
THEY THOUGHT I WAS HIS ILLEGITIMATE SON.
DEPARTURES
HIS WIFE WAS GLAD YOU SENT YOUR RESPECTS.
SHE LOST IT. SHE OPENED THE CASKET AND PULLED OFF HIS WEDDING RING.
THE TURNOUT WAS AMAZING.
THE COPS STORMED IN TO BREAK UP THE FIGHTING.
I WISH YOU COULD'VE BEEN HERE.
...TO SAVE ME FROM YOUR CRAZY-*#% FAMILY.
DARRIN BELL

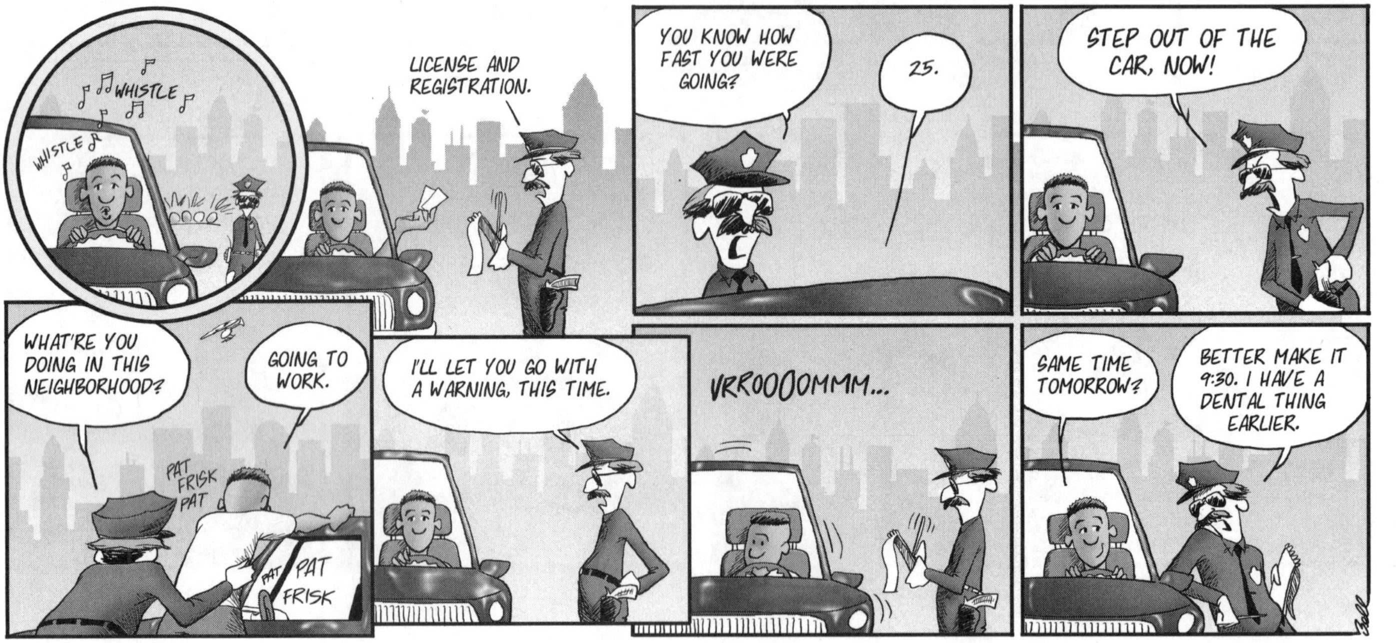
WHISTLE
WHISTLE
LICENSE AND REGISTRATION.
YOU KNOW HOW FAST YOU WERE GOING?
25.
STEP OUT OF THE CAR, NOW!
WHAT'RE YOU DOING IN THIS NEIGHBORHOOD?
GOING TO WORK.
PAT FRISK PAT
PAT PAT FRISK
I'LL LET YOU GO WITH A WARNING, THIS TIME.
VRROOOOMMM...
SAME TIME TOMORROW?
BETTER MAKE IT 9:30. I HAVE A DENTAL THING EARLIER.

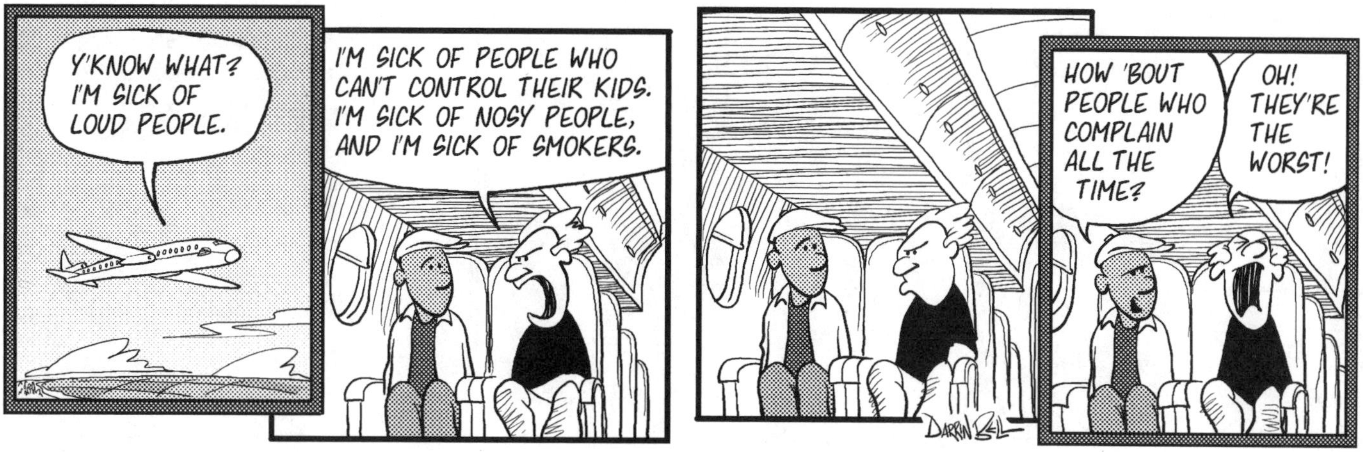
Y'KNOW WHAT? I'M SICK OF LOUD PEOPLE.
I'M SICK OF PEOPLE WHO CAN'T CONTROL THEIR KIDS. I'M SICK OF NOSY PEOPLE, AND I'M SICK OF SMOKERS.
HOW 'BOUT PEOPLE WHO COMPLAIN ALL THE TIME?
OH! THEY'RE THE WORST!

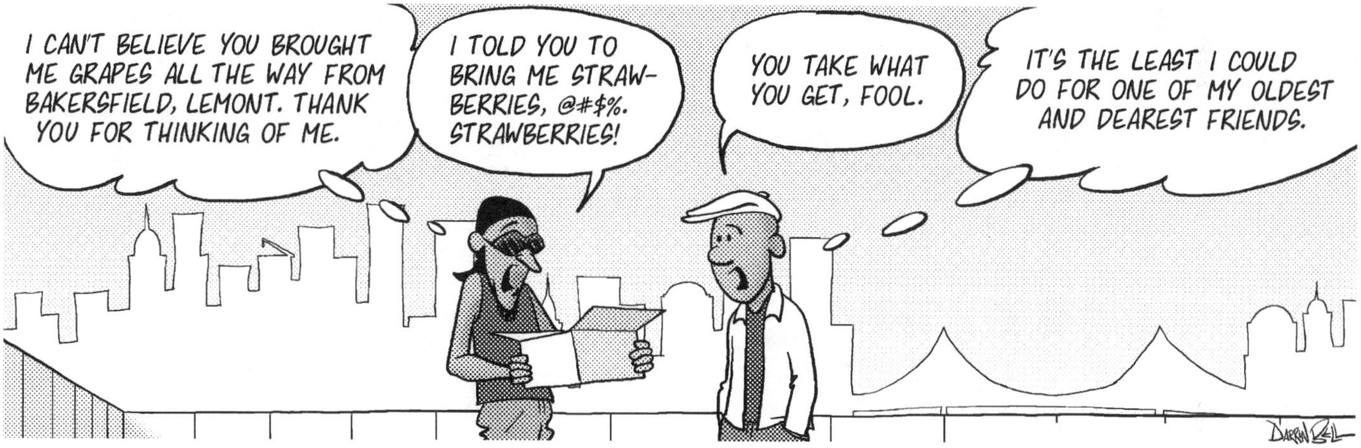
I CAN'T BELIEVE YOU BROUGHT ME GRAPES ALL THE WAY FROM BAKERSFIELD, LEMONT. THANK YOU FOR THINKING OF ME.
I TOLD YOU TO BRING ME STRAW-BERRIES, @#$%. STRAWBERRIES!
YOU TAKE WHAT YOU GET, FOOL.
IT'S THE LEAST I COULD DO FOR ONE OF MY OLDEST AND DEAREST FRIENDS.

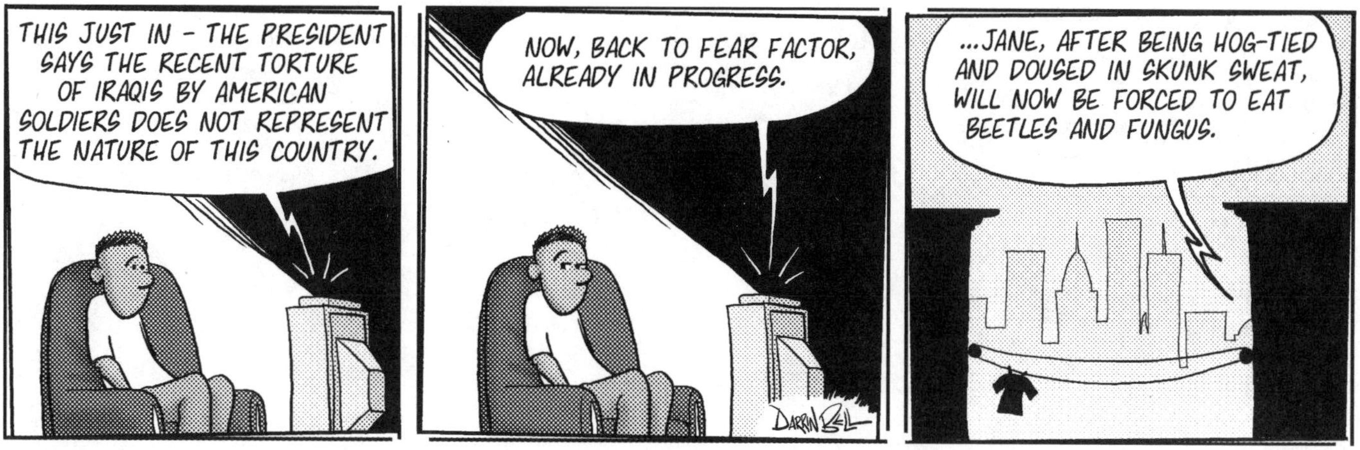
THIS JUST IN - THE PRESIDENT SAYS THE RECENT TORTURE OF IRAQIS BY AMERICAN SOLDIERS DOES NOT REPRESENT THE NATURE OF THIS COUNTRY.
NOW, BACK TO FEAR FACTOR, ALREADY IN PROGRESS.
...JANE, AFTER BEING HOG-TIED AND DOUSED IN SKUNK SWEAT, WILL NOW BE FORCED TO EAT BEETLES AND FUNGUS.

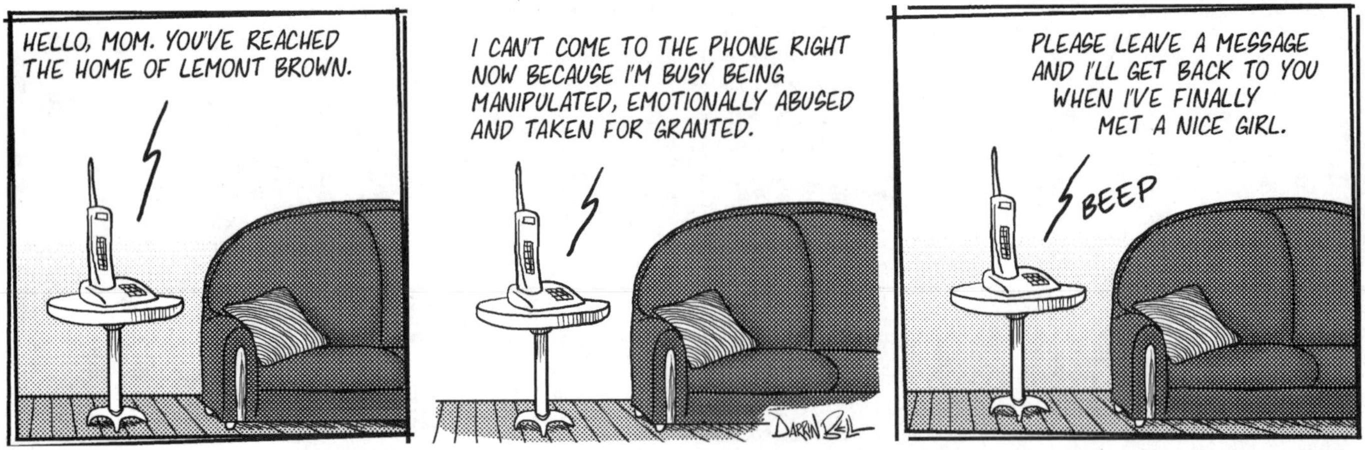

HELLO, MOM. YOU'VE REACHED THE HOME OF LEMONT BROWN.
I CAN'T COME TO THE PHONE RIGHT NOW BECAUSE I'M BUSY BEING MANIPULATED, EMOTIONALLY ABUSED AND TAKEN FOR GRANTED.
PLEASE LEAVE A MESSAGE AND I'LL GET BACK TO YOU WHEN I'VE FINALLY MET A NICE GIRL.
BEEP
DARRIN BELL

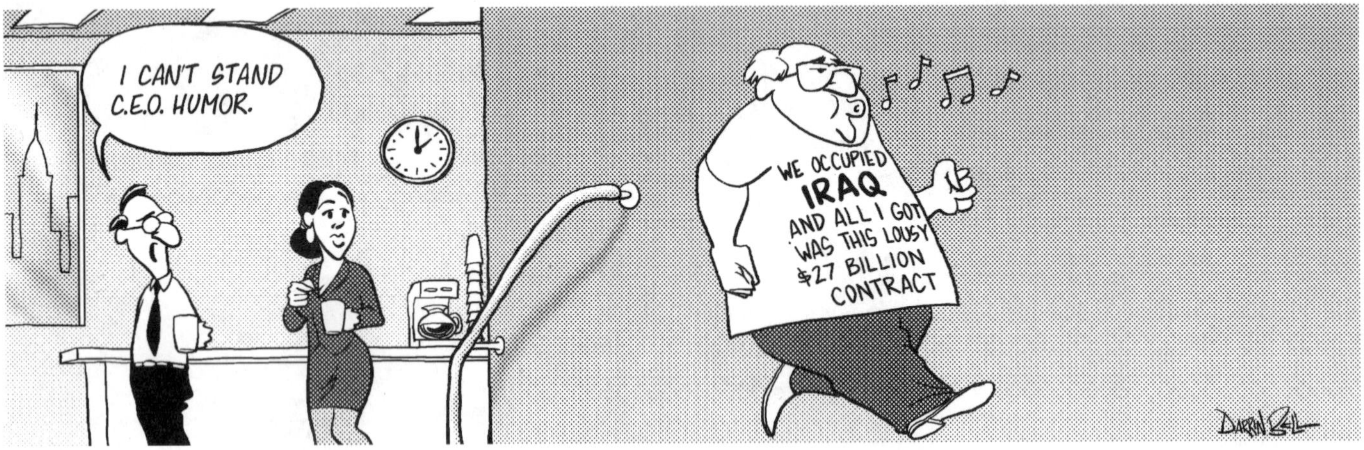

I CAN'T STAND C.E.O. HUMOR.
WE OCCUPIED IRAQ AND ALL I GOT WAS THIS LOUSY $27 BILLION CONTRACT
DARRIN BELL

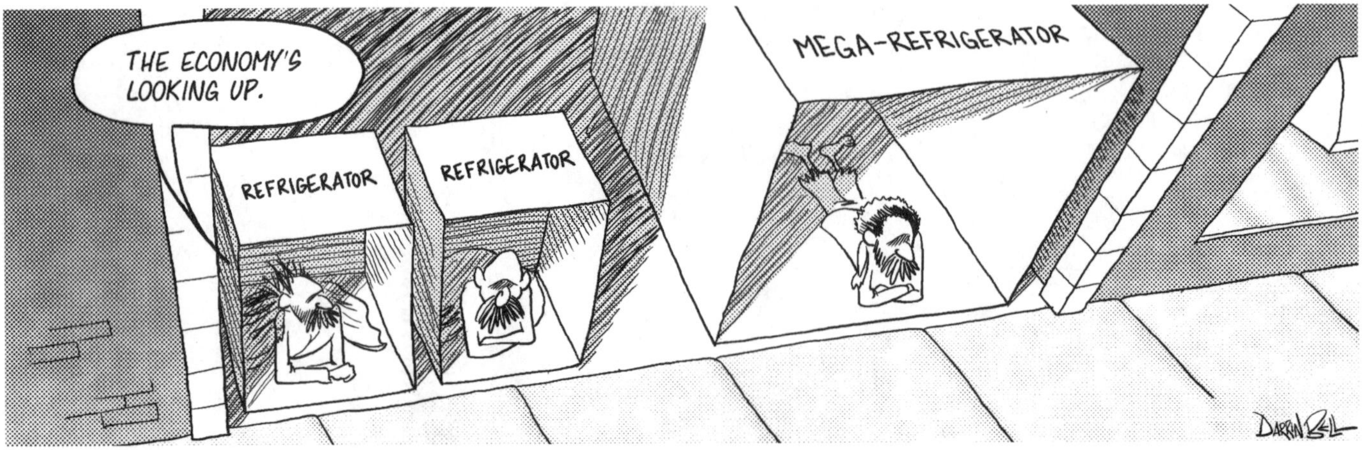

THE ECONOMY'S LOOKING UP.
REFRIGERATOR
REFRIGERATOR
MEGA-REFRIGERATOR
DARRIN BELL

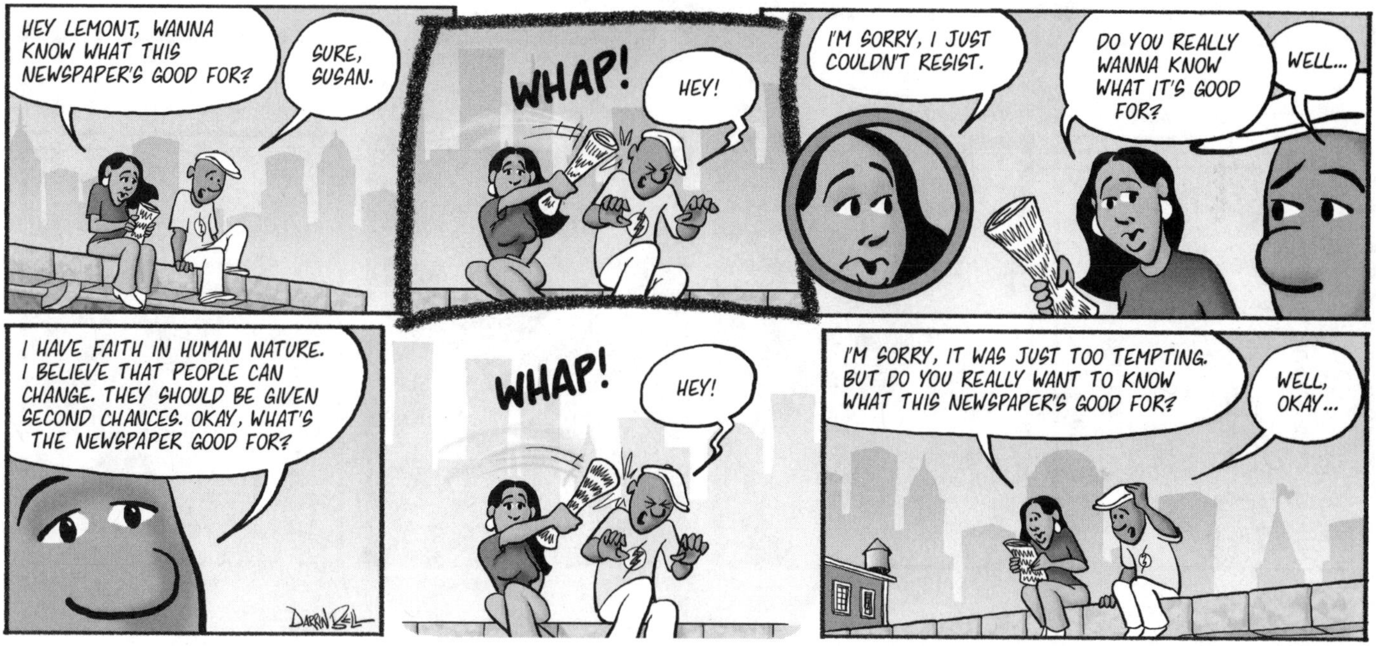
HEY LEMONT, WANNA KNOW WHAT THIS NEWSPAPER'S GOOD FOR?
SURE, SUSAN.
WHAP!
HEY!
I'M SORRY, I JUST COULDN'T RESIST.
DO YOU REALLY WANNA KNOW WHAT IT'S GOOD FOR?
WELL...
I HAVE FAITH IN HUMAN NATURE. I BELIEVE THAT PEOPLE CAN CHANGE. THEY SHOULD BE GIVEN SECOND CHANCES. OKAY, WHAT'S THE NEWSPAPER GOOD FOR?
DARRIN BELL
WHAP!
HEY!
I'M SORRY, IT WAS JUST TOO TEMPTING. BUT DO YOU REALLY WANT TO KNOW WHAT THIS NEWSPAPER'S GOOD FOR?
WELL, OKAY...

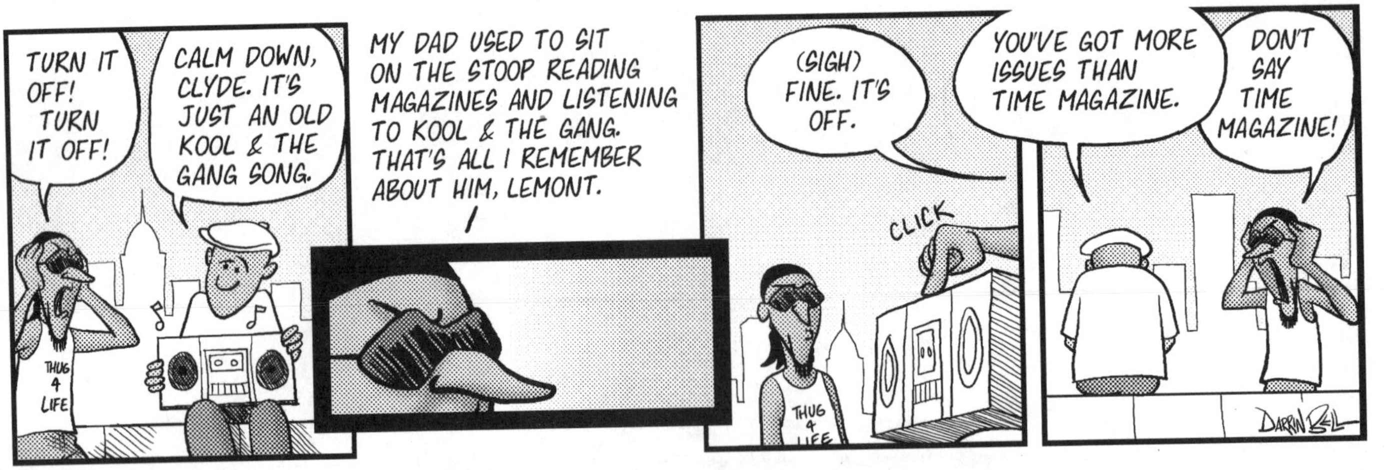
TURN IT OFF! TURN IT OFF!
CALM DOWN, CLYDE. IT'S JUST AN OLD KOOL & THE GANG SONG.
THUG 4 LIFE
MY DAD USED TO SIT ON THE STOOP READING MAGAZINES AND LISTENING TO KOOL & THE GANG. THAT'S ALL I REMEMBER ABOUT HIM, LEMONT.
(SIGH) FINE. IT'S OFF.
CLICK
YOU'VE GOT MORE ISSUES THAN TIME MAGAZINE.
DON'T SAY TIME MAGAZINE!
DARRIN BELL

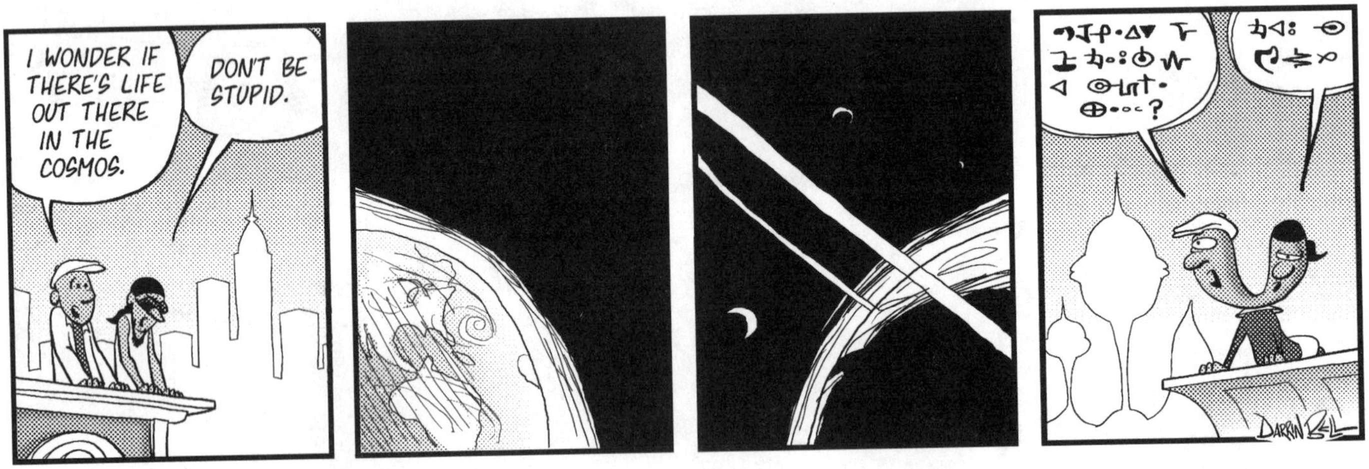
I WONDER IF THERE'S LIFE OUT THERE IN THE COSMOS.
DON'T BE STUPID.
DARRIN BELL

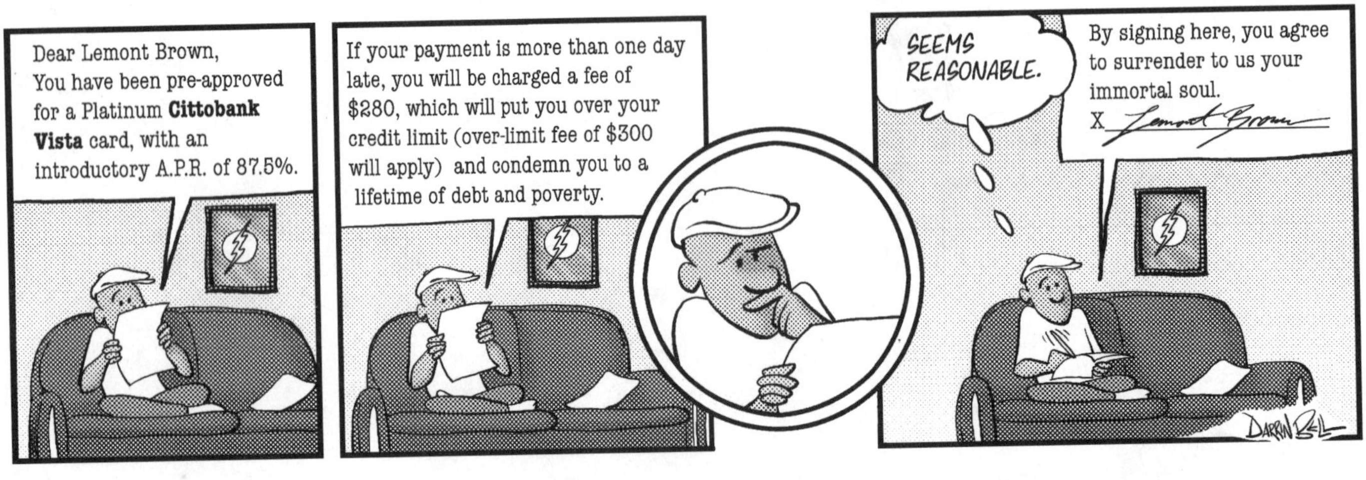
Dear Lemont Brown,
You have been pre-approved for a Platinum **Cittobank Vista** card, with an introductory A.P.R. of 87.5%.
If your payment is more than one day late, you will be charged a fee of $280, which will put you over your credit limit (over-limit fee of $300 will apply) and condemn you to a lifetime of debt and poverty.
SEEMS REASONABLE.
By signing here, you agree to surrender to us your immortal soul.
X Lemont Brown
DARRIN BELL

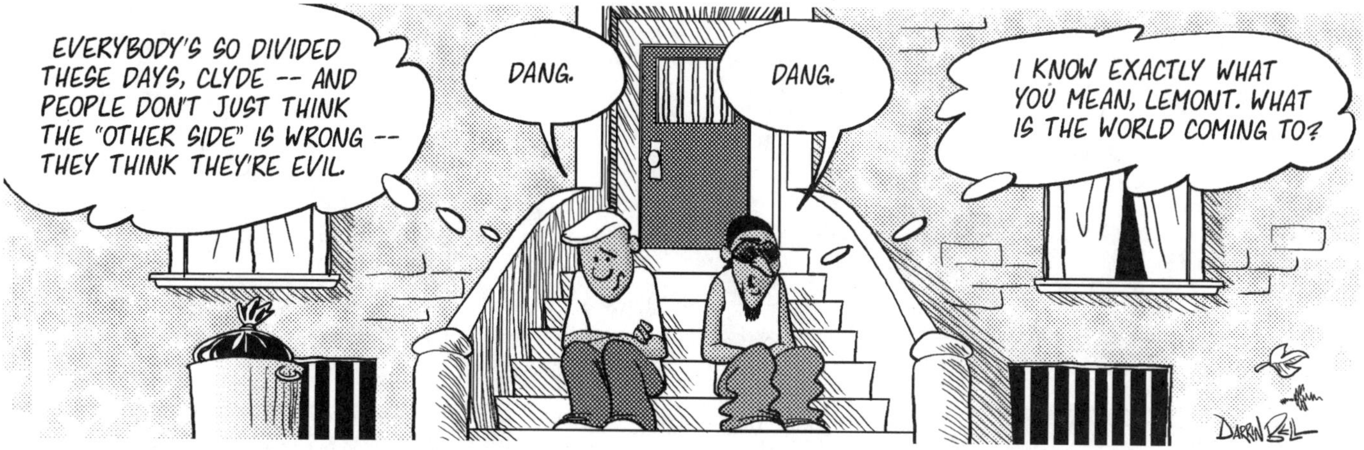
EVERYBODY'S SO DIVIDED THESE DAYS, CLYDE -- AND PEOPLE DON'T JUST THINK THE "OTHER SIDE" IS WRONG -- THEY THINK THEY'RE EVIL.
DANG.
DANG.
I KNOW EXACTLY WHAT YOU MEAN, LEMONT. WHAT IS THE WORLD COMING TO?

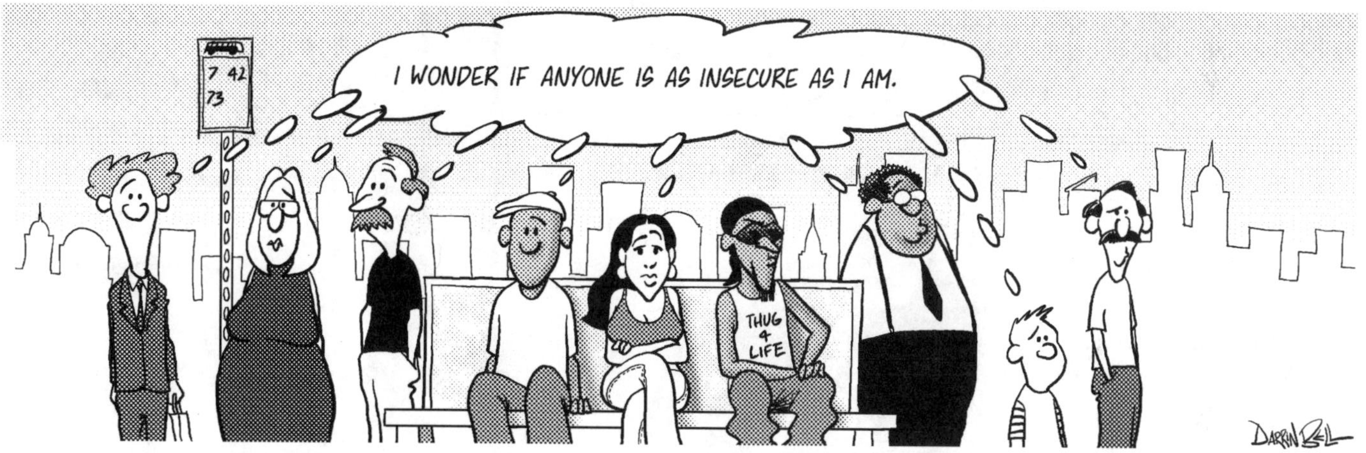
7 42
73
I WONDER IF ANYONE IS AS INSECURE AS I AM.
THUG 4 LIFE

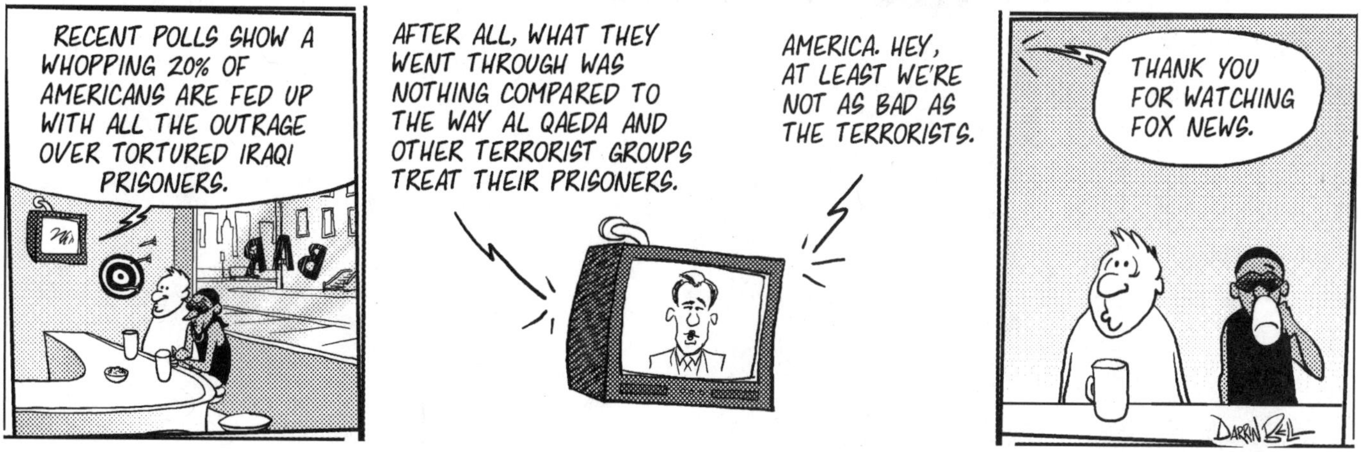
RECENT POLLS SHOW A WHOPPING 20% OF AMERICANS ARE FED UP WITH ALL THE OUTRAGE OVER TORTURED IRAQI PRISONERS.
AFTER ALL, WHAT THEY WENT THROUGH WAS NOTHING COMPARED TO THE WAY AL QAEDA AND OTHER TERRORIST GROUPS TREAT THEIR PRISONERS.
AMERICA. HEY, AT LEAST WE'RE NOT AS BAD AS THE TERRORISTS.
THANK YOU FOR WATCHING FOX NEWS.

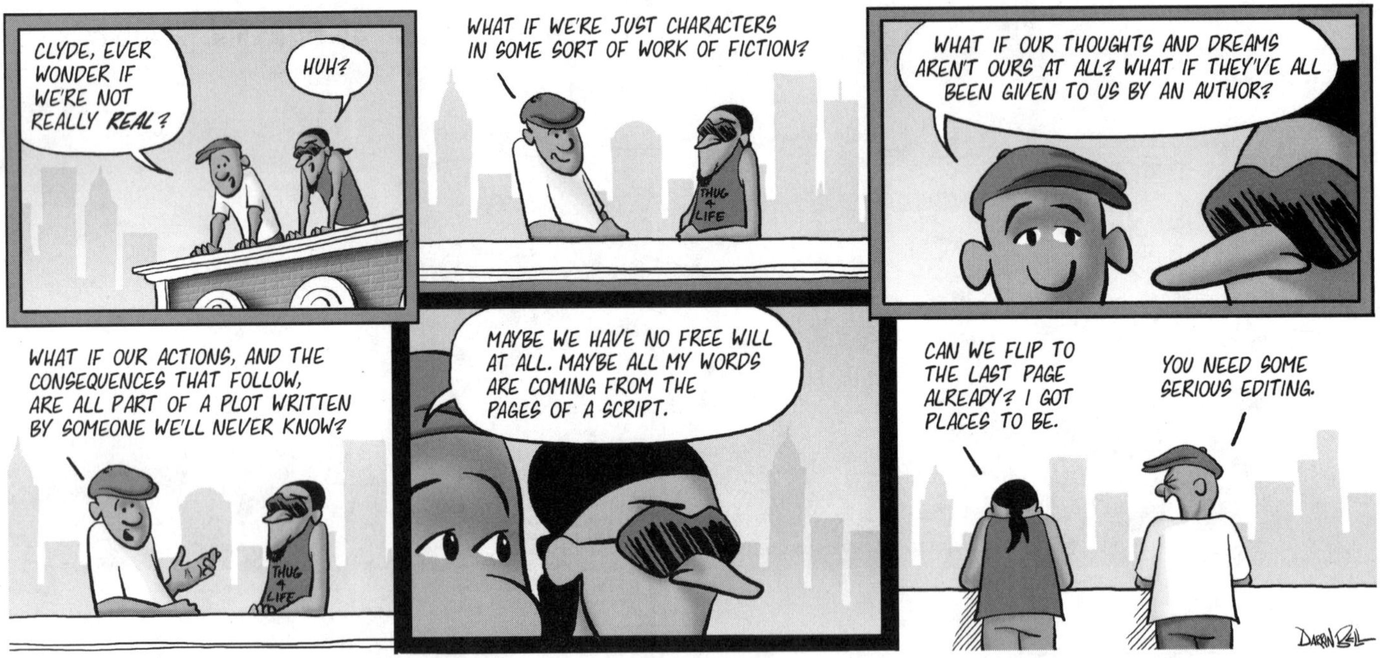
CLYDE, EVER WONDER IF WE'RE NOT REALLY REAL?
HUH?
WHAT IF WE'RE JUST CHARACTERS IN SOME SORT OF WORK OF FICTION?
THUG 4 LIFE
WHAT IF OUR THOUGHTS AND DREAMS AREN'T OURS AT ALL? WHAT IF THEY'VE ALL BEEN GIVEN TO US BY AN AUTHOR?
WHAT IF OUR ACTIONS, AND THE CONSEQUENCES THAT FOLLOW, ARE ALL PART OF A PLOT WRITTEN BY SOMEONE WE'LL NEVER KNOW?
THUG 4 LIFE
MAYBE WE HAVE NO FREE WILL AT ALL. MAYBE ALL MY WORDS ARE COMING FROM THE PAGES OF A SCRIPT.
CAN WE FLIP TO THE LAST PAGE ALREADY? I GOT PLACES TO BE.
YOU NEED SOME SERIOUS EDITING.
DARRIN BELL

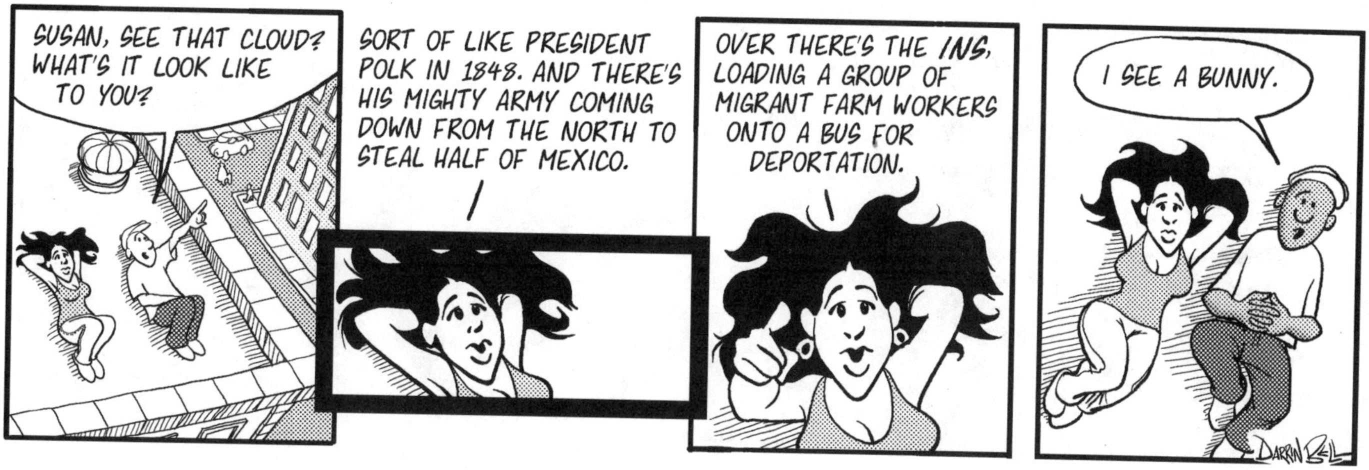
SUSAN, SEE THAT CLOUD? WHAT'S IT LOOK LIKE TO YOU?
SORT OF LIKE PRESIDENT POLK IN 1848. AND THERE'S HIS MIGHTY ARMY COMING DOWN FROM THE NORTH TO STEAL HALF OF MEXICO.
OVER THERE'S THE *INS*, LOADING A GROUP OF MIGRANT FARM WORKERS ONTO A BUS FOR DEPORTATION.
I SEE A BUNNY.
DARRIN BELL

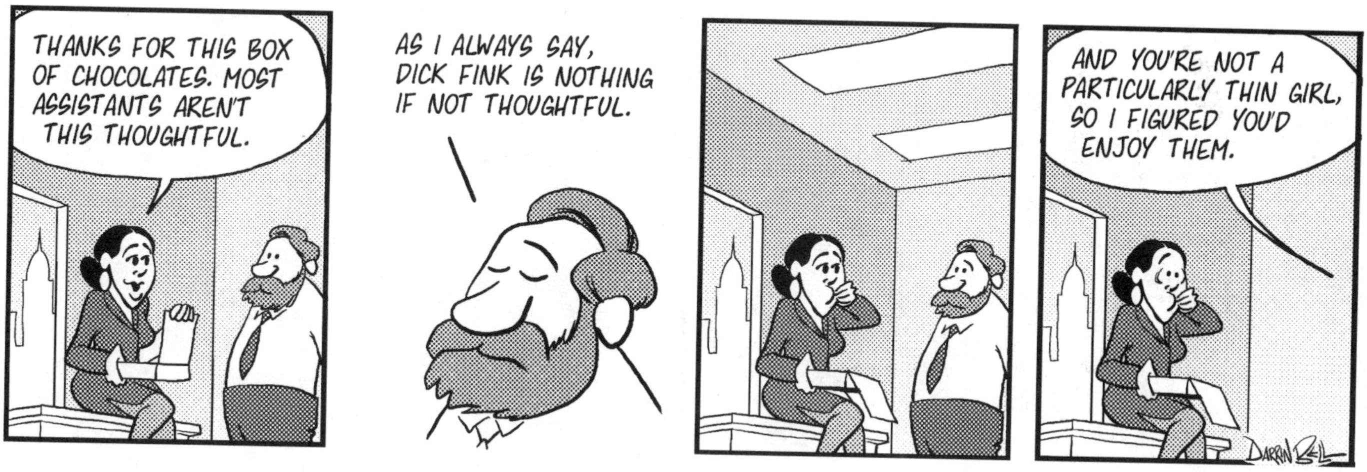
THANKS FOR THIS BOX OF CHOCOLATES. MOST ASSISTANTS AREN'T THIS THOUGHTFUL.
AS I ALWAYS SAY, DICK FINK IS NOTHING IF NOT THOUGHTFUL.
AND YOU'RE NOT A PARTICULARLY THIN GIRL, SO I FIGURED YOU'D ENJOY THEM.
DARRIN BELL

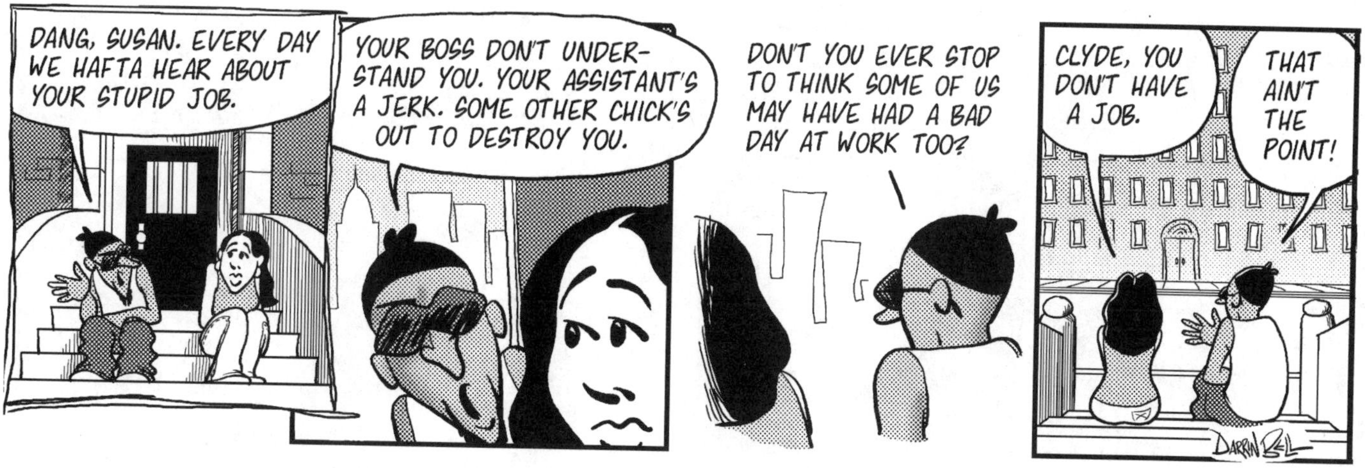
DANG, SUSAN. EVERY DAY WE HAFTA HEAR ABOUT YOUR STUPID JOB.
YOUR BOSS DON'T UNDERSTAND YOU. YOUR ASSISTANT'S A JERK. SOME OTHER CHICK'S OUT TO DESTROY YOU.
DON'T YOU EVER STOP TO THINK SOME OF US MAY HAVE HAD A BAD DAY AT WORK TOO?
CLYDE, YOU DON'T HAVE A JOB.
THAT AIN'T THE POINT!
DARRIN BELL

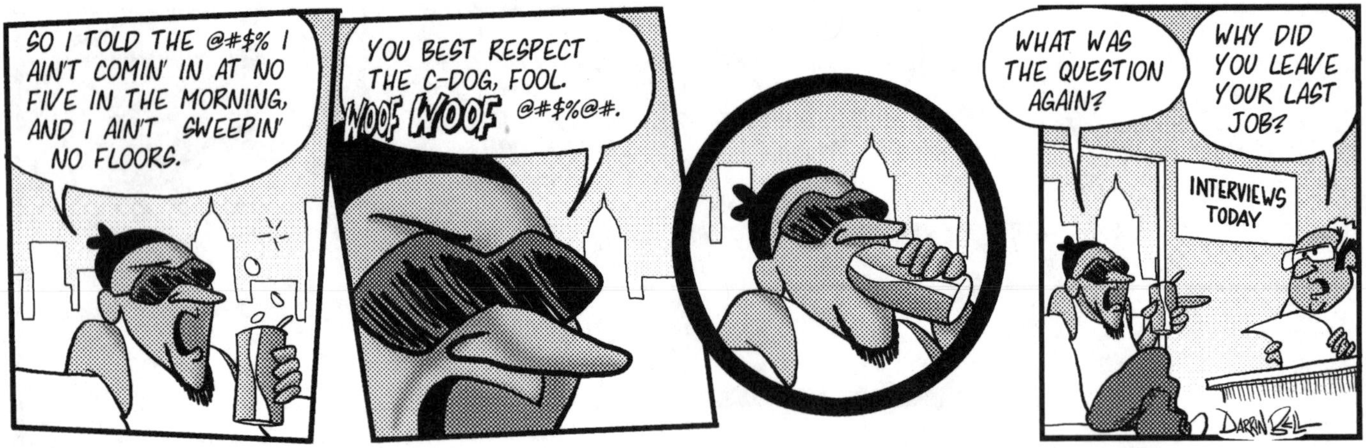
SO I TOLD THE @#$% I AIN'T COMIN' IN AT NO FIVE IN THE MORNING, AND I AIN'T SWEEPIN' NO FLOORS.
YOU BEST RESPECT THE C-DOG, FOOL. WOOF WOOF @#$%@#.
WHAT WAS THE QUESTION AGAIN?
WHY DID YOU LEAVE YOUR LAST JOB?
INTERVIEWS TODAY
DARRIN BELL

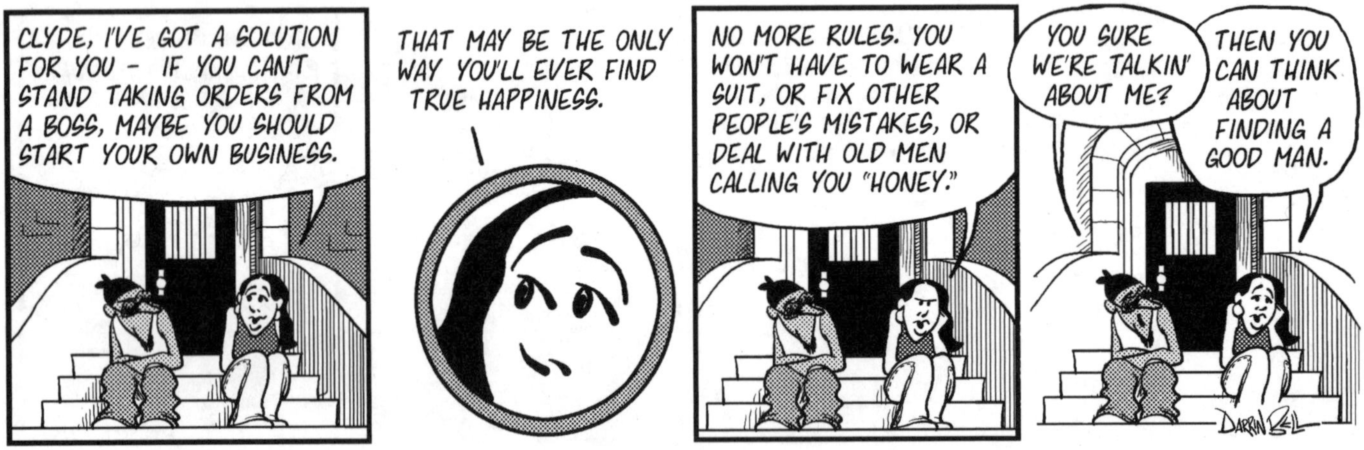
CLYDE, I'VE GOT A SOLUTION FOR YOU - IF YOU CAN'T STAND TAKING ORDERS FROM A BOSS, MAYBE YOU SHOULD START YOUR OWN BUSINESS.
THAT MAY BE THE ONLY WAY YOU'LL EVER FIND TRUE HAPPINESS.
NO MORE RULES. YOU WON'T HAVE TO WEAR A SUIT, OR FIX OTHER PEOPLE'S MISTAKES, OR DEAL WITH OLD MEN CALLING YOU "HONEY."
YOU SURE WE'RE TALKIN' ABOUT ME?
THEN YOU CAN THINK ABOUT FINDING A GOOD MAN.
DARRIN BELL

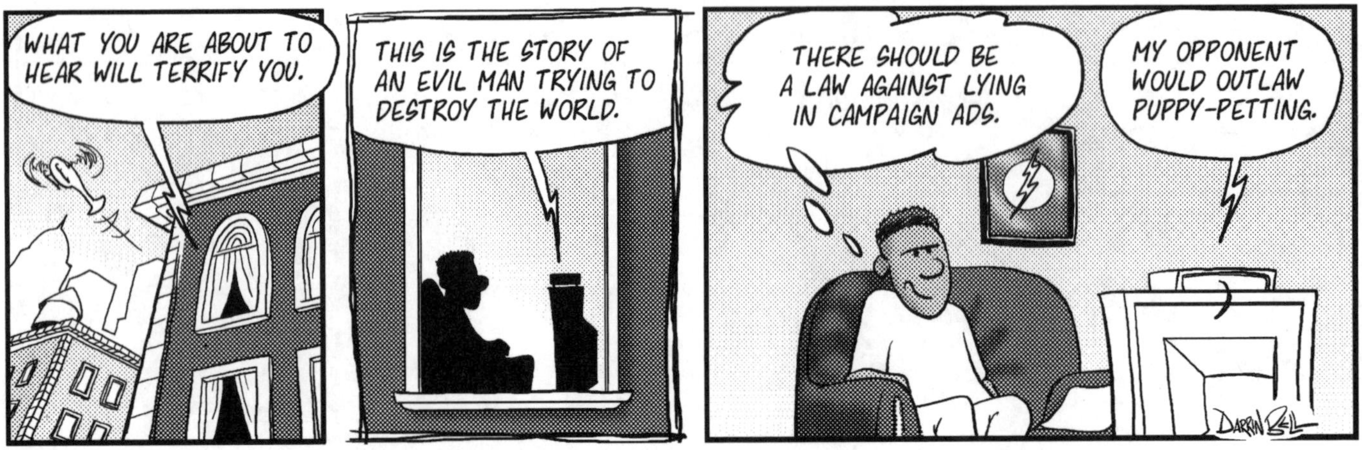
WHAT YOU ARE ABOUT TO HEAR WILL TERRIFY YOU.
THIS IS THE STORY OF AN EVIL MAN TRYING TO DESTROY THE WORLD.
THERE SHOULD BE A LAW AGAINST LYING IN CAMPAIGN ADS.
MY OPPONENT WOULD OUTLAW PUPPY-PETTING.
DARRIN BELL

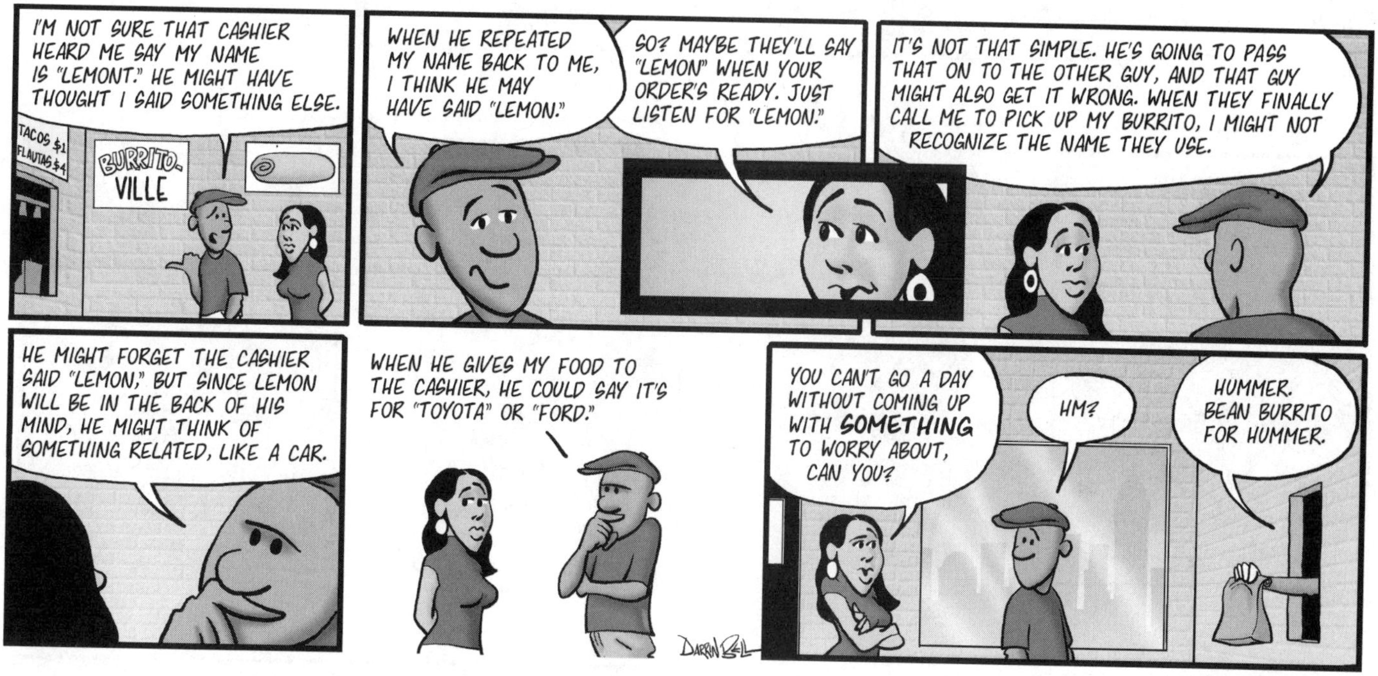
I'M NOT SURE THAT CASHIER HEARD ME SAY MY NAME IS "LEMONT." HE MIGHT HAVE THOUGHT I SAID SOMETHING ELSE.
TACOS $1
FLAUTAS $4
BURRITO-VILLE
WHEN HE REPEATED MY NAME BACK TO ME, I THINK HE MAY HAVE SAID "LEMON."
SO? MAYBE THEY'LL SAY "LEMON" WHEN YOUR ORDER'S READY. JUST LISTEN FOR "LEMON."
IT'S NOT THAT SIMPLE. HE'S GOING TO PASS THAT ON TO THE OTHER GUY, AND THAT GUY MIGHT ALSO GET IT WRONG. WHEN THEY FINALLY CALL ME TO PICK UP MY BURRITO, I MIGHT NOT RECOGNIZE THE NAME THEY USE.
HE MIGHT FORGET THE CASHIER SAID "LEMON," BUT SINCE LEMON WILL BE IN THE BACK OF HIS MIND, HE MIGHT THINK OF SOMETHING RELATED, LIKE A CAR.
WHEN HE GIVES MY FOOD TO THE CASHIER, HE COULD SAY IT'S FOR "TOYOTA" OR "FORD."
DARRIN BELL
YOU CAN'T GO A DAY WITHOUT COMING UP WITH **SOMETHING** TO WORRY ABOUT, CAN YOU?
HM?
HUMMER. BEAN BURRITO FOR HUMMER.

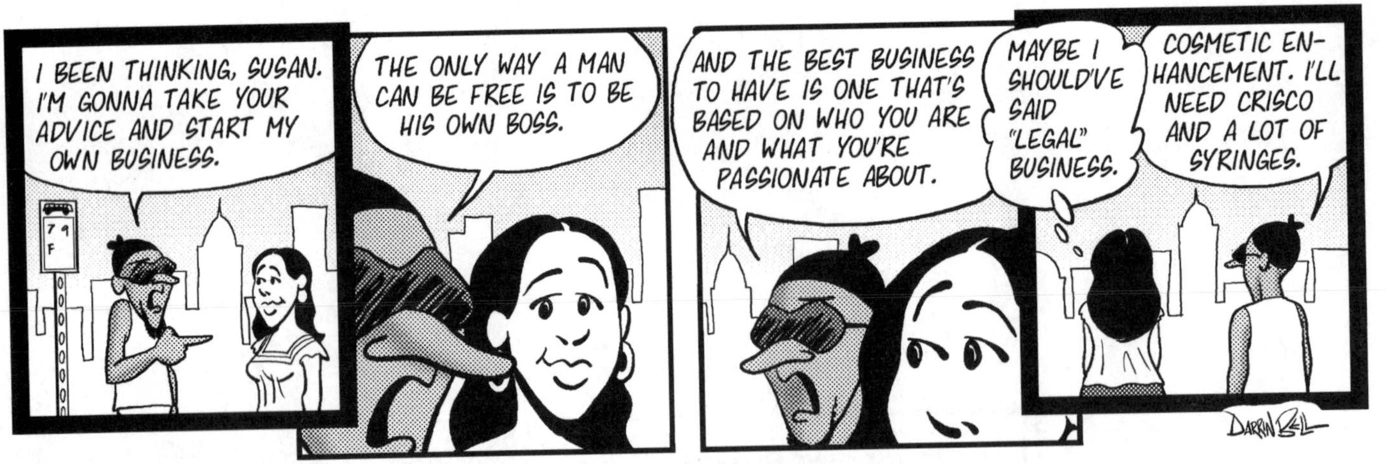
I BEEN THINKING, SUSAN. I'M GONNA TAKE YOUR ADVICE AND START MY OWN BUSINESS.
THE ONLY WAY A MAN CAN BE FREE IS TO BE HIS OWN BOSS.
AND THE BEST BUSINESS TO HAVE IS ONE THAT'S BASED ON WHO YOU ARE AND WHAT YOU'RE PASSIONATE ABOUT.
MAYBE I SHOULD'VE SAID "LEGAL" BUSINESS.
COSMETIC EN-HANCEMENT. I'LL NEED CRISCO AND A LOT OF SYRINGES.
DARRIN BELL

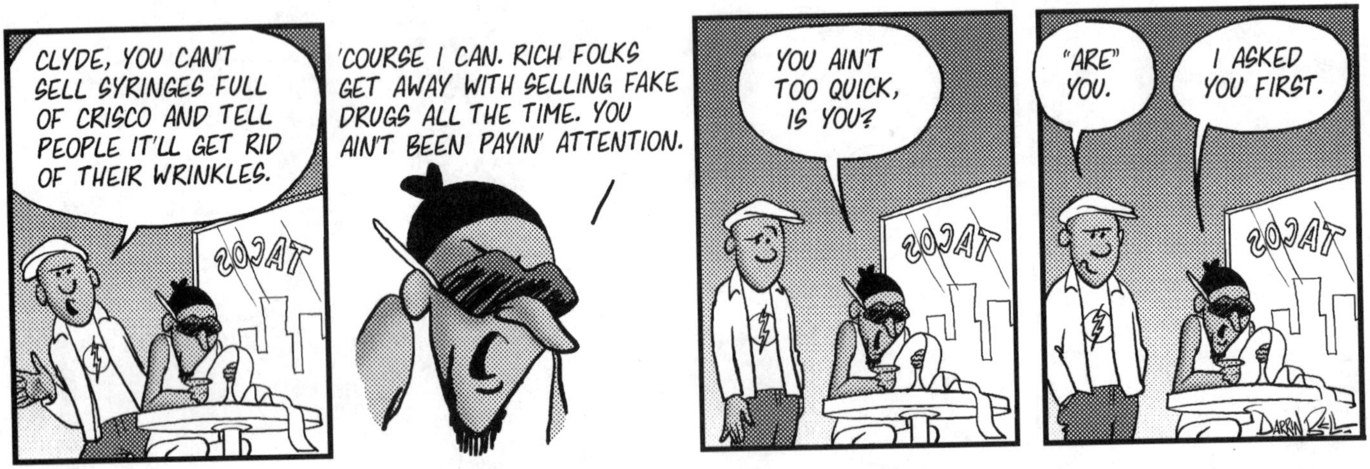
CLYDE, YOU CAN'T SELL SYRINGES FULL OF CRISCO AND TELL PEOPLE IT'LL GET RID OF THEIR WRINKLES.
TACOS
'COURSE I CAN. RICH FOLKS GET AWAY WITH SELLING FAKE DRUGS ALL THE TIME. YOU AIN'T BEEN PAYIN' ATTENTION.
YOU AIN'T TOO QUICK, IS YOU?
"ARE" YOU.
I ASKED YOU FIRST.
DARRIN BELL

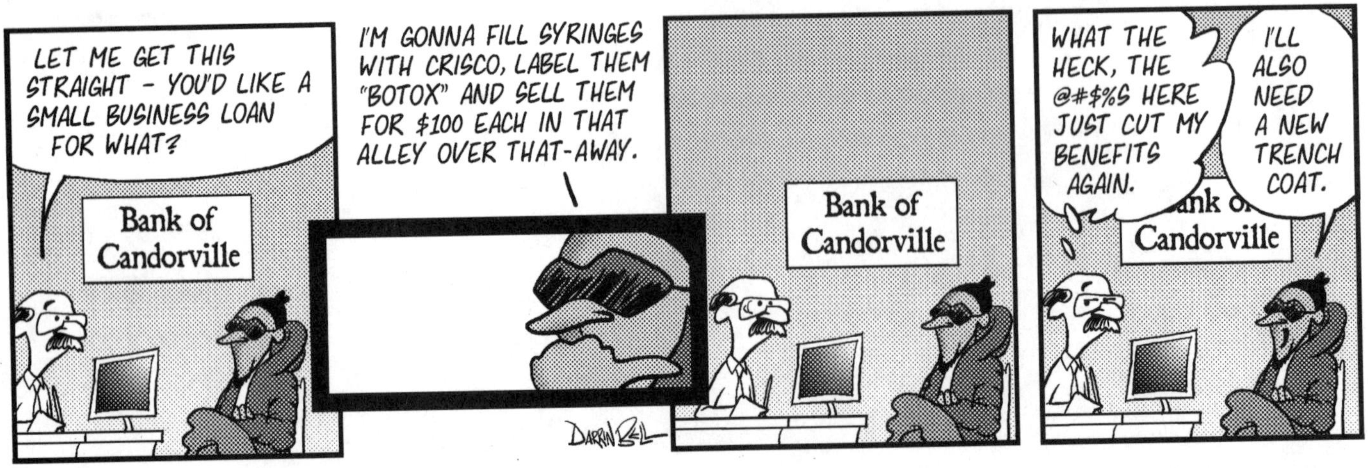
LET ME GET THIS STRAIGHT - YOU'D LIKE A SMALL BUSINESS LOAN FOR WHAT?
Bank of Candorville
I'M GONNA FILL SYRINGES WITH CRISCO, LABEL THEM "BOTOX" AND SELL THEM FOR $100 EACH IN THAT ALLEY OVER THAT-AWAY.
WHAT THE HECK, THE @#$%$ HERE JUST CUT MY BENEFITS AGAIN.
I'LL ALSO NEED A NEW TRENCH COAT.
DARRIN BELL

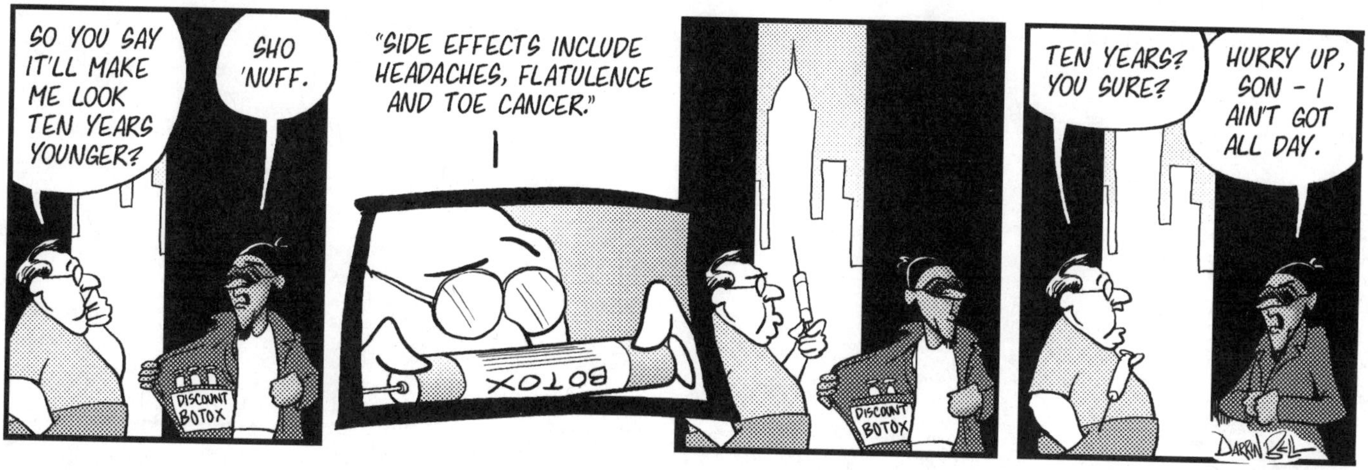
SO YOU SAY IT'LL MAKE ME LOOK TEN YEARS YOUNGER?
SHO 'NUFF.
DISCOUNT BOTOX
"SIDE EFFECTS INCLUDE HEADACHES, FLATULENCE AND TOE CANCER."
BOTOX
DISCOUNT BOTOX
TEN YEARS? YOU SURE?
HURRY UP, SON - I AIN'T GOT ALL DAY.
DARRIN BELL

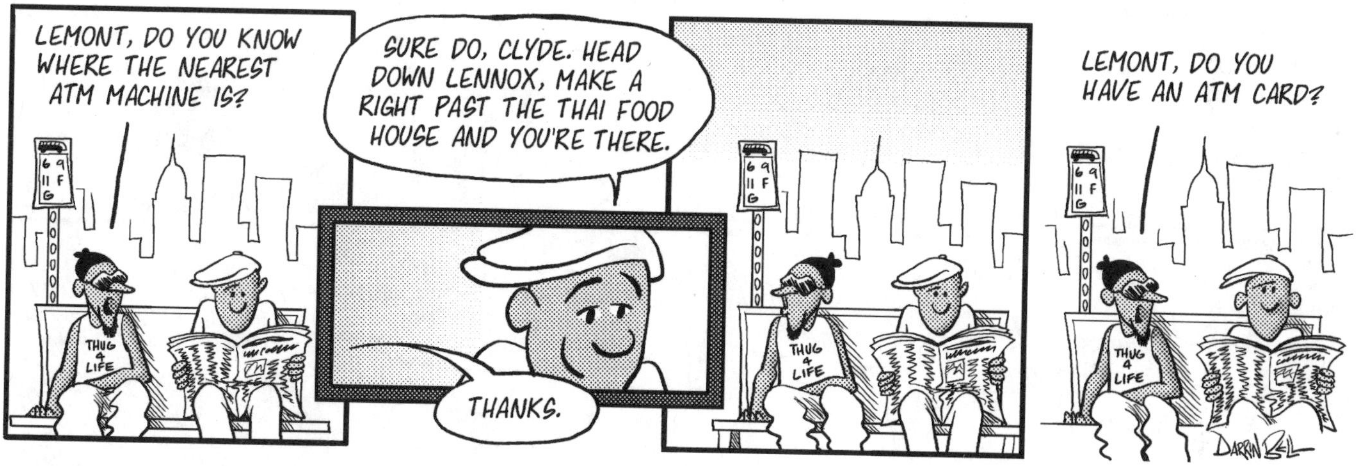
LEMONT, DO YOU KNOW WHERE THE NEAREST ATM MACHINE IS?
THUG 4 LIFE
SURE DO, CLYDE. HEAD DOWN LENNOX, MAKE A RIGHT PAST THE THAI FOOD HOUSE AND YOU'RE THERE.
THANKS.
LEMONT, DO YOU HAVE AN ATM CARD?
DARRIN BELL

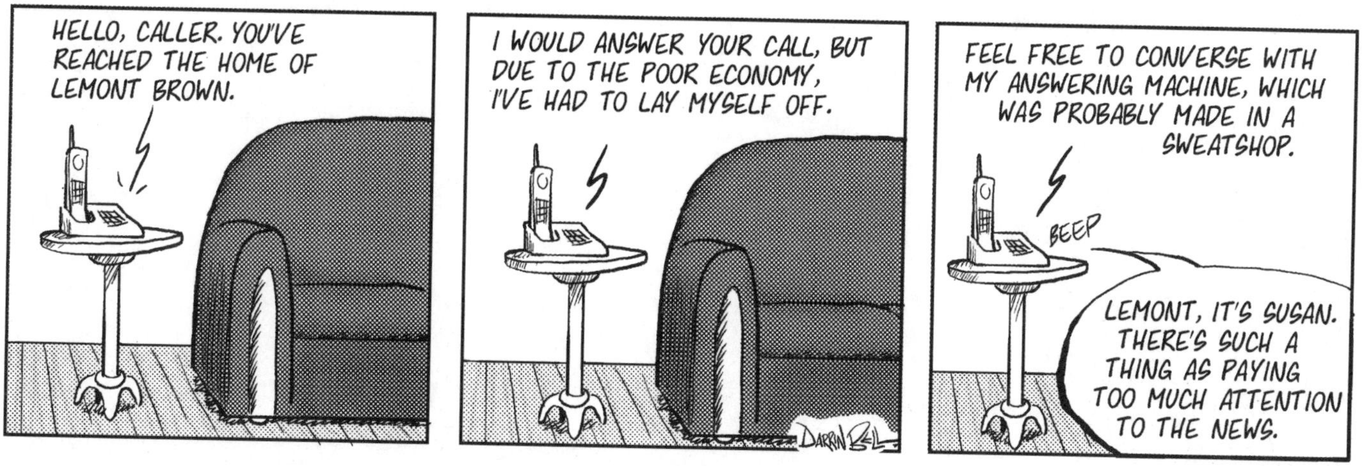
HELLO, CALLER. YOU'VE REACHED THE HOME OF LEMONT BROWN.
I WOULD ANSWER YOUR CALL, BUT DUE TO THE POOR ECONOMY, I'VE HAD TO LAY MYSELF OFF.
DARRIN BELL
FEEL FREE TO CONVERSE WITH MY ANSWERING MACHINE, WHICH WAS PROBABLY MADE IN A SWEATSHOP.
BEEP
LEMONT, IT'S SUSAN. THERE'S SUCH A THING AS PAYING TOO MUCH ATTENTION TO THE NEWS.

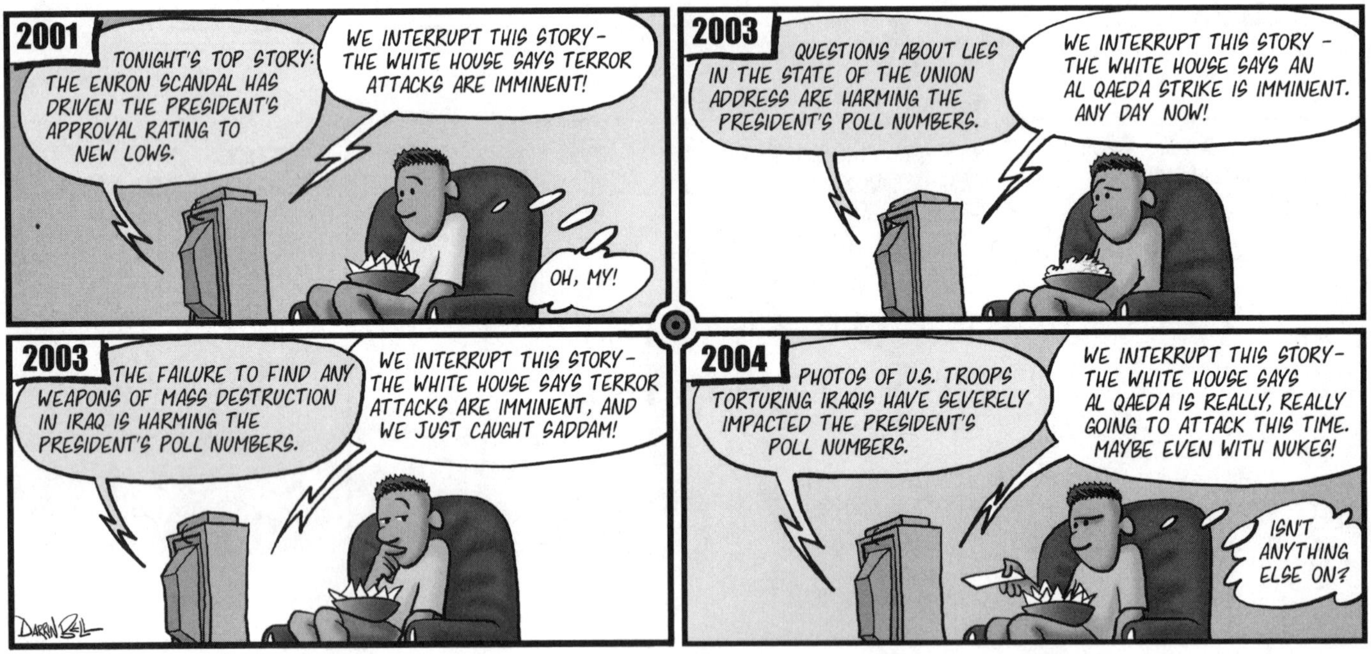
2001
TONIGHT'S TOP STORY: THE ENRON SCANDAL HAS DRIVEN THE PRESIDENT'S APPROVAL RATING TO NEW LOWS.
WE INTERRUPT THIS STORY - THE WHITE HOUSE SAYS TERROR ATTACKS ARE IMMINENT!
OH, MY!
2003
QUESTIONS ABOUT LIES IN THE STATE OF THE UNION ADDRESS ARE HARMING THE PRESIDENT'S POLL NUMBERS.
WE INTERRUPT THIS STORY - THE WHITE HOUSE SAYS AN AL QAEDA STRIKE IS IMMINENT. ANY DAY NOW!
2003
THE FAILURE TO FIND ANY WEAPONS OF MASS DESTRUCTION IN IRAQ IS HARMING THE PRESIDENT'S POLL NUMBERS.
WE INTERRUPT THIS STORY - THE WHITE HOUSE SAYS TERROR ATTACKS ARE IMMINENT, AND WE JUST CAUGHT SADDAM!
DARRIN BELL
2004
PHOTOS OF U.S. TROOPS TORTURING IRAQIS HAVE SEVERELY IMPACTED THE PRESIDENT'S POLL NUMBERS.
WE INTERRUPT THIS STORY - THE WHITE HOUSE SAYS AL QAEDA IS REALLY, REALLY GOING TO ATTACK THIS TIME. MAYBE EVEN WITH NUKES!
ISN'T ANYTHING ELSE ON?

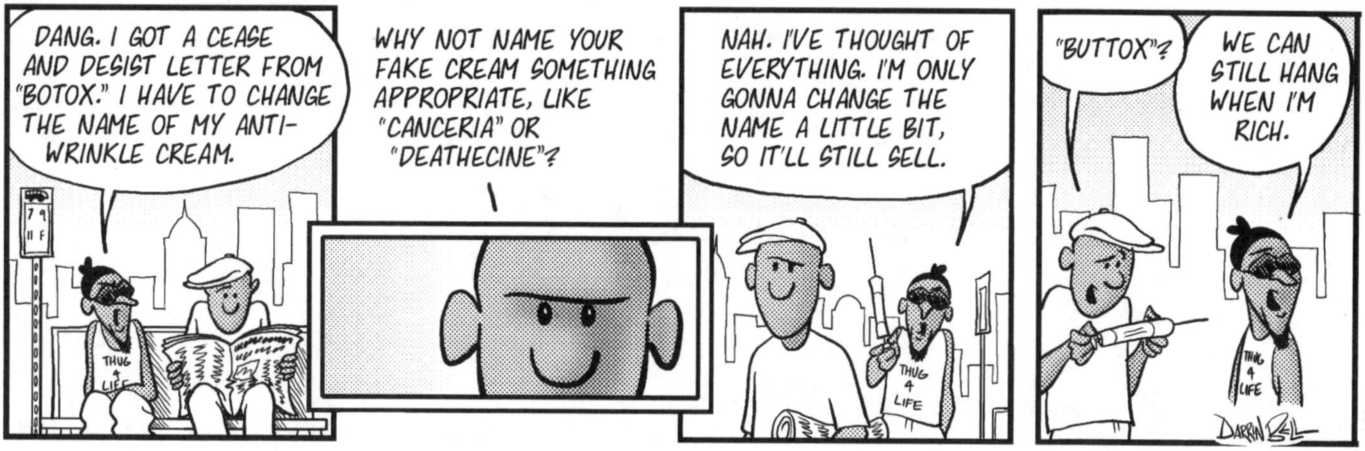
DANG. I GOT A CEASE AND DESIST LETTER FROM "BOTOX." I HAVE TO CHANGE THE NAME OF MY ANTI-WRINKLE CREAM.
THUG 4 LIFE
WHY NOT NAME YOUR FAKE CREAM SOMETHING APPROPRIATE, LIKE "CANCERIA" OR "DEATHECINE"?
NAH. I'VE THOUGHT OF EVERYTHING. I'M ONLY GONNA CHANGE THE NAME A LITTLE BIT, SO IT'LL STILL SELL.
THUG 4 LIFE
"BUTTOX"?
WE CAN STILL HANG WHEN I'M RICH.
THUG 4 LIFE
DARRIN BELL

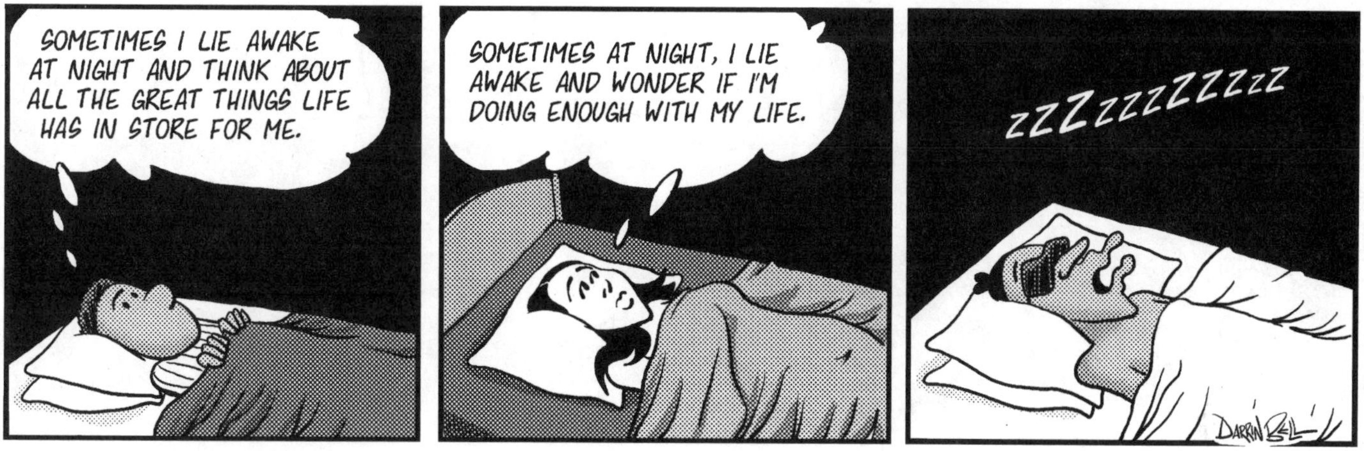
SOMETIMES I LIE AWAKE AT NIGHT AND THINK ABOUT ALL THE GREAT THINGS LIFE HAS IN STORE FOR ME.
SOMETIMES AT NIGHT, I LIE AWAKE AND WONDER IF I'M DOING ENOUGH WITH MY LIFE.
zZZzzzZZZzZ
DARRIN BELL

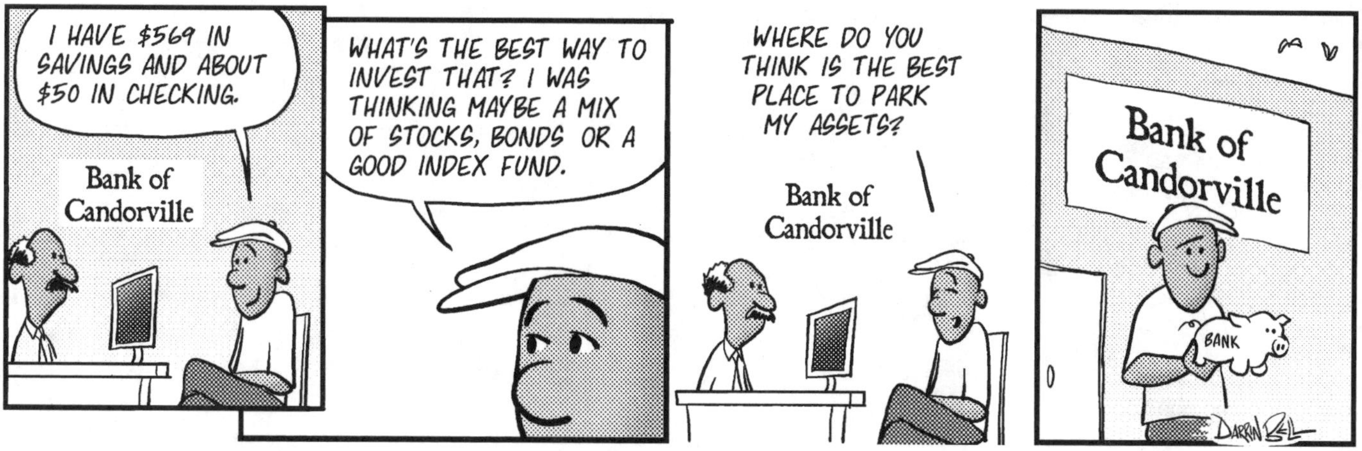
I HAVE $569 IN SAVINGS AND ABOUT $50 IN CHECKING.
Bank of Candorville
WHAT'S THE BEST WAY TO INVEST THAT? I WAS THINKING MAYBE A MIX OF STOCKS, BONDS OR A GOOD INDEX FUND.
WHERE DO YOU THINK IS THE BEST PLACE TO PARK MY ASSETS?
Bank of Candorville
Bank of Candorville
BANK
DARRIN BELL

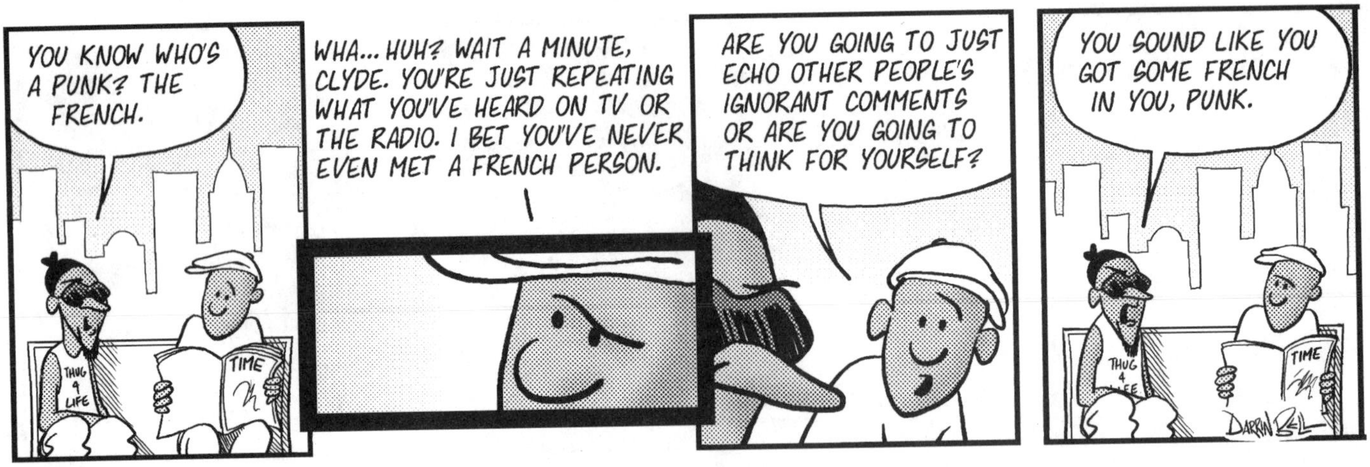
YOU KNOW WHO'S A PUNK? THE FRENCH.
WHA... HUH? WAIT A MINUTE, CLYDE. YOU'RE JUST REPEATING WHAT YOU'VE HEARD ON TV OR THE RADIO. I BET YOU'VE NEVER EVEN MET A FRENCH PERSON.
ARE YOU GOING TO JUST ECHO OTHER PEOPLE'S IGNORANT COMMENTS OR ARE YOU GOING TO THINK FOR YOURSELF?
YOU SOUND LIKE YOU GOT SOME FRENCH IN YOU, PUNK.
DARRIN BELL

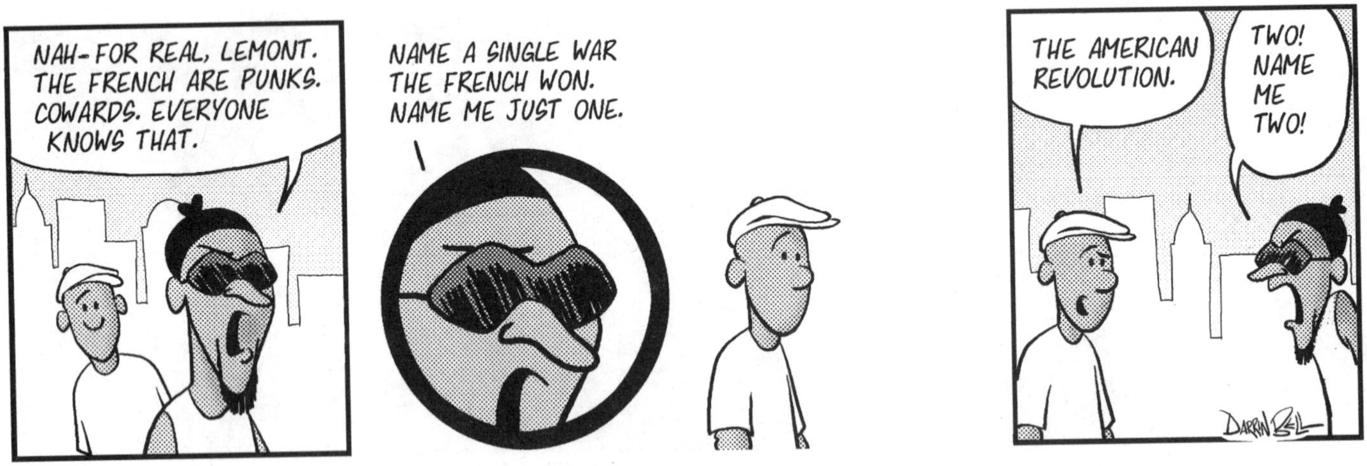
NAH-FOR REAL, LEMONT. THE FRENCH ARE PUNKS. COWARDS. EVERYONE KNOWS THAT.
NAME A SINGLE WAR THE FRENCH WON. NAME ME JUST ONE.
THE AMERICAN REVOLUTION.
TWO! NAME ME TWO!
DARRIN BELL

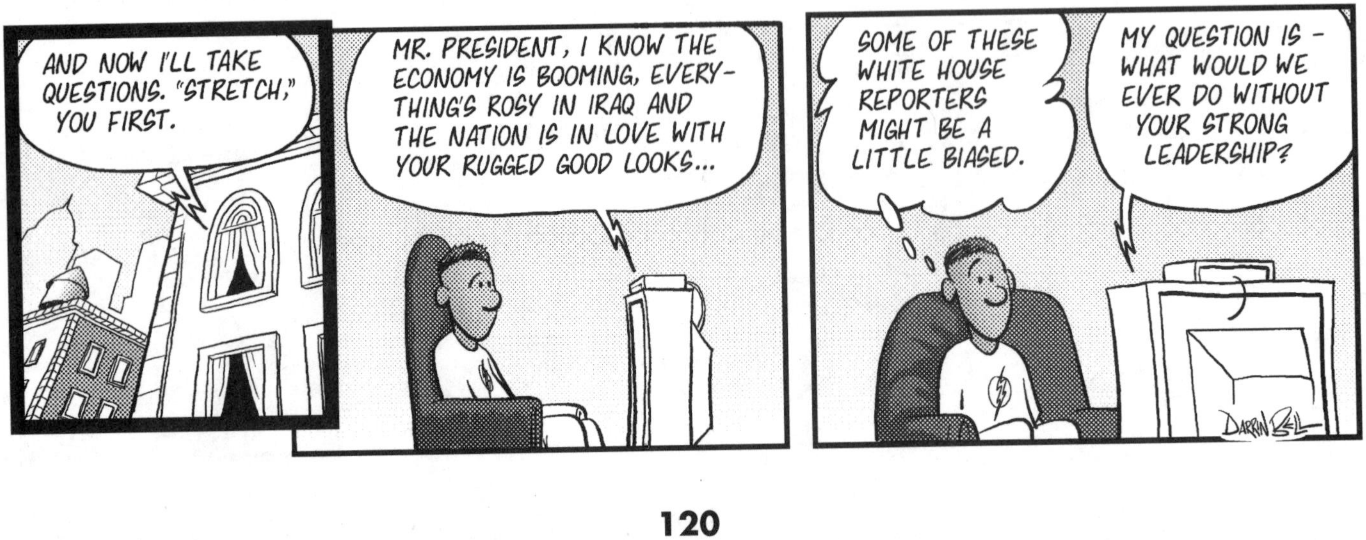
AND NOW I'LL TAKE QUESTIONS. "STRETCH," YOU FIRST.
MR. PRESIDENT, I KNOW THE ECONOMY IS BOOMING, EVERYTHING'S ROSY IN IRAQ AND THE NATION IS IN LOVE WITH YOUR RUGGED GOOD LOOKS...
SOME OF THESE WHITE HOUSE REPORTERS MIGHT BE A LITTLE BIASED.
MY QUESTION IS - WHAT WOULD WE EVER DO WITHOUT YOUR STRONG LEADERSHIP?
DARRIN BELL

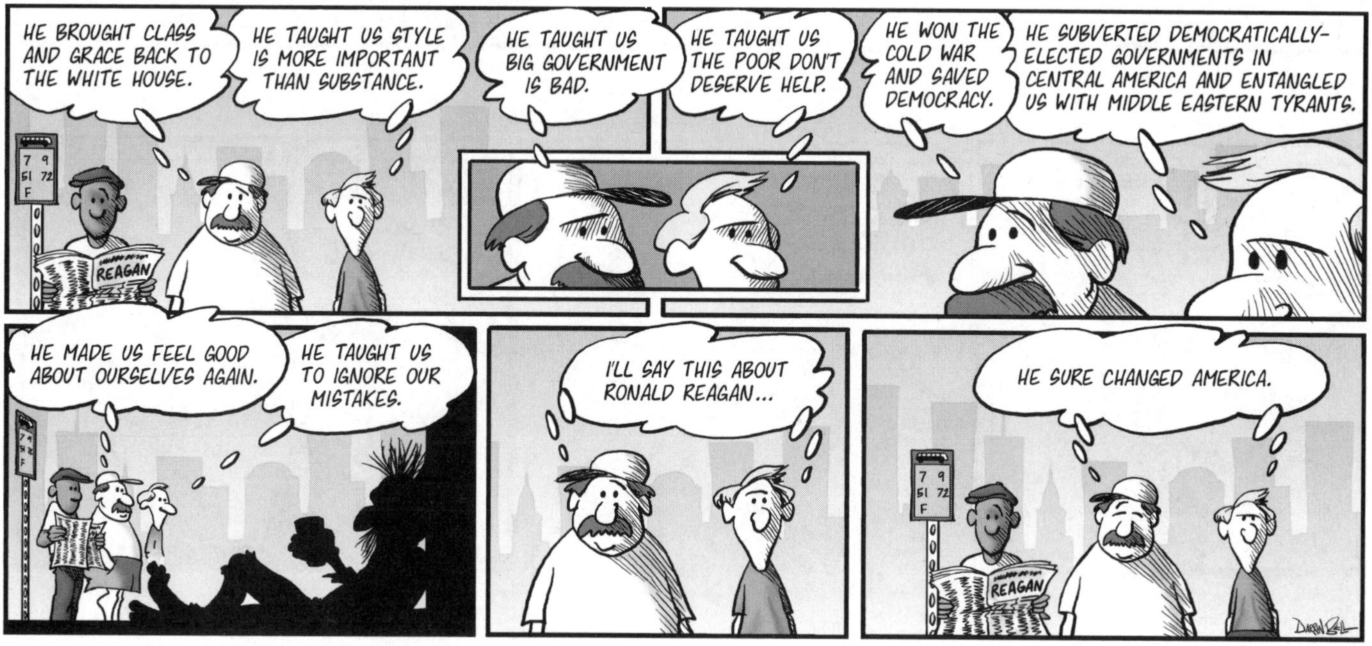
HE BROUGHT CLASS AND GRACE BACK TO THE WHITE HOUSE.
HE TAUGHT US STYLE IS MORE IMPORTANT THAN SUBSTANCE.
REAGAN
HE TAUGHT US BIG GOVERNMENT IS BAD.
HE TAUGHT US THE POOR DON'T DESERVE HELP.
HE WON THE COLD WAR AND SAVED DEMOCRACY.
HE SUBVERTED DEMOCRATICALLY-ELECTED GOVERNMENTS IN CENTRAL AMERICA AND ENTANGLED US WITH MIDDLE EASTERN TYRANTS.
HE MADE US FEEL GOOD ABOUT OURSELVES AGAIN.
HE TAUGHT US TO IGNORE OUR MISTAKES.
I'LL SAY THIS ABOUT RONALD REAGAN...
HE SURE CHANGED AMERICA.
REAGAN

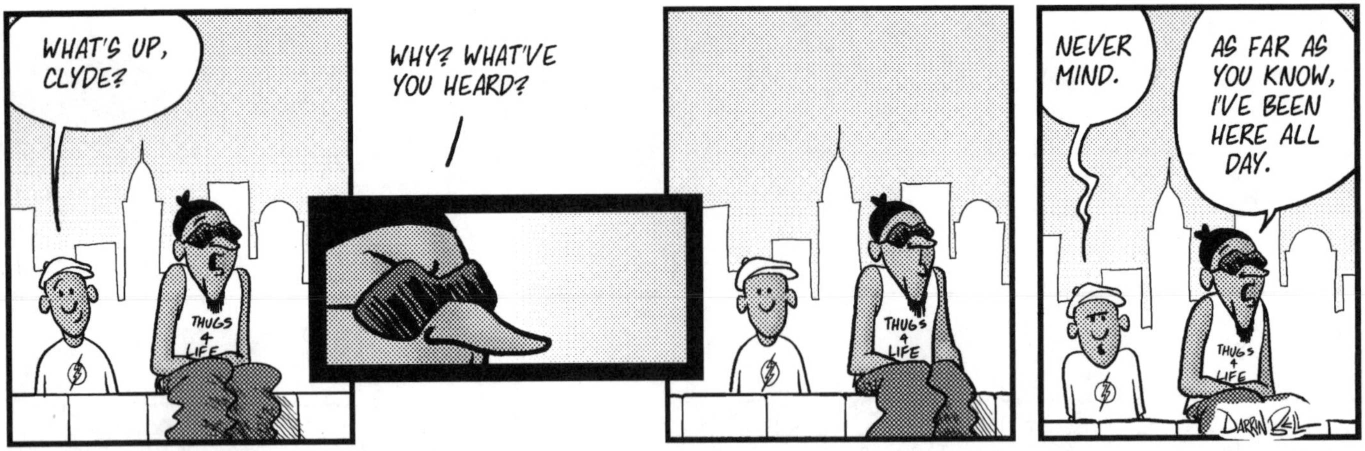
WHAT'S UP, CLYDE?
WHY? WHAT'VE YOU HEARD?
THUGS 4 LIFE
NEVER MIND.
AS FAR AS YOU KNOW, I'VE BEEN HERE ALL DAY.
DARRIN BELL

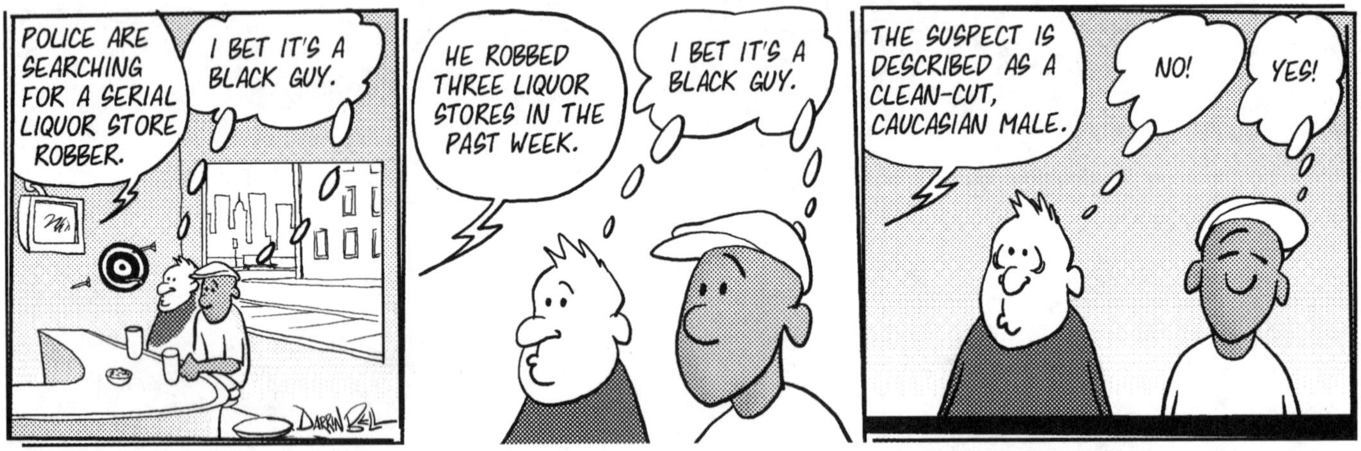
POLICE ARE SEARCHING FOR A SERIAL LIQUOR STORE ROBBER.
I BET IT'S A BLACK GUY.
HE ROBBED THREE LIQUOR STORES IN THE PAST WEEK.
I BET IT'S A BLACK GUY.
THE SUSPECT IS DESCRIBED AS A CLEAN-CUT, CAUCASIAN MALE.
NO!
YES!
DARRIN BELL

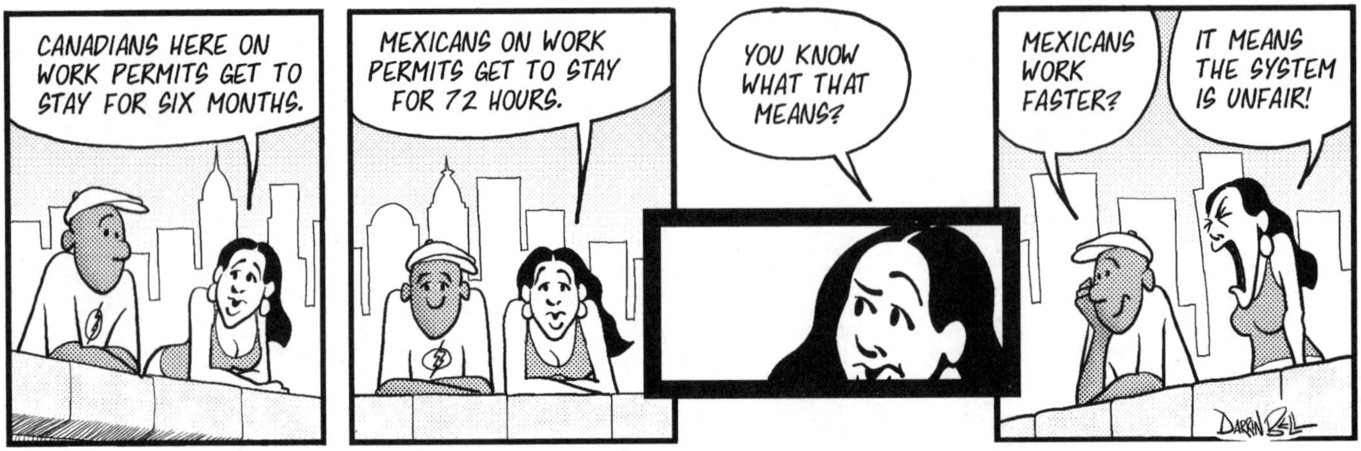
CANADIANS HERE ON WORK PERMITS GET TO STAY FOR SIX MONTHS.
MEXICANS ON WORK PERMITS GET TO STAY FOR 72 HOURS.
YOU KNOW WHAT THAT MEANS?
MEXICANS WORK FASTER?
IT MEANS THE SYSTEM IS UNFAIR!
DARRIN BELL

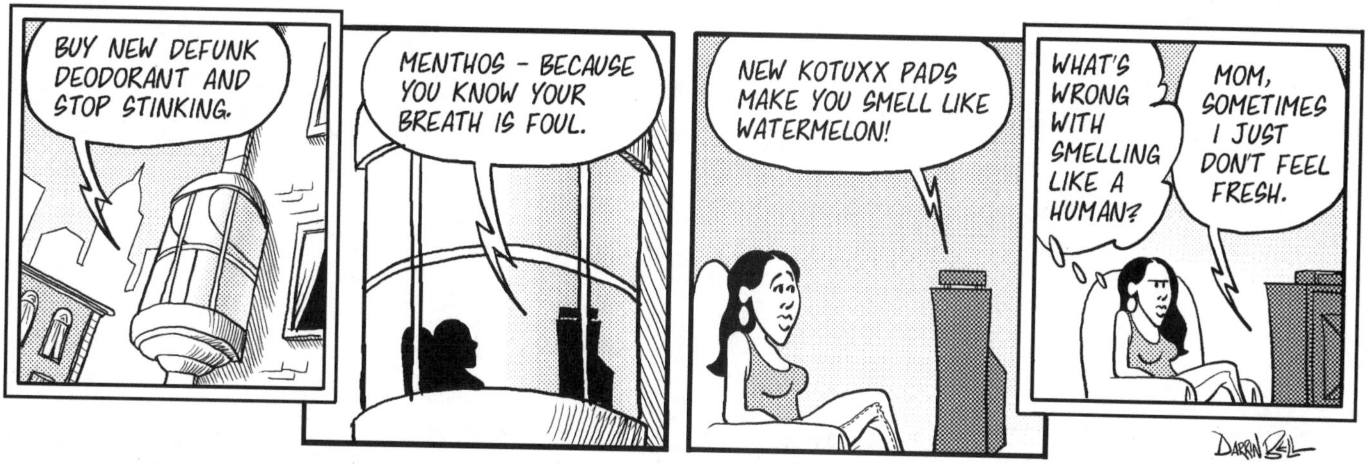
BUY NEW DEFUNK DEODORANT AND STOP STINKING.
MENTHOS - BECAUSE YOU KNOW YOUR BREATH IS FOUL.
NEW KOTUXX PADS MAKE YOU SMELL LIKE WATERMELON!
WHAT'S WRONG WITH SMELLING LIKE A HUMAN?
MOM, SOMETIMES I JUST DON'T FEEL FRESH.
DARRIN BELL

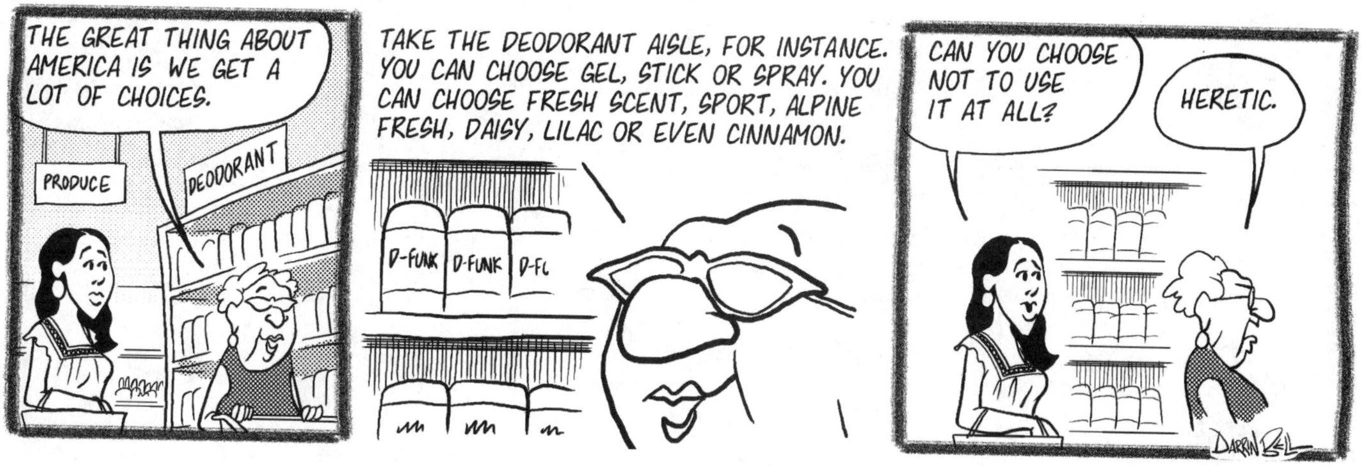
THE GREAT THING ABOUT AMERICA IS WE GET A LOT OF CHOICES.
PRODUCE
DEODORANT
TAKE THE DEODORANT AISLE, FOR INSTANCE. YOU CAN CHOOSE GEL, STICK OR SPRAY. YOU CAN CHOOSE FRESH SCENT, SPORT, ALPINE FRESH, DAISY, LILAC OR EVEN CINNAMON.
D-FUNK
D-FUNK
CAN YOU CHOOSE NOT TO USE IT AT ALL?
HERETIC.
DARRIN BELL

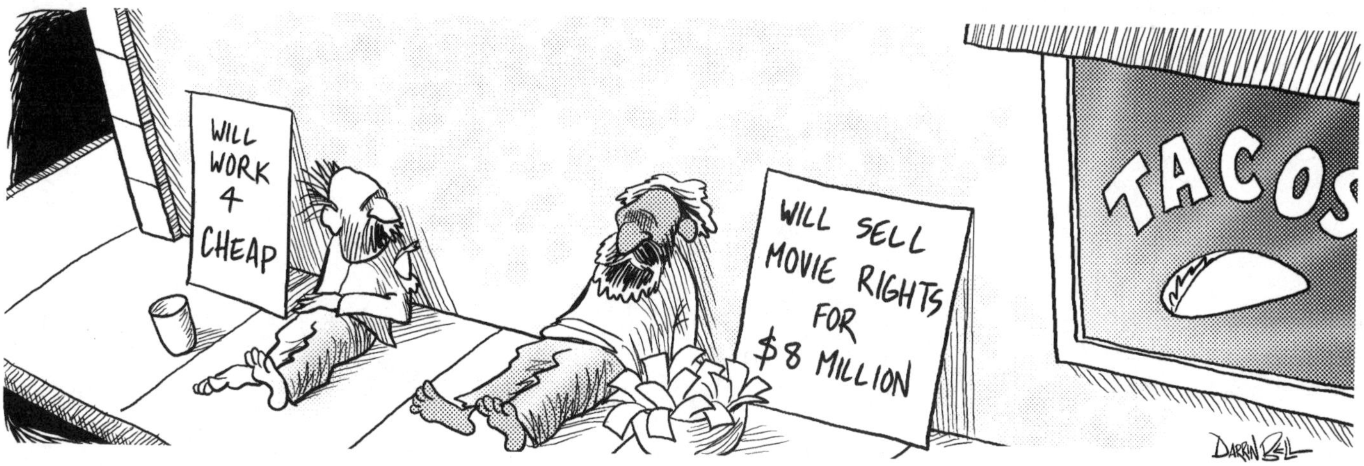
WILL WORK 4 CHEAP
WILL SELL MOVIE RIGHTS FOR $8 MILLION
TACOS
DARRIN BELL

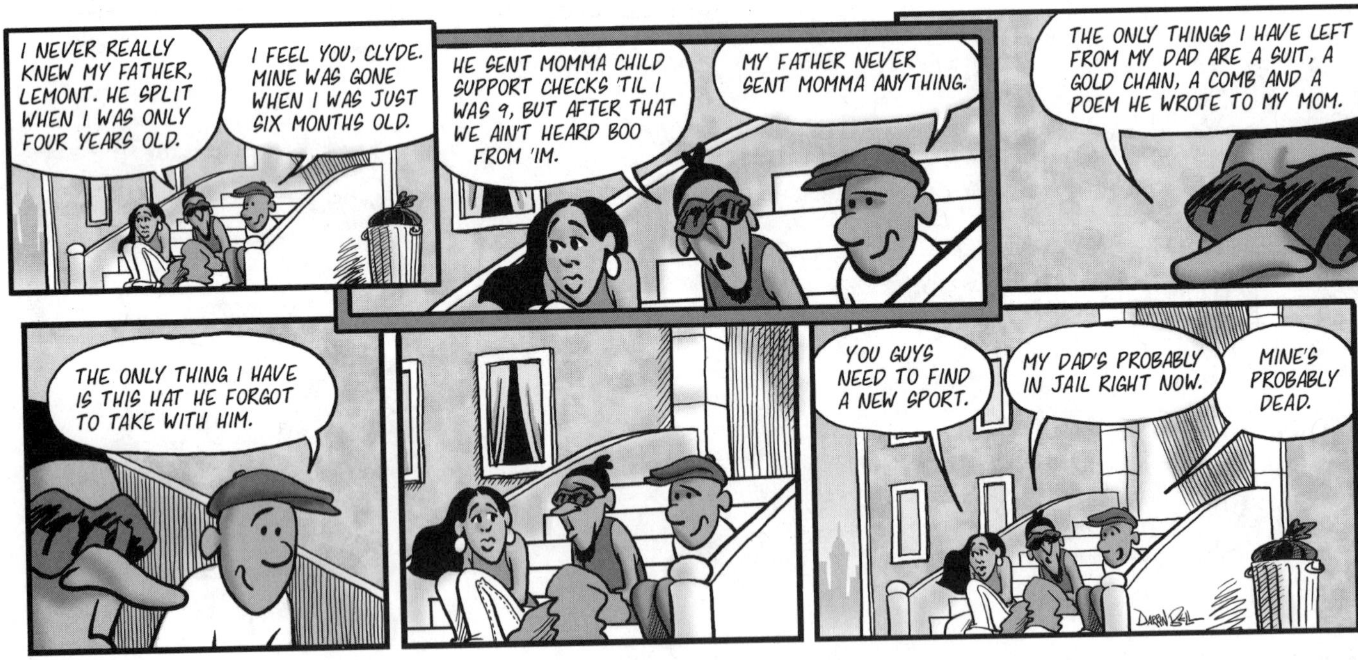
I NEVER REALLY KNEW MY FATHER, LEMONT. HE SPLIT WHEN I WAS ONLY FOUR YEARS OLD.
I FEEL YOU, CLYDE. MINE WAS GONE WHEN I WAS JUST SIX MONTHS OLD.
HE SENT MOMMA CHILD SUPPORT CHECKS 'TIL I WAS 9, BUT AFTER THAT WE AIN'T HEARD BOO FROM 'IM.
MY FATHER NEVER SENT MOMMA ANYTHING.
THE ONLY THINGS I HAVE LEFT FROM MY DAD ARE A SUIT, A GOLD CHAIN, A COMB AND A POEM HE WROTE TO MY MOM.
THE ONLY THING I HAVE IS THIS HAT HE FORGOT TO TAKE WITH HIM.
YOU GUYS NEED TO FIND A NEW SPORT.
MY DAD'S PROBABLY IN JAIL RIGHT NOW.
MINE'S PROBABLY DEAD.
DARRIN BELL

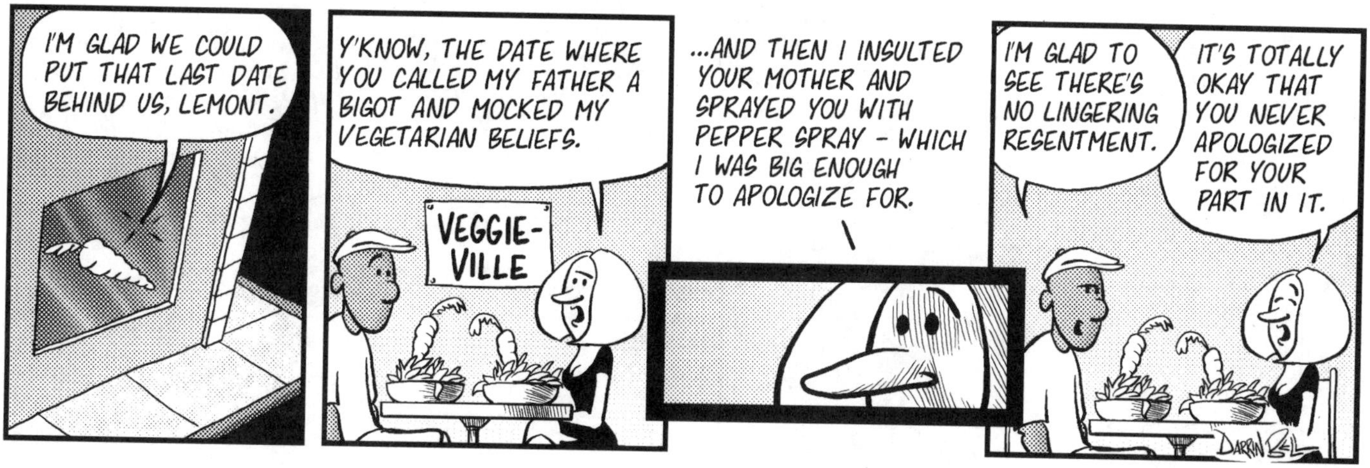
I'M GLAD WE COULD PUT THAT LAST DATE BEHIND US, LEMONT.
Y'KNOW, THE DATE WHERE YOU CALLED MY FATHER A BIGOT AND MOCKED MY VEGETARIAN BELIEFS.
VEGGIE-VILLE
...AND THEN I INSULTED YOUR MOTHER AND SPRAYED YOU WITH PEPPER SPRAY – WHICH I WAS BIG ENOUGH TO APOLOGIZE FOR.
I'M GLAD TO SEE THERE'S NO LINGERING RESENTMENT.
IT'S TOTALLY OKAY THAT YOU NEVER APOLOGIZED FOR YOUR PART IN IT.
DARRIN BELL

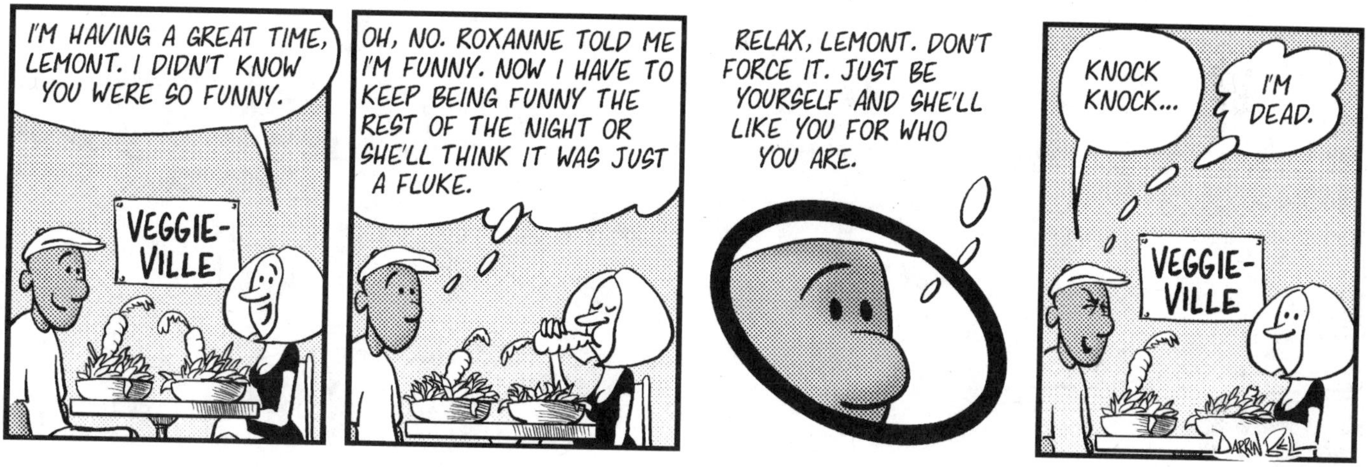
I'M HAVING A GREAT TIME, LEMONT. I DIDN'T KNOW YOU WERE SO FUNNY.
VEGGIE-VILLE
OH, NO. ROXANNE TOLD ME I'M FUNNY. NOW I HAVE TO KEEP BEING FUNNY THE REST OF THE NIGHT OR SHE'LL THINK IT WAS JUST A FLUKE.
RELAX, LEMONT. DON'T FORCE IT. JUST BE YOURSELF AND SHE'LL LIKE YOU FOR WHO YOU ARE.
KNOCK KNOCK...
I'M DEAD.
VEGGIE-VILLE
DARRIN BELL

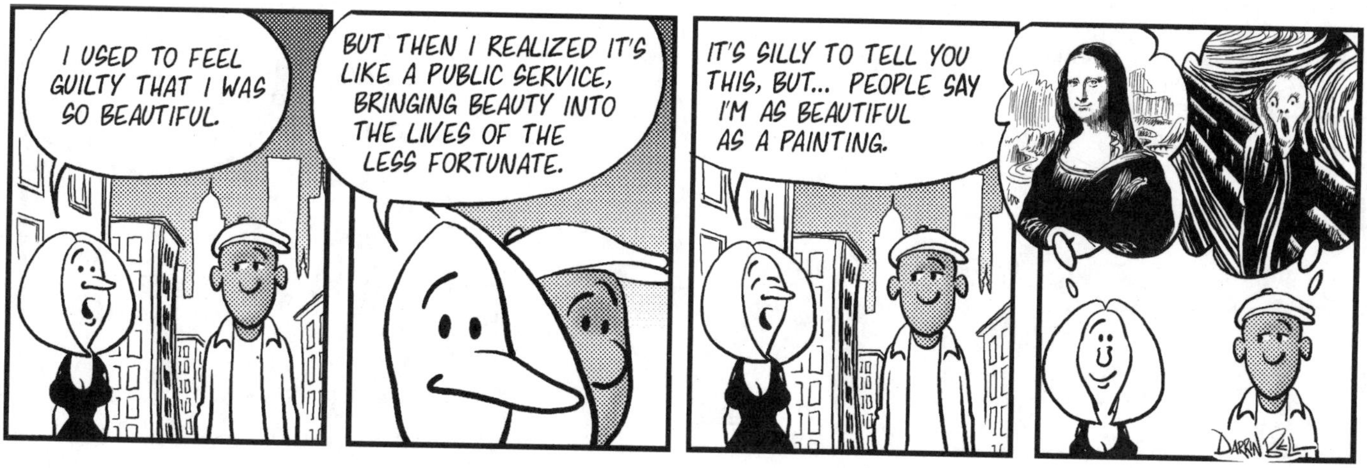
I USED TO FEEL GUILTY THAT I WAS SO BEAUTIFUL.
BUT THEN I REALIZED IT'S LIKE A PUBLIC SERVICE, BRINGING BEAUTY INTO THE LIVES OF THE LESS FORTUNATE.
IT'S SILLY TO TELL YOU THIS, BUT... PEOPLE SAY I'M AS BEAUTIFUL AS A PAINTING.
DARRIN BELL

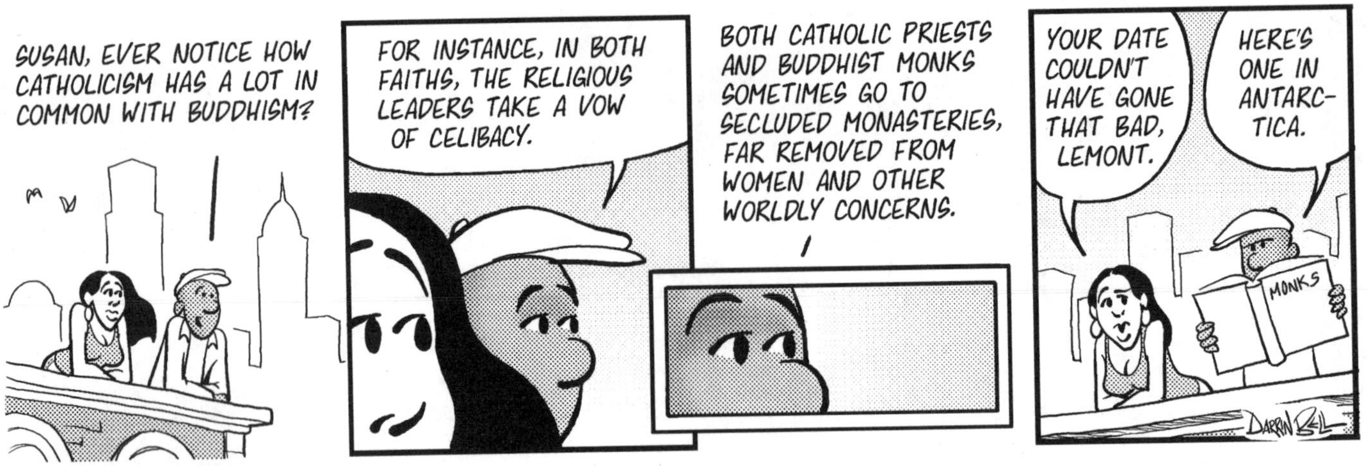
SUSAN, EVER NOTICE HOW CATHOLICISM HAS A LOT IN COMMON WITH BUDDHISM?
FOR INSTANCE, IN BOTH FAITHS, THE RELIGIOUS LEADERS TAKE A VOW OF CELIBACY.
BOTH CATHOLIC PRIESTS AND BUDDHIST MONKS SOMETIMES GO TO SECLUDED MONASTERIES, FAR REMOVED FROM WOMEN AND OTHER WORLDLY CONCERNS.
YOUR DATE COULDN'T HAVE GONE THAT BAD, LEMONT.
HERE'S ONE IN ANTARC-TICA.
MONKS
DARRIN BELL

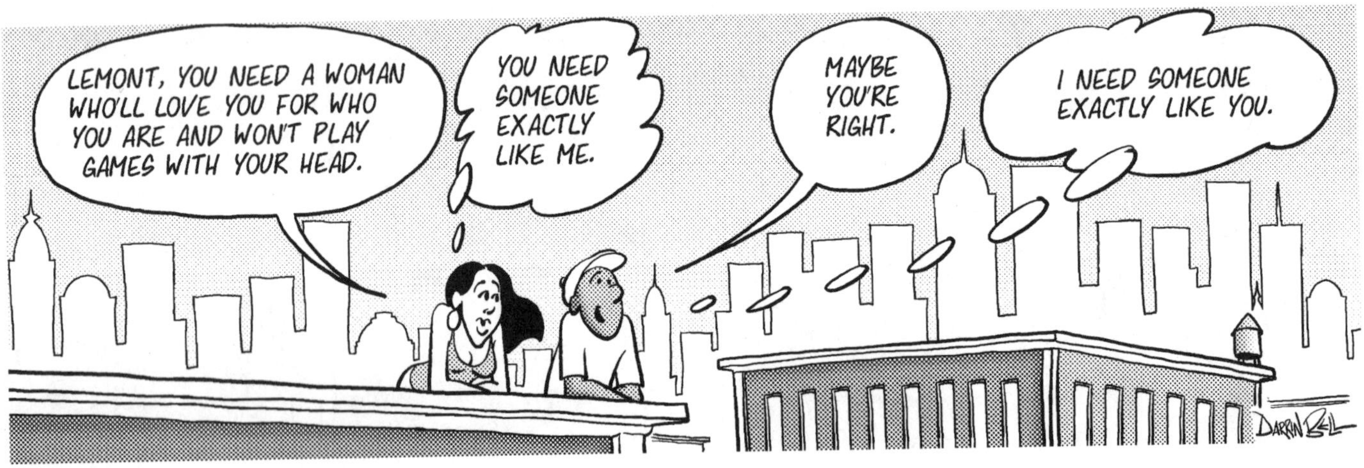
LEMONT, YOU NEED A WOMAN WHO'LL LOVE YOU FOR WHO YOU ARE AND WON'T PLAY GAMES WITH YOUR HEAD.
YOU NEED SOMEONE EXACTLY LIKE ME.
MAYBE YOU'RE RIGHT.
I NEED SOMEONE EXACTLY LIKE YOU.
DARRIN BELL

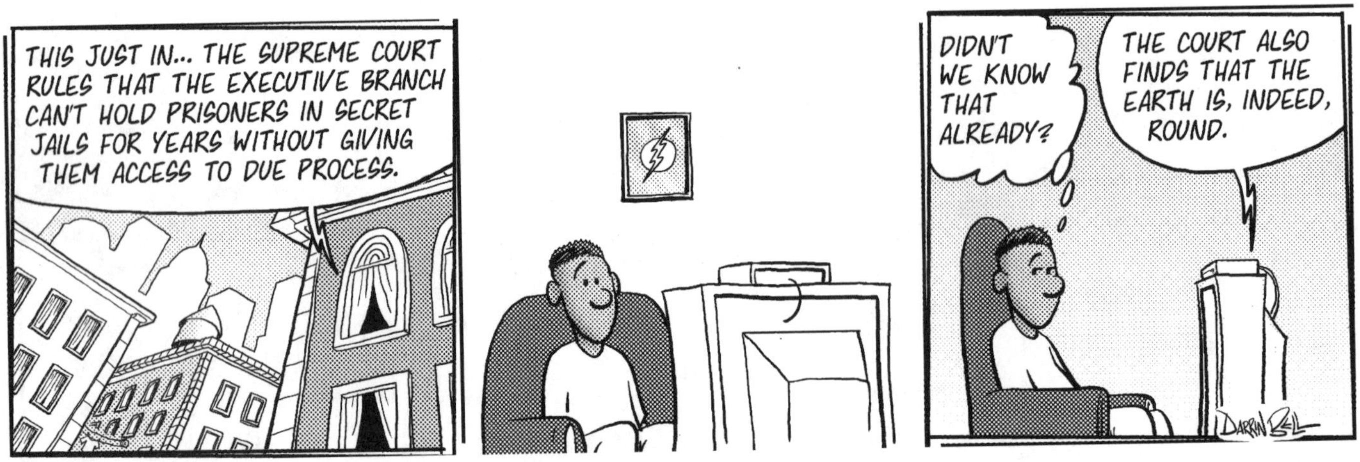
THIS JUST IN... THE SUPREME COURT RULES THAT THE EXECUTIVE BRANCH CAN'T HOLD PRISONERS IN SECRET JAILS FOR YEARS WITHOUT GIVING THEM ACCESS TO DUE PROCESS.
DIDN'T WE KNOW THAT ALREADY?
THE COURT ALSO FINDS THAT THE EARTH IS, INDEED, ROUND.
DARRIN BELL

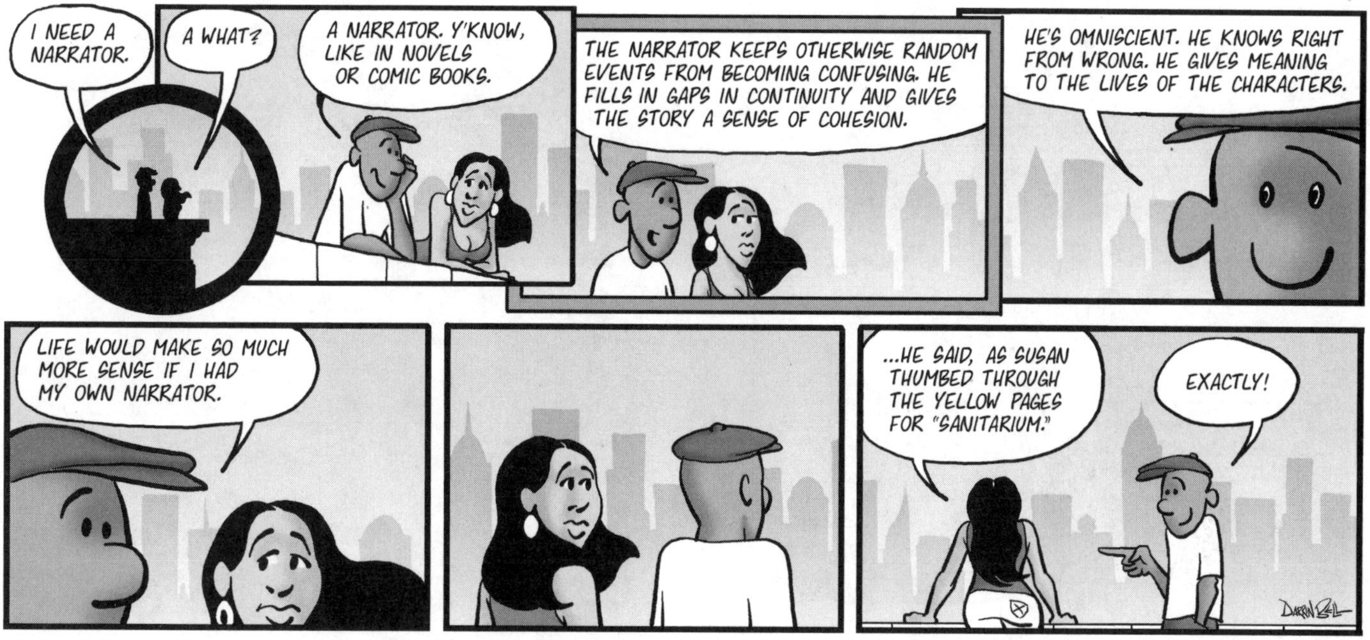
I NEED A NARRATOR.
A WHAT?
A NARRATOR. Y'KNOW, LIKE IN NOVELS OR COMIC BOOKS.
THE NARRATOR KEEPS OTHERWISE RANDOM EVENTS FROM BECOMING CONFUSING. HE FILLS IN GAPS IN CONTINUITY AND GIVES THE STORY A SENSE OF COHESION.
HE'S OMNISCIENT. HE KNOWS RIGHT FROM WRONG. HE GIVES MEANING TO THE LIVES OF THE CHARACTERS.
LIFE WOULD MAKE SO MUCH MORE SENSE IF I HAD MY OWN NARRATOR.
...HE SAID, AS SUSAN THUMBED THROUGH THE YELLOW PAGES FOR "SANITARIUM."
EXACTLY!
DARRIN BELL

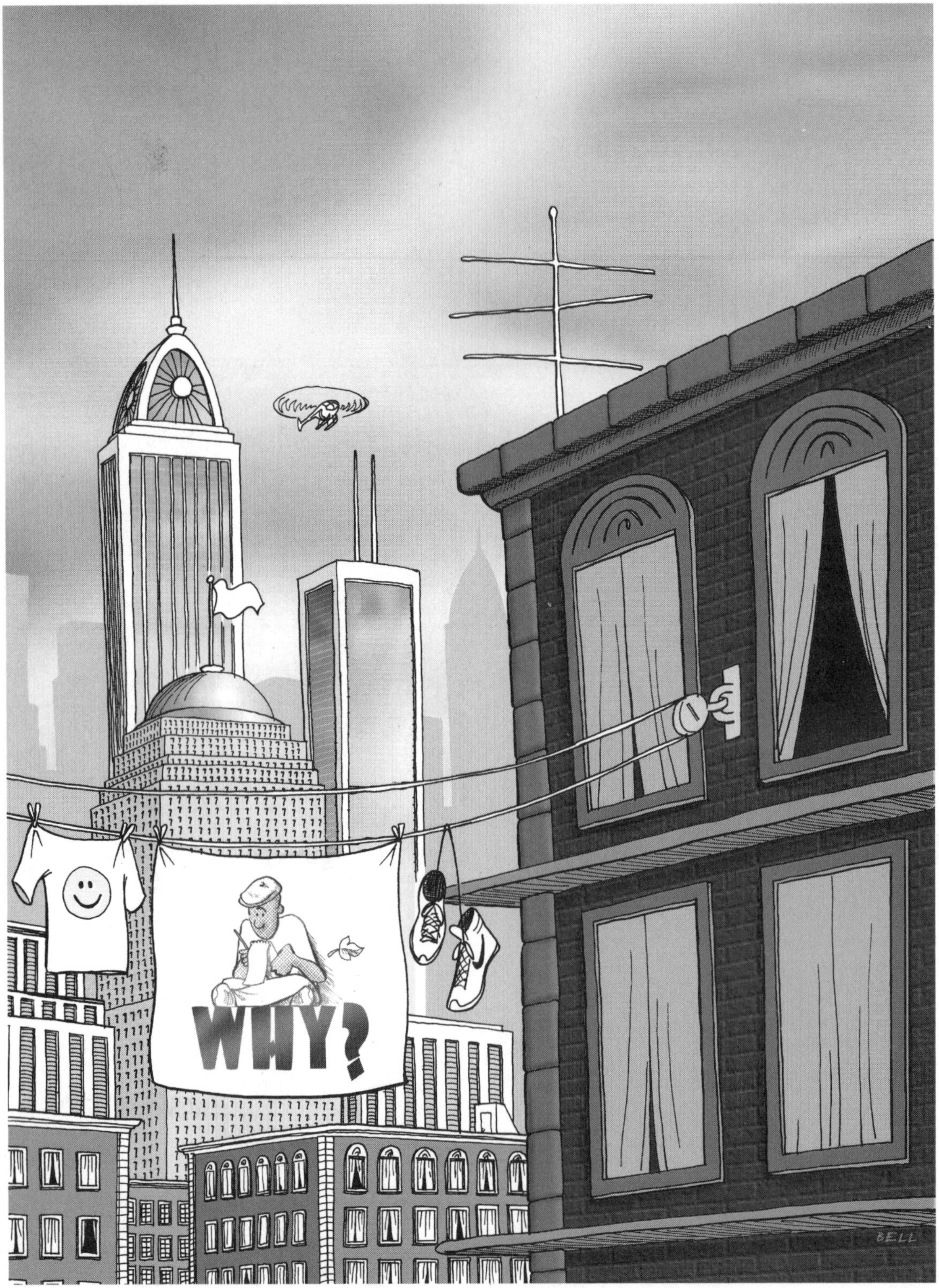
WHY?
BELL

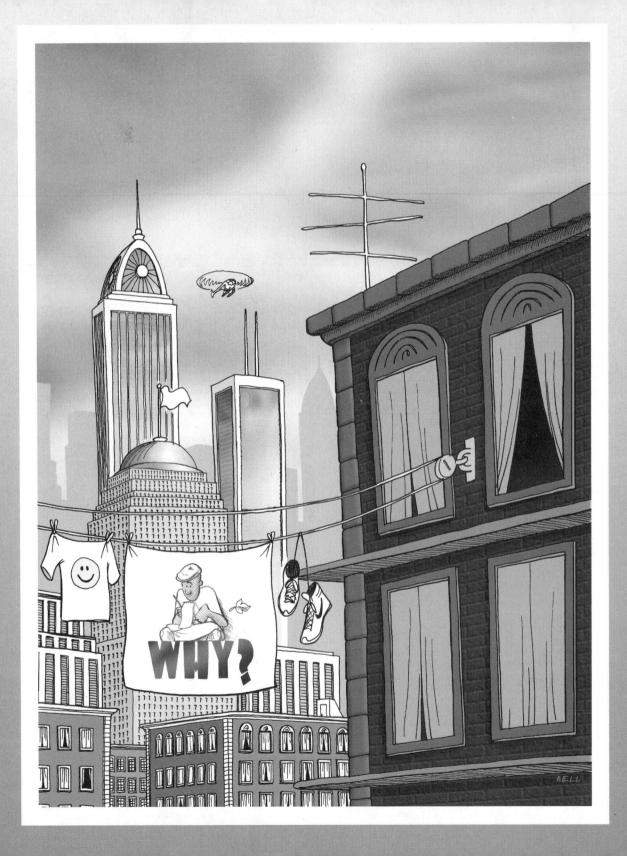